# Artificial Intelligence in Management
## Impact, Challenges and Developments


*Editors:*

**Alka Agnihotri**
Professor, School of Business
Galgotias University, Greater Noida, India

**Anuja Pandey**
Professor-Department of Marketing
All India Management Association, Delhi, India

**Balamurugan Balusamy**
Associate Dean-Academics
Shiv Nadar University, Greater Noida, India



CRC Press
Taylor & Francis Group
Boca Raton London New York

CRC Press is an imprint of the
Taylor & Francis Group, an **informa** business
A SCIENCE PUBLISHERS BOOK

First edition published 2026
by CRC Press
2385 NW Executive Center Drive, Suite 320, Boca Raton FL 33431

and by CRC Press
4 Park Square, Milton Park, Abingdon, Oxon, OX14 4RN



*Library of Congress Cataloging-in-Publication Data (applied for)*

ISBN: 978-1-032-88371-7 (hbk)
ISBN: 978-1-032-90799-4 (pbk)
ISBN: 978-1-003-55984-9 (ebk)

DOI: 10.1201/9781003559849

Typeset in Times New Roman
by Prime Publishing Services

# Preface

The use of computational systems to do tasks related to human intelligence is on a positive trend in current time and also several researches are underway world over to expand this domain. The curiosity as to how machines may perform the activities related to human intelligence and help humanity tap the unlimited potential for serving mankind has led to several AI and management interlinking opportunities of collaboration and leveraging in almost all areas of study. This book deals with implementation and impact of artificial intelligence (AI) on organisations with focus on society 5.0 and sustainability resonating with the aspirations of current human expectations for better services and sustainability centric growth and development. It also elaborates the implementation process of IA in different organisations in different fields of management including the impact studies of AI , symbiotics relationship with different management fields like HR, marketing, health, hospitality and innovation etc., bringing out the challenges and the current developments in the use of Artificial Intelligence.

# Contents

# List of Contributors

**Akshya Jothi**
Department of Computational Intelligence, School of Computing, SRM Institute of Science and Technology, Kattankulathur Campus, Chengalpattu, Tamil Nadu, India.

**Alka Agnihotri**
Professor, School of Business, Galgotias University, Greater Noida, Uttar Pradesh.

**Amir Hafizullah Khan**
Lecturer in Digital Marketing, Salford Business School, University of Salford, United Kingdom.

**Apurva Saxena**
Student, School of Commerce, Finance & Accountancy, Christ University, India.

**Bharani B R**
Department of Information Science and Engineering, Cambridge Institute of Technology, Bangalore, India.

**Bhavna Sharma**
Assistant Professor, School of Commerce, Finance & Accountancy, Christ University, India.

**Biswajit Mahanty**
Department of Industrial and Systems Engineering, IIT Kharagpur.

**D Loganathan**
Department of Information Science and Engineering, Cambridge Institute of Technology, Bangalore, India.

**Dharun Krishna K B**
Researcher, Department of Computer Science, SASTRA Deemed University, Thanjavur.

**Ganesan Muruganantham**
Professor, Department of Management Studies, National Institute of Technology, Tiruchirappalli.

**Gurunadham Goli**
Assistant Professor, School of Business, SR University, Warangal, Telangana-506371, India.

**Jayanthi MG**
Department of Computer Science and Engineering, Cambridge Institute of Technology, Bangalore, India.

**Karthik P**
Department of Information Science and Engineering, Cambridge Institute of Technology, Bangalore, India.

**Kaushik Samaddar**
Assistant Professor (Marketing), Symbiosis Institute of Business Management, Bengaluru.

**Krishna Kumar**
Department of Computer Science and Engineering, Sasi Institute of Technology and Engineering, Tadepalligudem, Andhra Pradesh, India.

**Kulbir Kaur Bhatti**
Assistant Professor, Manav Rachna International Institute of Research and Studies, Sector 43, Faridabad, Haryana.

**M Sundarrajan**
Department of Networking and Communications, School of Computing, SRM Institute of Science and Technology, Kattankulathur Campus, Chengalpattu, Tamil Nadu, India.

**M. Rajya laxmi**
Assistant Professor, School of Business, SR University, Warangal, Telangana-506371, India.

**M.V. Rama Prasad**
Professor, GITAM School of Business, GITAM (Deemed to be University), Bangalore.

**Mani Deepak Choudhry**
Department of Computing Technologies, School of Computing, SRM Institute of Science and Technology, Kattankulathur Campus, Chengalpattu, Tamil Nadu, India.

**Md Mahabub Alam**
Draup Business Solutions Private Limited, Bengaluru, Karnataka.

**Parihar Suresh Dahake**
Assistant Professor, School of Management, Ramdeobaba University Nagpur, India.

**Poorvi Agrawal**
Research Scholar, Galgotias University, Greater Noida, Uttar Pradesh.

**Preethi S**
Department of Electronics and Communication Engineering, Dr. N.G.P. Institute of Technology, Coimbatore, Tamil Nadu, India.

**Preethi S**
Department of Information Science and Engineering, Cambridge Institute of Technology, Bangalore, India.

**Priyanka Desai**
Department of Information Science and Engineering, Cambridge Institute of Technology, Bangalore, India.

**Pulok Ranjan Mohanta**
RCG School of Infrastructure Design and Management, IIT Kharagpur.

**Rachoru Himani Srihita**
Research Scholar, School of Business, SR University, Warangal, Telangana-506371, India.

**Rashmi Singel**
Associate Professor ,Manav Rachna International Institute of Research and Studies, Sector 43, Faridabad, Haryana.

**Richa Nangia**
Associate Professor, Sushant University, Sector 55, Gurugram, Haryana.

**S. Neaba**
Research Scholar, Department of Management Studies, National Institute of Technology, Calicut, Kerala, India.

**Sanjana Mondal**
Associate Professor (Marketing), CMS Business School, JAIN University, Bangalore, India.

**Sankar Mukherjee**
Associate Professor, M S Ramaiah Institute of Management, Bengaluru, Karnataka.

**Shruti Tyagi**
Student, School of Commerce, Finance & Accountancy, Christ University, India.

**Utpala Das**
Professor, Galgotias University, Greater Noida, Uttar Pradesh.

**Vivek Aggarwal**
Professor, School of Business, Galgotias University.

# 1 Artificial Intelligence and Human Resources: A Symbiotic Relationship for the Future

Rachoru Himani Srihita[1*], Gurunadham Goli[2] and M. Rajya Laxmi[3]

Human Resources (HR) is one of the quintessential parts of any business, since it directly affects the lives of the people who work for the company. For workers to be effective and productive, their workplace must have a healthy, well-communicated atmosphere. One of today's most cutting-edge and rapidly developing technologies, artificial intelligence has greatly enhanced the HR division. AI has the potential to revolutionize employee experiences in a wide variety of ways right from the hiring to retaining, by managing massive amounts of data swiftly and accurately. AI is becoming and playing a pivotal role in Human Resource Management Systems (HRMS) as a result of HRM's digitization. This chapter examines various AI applications employed by the HR department to attract and retain top talent, both in the past and present by applying a comprehensive literature review high lighting the transformative impact of AI on HR practices and employee experiences. It also underscores the significance of AI applications in transforming human resource management, by seamlessly integrating AI technologies into various HR functions. Additionally, it investigates the future aspects of AI in HRM and how they may impact the HR strategies of an organization.

## Introduction to HR

The concept of "human resource" was initially introduced by American institutional economist John R. Commons in his 1893 publication, The Distribution of Wealth. Today, Human Resources (HR) is essential for helping organizations navigate the fast-changing business landscape and meet the increasing demand for skilled professionals in the 21st century. For any organization human resources are the greatest asset in order to travel all the path and reach the planned objectives and designed goals (Okoye et al., 2013). It pertains to the personnel, who constitute the workforce, of an organization, business sector, industry, or economy. This term binds all individuals, who lend their skills and efforts working within these contexts showing the general appreciation of their collective importance as a

[1] Research Scholar, School of Business, SR University, Warangal, Telangana-506371, India.
[2,3] Assistant Professor, School of Business, SR University, Warangal, Telangana-506371, India.
Email: mbagurunath@gmail.com[2]; laxmi.gunna@gmail.com[3]
* Corresponding author: himanirachoru@gmnail.com

DOI: 10.1201/9781003559849-1

critical asset of the organization. HRs manages correctly by highlighting the thirst of an organization to achieve its strategic objectives for long-term growth (Enz et al., 2000).

## Importance of HR in Organization

HR is essential to any organization and reflects one of the most critical functions within it. The management of probably the single most valuable asset: the people. Not only do human resource professionals simply engage in recruiting and discharging employees, but they play a strategic role in shaping the future of any organization through comprehensive management of worker capabilities, leadership qualities, and continuous motivation of the workforce (Vishwanath and Vaddepalli, 2023a).

Human Resources is more than just another department in an organization; it binds it together by empowering, supporting, and managing its human capital to increase productivity and happiness. Its roles are diverse and dynamic, comprising strategic planning and talent management on the one hand, and delivering a competitive advantage by delivering comprehensive benefits on the other. Therefore, investing in sound HR practices becomes imperative and not merely significant for an organization to emerge victorious among its competitors.

Table 1 summarizes the key developments in the evolution of Human Resources (HR). This condensed table captures the essential milestones in HR's evolution.

**Table 1** Evolution of Human Resources.

| *Period* | *Key Developments* | *Source* |
|---|---|---|
| Late 18th Century | The Industrial Revolution highlighted the need for human labor, and discussions on employee engagement. | Smith, 1994 |
| Early 20th Century | Emergence of employment clerks; by 1915, 5% of large U.S. companies had personnel departments. | Jacoby, 2004 |
| 1920s | The Human Relations Movement focused on psychological well-being by 1929, a third of large U.S. companies had personal departments. | Mayo, 2004 |
| 1940s | Formalization of HR; establishment of ASPA in 1948; Peter Drucker introduced "human resources" in 1954. | Gazell, 2000 |
| 1960s | The Civil Rights Movement led to anti-discrimination laws and the establishment of the EEOC. | Kochan et al., 1982 |

*Source:* Author

## Introduction to Human Resource Management

In the early days HRM is referred to as "Personnel Administration", as time went on, the field of HRM continued to evolve, and the term "Personnel Administration" was eventually replaced by the more contemporary and encompassing term of

"Human Resource Management" (HRM) (Poole, 1999). It is the process of recruiting, developing, and motivating employees in order to achieve the goals of an organization. It involves utilizing human resources effectively to achieve the desired outcomes. This process is an essential part of any organization's operations, ensuring the smooth functioning and productivity of all departments and teams. Just like a well-oiled machine, this process is the backbone of any organization, allowing all parts to work seamlessly together for optimal efficiency and success (Rohit et al., 2024). It influences employee's behaviours, attitudes, and performance of the personnel encompassing a range of policies, practices, and systems. HRM is a strategic approach to oversee company employees, optimize the performance of employees and the work environment by creating a positive and productive work culture. This often involves using metrics to evaluate the effectiveness of the workforce (Sharma, 2023). To be a valuable asset, HRM focuses on recruitment, development, and positioning of people with relevant skills to work collaboratively towards attainment of organizational objectives. This includes identifying the specific needs of an organization and matching those with the right kind of talent. By ensuring adequate skills among workers and motivating them to work in a bonding manner as one unit, the HRM enhances team cohesion aligning with the company's goals. This not only maximizes productivity and efficiency but also fosters supporting work environments wherein individuals feel empowered to give their best in hitting shared goals (Aswal D.K. 2020).

## Overview of Artificial Intelligence

The development of AI, from its inception to current-day practical uses encompasses some of the milestones, major breakthroughs, and shaped the evolution of AI (Cena and Joshua, 2024). The definition of AI has changed many times during the 19th and 20th centuries with changing developments in this field. These definitions emphasize that the early perceptions of AI were related simply to emulating human intelligence and behavior through machines, placing much of the focus on the intention to develop systems that could do things that normally require human cognitive abilities. It provided grounds for the modern understandings of AI, which nowadays also include the system's ability to interpret external data, further learn from it, and be flexible in the job of achieving certain predefined goals and tasks.

Table 2 depicts the various authors definitions of AI:

**Table 2** Various Authors Definitions of AI.

| *Definition* | *Source* |
|---|---|
| The Dartmouth Research Project, as far back as 1955, defined artificial intelligence as the challenge of making a machine do things that would be considered intelligent if a human were performing them. | McCarthy et al., 1955 |
| Marvin Minsky, who is a Cognitive Scientist, characterized AI as "the science of enabling machines to carry out tasks that would typically require human intelligence". | Minsky, 1968. |

*Contd.*

**Table 2** *Contd.*

| | |
|---|---|
| One common definition of artificial intelligence is to relate it to human intelligence, often characterized by the ability to process information, solve issues, or produce valuable items within a cultural context. | Gardner, 1999. |
| AI is the potential of a machine to learn from given contexts, understand appropriately, and channel such learning toward specific goals, with flexible adaptability. | Kaplan and Haenlein, 2019. |
| In other terms it is coined as the expression of the real world in the form of non-human machines or artificial entities capable of doing, reasoning, communicating, interacting, and even acting logically like biological humans. As can be seen from the definition, AI demonstrates human behaviour and intelligence through a series of actions and interactions. | Gil de Zúñiga et al., 2024. |

*Source:* Author

## Methodology

This chapter examines the revolutionary role of artificial intelligence in Human Resource Management employing a thorough analysis of pre-existing studies. This chapter categorizes AI applications historically and in current practice, analyzing their impact on improving HR strategies and enhancing employee experiences. It also explores emerging trends, challenges and future aspects of AI in HR practices. This thorough analysis of AI-powered applications provides insights into the integration of AI and its potential to rethink HR procedures for increased organizational success.

### *Objectives*

- Examine how the evolution of HR integrates AI and automation in recruitment.
- Explore how AI-powered adaptive learning enables personalized and continuous employee development.
- Examine AI-driven insights of compensation and payroll management for personalized career paths to enhance retention.
- Analyze the latest HR innovations integrated with AI for enhancing employee well-being and ethical considerations for the future of work.

## Transformation of Human Resources

Figure 1 represents the transformation of HR across four waves: (Masud et al., 2018)

1. **HR Administrative Wave:** The First wave focused on administrative responsibilities, HR service delivery, and regulatory functions. This phase aimed to enhance administrative efficiency and often delegated HR tasks to line managers, emphasizing streamlined processes and compliance.

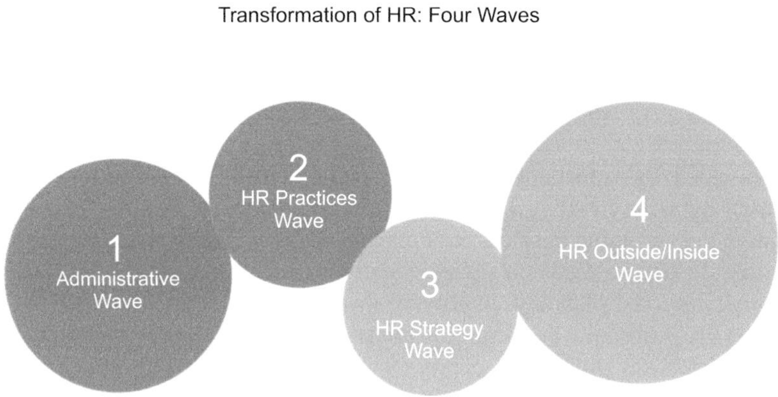


**Fig. 1** Transformation of HR: Four Waves.
*Source:* Author

2. **HR Practises Wave:** The Second wave centres on developing fundamental HR practices such as recruitment, career development, organizational structure, and work processes. In this phase, HR professionals act as competent specialists who customize and implement HR practices to meet the specific needs of the organization, ensuring effective alignment with its goals and requirements.
3. **HR Strategy Wave:** The Third wave focuses on aligning HR practic es with business strategies to enhance organizational success. In this phase, HR not only implements effective practices but also actively resolves organizational issues and creates value, ensuring that HR functions are integral to achieving strategic business goals.
4. **HR Outside/Inside Wave:** The Fourth wave connects HR with the broader external context by responding to external needs and aligning internal efforts with these expectations. This approach ensures HR practices meet market trends and societal demands, enhancing the organization's adaptability and reputation.

## Overview of AI's Integration into Human Resource

The introduction of AI to the business greatly benefited the HR department by efficiently organizing data and accurately matching employees with suitable job profiles. This technological improvement has streamlined HR processes, making it easier to align talent with organizational needs.

The use of AI technology has enhanced the efficiency of recruitment and talent management procedures by automating tasks such as candidate evaluation and data handling, thereby saving valuable time and effort (Alsaif and Sabih Aksoy 2023). Because AI-driven tools automate all routine tasks, like resume screening, scheduling interviews, and the onboarding process, HR professionals can shift their attention to more significant and high-order goals. Additionally, AI can predict future needs, pinpoint skill deficiencies within an organization, and offer valuable insights into the performance of employees and workplace engagement. By leveraging AI, HR departments can enhance their decision-making processes, boost employee contentment, and thus contribute to overall organizational success (Gupta, 2024). This technological advancement doesn't just increase efficiency, but also helps in creating a more nimble and responsive HR function that is adaptive to a changing business environment. By automating repetitive tasks, AI will free up HRs to focus on strategic activities such as employee development and organizational planning, improving the effectiveness and value of the HR function (Kambur and Yildirim, 2023). AI facilitates real-time communication through chat boxes or virtual meetings, allowing for prompt resolution of employee queries and complaints. Furthermore, AI assists HR set measurable goals for employees, monitor emotions and performance, and take corrective actions, thereby strengthening the organisation-employee bond and increasing engagement (Saju et al., 2021). Human Resources (HR) has undergone much more transformation with the integration of advanced technologies such as big data analysis, natural language processing, pattern recognition, and cloud computing. These innovations enable HR professionals to process and analyse vast amounts of data swiftly and effectively, offering keen insights into employee performance, engagement, and talent acquisition (Kaur and Kaur, 2022). For instance, big data analysis can reveal patterns and trends in employee data, such as turnover rates, satisfaction levels, and productivity metrics. This will, in turn, contribute to making data-driven decisions that optimize strategies in employee retention, increasing employee engagement, and thus, talent acquisition. The review of Natural language processing (NLP) can be used to analyse employee feedback and sentiment analysis to identify areas where employees may need additional support or training. Finally, cloud computing allows HR professionals to access employee data from anywhere, at any time, making it easier to manage remote teams and ensure that employees have the resources they need to be successful (Vishwanath and Vaddepalli, 2023b).

## AI in Today's HR Applications

### *Evolution of Recruitment: From Traditional to Digital*

The process of recruitment is crucial in the hiring process for any organization as it stands as the cornerstone of any organization's growth, encompassing a meticulous journey pivotal to securing top-tier talent. It involves several steps such as job requirements, sourcing suitable candidates and selecting the best applicants. The ultimate aim of recruitment is to track the right candidate who would help the organization meet its needs and thus enable it to achieve its goals (Sills, 2014). Figure 2 depicts two methods of hiring:

Recruitment can be both:

1. Internal, by identifying talent within the company, or
2. External, by hiring qualified candidates from outside the organization.

**Fig. 2** Types of Recruitment.
*Source:* Author

Ensuring that the right talent is attracted and hired remains a critical aspect of the recruitment process in today's competitive market.

The late 20th century marked the start of digital transformation in recruitment, a trend that rapidly advanced into the 21st century. This revolution has achieved numerous significant milestones. Traditionally, job openings were announced by posting notices on HR bulletin boards, where the term 'job posting' originated. Nowadays, organizations often post job vacancies electronically through intranets or notify employees via email. Additionally, some managers believe that the most effective way to get top talent is to hire those whom existing employees refer to the organizations personally (Vimaladevi et al., 2024).

An increase in online recruiting has been the most important change in recruiting practices. Since the beginning of the 1960s, one of the instances in which practices of human resource management have been developed to a great extent is fast artificial intelligence. AI technologies were already in place for applicant-tracking solutions that were going to systematize the work of recruitment by the early 2000s. During the 2010s, the capabilities of AI, machine learning, and predictive analytics went further to improve the ability of HR to manage talent effectively (Madanchian et al., 2023). It has been reshaping HR roles by automating more routine tasks, for instance, the initial screening of résumés, hence the increasing ability of HR professionals to focus on more strategic initiatives on talent development and organizational strategy (Maganti Sridevi, 2023). The introduction of online job boards and career portals allowed employers to list openings digitally, expediting the application process for candidates. Many organizations now advertise job openings on their websites, or on specialized sites such as career builder.com, naukri.com, monster.com, eliminating the hard copy application completely. Social media sites such as LinkedIn have developed as vital tools for recruiters, allowing them to source, network and screen candidates (Halid et al., 2024). Other technologies participated in this race wherein Applicant Tracking Systems (ATS) proliferated to automate several areas of recruiting, diversified into resume screening, candidate tracking and communication. These advancements underscore how AI-driven technologies have revolutionized recruitment, making it more efficient, responsive and accessible in the digital age (Arifuzzaman et al., 2023).

In Table 3 there is a tabular comparison, high lighting the evolution of recruitment from traditional to modern AI recruitment methods, showcasing the transformation of technology in the talent acquisition process.

**Table 3** Traditional to Latest Recruitment Methods.

| *Traditional Recruitment Methods* | *Latest Recruitment Methods* |
|---|---|
| Newspaper Ads and Bulletin Boards | Online Job Boards |
| Printed Ads in newspaper, Physical bulletin boards | Platforms like Monster, LinkedIn, and Indeed |
| Word of Mouth | Social Media Recruiting |
| Personal recommendations and network | Recruiters source candidates via LinkedIn, Naukri, Indeed and showcasing culture |
| Paper Resumes | Applicant Tracking Systems (ATS) |
| Hand-delivered resumes, extensive filing | Streamlines resume collection and organization |
| Face-to-Face Interviews | Video Interviews |
| In-person interviews, time consuming and costly | Initial interviews conducted remotely, saves time and resources |
| Manual Screening | Big Data and Analytics |
| HR manually screens resumes, subjective and time-intensive | Data-driven strategies, identify trend analysis |
| Job Fairs and Walk-ins | Mobile Recruiting |
| Physical attendance, on the spot interviews | Mobile-optimized applications |
| Recruitment Agencies | AI and Chatbots |
| Relying on third-party-agencies, costly | AI for first screening, questioning, inviting for interviews and increasing efficiency |

*Source:* Author

## Case Study

### Unilever's AI-Driven Recruitment Practices (Hu, 2023)

Unilever's AI-driven recruitment practices, revolutionized its recruitment process with advanced technologies and collaboration with platforms like HireVue and Pymetrics to transform traditional hiring processes with enhanced efficiency, diversity and inclusiveness.

**Key features**

1. Gamification: Candidates are evaluated through neuroscience-based games developed by Pymetrics to assess traits like focus and risk tolerance.
2. NLP in video Interviews: HireVue facilitates AI-driven video interviews that analyse verbal and non-verbal cues, including tone, body language, and word choice to identify top talent.
3. Scalability: The fully digital system enables candidates to access the applications globally. The process is operated in 68 countries via digital devices.

**Impact:**

1. Efficiency: Saved 50,000 hours annually and reduced costs by £1 million.
2. Diversity and Inclusion: Promoted diversity by reducing human bias, resulting in the company's most diverse class of hires.
3. Positive Feedback: Over 80% of applicants provided positive feedback, with the process rated highly for its fairness, transparency, and engagement.

The use of AI in hiring by Unilever is an example of how technology can promote inclusivity and efficiency in the employment process establishing a standard for creative HR practices in the digital age.

## On-boarding Process

Employee onboarding is a crucial social interaction process that has a significant impact on employee motivation, job satisfaction, and loyalty to the organization, making it a vital component of any company's human resources strategy (Ziden and Joo, 2020).

## Traditional On-boarding

Traditional on-boarding featured many face-to-face induction programs, where new hires would gather in a physical location for a series of orientation sessions and introductions (Bradt and Vonnegut, 2009). These programs often included classroom-based training sessions led by instructors, providing foundational knowledge and skills necessary for the job. Documentation and compliance processes were typically paper-based, requiring new employees to fill out numerous forms manually, which were then processed and filed by HR staff. Most of the communication in this period was through emails and physical meetings. Progress tracking was also manual, involving frequent check-ins and updates that had to be recorded and monitored by hand. This approach made it a longer and rather inflexible process (Bauer, 2010).

## AI-integrated On-boarding

The evolution of onboarding processes from traditional to modern methodologies reflects a significant shift driven by AI technological advancements and changing workforce expectations (Ritz et al., 2023). AI-powered onboarding process utilizes digital tools and platforms to a great extent in most cases to make the process easier and better (Das, 2019a). Virtual orientation and e-learning modules integrated with artificial intelligence provide engaging and interactive training, while onboarding portals and mobile apps make access easy to resources and documentation (Verma et al., 2023). Real-time feedback mechanisms and automated progress tracking delivers continuous improvement and adaptability to the onboarding process. Virtual mentorship programs with online activities for social integration also make employee engagement easier and expedite their assimilation into the company culture. They can enable focused, flexible, and responsive onboarding experiences at various levels to meet new employees' needs towards maximum satisfaction and productivity by implementing modern onboarding techniques (Hajjami and Crocco, 2024).

### *The Foundations of Effective On-boarding*

On-boarding lays the foundation for a new hire's transition into their company. Figure 3 represents the effective foundations that are laid down for an on-boarding (Bauer 2010, Stoiber et al., 2021).

**Fig. 3** The Foundations of Effective On-Boarding.
*Source:* Author

1. **Job Role:** The process of on-boarding outlines the responsibilities of a new hire, illustrates the desired level of performance, and delineates the objectives they are expected to achieve. This gives a clear understanding of the role and the manner in which the individual contributes to the organization's success (Kumar and Pandey, 2017).
2. **Work processes:** Comprehensive training on tools, systems, and standard operating procedures equips new employees with an overview of the company's working processes, enabling them to perform their job responsibilities efficiently and effectively (Ju et al., 2021).
3. **Relationships:** Onboarding is a valuable chance to get to know individuals within the organization. The support network, which includes colleagues, immediate supervisors, and mentors, will help them integrate and easily fit into the team with a sense of belonging (Hassan, 2020).
4. **Company Culture:** The onboarding process enables new hires to feel the company culture by communicating its values, mission, and expected behaviours. With this information, employees can gain a deeper understanding of the company's ethos and become more engaged in their roles (Hall-Jones et al., 2018).

Table 4 highlights the key differences between traditional and modern onboarding processes, showcasing how technology and new methodologies are transforming the way organizations introduce and integrate new employees (Dominic Teena and Kumar Ravi, 2024, Ziden and Joo, 2020).

**Table 4** Traditional and AI-Enhanced On-Boarding.

| *Aspect* | *Traditional Onboarding* | *Modern Onboarding with AI* |
|---|---|---|
| **Orientation Format** | In-person sessions and presentations | Virtual orientation with interactive multimedia content |
| **Documentation** | Paper-based and manual processes | Digital forms and automated workflows |
| **Training Delivery** | Classroom-based | E-learning modules and virtual training |
| **Engagement Tools** | Face-to-Face and physical handbooks | On-boarding portals and mobile apps |
| **Communication** | Email and in-person meetings | Instant messaging, video conferencing and collaboration platforms |
| **Mentorship** | Assigned mentors for shadowing and guidance | Virtual mentorship and online mentoring platforms |
| **Access** | Physical manuals | Online knowledge bases and digital libraries |
| **Process Tracking** | Manual tracking | Streamlined, automating tracking analytics |
| **Social Integration** | In-person social events and team-building activities | Virtual meet-and-greets, social platforms and online team-building activities |
| **Progress Tracking** | Manual tracking | Automated progress tracking and analytics |
| **Personalization** | Standardized approach | Personalized onboarding experiences based on role and individual needs |
| **Technical Setup** | Manual setup of workstations and equipment | Remote setup assistance and virtual IT support |

*Source:* Author

## Training and Development

They are the very basis of skill, knowledge, and performance enrichment of employees. Any organization that spends some of its resources in staff development is likely to enjoy many benefits, including high levels of job satisfaction, lower turnovers, improved productivity, and increased innovation.

## Traditional Training and Development Practises

In the past, traditional training relied heavily on in-person classroom instruction, paper-based materials, and standardized programs. Key modes of instruction revolve around focused lectures in which the subject matter experts deliver structured content in a classroom setting to the audience to provide foundational knowledge and theoretical insights into the conceptual framework. Infrequent workshops supplement some of these lectures with hands-on experience and collaborative learning to help employees apply concepts learned through lectures in practical scenarios (Sonnentag S. et al., 2004). On-the-job training is a method of directly exposing the employee to the work they do, guided by other staff or mentors who have previous experience in such work. In this methodology, knowledge acquired is immediately applied and a more in-depth understanding is promoted with regard to tasks and procedures required in any particular job. These traditional methods combine to provide a balanced training program—instructional in theory, practical in application, with real experience that will successfully enhance the competencies and resulting performance of employees (Licy Varghese et al., 2023, Latham, 1988).

### *Training and Development Incorporated with AI*

In these high-tech times, this is the progression toward e-learning and online training being deemed cost-effective and is much more flexible for professionals than the traditional approaches. AI-driven technologies integrated in different employee development training methods that include the use of technology through Virtual Reality (VR) and Augmented Reality (AR) open new vistas (Bhatt and Muduli, 2023). The evolution of training and development practices has transformed significantly from traditional methods to modern, technology-driven approaches. AI- powered Learning Management Systems (LMS) and real-time analytics offers immediate feedback and tracks learning progress, which was not possible with the mechanisms of the past. The rigid schedules associated with traditional training have been replaced by flexible, self-paced learning opportunities, and digital coaching platforms, enhanced by AI have expanded mentorship possibilities beyond the confines of the organization (Maity, 2019).

The emergence of digital learning platforms and innovative AI training technologies has transformed these practices, making training more flexible, accessible, and tailored to individual learning needs (Das, 2019b). The role of AI in modern training solutions reflects an enhanced recognition for continuous learning and development amidst today's rapidly changing business environment. Equipped with AI, it is all-rounded to ensure that the staff are not only skilled but also motivated and aligned to the organizational goals, hence driving business success and competitive advantage (Davis, 2000).

AI brings forth a continued process of employee training and development. It is only with the evolving business needs that an effective training program leads to long-term success. In most industries today, things are changing so fast that continuous learning facilitated by AI has become a part of the culture. Training of employees should not be viewed as a single occurrence but rather as an ongoing procedure.

Table 5 illustrates how AI has transformed training and development practices from traditional methods to advanced technologies and more personalized approaches to better meet the needs of modern learners and organizations (Ilie, 2019; Bretz, Jr and Thompsett, 1992; Yusuf et al., 2024).

**Table 5** Traditional vs AI-driven Training and Development Practices.

| *Traditional Training and Development Practices* | *AI-Driven Training and Development Practices* |
|---|---|
| **In-person Classroom Training** | **AI- powered Online Learning Platforms** |
| Face-to-Face instructions, set schedules and locations | E-learning platforms like Coursera, Udemy, flexible and on-demand access |
| **Paper-based Materials** | **Digital Learning Materials curated by AI** |
| Printed handouts and textbooks | Interactive PDFs, eBooks, multimedia content |
| **Lectures and Seminars** | **Interactive Webinars and Virtual Classrooms facilitated by AI** |
| Passive learning through listening | Active participation, real-time feedback |
| **On-the-Job-Training (OJT)** | **Virtual Reality (VR) and Augmented Reality (AR) Training powered by AI** |
| Physical, hands-on experience | Immersive AI simulations and virtual environments |
| **Standard Training Programs** | **Personalized Learning Paths using AI** |
| Fixed schedules, limited customization | Tailored, adoptive content |
| **Instructor-Led-Training (ILT)** | **Blended Learning** |
| Classroom-based, synchronous learning | ILT combined with online modules |
| **Employee Manuals and Handbooks** | **AI-driven Learning Management Systems (LMS)** |
| Static, Physical documents | Dynamic, track learning progress |
| **Limited Feedback Mechanisms** | **Real-time AI Analytics and Feedback** |
| Feedback collected post-training | Immediate AI performance analytics and personalized feedback |
| **Traditional Mentorship** | **Digital Coaching and Mentorship** |
| In-person, limited mentors | Virtual mentoring, AI-matched exports |

*Source:* Author

## Case Study

### AI-Based Training and Development Across Industries (Ashwani Kumar Upadhyay and Komal Khandelwal, 2018)

The application of AI in training and development is revolutionizing how organizations and intuitions deliver learning experiences. Several companies and institutions such as Air Methods, Associated Press, Yahoo, Fox, Aristocrat Technologies, and Georgia Institute of Technology illustrate how AI can enhance efficiency, engagement, and learning outcomes across diverse industries.

**Key Applications**

1. **Air Methods:** AI was used to improve engagement and personalization in adaptive medical transport training for employees.
2. **Georgia Institute of Technology:** Introduced virtual teaching assistants and improved efficiency in addressing student queries and enhanced performance tracking through detailed analytics.
3. **Associated Press, Yahoo, and Fox:** Leveraged AI to generate news content efficiently. This streamlined content production and allowed human resources to focus on higher-level editorial tasks.
4. **Aristocrat Technologies:** Developed an AI-powered chatbot for safety training. Made training sessions interactive and ensured the effective delivery of critical safety protocols.

**Outcomes**

- Personalized learning pathways and real-time feedback.
- Increased efficiency and reduced costs.
- Interactive, scalable, and adaptive training programs.

AI-based training and development programs offer substantial benefits, from cost savings to improved learner satisfaction and open new avenues for innovative training solutions across various industries.

## Performance Management

Over time, the development of performance management has been influenced by many historical and economic factors. At the beginning of the year 2000, the appraisal form was increasingly used by organizations to hold employees accountable but also to reward meritorious and outstanding performance. Good performance management can help align individuals working for an organization towards its goals, enhancing productivity and promoting a culture of accountability and excellence in performance, as part of a broader realization (Cappelli and Tavis, 2016).

Performance management is a continuous process that entails identifying, evaluating, and improving the performance of individuals and teams in order to align with and attain an organization's strategic goals (Aguinis et al., 2012). Recognizing the role of individual performance in organizational success, all global organizations virtually have implemented these systems (Aguinis et al., 2011).

## Traditional Practices of Performance Management

Traditional performance management practices mainly relied on annual or half-yearly evaluations, focusing on set, long-term objectives with supervisors providing feedback from the top down. This approach involved utilising paper-based appraisal forms and concentrated on past performance and metrics, often resulting in a formal and bureaucratic process (Pulakos, 2009). Employee engagement was restricted, with occasional and role-specific training and development opportunities, and development opportunities, and minimal technological application (Cappelli and Tavis, 2016). The review meetings were organized and formal, leading to performance evaluations and rankings, fostering a competitive and individual-centred culture.

## Performance Management System Integrated by AI

In contrast, contemporary performance management practices emphasise ongoing feedback and regular check-ins, with dynamic, short-term, and adaptable goals (Das, 2019c). Feedback is obtained from multiple sources, including peers and subordinates, utilizing digital performance management systems (Buck and Morrow, 2018). Employees actively participate in goal-setting and feedback, supported by AI and analytics for insights. Informal, frequent touchpoints facilitated by AI-driven platforms replace scheduled meetings, leading to development-focused outcomes and real-time adjustments (Adler et al., 2016). This approach fosters a collaborative, team-oriented culture, with real-time recognition and rewards enhancing employee motivation and engagement (Schraeder and Jordan, 2011).

Table 6 shows traditional vs modern performance management practices enhanced by AI.

**Table 6** Traditional vs AI-Enhanced Performance Management

| *Aspect* | *Traditional Performance Management* | *AI Enhanced Performance Management* |
|---|---|---|
| **Frequency** | Annual or semi-annual reviews | Continuous feedback and regular check-ins |
| **Goals** | Fixed, long-term objectives | Dynamic, and adaptable goals |
| **Feedback** | Top-down feedback from supervisors | 360-degree feedback from peers, subordinates, and supervisors |
| **Documentation** | Paper-based appraisal forms | Digital performance management systems |
| **Criteria** | past performance metrics | Future development and potential |

*Contd.*

**Table 6** *Contd.*

| *Aspect* | *Traditional Performance Management* | *AI Enhanced Performance Management* |
|---|---|---|
| **Engagement** | Formal and bureaucratic | Collaborative and ongoing conversations |
| **Employee Involvement** | Limited engagement | Active employee participation in goal-setting |
| **Review Meetings** | Scheduled, formal meetings | Informal, frequent touchpoints |
| **Technology** | Minimal use | AI and analytics-driven |
| **Outcome** | Performance ratings and rankings | Development-focused and real-time adjustments |
| **Rewards and Recognition** | Based on annual performance | Real-time recognition and rewards |

*Source:* Author

## Wages and Compensation

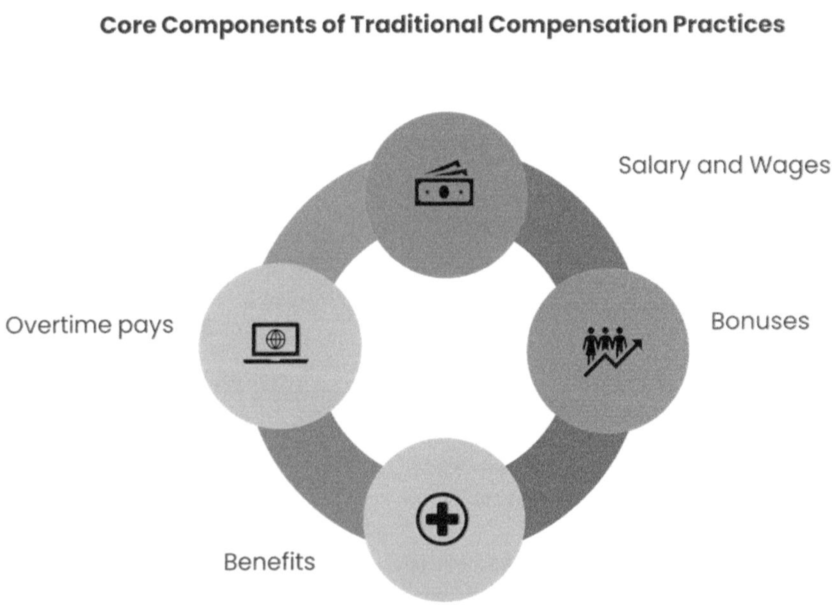


**Fig. 4** Core Components of Traditional Compensation Practices.
*Source:* Author

Traditional labour practices encompass fundamental elements as shown in Fig. 4 have historically structured employment relationships, defining how workers are compensated, managed, and supported within organizations.

1. **Salary and Wages:** These are the fundamental forms of compensation, where workers are paid a fixed amount of money, either on a fixed annual basis, salary, or on per hour worked wage. Salaries are typically set based on job roles, industry standards, and individual experience, providing financial stability (Sharma and Sharma, 2024).
2. **Bonuses:** Apart from the fixed salaries, many organizations provide their highly meritorious services with performance incentives or bonuses. These bonuses can be awarded annually, quarterly, or based on the attainment of specific milestones, and are designed to incentivize staff members to beat their targets for the sake of overall success throughout the organization (Taras 2012, Bryant and Allen, 2013).
3. **Benefits:** This refers to non-monetary or fringe benefits, which cover medical insurance, retirement plans and paid time off in the form of PTOs. These are essential in terms of putting a backbone into the general well-being and work-life balance of employees (Nazareno and Schiff, 2021).
4. **Overtime pays:** Employees who work beyond the standard workweek are entitled to overtime pay. This practise ensures fair compensation for extra hours worked and helps manage workload demands (Liang, 2024).

AI-Enhanced Compensation and Payroll Management

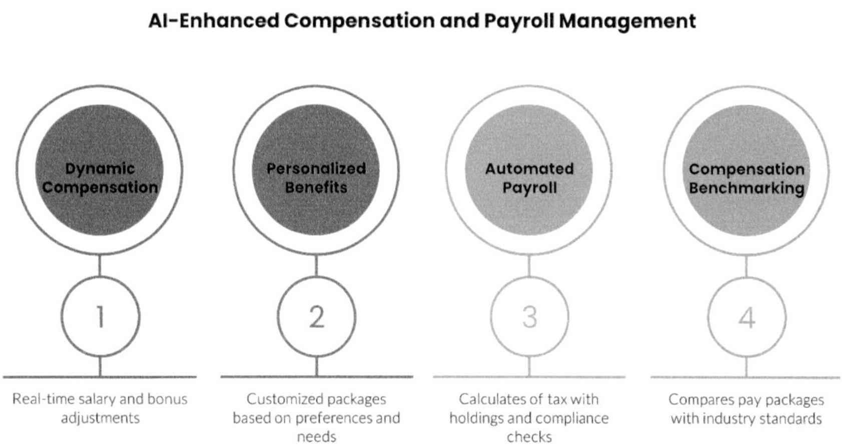


**Fig. 5** AI-Enhanced Compensation and Payroll Management.
*Source:* Author

The practices depicted in Fig. 5 integrated with AI, leverages advanced algorithms to automate AI payroll processing. This improves accuracy, efficiency, and competitiveness, while freeing HR for other tasks (Liang, 2024).

1. **Dynamic Compensation:** AI adjusts salary and bonus in real-time according to the market trend and performance of each employee, so that they can be competitive and aligned with external benchmarks and internal achievements (Aggarwal et al., 2022).

2. **Personalized Benefits:** AI customizes packages to employees based on preferences and needs, making them more relevant and attractive by such plans as targeted health plans that boost satisfaction and engagement (Thite and Sandhu, 2014).
3. **Automated Payroll:** AI enforces payroll calculations, tax withholding, and compliance in a framework that minimizes errors and speed-up on-time payments, freeing HR for strategic tasks (Ahmed et al., 2023).
4. **Compensation Benchmarking:** AI compares company pay packages with industry standards in real-time, ensuring competitive pay and adjusting strategies to attract top talent and retain them (Callewaert and Vennekens, 2024).

## Retention Strategies

Employees are a company's most valuable asset, and retaining them poses one of the greatest challenges for managers. Losing an employee can mean losing vital aspects of company culture, core values, and essential skills, which can be detrimental to the organization. The expense of replacing an employee is substantial, making it imperative to focus on retaining current staff for the firm's growth and stability (Singh, 2019). Figure 6 shows traditional retention strategies.

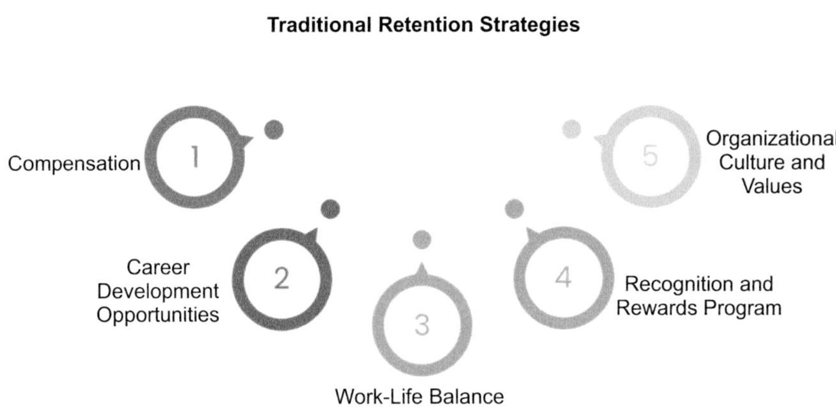


**Fig. 6** Traditional Retention Strategies.
*Source:* Author

1. **Compensation:** Compensation is, therefore, the real reason any organization can retain its employees. It's a potent factor for showing commitment to the workers and making them stick around. Most successful organizations emphasize this in a number of ways, such as security plans, scholarships, medical allowances, career growth, stock options, and several other incentives (Hannay and Northam, 2000).

2. **Career Development Opportunities:** By providing growth opportunities through training and mentorship ensure that employees are engaged and motivated. Investing in these aspects not only enhances job satisfaction and loyalty but also aligns individual goals with organizational objectives (Crawshaw et al., 2012, Hosen et al., 2024).
3. **Work-Life Balance:** WLB initiatives like flexible working hours, extensive leave options, dependent care support, and family-related services enhance an organization's reputation. These programs help alleviate conflicts between work and family life, promote diversity, and encourage organizational commitment, all of which contribute to higher employee satisfaction and engagement (Smith and Gardner, 2007; Tahir, 2024).
4. **Recognition and Rewards Program:** Workers are acknowledged and compensated for their efforts through the thoughtful allocation of financial and non-financial benefits. Reward and Recognition programs are the crucial element of HRM designed to create, implement, and sustain reward systems that correspond with the organization's objectives. These programs are intended to attract, cultivate, and hold onto exceptional talent (Bolatito and Mohamoud, 2024).
5. **Organizational Culture and Values:** Organizational culture is one of the most important drivers of success in today's fast-changing business environment. It defines an organization's identity and brand and is, therefore, the set of shared values, beliefs, norms, and behaviors. Through its impact on attitudes, behaviors, and performance at large, this culture has a bearing on employees.

An organizational culture of positivism, guided by values such as integrity, professionalism, and accountability, provides the working environment with support and sets. A strong culture in company's moves hand-in-hand with the fostering of innovation for long-term success and adaptability in a dynamic business environment (Alateeg and Alhammadi, 2024).

### *AI-Integrated Retention Strategies*

These strategies as shown in Fig. 7 use data analytics to predict turnover risks and tailor solutions, they help organizations proactively manage talent, improve job satisfaction, and foster long-term employee loyalty (Maulita and Mesra, 2024; Brown et al., 2024).

1. **Predictive Analysis for C ompensation Analysis:** This encompasses all types of rewards that employees derive from working for the organization, starting from salary and bonuses to company-subsidized health insurance and paid time off. This is a comprehensive package intended to attract, retain, and motivate staff (Yanamala, 2024).
2. **AI-Driven Personalized Career Pathing:** AI-driven personalized career pathing utilises artificial intelligence to come up with individual-centric career development plans that are tailored with individual employee's unique

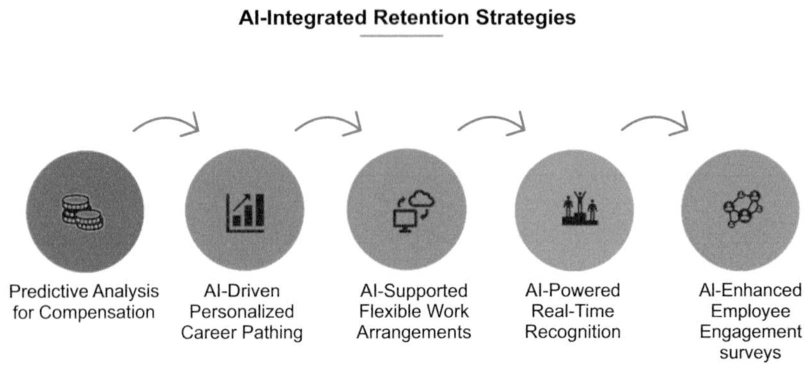


**Fig. 7** AI-Integrated Retention Strategies.
*Source:* Author

skills and aspirations. It considers factors such as employee performance data and career goals to create personalized training and job recommendations, improving employee satisfaction and fueling growth in a manner consistent with organizational needs (Bankins et al., 2024).

3. **AI-Supported Flexible Work Arrangements:** AI algorithms can thus optimize flexible work schedules by using attendance, preference, and workload data to derive dynamic, efficient schedules that adjust in real-time to changes and ensure effective resource allocation, high satisfaction for the employees, and enhancement of general productivity (Roberto et al., 2023).
4. **AI-powered Real-Time Recognition:** AI tools allow for real-time engagement and recognition through performance data analysis in real time, providing insights and personalized acknowledgments. This acts as a motivation booster for continuous development in a much more responsive and engaging work environment (Madhumita et al., 2024).
5. **AI-Enhanced Employee Engagement Surveys:** Integrating AI into retention strategies enhances their effectiveness by leveraging data-driven insights, automation, and personalization to meet the evolving needs and expectations of employees in today's workforce (Azash et al., 2024).

## Traditional vs AI-Integrated Administrative Tasks

The traditional tasks performed include record-keeping, scheduling, and document management. This involves piles of paperwork and manual updating, which can be time-consuming and prone to errors. HR staff spend many hours maintaining personnel records, organizing working schedules, and complying with regulations (Zhang and Chen, 2024).

The development of the digital administration state represents a major opportunity and advancement in it (Egidy, 2024). AI transforms these routine HR tasks by automating processes like record maintenance, scheduling, and compliance management. AI systems streamline data entry, update records in real time, and handle scheduling conflicts with minimal human intervention. This automation enhances overall efficiency, accuracy, and productivity, and allows HR professionals to concentrate on strategic and value-added activities (Ravshanbekov, 2024).

## Future Trends and Innovations in AI for HR

At the junction of technology, globalization, and changing social expectations lies the reshaping of the future of work in this dynamic 21st century. In the face of unprecedented change, the role of HR has become integral in reshaping the future of work. The integration of automation, in a really short period has transformed traditional HR practices (Ayanponle et al., 2024). Figure 8 is an iconic representation of AI's transformative penetration on HR, showcasing the trends and innovations driving this change.

**Fig. 8** Transformation of HR Traditional Practices to Innovative HR.
*Source:* Author

1. **Advanced Predictive Analytics:** (Reena et al., 2019a)
   - **Trend:** This helps the HR of an organization make decisions on the basis of data, predict employee behaviour and forecast workforce needs.
   - **Innovation:** Offers insights into turnover risks and career progression, enabling proactive HR management.

2. **AI-powered Talent Acquisition** (Ali and Kallach, 2024, Davenport and Ronanki, 2018)
   - **Trend:** Enhances recruitment by sourcing, screening and interviewing candidates.
   - **Innovation:** AI chatbots and virtual tools will streamline candidate interactions and accelerates hiring.

3. **Personalized Learning and Development** (Chaturvedi, 2016, Coolen et al., 2023)
   - **Trend:** Helps in providing personalized training based on employee needs and goals, identifies emerging skill demands in the market, skill gaps of the employees, learning preferences and industry shifts.
   - **Innovation:** Adaptive platforms will provide bespoke learning experiences and skill recommendations.

4. **Enhanced Employee Experience** (Reena et al., 2019b; Prakash et al., 2021)
   - **Trend:** Integration of AI in HR can significantly impact employee experience, performance and engagement with real-time feedback and personalized support.
   - **Innovation:** AI can identify patterns, and factors with the feedback and recommend ways for enhancing satisfaction and productivity.
5. **Automated HR Operations** (Prakash et al., 2021)
   - **Trend:** AI-powered chatbots and virtual assistants automates or streamlines administrative tasks and improvises employee support.
   - **Innovation:** This makes operations smoother, reduces errors, and free HR to focus on strategic work.
6. **AI-Driven Diversity and Inclusion** (Kakulapati et al., 2020)
   - **Trend:** AI will improve diversity and inclusion by fostering collaborations between teams, encouraging open communication, and bringing out creative ideas.
   - **Innovation:** This will ensure equal opportunities through the analysis of the hiring and promotion patterns.

**Fig. 9** AI in HR Strategies.
*Source:* Author

AI is set to revolutionize HR Strategies and policies across various functions. Recruitment process will be streamlined as AI automates from candidates sourcing to interviewing, reducing time-to-hire. For employee management, it will enable personalized onboarding, continuous performance tracking, and tailored learning paths (Petrika-Lindroos, 2022). AI will drive data-driven decision-making in compensation, benefits, and workforce planning. It will improve employee engagement through sentiment analysis and predictive retention strategies. In compliance and risk management, AI will ensure adherence to regulations and detect potential issues (Zehir et al., 2020). It will help initiatives towards diversity and inclusion by finding and mitigating biases. Additionally, AI will support data-driven policy development by analyzing trends and outcomes from various HR practices, leading to more effective and evidence-based policies. As organizations navigate this shift, they'll need to reimagine HR policies to account for AI's growing influence while ensuring they maintain the human touch in people management (Plastino and Purdy, 2018). Figure 9 illustrates integration of AI in HR strategies.

## Ethical Considerations of AI in HR

Figure 10 shows the ethical dimensions of AI, detailing the crucial considerations involved.

- **Ethical Implications:** There are several concerns related to privacy, bias, and accountability that are raised with regard to AI in HR. One should be concerned with the algorithms of AI working not to reinforce existing biases or violate the privacy of an employee. There needs to be transparency regarding AI decision-making and the data used so that ethical standards and trust can be upheld (Andrieux et al., 2024).
- **Fairness and Transparency:** The challenges embedded with fairness, transparency, privacy, accountability and the decision-making process of AI are beyond technical considerations. To ensure fairness, AI systems should be regularly audited for biases and discriminatory practices. On the other hand, transparent processes, including clear explanations of how AI made decisions and the criteria should be made available. This is essential in maintaining trust and ensuring equitable treatment of all employees (Shah Awais and Thrun Sebastian 2024).

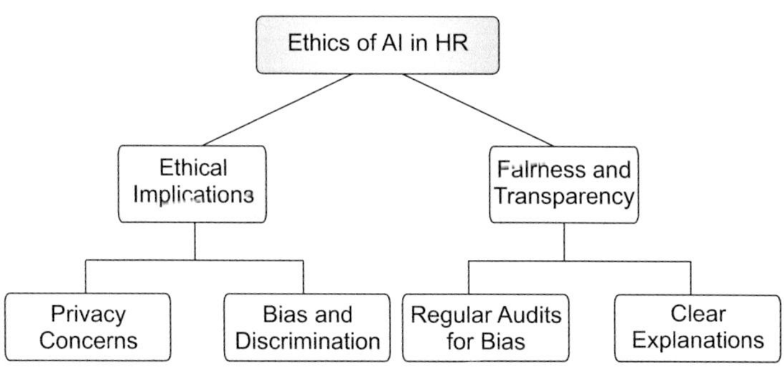


**Fig. 10** Ethics of AI in HR.
*Source:* Author

## Conclusion

This chapter explores the transformative era of Human Resources (HR) as it integrates with Artificial Intelligence (AI), tracing the evolution from traditional methods to advanced AI-enhanced practices. AI has significantly impacted HR by revolutionizing processes from recruitment through to retention strategies. Historically reliant on manual processes, HR practices have been transformed by AI, which streamlines tasks such as resume screening, matching the candidate, onboarding to training and retaining the top talented employee. This shift has allowed HR professionals to save time and redirect their focus towards strategic objectives that contribute to organizational success. Looking ahead, future trends and innovations indicate that AI will continue to refine HR practices with even greater precision. Enhanced predictive analytics will enable proactive workforce planning and personalized employee development. There will be a heightened emphasis on ethical AI to ensure fairness and transparency, while AI-driven tools will increasingly support employee well-being by monitoring and addressing mental health and work-life balance. These advancements will not only optimize HR functions but also elevate the overall employee experience, positioning organizations to adapt effectively to an evolving business landscape.

### *Novelty*

The novelty of this chapter lies in its extensive examination of the progression of human resources, viewed through the prism of artificial intelligence (AI). It charts the transition from traditional manual processes to cutting-edge, AI-enhanced applications and tools. The chapter emphasises the influence of AI, right from the hiring most suitable candidate to retaining the top talent empowering HR professionals to concentrate on strategic duties. The future trends indicate that AI will continue to influence and advance the practices of HR people. The integration of AI in these practices will continue to reshape and enhance organizational success in a dynamic business environment.

## References

Adler, S., Campion, M., Colquitt, A., Grubb, A., Murphy, K., Ollander-Krane, R. and Pulakos, E.D. (2016). Getting rid of performance ratings: Genius or folly? A debate. *Industrial and Organizational Psychology*, *9*(2), 219–252.

Aggarwal, T., Tiwari, S., Kumar, A. and Yadav, S.S. (2022, December). Design and Implementation: A Review of Payroll Management System. In *2022 4th International Conference on Advances in Computing, Communication Control and Networking (ICAC3N)* (pp. 26–32). IEEE.

Aguinis, H., Gottfredson, R.K. and Joo, H. (2012). Delivering effective performance feedback: The strengths-based approach. *Business Horizons*, *55*(2), 105–111.

Aguinis, H., Joo, H., and Gottfredson, R.K. (2011). Why we hate performance management—And why we should love it. *Business Horizons*, *54*(6), 503–507.

Ahmed, A.M., Mohammed, C.N., and Ahmad, A.M. (2023). Web-based payroll management system: design, implementation, and evaluation. *Journal of Electrical Systems and Information Technology*, *10*(1), 17.

Alateeg, S., and Alhammadi, A. (2024). The impact of organizational culture on organizational innovation with the mediation role of strategic leadership in Saudi Arabia. *Journal of Statistics Applications & Probability*, *13*(2), 843–858.

Ali, O. and Kallach, L. (2024). Artificial Intelligence Enabled Human Resources Recruitment Functionalities: A Scoping Review. *Procedia Computer Science*, *232*, 3268–3277.

Alsaif, A. and Sabih Aksoy, M. (2023). AI-HRM: artificial intelligence in human resource management: a literature review. *Journal of Computing and Communication*, *2*(2), 1–7.

Andrieux, P., Johnson, R.D., Sarabadani, J. and Van Slyke, C. (2024). Ethical considerations of generative AI-enabled human resource management. *Organizational Dynamics*, *53*(1), 101032.

Ansari, R.M.M. and Jayakrishnan, S.S. (2019, December). Emerging trends in human resource analytics in upcoming decade.

Arifuzzaman, M., Islam, M.S., Masum, M.Y. and Annona, J.S. (2023). The use of e-recruitment Process with comparison of Traditional Recruitment Process in Bangladesh: A case Study on BRAC Bank Ltd. *Journal of Education, Management and Development Studies*, *3*(2), 15–25.

Aswal, D.K. (Ed.). (2020). *Metrology for inclusive growth of India*. Springer Nature.

Ayanponle, L.O., Elufioye, O.A., Asuzu, O.F., Ndubuisi, N.L., Awonuga, K.F. and Daraojimba, R.E. (2024). The future of work and human resources: A review of emerging trends and HR's evolving role. *International Journal of Science and Research Archive*, *11*(2), 113–124.

Azash, S.M.D., Subbaiah, P.V. and Vilcekova, L. (2024). Predictive Analytics: A Tool for Strategic Decision of Employee Turnover. *Intelligent Techniques for Predictive Data Analytics*, 231.

Bankins, S., Jooss, S., Restubog, S.L.D., Marrone, M., Ocampo, A.C. and Shoss, M. (2024). Navigating career stages in the age of artificial intelligence: A systematic interdisciplinary review and agenda for future research. *Journal of Vocational Behavior*, 104011.

Bauer, T.N. (2010). Maximizing success. *SHRM Foundation's Effective practice guidelines series*.

Bhatt, P., and Muduli, A. (2023). Artificial intelligence in learning and development: a systematic literature review. *European Journal of Training and Development*, *47*(7/8), 677–694.

Bolatito, A.O.S. and Mohamoud, Y. A. (2024). Reward Management and Employee Performance: A Review of Job Satisfaction in Somalia. *TWIST*, *19*(1), 128–137.

Bradt, G.B. and Vonnegut, M. (2009). *Onboarding: How to get your new employees up to speed in half the time*. John Wiley & Sons.

Bretz Jr, R.D. and Thompsett, R.E. (1992). Comparing traditional and integrative learning methods in organizational training programs. *Journal of Applied Psychology*, *77*(6), 941.

Brown, J., Burke, J. and Sauciuc, A. (2024). Using Artificial Intelligence to Evaluate Employees: The Effects on Recruitment, Effort, and Retention. *Kelley School of Business Research Paper*, (2021–25).

Bryant, P.C. and Allen, D.G. (2013). Compensation, Benefits and Employee Turnover. *Compensation & Benefits Review, 45(3), 171–175.* doi:10.1177/0886368713494342.

Buck, B. and Morrow, J. (2018). AI, performance management and engagement: keeping your best their best. *Strategic HR Review*, *17*(5), 261–262.

Callewaert, B. and Vennekens, J. (2024). Answer Set Programming for Flexible Payroll Management. *arXiv preprint arXiv:2403.12823*.

Cappelli, P. and Tavis, A. (2016). The performance management revolution. *Harvard Business Review*, *94*(10), 58–67.

Cena, Joshua. (2024). Exploring the Evolution of Artificial Intelligence: From Early Concepts to Modern Applications. Artificial Life.

Chaturvedi, V. (2016, July). Talent Analytics as an Indispensable Tool and an Emerging Facet of HR for Organization Building. *FIIB Business Review*, 5(3), 13–20.

Coolen, P., Heuvel, S.V.D., Voorde, K.V.D. and Paauwe, J. (2023, December). Understanding the adoption and institutionalization of workforce analytics: A systematic literature review and research agenda. *Human Resource Management Review*, 33(4), 100985.

Crawshaw, J.R., Van Dick, R. and Brodbeck, F.C. (2012). Opportunity, fair process and relationship value: career development as a driver of proactive work behaviour. *Human Resource Management Journal*, *22*(1), 4–20.

Das, G. (2019). Impact of Artificial Intelligence on Human Resource Management in Today's Era. *Think India Journal*, *22*(20), 273–288.

Davenport, T.H. and Ronanki, R. (2018). Artificial intelligence for the real world. *Harvard business review*, *96*(1), pp. 108–116.

Davis, J.H.S. (2000). Traditional vs. On-line learning: It's not an either/or proposition. *Employment Relations Today, 27*(1), 47–60. doi:10.1002/ert.3910270105.

Dominic, T. and Kumar, R . (2024). *Recruitment and Onboarding in IT Companies with Integration of AI Technologies*. 2455–6211.

Egidy, S. (2024). Resilient Administrative Technology. *Georgia Law Review*, *58*(3), 7.

Enz, C. A. and Siguaw, J.A. (2000). Best practices in human resources. *Cornell Hotel and Restaurant Administration Quarterly*, *41*(1), 48–61.

Gardner, H. (1999). Intelligence reframed: Multiple intelligences for the 21st century. New York, NY: Basic Book.

Gazell, J.A. (2000). Drucker on effective public management. *Journal of Management History (Archive), 6*(1), 48–62. doi:10.1108/13552520010316619.

Gil de Zúñiga, H., Goyanes, M. and Durotoye, T. (2024). A scholarly definition of artificial intelligence (AI): advancing AI as a conceptual framework in communication research. *Political Communication*, *41*(2), 317–334.

Gupta, R. (2024). Impact of Artificial Intelligence (AI) on Human Resource Management (HRM). *International Journal For Multidisciplinary Research, doi, 10.*

Hajjami, O., and Crocco, O.S. (2024). Evolving approaches to employee engagement: comparing antecedents in remote work and traditional workplaces. *European Journal of Training and Development*, *48*(3/4), 375–392.

Halid, H., Ravesangar, K., Mahadzir, S.L., and Halim, S.N.A. (2024). Artificial Intelligence (AI) in Human Resource Management (HRM). In *Building the Future with Human Resource Management* (pp. 37–70). Cham: Springer International Publishing.

Hall-Jones, J., Simmons, T., Stermer, E., van Hemert, J.P. and Vogel, M. (2018). Onboarding employees through shared values. *Journal of Research, Assessment, and Practice in Higher Education*, *3*(1), 9.

Hannay, M. and Northam, M. (2000). *Low-Cost Strategies for Employee Retention. Compensation & Benefits Review, 32*(4), 65–72. doi:10.1177/08863680022097920.

Hassan, S.H. (2020). Impacts of implementation of extensive onboarding process on employee retention–a casestudy from transferwise. *Master's Thesis. Tallinn University of Technology, Tallinn, Estonia.*

Hosen, S., Hamzah, S.R.A., Ismail, I.A., Alias, S.N., Abd Aziz, M.F. and Rahman, M.M. (2024). Training & development, career development, and organizational commitment as the predictor of work performance. *Heliyon*, *10*(1).

Hu, Q. (2023). Unilever's Practice on AI-based Recruitment. *Highlights in Business, Economics and Management*, *16*, 256–263.

Ilie, V. (2019). Traditional learning versus e-learning. *European Proceedings of Social and Behavioural Sciences.*

Jacoby, S.M. (2004). *Employing bureaucracy: Managers, unions, and the transformation of work in the 20th century*. Psychology Press.

Ju, A., Sajnani, H., Kelly, S. and Herzig, K. (2021, May). A case study of onboarding in software teams: Tasks and strategies. In *2021 IEEE/ACM 43rd International Conference on Software Engineering (ICSE)* (pp. 613–623). IEEE.

Kakulapati, V., Chaitanya, K.K., Chaitanya, K.V.G. and Akshay, P. (2020, July). Predictive analytics of HR - A machine learning approach.

Kambur, E., and Yildirim, T. (2023). From traditional to smart human resources management. *International Journal of Manpower*, *44*(3), 422–452.

Kaplan, A. and Haenlein, M. (2019). Siri, Siri, in my hand: Who's the fairest in the land? On the interpretations, illustrations, and implications of artificial intelligence. *Business Horizons*, *62*(1), 15–25. https://doi.org/10.1016/j.bushor.2018.08.0.

Kaur, G. and Kaur, R. (2022, October). A critical review on analysis of human resource functions using AI technologies. In *AIP Conference Proceedings* (Vol. 2555, No. 1). AIP Publishing.

Kochan, T.A. and Cappelli, P. (1982). The transformation of the industrial relations and personnel function.

Kumar, N. and Pandey, S. (2017). New employee onboarding process in an organization. *International Journal of Engineering Development and Research*, *5*(1), 198–206.

Latham, G.P. (1988). Human resource training and development. *Annual Review of Psychology*, *39*(1), 545–582.

Liang, Y. (2024). The Impact of Artificial Intelligence on Employment and Income Distribution. *Journal of Education, Humanities and Social Sciences*, *27*, 166–171.

Licy Varghese, D.U.U., Kambar, M.Y., Natvarbhai, S.J. and Jha, S. (2023). Employee Training and Development: Assessing The Effectiveness of Various Training Methods. *Remittances Review*, *8*(4).

Madanchian, M., Taherdoost, H. and Mohamed, N. (2023). AI-Based Human Resource Management Tools and Techniques; A Systematic Literature Review. *Procedia Computer Science*, *229*, 367–377.

Madhumita, G., Diana, P.D., Neena, P.C., Kiran, P.N., Aggarwal, S. and Nargunde, A.S. (2024, April). AI-powered Performance Management: Driving Employee Success and Organizational Growth. In *2024 5th International Conference on Recent Trends in Computer Science and Technology (ICRTCST)* (pp. 204–209). IEEE.

Maganti, Sridevi. (2023). Transformative Impact Exploring the Integration of AI on HRM. 10.13140/RG.2.2.19979.87844.

Maity, S. (2019). Identifying opportunities for artificial intelligence in the evolution of training and development practices. *Journal of Management Development*, *38*(8), 651–663.

Masud, H., Daud, W.N.W., Zainol, F.A., Rashid, N. and Afthanorhan, A. (2018). Past and Future of Human Resource Functions: Are We Done? *International Journal of Academic Research in Business and Social Sciences*, *8*(11), 1149–1171.

Maulita, C. and Mesra, B. (2024, January). Analysis of Compensation, Work Environment on Employee Performance with Satisfaction Employment as an Intervening Variable. In *Proceeding of International Conference on Artificial Intelligence, Navigation, Engineering, and Aviation Technology (ICANEAT)* (Vol. 1, No. 1, pp. 175–178).

Mayo, E. (2004). *The human problems of an industrial civilization*. Routledge.

McCarthy, J., Minsky, M.L., Rochester, N. and Shannon, C.E. (1955). A proposal for the Dartmouth summer research project on artificial intelligence. Available at http:// www-formal.stanford.edu/jmc/history/dartmouth/ dartmouth.html.

Minsky, M.L. (1968). Semantic information processing. Cambridge, MA: MIT Press.

Nazareno, L. and Schiff, D.S. (2021). *The impact of automation and artificial intelligence on worker well-being. Technology in Society, 67, 101679.* doi:10.1016/j.techsoc.2021.101679.

Okoye, P.V.C. and Ezejiofor, R.A. (2013). The effect of human resources development on organizational productivity. *International Journal of Academic Research in Business and Social Sciences*, *3*(10), 250.

Petrika-Lindroos, I. (2022). Unlocking the power of AI in HR: how Artificial Intelligence can elevate the HR strategy in knowledge-based organizations.

Plastino, E. and Purdy, M. (2018). Game changing value from Artificial Intelligence: eight strategies. *Strategy & Leadership*, *46*(1), 16–22.

Poole, M. (Ed.). (1999). *Human resource management: critical perspectives on business and management* (Vol. 2). Taylor & Francis.

Prakash, K.B., Reddy, A.A.S. and Yasaswi, R.K.K., (2021, December). AI-Powered HCM: The Analytics and Augmentations. IntechOpen eBooks.

Pulakos, E.D. (2009). *Performance Management: A New Approach for Driving Business Results*. John Wiley & Sons.

Rahmawati, N.D. (2024). Human Resource Planning at Baitul Maal Wat Tamwil. *Journal of Economic, Religious, and Entrepreneurship (JoERE)*, *2*(1), 46–54.

Ravshanbekov, B. (2024). Transition from Traditional Public Administration to Digital Public Administration and Adaptation of Public Administration to Emerging Technologies. *International Journal of Law and Policy*, *2*(5), 7–15.

Reena., K, M. M. A. and Jayakrishnan, S.S. (2019, December). Emerging trends in human resource analytics in upcoming decade.

Ritz, E., Donisi, F., Elshan, E. and Rietsche, R. (2023, January). Artificial Socialization? How Artificial Intelligence Applications Can Shape A New Era of Employee Onboarding Practices. In *HICSS* (pp. 155–164).

Roberto, R., Penna, M., Felici, B. and Rao, M. (2023). Smart working and flexible work arrangements: opportunities and risks for sustainable communities. In *Intelligent Environments* (pp. 243–283). North-Holland.

Rohit, A.K., Saini, M. and Pawar, M. (2024). Integration of Artificial Intelligence In Human Resource Information System. *International Journal of Innovative Research in Technology and Science*, *12*(2), 177–183.

Saju, M.D., Oswal, N. and Ateeq, K. (2021), "Artificial intelligence (AI): bringing a new revolution in human resource management (HRM)", *Grenze International Journal of Engineering and Technology*, Vol. 7, pp. 211–218.

Sawaneh, I.A. and Kamara, F.K. (2019). Evaluating employee retention strategies on job performance. *Science Journal of Business and Management*, *7*(3), 67–73.

Schraeder, M. and Jordan, M. (2011). Managing performance: A practical perspective on managing employee performance. *The Journal for Quality and Participation*, *34*(2), 4.

Shah, Awais and Thrun, Sebastian. (2024). Ethical Considerations in Artificial Intelligence Implementation for Human Resources Management. 10.13140/RG.2.2.23622.89923.

Sharma, F.C. (2023). *Human Resource Management*. SBPD Publications.

Sharma, R.C., and Sharma, S. (2024). *Compensation and Reward Management: Wage and Salary Administration and Benefits*. Taylor & Francis.

Sills, M. (2014). E-recruitment: A comparison with traditional recruitment and the influences of social media: A qualitative and quantitative review.

Singh, D. (2019). A literature review on employee retention with focus on recent trends. *International Journal of Scientific Research in Science and Technology, 6*(1), 425, 431.

Smith, J., and Gardner, D.H. (2007). Factors affecting employee use of work-life balance initiatives.

Smith, V. (1994). *Braverman's Legacy. Work and Occupations, 21*(4), 403–421. doi:10.1177/0730888494021004004.

Sonnentag, S., Niessen, C. and Ohly, S. (2004). Learning at work: training and development. *International Review of Industrial and Organizational Psychology*, *19*, 249–290.

Stoiber, C., Walchshofer, C., Grassinger, F., Stitz, H., Streit, M. and Aigner, W. (2021, September). Design and comparative evaluation of visualization onboarding methods. In *Proceedings of the 14th International Symposium on Visual Information Communication and Interaction* (pp. 1–5).

Tahir, R. (2024). Work–life balance: is an entrepreneurial career the solution?. *Journal of Entrepreneurship in Emerging Economies*, *16*(4), 845–867.

Taras, V. (2012). *Direct Versus Indirect Compensation. Compensation & Benefits Review, 44*(1), 24–28. doi:10.1177/0886368712445666.

Thite, M. and Sandhu, K. (2014). Where is my pay? Critical success factors of a payroll system–A system life cycle approach. *Australasian Journal of Information Systems*, *18*(2).

Upadhyay, A.K. and Khandelwal, K. (2018) "Artificial intelligence-based training learning from application", *Development and Learning in Organizations: An International Journal*, https://doi.org/10.1108/DLO-05-2018-0058.

Verma, A., Mahanandia, R. and Dixit, A. (2023). Emerging Impact of Artificial Intelligence in Human Resources. *Journal of Research Administration*, *5*(2), 399–405.

Vimaladevi, S., Gopi, V., Kumar, R. and Rajalakshmi, M. (2024). The Role of AI in Workforce Planning and Optimization: A Study on Staffing and Resource Allocation. *Asian And Pacific Economic Review*, *17*(2), 123–144.

Vishwanath, B. and Vaddepalli, S. (2023). The Future of Work: Implications of Artificial Intelligence on Hr Practices. *Tuijin Jishu/Journal of Propulsion Technology*, *44*(3), 1711–1724.

Yanamala, K.K.R. (2024). Artificial Intelligence in talent development for proactive retention strategies. *Journal of Advanced Computing Systems*, *4*(8), 13–21.

Yusuf, S.O., Abubakar, J.E., Durodola, R.L., Ocran, G., Paul-Adeleye, A.H. and Yusuf, P.O. (2024). Impact of AI on continuous learning and skill development in the workplace: A comparative study with traditional methods.

Zehir, C., Karaboga, T. and Basar, D. (2020). The transformation of human resource management and its impact on overall business performance: big data analytics and AI technologies in strategic HRM. *Digital Business Strategies in Blockchain Ecosystems: Transformational Design and Future of Global Business*, 265–279.

Zhang, J. and Chen, Z. (2024). Exploring human resource management digital transformation in the digital age. *Journal of the Knowledge Economy*, *15*(1), 1482–1498.

Ziden, A.A. and Joo, O.C. (2020). Exploring digital onboarding for organizations: A concept paper. *International Journal of Innovation, Creativity and Change*, *13*(9), 734–750.

# 2 The Future of Insurance: How AI is Shaping the Sector

Shruti Tyagi[1], Apurva Saxena[2] and Bhavna Sharma[3*]

**The combination of AI and insurance was once an idyllic idea, but it has now become an imperative, transforming how insurers analyze, manage, and mitigate risks. AI benefits the insurance sector in a variety of ways. It aids in accelerated underwriting, hazard assessment, more equitable pricing, and tailored policies. AI helps to speed up claim processing and detect fraudulent activity.** Furthermore, AI enables the performance of operations by means of lowering administrative overhead via automation. The purpose of the study is to examine the current and potential AI applications in the insurance sector and also to analyse the impact of AI in the insurance sector. The study employed a descriptive research design and the data has been collected through secondary sources like journals, books, reports, websites, etc. The study found that AI has enabled insurers to streamline processes, enhance efficiency, and offer extra customized danger evaluation for its clients. This has led to a seamless and handy revel in for policyholders, in addition to extra correct underwriting and pricing for insurers. Additionally, AI has facilitated the automation of claims processing, taking into account quicker and extra correct claims settlements. However, the implementation of AI within the coverage enterprise also presents demanding issues that need to be solved.

## Introduction

Artificial Intelligence (AI) refers to simulation of human intelligence in machines. It consists of the development of algorithms, software, and hardware that allow machines to perform duties generally requiring human intelligence. These duties can embody problem-solving, perception, natural language understanding, and decision-making (Ali et al., 2023). From the 1980s to the 1990s, the insurance industry began to use AI for data analysis and risk assessment. Expert structures and rule-primarily based total algorithms had been used to automate underwriting and claims processing, though they had been noticeably fundamental in comparison

[1,2] Student, School of Commerce, Finance & Accountancy, Christ University, India.
[3] Assistant Professor, School of Commerce, Finance & Accountancy, Christ University, India.
Email: shruti.tyagiji@gmail.com[1]; apurva.saxena62@gmail.com[2]
* Corresponding author: u.bhavna@gmail.com

DOI: 10.1201/9781003559849-2

to fashionable AI. In the early 2000s, the enterprise commenced incorporating greater superior predictive analytics models.The deployment of chatbots and digital assistants inside the coverage region became more common within the 2010s (Ladva, 2023). In today's swiftly converting technological landscape, the coverage agencies locate themselves at a vital crossroads, assured to leverage the transformative capacity of Artificial Intelligence (AI). The combination of AI and insurance was once an idyllic idea, but it has now become an imperative, transforming how insurers analyze, manage, and mitigate risks. AI is helping coverage agencies in a variety of ways. First of all, it may assist in stepped forward underwriting, permitting hazard assessment, fairer pricing and personalised policies. Second, AI helps to expedite claim processing and detect fraudulent activity. Furthermore, AI enables the performance of operations by means of lowering administrative overhead via automation. Finally, AI gives 24/7 purchaser offerings via chat bots improving purchaser experience (Banu, 2022). A Chat bot is a laptop designed utility that uses auditory and textual manners to stimulate an effective conversation with human clients (Ladva, 2023). Chat bots allow you to communicate with clients in the language they understand, making the conversation more personal. Prominent examples of the latest generation used in AI conversation bots embody methodologies for learning word representations and text classification. (Zia and Kalia, 2022), (Ahmad and Saxena, 2022). The purpose of the study is to examine the current and potential AI applications in the insurance sector and also to analyse the impact of AI in the insurance sector.

## Review of Literature

**Banu (2022) demonstrated that big data applications are growing in the insurance market, providing insight from massive data sets and improving results while lowering costs.** Eckert et al., (2022) outlined a review of digital apps and their advantages for insurers in controlling client happiness. The results demonstrated how digital applications may enhance sales and marketing by accelerating and simplifying (standard) operations, as well as by creating user-friendly procedures that increase productivity and improve the density of client encounters. The insurance industry benefited from higher client satisfaction levels. Sharma et al., (2022) investigated the role of synthetic intelligence within India's coverage zone. The study, conducted from 2017 to 2021, discovered that the coverage enterprise is growing inside the country; hence, AI is critical for the growth of each region, and the coverage business is rapidly implementing AI-era tactics for state efficiency. They stated that insurance and technology are moving the era into the realm of coverage. They highlighted the area by identifying important and decisive factors for learning. The researcher found that bringing technology that involves machine learning into the sphere of coverage might be quite beneficial. They also emphasized that insurance and technology work together to provide a much more comprehensive service to consumers.

Johnson et al., (2023) provided the use of Design Science Research (DSR) paradigm and developed a Responsible Artificial Intelligence (RAI) answer assisting medical institution directors to pick out probably denied claims. They highlighted that, strategies i.e., the PI and PDP algorithms are higher to make betterment within the society. They endorsed that AI may be used to discover fraudulent claims. Kumar et al., (2023) conducted a quantitative literature evaluation of machine learning and artificial intelligence in the insurance industry. From 2012 to 2021, data was collected from secondary sources using the Scopus database. The investigation was carried out using bibliometric approaches to detect important gaps and conduct scientific evaluations of artificial intelligence and machine learning in insurance. The findings found that the United States and the United Kingdom have made significant contributions to AI and insurance, whereas southern and eastern Asia have lagged behind. Hayes et al., (2014) mentioned the huge virtual technology which has a huge strategic effect on insurance companies` virtual transformation. The findings supported that, an incorporated strategic attitude is needed to put in force virtual technology with coverage use instances because of their robust interdependencies and this doesn't rely upon any individual virtual generation. They additionally concluded that digitalization is explicitly creating an upward push within the importance of comprehensively coping with the IT of the coverage agency.

Singh et al., (2023) mentioned how generation affects hazard evaluation and the coverage contract. They discovered that the coverage of block chain and robo advisors, gadget learning, The insurance industry has been significantly impacted by artificial intelligence. Finally, they found that the policyholder must accept that the insurer is protecting his private information and is not constantly misusing it, therefore the principle of maximum desirable religion should most likely be implemented, regardless of the capability of regulatory measures. Bulte (2016) identified three major types of alternate launched by use of synthetic intelligence systems. First, the manner wherein coverage businesses engage with their customers (e.g. sales, client service) is being transformed. While client offerings historically required non-public interplay with an agent, broking or financial institution for client queries and product statistics because of a loss of channels, the statistics to be had has stepped forward notably over the net and/or through chat bots. At last, they concluded that using AI allows in chance discount which additionally advantages the coverage enterprise from frauds.

Ladva et al., (2023) discussed the influence of index coverage and the linkages between coverage and credit score. They provided a meta-analysis that outlines the most relevant results about the possibility of index coverage to improve credit score delivery for smallholders and thereby farm output. They stated that it isn't always the case, but they demonstrated that coverage demand is unquestionably hump-backed in risk aversion. They also stated that the impact of acceptance and training on actual hobbies isn't usually as significant as expected. The findings revealed that the relationship between premise chance and price is an important component of the plan for reporting safety items. They decided that there is room for improvement within the overall coverage and credit score.

Corea (2019) investigated if sales coverage would be greater green since it would provide subsidies while sales are low and marginal software is high, and it is far one of the most relevant to producers. They highlighted the involvement of the presidency in giving profits safety. They additionally located that, development of nation yield contracts at the Chicago Leading Organization of Exchange increases the opportunity that examiners may want to provide non-public reinsurance. They concluded that a sales coverage is a sort of scheme that ensures 75% of predicted sales to chance-averse producers. Mahajan (2021) talked about the bid facts for the coverage region and the way its utility has opened the door for brand new and progressive adjustments within the coverage enterprise. It became a secondary record series associated with the huge records analytics within the discipline of coverage zone. He discussed the blessings, architectural framework and its demanding situations and possibilities within the coverage zone. It was found out that analytics is evolving within the discipline of coverage zone and is improving to offer perception from the massive records units and enhancing consequences whilst decreasing value within the region of coverage zone. Sood et al., (2022) highlighted the block chain because the maximum sizable technological innovation in this era and maximum character are unaware of approximately its uses within the coverage zone. It became a secondary record series through specific papers. The findings found out that a few coverage organizations are actually investigating and making use of block chain generation for coins' waft tracking, fraud detection, and automatic claims. It additionally found out that the coverage enterprise is now starting to undertake block chain generation, and there are nonetheless quite a few critical issues that want to be resolved. Distributed ledger generation (DLT) makes it easy for all events concerned to speak pertinent records in actual time. Through this block chain generation is assisting all coverage carriers in minimising disparities regarding fraudulent claims.

Ahmad et al., (2023) proposed that the coverage zone is at the verge of a brand-new age due to the technology programs like block chain, the Internet of Things, and synthetic intelligence.It became a secondary record review of the technology inside the coverage zone. Economic progress has had an impact on the monetary hobby in a variety of ways, and the coverage zone is built on blockchain, while AI is also expected to grow in the future. They discussed the most essential role that blockchain and artificial intelligence play in the evolution of the insurance industry. The investigation discovered the advantages that accrue to both the issuer and the consumer with the objective of demonstrating the concepts and significance of block chain generation and synthetic intelligence within the insurance industry. Zarifis et al., (2022) talked about the effect of Fintech and Insur-tech. They indicated that they agree with a specific affiliation and the self-belief required within the invention, such as synthetic intelligence. The data was acquired using an online survey with 236 responses related to topics such as taking out a loan and purchasing coverage insurance. They used variables such as partial least squares structural equation modeling (PLS-SEM), multi-organizational evaluation (MGA), and so on. The studies revealed that Fintech and Insur-tech are equally suited to each location, and the current period is betting big on the advancement of both industries. They also stated that Fintech and Insurtech's emerging, pivotal roles are changing customer relationships. In this era of AI-driven virtual transformation, insurers and businesses rely on customer agreement.

Zia et al., (2022) mentioned the rising technology along with synthetic intelligence (AI), bid facts, block chain, the net of things (IoT), chat-bots, drones etc. in the context of coverage area. The facts became determined from the net of science (WoS) coral database. They have used R-studio for the fact's valuation and visualisation. The findings said that the most important range of exam articles allotted are related with widespread information, trailed through man-made intelligence and net-primarily based totally entertainment. They additionally said that the important article on man-made intelligence in safety confirmed up in 1975 (Web-primarily based totally entertainment) is the maximum improved mentioned new innovation, though the low codes are the unseen worldview for the safety place without an allotted exam. They cautioned that the impact of chat-bots, robots, and flexible innovation within the side of the safety commercial enterprise is presently at an early level and it's also assisting the coverage area to grow.

## Methodology

The study employed a descriptive research design and the data has been collected through secondary sources like journals, books, reports, websites, etc.

## Applications of AI in Insurance Sector

### *Artificial Intelligence in Insurance Operations*

Artificial Intelligence (AI) has emerged as a driving stress in insurance operations, reframing the way insurers assess, manage, and optimize their processes. With AI's capacity to examine massive volumes of data, each dependent and unstructured, coverage corporations can now make extra knowledgeable and well timed decisions. From underwriting to claims processing, AI automates and hurries up important tasks, decreasing administrative overhead and enhancing accuracy. Furthermore, AI assists insurers to discover risks, recommend policyholders on preventive measures, and personalised coverage offerings. This strengthens the operational performance and patron courting with the aid of presenting services. AI facilitates insurers in fraud detection stopping fraudulent activities (Ostrowska, 2021).

**Table 1** Global Insurtech Market (USD in Billion).

| *Year* | *Insurtech Market Revenue* |
|---|---|
| 2022 | 11.8 |
| 2023 | 16.6 |
| 2024 | 22.6 |
| 2025 | 34.3 |
| 2026 | 50.1 |

*Contd.*

**Table 1** *Contd.*

| *Year* | *Insurtech Market Revenue* |
|---|---|
| 2027 | 68.1 |
| 2028 | 85.2 |
| 2029 | 120.2 |
| 2030 | 163.1 |
| 2031 | 229.9 |
| 2032 | 336.5 |

*Source:* (Deloitte 2019)

## AI and Risk Assessment

AI's effect on chance valuation within the coverage businesses is profound. Traditional chance valuation methodologies had been frequently time-ingesting and relied closely on historic records. One of the important benefits of AI is its hotel chance evaluation is its cap potential to examine great datasets in real-time. It can system established records, consisting of historic claims statistics and policyholder information, in addition to unstructured records from assets like social media, climate reviews and IoT devices. AI's function in chance evaluation within the coverage businesses is transformative. It now no longer best facilitates insurers to examine an array of records assets, adapt to converting risks, and offer policyholders with particularly customized insurance however additionally complements purchaser revel in via means of offering fairer pricing and greater applicable coverage policies (Ostrowska, 2021).

## AI and Claims Processing

AI-powered chat bots and digital assistants are more and more getting used to address the preliminary level of claims processing. They engage with policyholders, gather initial facts approximately the declare, and manual them via the manner. This now no longer best assists to hurry up claims however additionally complements the general level of policyholders with the aid of imparting them with instant assistance. AI structures can manner and extract facts from numerous documents, inclusive of clinical reports, twist of fate records, and photos. AI's facts analytics talents are instrumental in detecting fraudulent claims. AI-pushed predictive fashions can help in figuring out suitable declared settlements (Ostrowska, 2021).

## AI and Underwriting

AI-pushed underwriting allows the introduction of fairly personalized coverage policies. Policies may be tailor-made to an individual's or company's precise chance profile, making sure that charges are in shape intently with the real dangers confronted through policyholders. AI in underwriting reduces administrative overhead through automating habitual obligations like facts access and report processing. This not only simplifies the underwriting process, but it also lowers insurers' operational costs. AI enhances the decision-making process by providing underwriters with fact-based suggestions. This allows underwriters to make greater knowledgeable and suitable decisions, particularly while handling complicated or high-fee policies (Ostrowska, 2021).

## AI and Customer Insights and Retention

**This early warning system enables insurers to take proactive steps to retain clients. AI enables insurers to provide tailored conversations to policyholders. This includes providing individualized renewal reminders, coverage updates, and centered offers. These custom-designed encounters help consumers feel appreciated and understood, hence increasing their loyalty to the insurer. AI helps insurers track the competitive landscape by analyzing market trends and competitor behaviors.** This statistic allows insurers to confirm their techniques and services to stay aggressive, keeping clients who may also bear in mind switching (Ostrowska, 2021).

**Table 2** Insurtech Market Share.

| *Technology* | *Market Share* |
|---|---|
| Cloud Computing | 23% |
| Block chain | 20% |
| IoT | 17% |
| Machine Learning | 15% |
| Robo Advisory | 11% |
| Other Technologies | 14% |

*Source:* (Infosys 2019)

**Companies using AI**

- Swiss Re makes use of AI for precise lifestyles coverage danger assessments, streamlining the underwriting process. Swiss Re makes use of AI for precise lifestyle coverage danger assessments.
- Geico's digital assistant Kate (mobile's AI-enabled Chabot) allows clients with coverage questions and updates anytime.
- Lemonade's AI, Jim, evaluates claims and cross-references them towards coverage details, frequently settling claims in mere seconds.
- One of America's biggest coverage firms, All state makes use of AI equipment to scrutinize claims for abnormal patterns, efficiently figuring out fraudulent claims.
- ICICI Lombard makes use of AI for short evaluation of motor coverage claims, the use of photographs and movies of the damage.

- Zurich Insurance has computerized lots of its records processing tasks, improving operational efficiency (Smart Tek 2024).

## Benefits of AI in Insurance Sector

**AI can automate repetitive tasks within the claims process, including as record entry, record inspection, and preliminary declaration validation. This frees up adjusters to focus on complicated claims and provide better customer service. AI can study large amounts of data to generate more detailed information about an individual's risk profile. This enables insurers to determine fairer and more competitive rates based only on each customer's individual scenario.**

AI-powered Chabot`s and digital assistants can offer instant purchaser support, solution questions on policies, or even provide customized suggestions for insurance options. AI can examine records to pick out styles and crimson flags that would imply fraudulent claims. This allows insurers to save money by reducing fraud, which may then be passed on to policyholders in the form of reduced rates. AI may be used to broaden new coverage services and products which can be tailor-made to unique purchaser needs. For example, AI-powered usage-primarily based totally automobile coverage can provide decrease costs to secure drivers (Banu, 2022).

## Impact of AI in Insurance Sector

AI has brought more personalized services, advertisement facilities with new data source services. The efficiency has been increased up to 60% through usage of AI in the insurance sector. To overcome the slow insurance procedure especially in property sector, in 2017, insurer invested in AI to improve the efficiency by automating claims and processing and 24*7 customer service (Chatbot). AI has brought more efficient and useful products of insurance to customers which also helped them in detection of fraud activities as well. Insurance firms can detect any risk related to their company, and using AI makes it easier and faster. The AI assists analysts by maintaining a steady state of discussion and giving them the simplicity of data operation. AI helps insurance companies audit massive amounts of data in seconds. By adding another data point, AI provides analysts with greater insights (Mahajan, 2021).

## Challenges Faced by AI in Insurance

**The protection of insurance data relies heavily on information, and artificial intelligence models require massive amounts of quality information to produce precise predictions. Providing accurate and timely information can be a considerable challenge. Insurance firms manage confidential client information.** Keeping up with information protection and security while utilizing simulated intelligence is a basic test, particularly with expanding guidelines like

GDPR and CCPA. The protection business is intensely directed, and simulated intelligence frameworks should agree with these guidelines. Guaranteeing that computer-based intelligence models fulfil legitimate and moral guidelines can be mind boggling and exorbitant.

Artificial intelligence fashions mainly profound getting to know fashions which might be regularly considered as "mystery elements," deciding on it looking to resolve their alternatives for customers and controllers. Interpretability and ease are essential within the safe place to gather trust. While AI can further develop extortion recognition, fraudsters can likewise utilize computer-based intelligence to turn out to be more refined. It's always hard to keep up with new ways to commit fraud. Developing and maintaining computer-based artificial intelligence frameworks necessitates a skilled workforce. Finding and preserving cap potential with flair in each simulated intelligence and safety is a task. Executing computer-based total intelligence plans across a large security organization with complex historical frameworks can be a critical strategic test. Furthermore, improving and maintaining AI machines can be costly. Offsetting the likely benefits with the frank and rising pricing is somewhat difficult for the dominant majority coverage agency. (Eling and Lehmann, 2018), (Johnson et al., 2023), (Rawat et al., 2021).

## Conclusion

**The incorporation of Artificial Intelligence (AI) has had a major impact on the coverage sector, resulting in significant changes in operations and customer reporting.** AI has enabled insurers to streamline processes, enhance efficiency, and offer extra customized danger evaluation for their clients. As a result, policyholders now have a more streamlined and convenient experience, while insurers have more accurate underwriting and pricing. Additionally, AI has facilitated the automation of claims processing, taking into account quicker and extra correct claims settlements. However, the adoption of AI within the coverage enterprise additionally provides demanding situations that want to be addressed. One of the worries is records privacy, as AI structures depend upon significant quantities of records to make knowledgeable selections. Insurers have to make certain that they're gathering and the usage of purchaser records in an accountable and moral manner, in compliance with guidelines inclusive of the General Data Protection Regulation (GDPR). Transparency is any other issue, as AI algorithms can now and again be visible as black boxes, making it tough to apprehend how selections are being made. Insurers want to discover methods to make their AI structures extra obvious and explainable to each client and regulator. Furthermore, AI has additionally raised concerns about fraud detection, as state-of-the-art fraudsters can also additionally try to manage AI structures to their advantage. Insurers want to constantly replace and enhance their AI fashions to live in advance of fraudulent activities. Lastly, the combination of AI into the coverage zone has created a call for expertise with understanding in each coverage and AI. Insurers want to spend money on schooling and recruiting specialists who can efficiently leverage AI technology to pressure innovation and growth. Despite those demanding situations, the collaboration among AI and coverage is right here to live, shaping the destiny of the enterprise. Finding the proper stability among innovation and addressing demanding situations might be critical for insurers seeking to completely leverage the transformative ability of AI. By navigating those limitations and embracing the possibilities provided via way of means of AI, insurers can keep to beautify their operations and supply higher reports for his or her clients.

## Future Research Scope

Exciting prospects are unfolding for AI within the realm of future research masking this region. I n addition, investigation into moral issues along with algorithmic transparency, bias in AI selection-making, and consumer acceptance of such era gives new avenues to be filled through the development of interpretable AI models. As markets rise, there is a need to recognize how AI can evolve tailored micro insurance products and enhance coverage access in under represented regions, mainly concerning climate risk management. There is also a need to find out the ability of regulatory frameworks to keep pace with AI development in such a manner that balances progress within customer protection. Further, research ought to have observed AI's role in actual-time hazard control the usage of IOT and telematics, allowing dynamic pricing models and adaptive rules. Additionally, the impact of AI-driven personalization on customer engagement and long-time period pricing fairness warrants interest, specifically in phrases of social fairness. As AI reshapes activity roles, destiny research should explore its effect on employment styles and talent necessities, figuring out new opportunities and addressing the hazard of job displacement. AI's contribution to sustainability in insurance additionally holds capability, with research focusing on inexperienced coverage products and AI's function in assessing climate-associated dangers. Finally, with quantum computing on the horizon, research ought to examine how its integration with AI ought to revolutionize hazard control and similarly remodel coverage operations. This complete exploration of AI's future in insurance will offer treasured insights into its long-term influences on the enterprise and society.

## References

Ahmad, S. and Saxena, C. (2022, May). Artificial intelligence and blockchain technology in insurance business. In *The International Conference on Recent Innovations in Computing* (pp. 61–71). Singapore: Springer Nature Singapore.

Ahmad, S.F., Han, H. et al. (2023). Impact of Artificial Intelligence on Human Loss in Decision Making, Laziness and Safety in Education. *Humanities and Social Sciences Communications*, 10, 1–14.

Banu, A. (2022). Big data analytics–tools and techniques–application in the insurance sector. In *Big data: A game changer for insurance industry* (pp. 191–212). Emerald Publishing Limited.

Corea, F. and Corea, F. (2019). How AI is changing the insurance landscape. *Applied artificial intelligence: where AI can be used in business*, 5–10.

Deloitte (2019). doi:https://www2.deloitte.com/content/dam/Deloitte/de/Documents/risk/article-risk-and-compliance-implications-of-ai.pdf

Eckert, C., Neunsinger, C. and Osterrieder, K. (2022). Managing customer satisfaction: digital applications for insurance companies. *The Geneva Papers on Risk and Insurance-Issues and Practice*, *47*(3), 569–602.

Eling, M. and Lehmann, M. (2018). The impact of digitalization on the insurance value chain and the insurability of risks. *The Geneva papers on risk and insurance-issues and practice*, *43*, 359–396.

Infosys. (2019). Infosys. Retrieved 2023, from https://www.infosys.com/about/knowledge-institute/insights/documents/ai-insurance.pdf

Johnson, M., Albizri, A. and Harfouche, A. (2023). Responsible artificial intelligence in healthcare: Predicting and preventing insurance claim denials for economic and social wellbeing. *Information Systems Frontiers*, *25*(6), 2179–2195.

Kumar, P., Taneja, S., Özen, E. and Singh, S. (2023). Artificial intelligence and machine learning in insurance: A bibliometric analysis. In Smart *Analytics, Artificial Intelligence and Sustainable Performance Management in a Global Digitalised Economy* (pp. 191–202). Emerald Publishing Limited.

Ladva, P. (2023). Benefits and use cases of AI in insurance. Retrieved September 2023, from https://www.swissre.com/risk-knowledge/advancing-societal-benefits-digitalisation/opportunities-ai-insurance.html

Mahajan, A. (2021). Role of chatbots in insurance industry: an overview. *AAYAM: AKGIM Journal of Management*, *11*(2), 21–24.

Ostrowska, M. (2021). Does new technology put an end to policyholder risk declaration? The impact of digitalisation on insurance relationships. *The Geneva Papers on Risk and Insurance-Issues and Practice*, *46*, 573–592.

Rawat, S., Rawat, A., Kumar, D. and Sabitha, A.S. (2021). Application of machine learning and data visualization techniques for decision support in the insurance sector. *International Journal of Information Management Data Insights*, *1*(2), 100012.

Sharma, V. and Sood, D. (2022). The role of artificial intelligence in the insurance industry of India. In *Big data analytics in the insurance market* (pp. 287–297). Emerald Publishing Limited.

Smart Tek. 2024. https://smarttek.solutions/blog/artificial-intelligence-in-insurance/#:~:text=Risk%20Assessment %20and%20Underwriting&text=Consequently%2C%20it%20leads%20to%20better,detailed%20life%20insurance%20risk%20assessments

Sood, K., Kaur, B. and Grima, S. (2022). Revamping Indian non-life insurance industry with a trusted network: Blockchain technology. In *Big Data: A game changer for insurance industry* (pp. 213–228). Emerald Publishing Limited.

Zarifis, A. and Cheng, X. (2022). A model of trust in Fintech and trust in Insurtech: How Artificial Intelligence and the context influence it. *Journal of Behavioral and Experimental Finance*, 36, 100739.

Zia and Kalia (2022), "Emerging Technologies in Insurance Sector: Evidence from Scientific Literature", *Big Data: A Game Changer for Insurance Industry (Emerald Studies in Finance, Insurance, and Risk Management)*, pp. 43–63. https://doi.org/10.1108/978-1-80262-605-620221004

# 3 | Strategic Management with Artificial Intelligence: Predictive Analytics Tools, Methods, and Applications

Dr. Parihar Suresh Dahake[1*] and Dr. Amir Hafizullah Khan[2]

**Purpose:** This chapter aims to explore the integration of artificial intelligence (AI) in strategic management, focusing specifically on the tools, methods, and applications of predictive analytics. By delving into the various facets of AI-driven predictive analytics, the chapter seeks to highlight its potential to revolutionize strategic decision-making processes in contemporary business environments.

**Background and Scope:** The advent of AI has introduced transformative capabilities across various industries, with predictive analytics emerging as a pivotal tool for strategic management. This chapter provides a comprehensive overview of the current landscape, examining the theoretical underpinnings and practical applications of predictive analytics in crafting and executing business strategies. The scope encompasses a wide range of industries, demonstrating the versatility and adaptability of AI in different strategic contexts.

**Methodology:** The chapter employs a multidisciplinary approach, integrating literature reviews and empirical and exploratory research to present a holistic view of predictive analytics in strategic management. Through qualitative and quantitative analyz es, the study evaluates the effectiveness of various AI tools and methods, offering insights into their practical implementation and impact on strategic outcomes.

**Originality:** This chapter contributes to the burgeoning field of AI in management by offering a focused examination of predictive analytics as a strategic tool. It differentiates itself by providing a detailed analysis of specific AI methodologies and their applications in real-world scenarios. The originality lies in the synthesis of theoretical insights and practical examples, creating a valuable resource for academics and practitioners alike.

**Implications and Future Directions:** The findings underscore the transformative potential of AI-driven predictive analytics in enhancing strategic decision-making, risk management, and competitive advantage. The chapter discusses the

1 Assistant Professor, School of Management, Ramdeobaba University Nagpur, India.
2 Lecturer in Digital Marketing, Salford Business School, University of Salford, United Kingdom. Email: a.h.khan4@salford.ac.uk
* Corresponding author: parihar.dahake@gmail.com

DOI: 10.1201/9781003559849-3

implications for managers and policymakers, emphasizing the need for adopting and integrating advanced AI tools in strategic planning processes. Future research directions are suggested, highlighting the importance of continuous innovation and the development of more sophisticated AI techniques to address emerging challenges in strategic management.

## Introduction

Companies are employing state-of-the-art innovation to remain competitive in the contemporary business environment. Strategic management has been revolutionized by AI. AI and machine learning are transforming strategic management through data-driven decision-making and performance optimisation (Miller 2023). Organizations utilize predictive analytics to make decisions that are informed by consumer behaviour, market dynamics, operational efficiency, and risk management. Strategic management leverages AI for predictive analytics, automation, and decision-making. AI technology has the great potential to solve problems, but its practical implementation and strategic usage to generate commercial value are still obstacles (Kitsios and Kamariotou, 2021). Strategic management leverages AI for predictive analytics, automation, and decision-making. AI Considers strategic management theory holistically (Hill and Jones, 2008). All of the above Strategic Decisions discusses the implementation of AI in strategic management and how robots and robotics might be used to solve business policy problems (Holloway, 1983). This chapter demonstrates the transformative potential of AI through predictive analytics. In predictive analytics, occurrences and patterns are predicted by machine learning algorithms and historical data. The application of artificial intelligence (AI) to strategic management AI alters the decision-making process in strategic management. Traditional strategic planning relied on intuition and historical data; however, AI-powered technologies and procedures have significantly improved the accuracy of predictions. The manner in which organiz ations plan, allocate resources, evaluate performance, and adapt to market changes is being transformed by AI and strategic management. The emergence of predictive analytics is behind this transition being driven by AI-powered predictive analytics, which forecasts future outcomes based on historical data. Predictive analytics algorithms can identify concealed trends, correlations, and anomalies by analysing vast quantities of structured and unstructured data. By accurately predicting future events, businesses can enhance operations, mitigate risks, and establish a competitive advantage. There are numerous strategic management applications of predictive analytics. There are Fuzzy rule-based models available for predicting customer behaviour (Tettamanzi et al., 2007)

Predictive analytics can be employed by CRM and marketing to identify potential clients, modify communication, and anticipate client loss. Supply networks, resource allocation, and demand prediction are optimized by operations management. It is capable of predicting the stability of the finance and risk management industry, detecting deception, and predicting loan defaults.

Strategic decisions across industries are facilitated by predictive analytics. This chapter delves into the strategic management and AI integration applications, approaches, and instruments of predictive analytics. In this chapter, the theoretical foundation, practical applications, and future perspectives of AI-driven predictive analytics are presented. Readers will acquire the knowledge necessary to navigate strategic management in the AI era. This chapter investigates the application of AI in management by means of empirical research, literature evaluations, and case studies. This resource is advantageous to academicians, practitioners, and policymakers. The theoretical foundation of AI and predictive analytics in strategic management is their fundamental principles and concepts.

What are the most effective AI predictive analytics methodologies for strategic management?

What is the most effective method for incorporating AI-driven predictive analytics into a company's strategy?

## Review of Literature

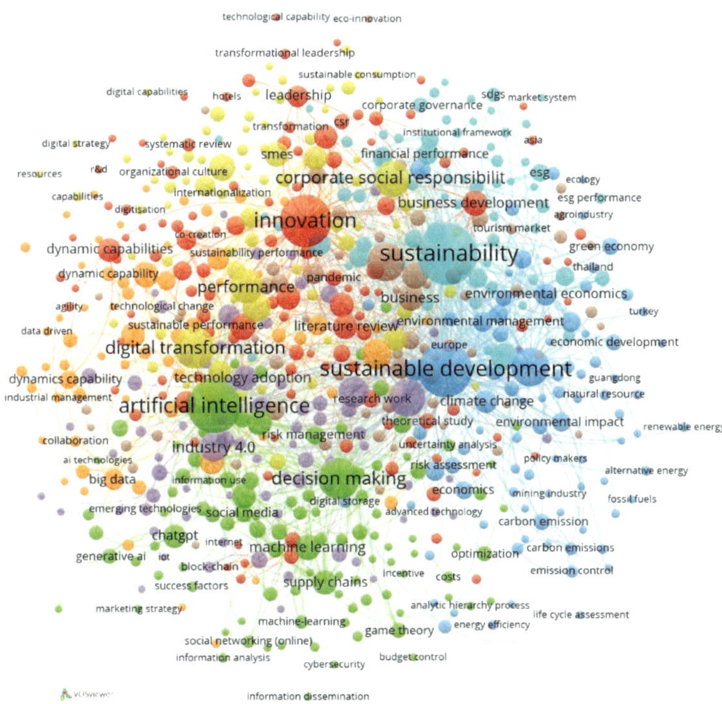


**Fig. 1** Keywords Analysis by VOSviewer.

The VOSviewer keyword co-occurrence network visualisation provides useful insights into "Strategic Management with Artificial Intelligence: Predictive Analytics Tools, Methods, and Applications." research subjects. The visualisation shows term clusters that indicate study trends and potential research fields.

These subjects emphasise the necessity of innovation and sustainability in strategic management. AI and digital transformation are increasingly influencing organisational strategies as interconnected concepts. Furthermore, these clusters demonstrate the effectiveness of AI-powered predictive analytics in enhancing organisational performance and facilitating decision-making. AI and predictive analytics are highlighted, but strategic management integration studies are scarce. Research might study how AI tools and methodologies can be integrated into strategic decision-making frameworks. The figure highlights AI and digital transformation but not strategic management predictive analytics. Future research may examine machine learning, data mining, and strategic applications. "Organisational culture" and "leadership" suffer. This reveals a research need on how AI-driven predictive analytics affect strategic management culture and leadership. Strategic management AI and predictive analytics integration should be studied due to the flaws in the system. Exploring specific tools, approaches, and applications can address critical gaps and expand the literature on how AI-driven analytics may change strategic decision-making. Innovation and sustainability require strategic frameworks that leverage AI for sustainable business operations, making the study important. On that ground (Dwivedi, Kshetri, et al., 2023) highlighted that Artificial intelligence (AI) holds great potential for resolving problems, but effectively using it and strategically leveraging it to create economic value remain obstacles also by the comprehensive analysis of (Dwivedi, Hughes et al., 2023) they argued that the way a product feels can have a significant impact on how consumers perceive it and marketing is an integral part of strategic management in the similar vein (Breese et al., n.d.). Bayesian networks and correlation approaches enhance strategic decision-making in collaborative filtering systems by accurately anticipating user preferences, resulting in tailored recommendations and increased user satisfaction. Subsequently, (Tools and Algorithms for the Construction and Analysis of Systems, 2009) presents a meta-modelling framework for modelling and testing modelled systems' resilience, using several validated methods. Parallelly (Jiakui et al., 2023) examined how green finance, financial development, and technical innovation affect green total factor productivity. This study has major consequences for China's green finance and environmental strategy, moreover (Carvalho and Ivanov, 2024) underlines how artificial intelligence and big language models, are revolutionising industries like tourism and cites ChatGPT's benefits for tourist stakeholders, such as increased customer service and productivity. Since the customer is the king of the market and achieving goals and the mission fulfilment of the customers demand is always the priority of every business and it is an integral part of strategic management and hence (Wang et al., 2022) mentioned that Green technology and managerial breakthroughs boost company sustainability. Moreover (Kitsios and Kamariotou, 2021) Demonstrated the models where, AI and machine learning can combine organisational strategy, knowledge management, decision-making, and service innovation to create economic value. Subsequently (Alerasoul et al., 2022) integrates Organisational Learning (OL), land learning orientation into a coherent framework, showing a profound grasp of their relationships. Recognises HR methods, environmental scanning, and internal/external communications as OL enhancements. It is notable that (Jan et al., 2023) discussed that Industry sectors deploy AI technology for Industry 4.0 differently according to strategic concerns and data availability. Similarly, (Attaran and Attaran, 2018) stated that while predictive analytics adoption benefits businesses, it requires strategic planning and data availability. However, (Aldoseri et al., 2023) addresses data quality, privacy, bias, and technical knowledge concerns in AI data use and provides advice. The Literature assesses past literatures and offers future study directions. The research in distinct areas of domestic literature is described under relevant topics. It seeks to expand on how the contemplation brings significant benefits to the existing body of literature, as well as to advance understandings of how breakthroughs in artificial intelligence (AI) technologies reform strategic management. In India, several AI-based predictive analytics tools and methods have been structured and implemented with case studies. The contemplation begins by exposure that the emergence of strategic management as a considered profession, academic discipline, and compulsory function of organizations has only been conceivable through the combined intervention of a congregation of consecutive technological revolutions since the fifties.

However, rapid advances in digital technologies during the last decades have governed an exponential pace of those transformations. It is tough for strategic management processes to keep abreast with new business models empowered by emerging technologies. Major contributions are widely held to have been made by big data analytics (BDA) enhancement and deployment to a broadening scope of target processes. What are the corresponding advancements in wider and wider deep learning, machine learning and other AI use? This foremost has is to inspect use-case and case-study based literature, as a step in trenching the way for a wide research quest (Kobbacy and Vadera, 2011)

## Thematic Analysis

**Conceptual contributions to the "Strategic Management with Artificial Intelligence" framework. The term "circular economy" refers to a new economic model based on resource sustainability and ever-changing clean technologies. The notion has been recognized as a priority for sustainable development and environmental management in the context of the green economy. In Europe, there has been an increase in research on circular economies. This topic is relevant from both European and global viewpoints because many topics in the literature can be applied to machine learning approaches.** India is one of the largest and fastest-growing economies and one of the largest emissions producers. Still, there is little attention to the development of the circular economy in India in the research arena. In India, a rise in the rate of material consumption by 3 times is an indication that material consumption is growing. Taking good practices, management recommends that the transition to the circular economy involves aspects at the level of the design of products, the definition of production processes less polluting and polluting of workspace and products, and respect for health and environment and the changing of consumption patterns. Measures to promote the circular economy are at the level of investments in waste treatment plants, designing products and processes that reduce environmental impacts over their life cycle, such as recycling products, use of renewable energy, and clean production technologies. Sociodemographic aspects are needed to drive a change of consumption models. There are five priorities for investment (defining priority sectors, supporting innovation, adoption and use of technology, creating commercial markets, including civil society, and establishing regular industrial dialogue) to afford changes at the industrial level. To maximize resource savings, it monitors waste streams and sets rules for the management of municipal waste and waste from hazardous and waste industrial activities. Employ AI the platform that includes predictive analytics tools, methodologies, and business applications to improve decisions on strategic management. Although several experiences with AI in industry are recorded, there is a gap in research with predictive analytics in terms of strategic management, resulting in machine learning techniques. These are characterized by a 17-year bibliographic and 5-year co-citation network analysis.

## Research Methodology

The study explores the potential impact of AI and predictive analytics on business. Enterprises have significant strategic decision-making obstacles in an age of swift technology progress and intricate market dynamics. AI-powered predictive analytics addresses these challenges by offering in-depth insights, improving decision precision, and strengthening competitiveness. The examination begins by looking at the literature on AI, predictive analytics, and strategic management. We do a complete examination that includes scholarly articles, industry reports, and case studies from many sectors in order to find areas where our research can provide fresh insights. Strategic management. AI tools and procedures are evaluated using both qualitative and quantitative approaches. Comprehensive interviews with industry experts, managers, and AI practitioners explain the obstacles and benefits of using predictive analytics to make strategic decisions. A thematic code is a tool for identifying and categorising reoccurring themes and patterns that arise during interviews. Companies that use AI-driven predictive analytics for strategic operations provide quantitative data. Many companies use systematic surveys to evaluate decision-making, risk management, and competitive advantage. Regression analysis assesses the strategic impact of predictive analytics. Exploratory research combines literature reading, qualitative interviews, and quantitative data analysis to get a thorough grasp of strategic management predictive analytics. The efficacy of AI applications reveals the potential for transformative effects on strategic decision-making by leveraging predictive analytics. Using several data sources improves the reliability and quality of a study. Ethical rules preserve participant privacy. This study's in-depth evaluation of AI techniques and their practical applications is unprecedented and beneficial to both scholars and practitioners. AI-powered predictive analytics has the potential to improve strategic decision-making, risk management, and competitive advantage. This chapter calls for the use of sophisticated artificial intelligence in strategic planning, as well as for managers and policymakers to examine strategic management difficulties.

**Objectives of the Study:**

1. To examine how AI, particularly predictive analytics, is changing strategic management.
2. To Understand AI management expertise by emphasizing predictive analytics' strategic implications.
3. To demonstrate AI-driven predictive analytics' sector-wide applicability.

**Hypothesis:**

H1: AI-powered predictive analytics improves strategic management decision-making.

H2: Strategic concerns and data availability will determine how AI-powered predictive analytics tools and approaches operate across industries.

## The Application of Predictive Analytics in Strategic Management

As per the collected data processed in the Orange Software for accuracy, the tree branches show the most important purchase variables. "Comfort, Economy, or Technology" is the root node, indicating it is the most significant. Later splits emphasize "Accuracy Product Show," "Influence," and other aspects.

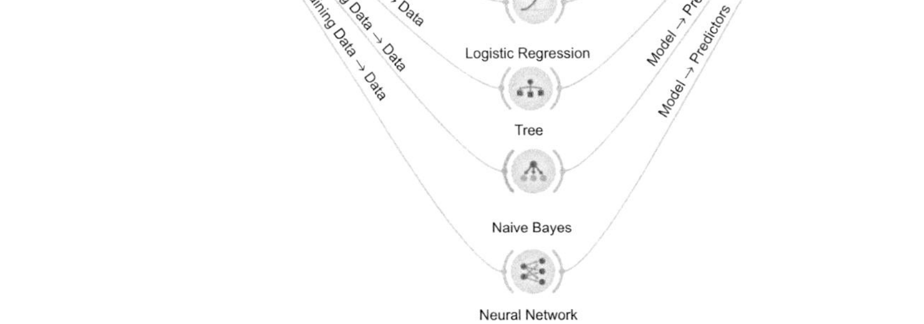


**Fig. 2** Orange workflow for using different predictive models.
*Source:* Predictive Analytics by Orange

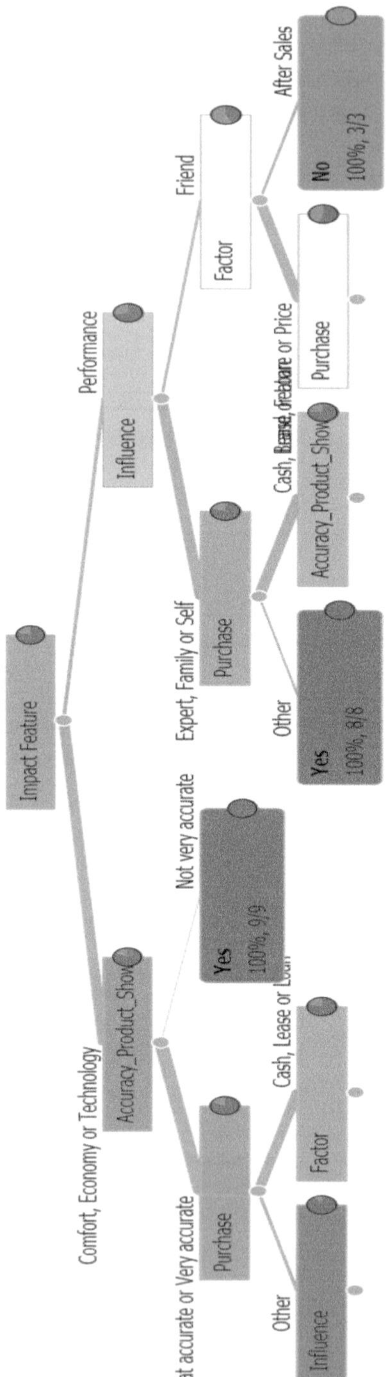


**Fig. 3** Orange Tree Diagram to check accuracy of predictive models for Strategic Decisions.
*Source:* Predictive Analytics by Orange

Generalizability and performance of prediction models require internal and external evaluation (Taylor et al., 2008) and to evaluate this login in this diagram. The decision logic is easier to understand when each node provides a percentage of "Purchase" (Yes) instances. Predictions end at leaf nodes. They provide percentages like "100%, 9/9," which indicate the model's accuracy for that category. All 9 instances in that node were "Yes" purchases. The "No" (100%, 3/3) leaf predicts "No" purchases perfectly. Figure 3 displays the model's decision-making process and estimates its accuracy at different nodes and overall. This is necessary to validate the model's prediction and decision-making abilities and to ensure the accuracy of a model and the quality of decision-making based on it, it is necessary to do model verification and validation (Sargent, 2015). This analysis shows data-driven decision-making works. Managers may use AI to analyze vast amounts of data and acquire insights instead of guessing. Strategy can be improved. The decision tree study shows AI-driven predictive analytics helps strategic management. The study finds that AI improves decision-making and understanding . Research and practice are needed to prove this. Business analytics and decision science, especially AI-powered predictive analytics, improve strategy (Chidera Victoria Ibeh et al., 2024) and Predictive Analytics and AI integration into business strategies may improve performance and decision-making (Kaggwa et al., 2024).

Table 1 and Fig. 4 showcase the performance indicators of the logistic regression and classification models. Understanding these metrics is essential for grasping the impact of artificial intelligence (AI), particularly predictive analytics, on strategic management. These metrics are commonly used in evaluating model performance:

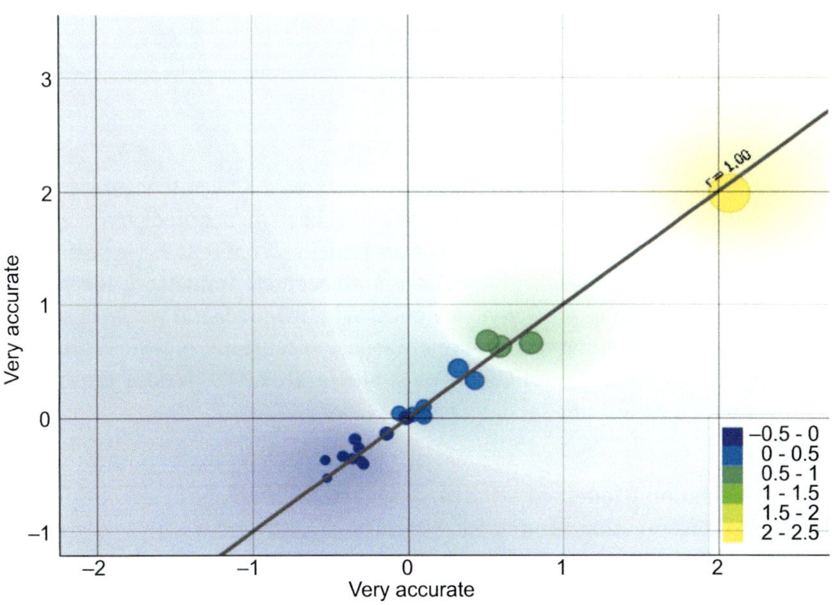


**Fig. 4** Graphical Representation of Logical Regression Model for the Predictive Analytics

Area Under the Curve (AUC), Classification Accuracy (CA), F1 score, Precision, Recall, and Matthews Correlation Coefficient (MCC). By examining these values in relation to the study goal, we can gain a deeper understanding of how predictive analytics can impact strategic decision-making.

**Table 1** Logical Regression Model for the Predictive Analytics.

| *S.No* | *Model* | *AUC* | *CA* | *F1* | *Prec* | *Recall* | *MCC* |
|---|---|---|---|---|---|---|---|
| 1 | Classification | 0.92 | 0.819 | 0.814 | 0.812 | 0.819 | 0.878 |
| 2 | Logistic Regression | 0.824 | 0.943 | 0.927 | 0.933 | 0.924 | 0.997 |

## Interpretation of Model Performance Metrics

### Area Under the Curve (AUC)

- **Classification Model:** AUC = 0.92
- **Logistic Regression Model:** AUC = 0.824

Having a solid grasp of the AUC is essential when it comes to assessing a model's ability to distinguish between different classes. Having a higher AUC suggests better performance in distinguishing between positive and negative classes. The classification model showcases its impressive effectiveness in predicting outcomes with an AUC of 0.92. This indicates a significant opportunity for leveraging AI technology to make strategic decisions. On the other hand, the logistic regression model shows a slightly lower AUC of 0.824, indicating that it might not be as robust as the classification model in specific strategic scenarios, although it remains effective.

### Classification Accuracy (CA):

- **Classification Model:** CA = 0.819
- **Logistic Regression Model:** CA = 0.943

The metric for Classification Accuracy measures the overall accuracy of the model's predictions. The logistic regression model has a higher predictive accuracy (CA) of 0.943 compared to the classification model's CA of 0.819. These findings suggest that logistic regression provides a more accurate framework for making strategic decisions using predictive analytics. With the precision we've observed, it seems that incorporating artificial intelligence, specifically logistic regression, could greatly enhance the reliability of strategic decisions, reduce errors, and improve overall organisational outcomes.

### F1 Score:

- **Classification Model:** F1 = 0.814
- **Logistic Regression Model:** F1 = 0.927

Having a good grasp of the F1 score is crucial for evaluating a model's performance in real-world situations, where the consequences of false positives and false negatives can be significant. The logistic regression model achieves an impressive F1 score of 0.927, surpassing the classification model's score of 0.814. It appears that logistic regression is more effective in achieving a balance between precision and recall in strategic decision-making. Being able to make accurate predictions is of utmost importance in strategic management, as the consequences of making incorrect ones can be quite costly.

**Precision:**

- **Classification Model:** Precision = 0.812
- **Logistic Regression Model:** Precision = 0.933

Having accurate predictions is essential for effective strategic management, particularly when aiming for specific objectives such as market entry or resource allocation. With an impressive precision of 0.933, the logistic regression model clearly outperforms the classification model (0.812), demonstrating its superior predictive capabilities for positive outcomes. This tool is highly reliable for making strategic decisions that require accurate outcome predictions.

**Recall:**

- **Classification Model:** Recall = 0.819
- **Logistic Regression Model:** Recall = 0.924

Recall is a measure that assesses the ability of a model to accurately identify all the significant positive instances, The recall of the logistic regression model is 0.924, whereas the classification model's recall stands at 0.819. It is clear that logistic regression is highly effective in identifying relevant positive outcomes in strategic contexts, making it a reliable tool for comprehensive strategic planning and risk management.

**Matthews Correlation Coefficient (MCC):**

- **Classification Model:** MCC = 0.878
- **Logistic Regression Model:** MCC = 0.997

The Mean Squared Correlation (MCC) is a comprehensive measure that considers both true and false positives and negatives to evaluate the precision of a model. Similarly, the logistic regression model exhibits its efficacy in strategic applications with an almost flawless Mean Squared Correlation coefficient (MCC) of 0.997. This underscores its remarkable capacity to deliver precise and well calibrated forecasts. Proficiency in data analysis and the ability to make well-informed judgements are essential in strategic management, especially when dealing with intricate corporate landscapes.

Using predictive analytics driven by AI, particularly through logistic regression, has proven to significantly enhance strategic management, as evident from the performance metrics. Organizations can make confident and informed decisions by relying on the accuracy, precision, and recall of the logistic regression model's predictions. Approaching tasks allows for more precise allocation of resources, better management of risks, and improved strategic planning by reducing uncertainty. Furthermore, the logistic regression model's higher MCC suggests its ability to create well-rounded strategies that consider multiple factors and potential outcomes. In today's dynamic and ever-evolving business landscape, the capacity to swiftly adjust and effectively navigate through shifting circumstances is paramount for achieving sustainable growth. The meticulous examination of these metrics reveals the profound impact of AI, particularly predictive analytics, on strategic management. Utilising models like logistic regression, organizations can enhance their strategic decision-making capabilities, leading to more sustainable and competitive business practices.

## A Process of Powerful Transformation of AI Tools in Strategic Management

**Data Collection:** This method uses corporate databases, market data, and social media to gather data and Orange Software employs social media analysis to gather competitive intelligence (He et al., 2015) and through social media data extraction, product qualities and user comments can be revealed. This expertise can help build future products (Tuarob and Tucker, 2015). AI is great at gathering enormous data on market trends, competitive analysis, customer behaviour, and internal operations. AI helps marketers identify large quantities of data and predict consumer behaviour (Dimitrieska et al., 2018) thus data analysis by smart computers can reveal patterns, connections, and insights humans miss. A marketing AI study found that advanced algorithms can uncover market trends, competitiveness, and customer behaviour (Kopalle et al., 2022).

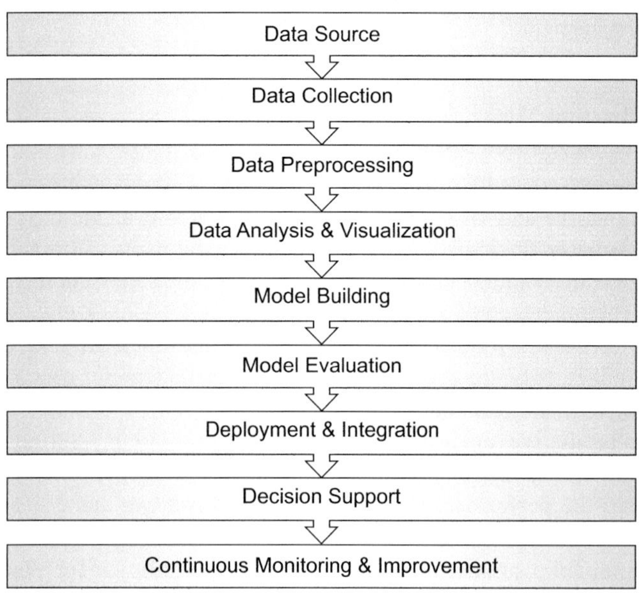


**Fig. 5** A Process of Powerful Transformation of AI Tools in Strategic Management.

**Data Preprocessing:** Orange Data Mining technologies clean, convert, and qualify data for analysis and for effective data analysis which requires data pretreatment (Joshi and Patel, 2021). AI-powered prediction models use historical data and patterns to predict future events. Strategic managers can better evaluate risks, make decisions, and adjust strategy additionally AI can accelerate processing, enhance predictions, and reduce labor (Dewitte et al., 2021), resulting in this Smart scenario generator for strategic business planning (Li et al., 1997) and its changing relationships to see affects enables experimentation (Jackson and Brownie, 1992).

**Feature Engineering:** To improve predictive accuracy and learning, select, extract, and convert key data elements. Learning efficient feature transformations from past experiences automates categorization under feature engineering (Nargesian et al., 2017).

**Model Building:** Orange Data Mining uses regression, classification, clustering, and other machine learning algorithms to create prediction models. Advanced automated prediction methods improve model performance and scalability (Hong and Weiss, 1999).

**Model Evaluation:** When it comes to evaluating machine learning models, it is essential to consider algorithm selection and validation measures such as accuracy, precision, recall, and F1 score. These measures play a vital role in assessing the accuracy of the model (Raschka, 2020).

**Model Deployment:** Use the best model in strategic decision-making tools. Four strategic decision-making frameworks covered decision variability. Models begin strategic decision process taxonomy (Shrivastava and Grant, 1985).

**Monitoring and Feedback:** Monitoring and Feedback includes device lifespan proportionate to parameters, promising reliability (Chenming Hu et al., 1985), constant model performance monitoring, feedback collection, and model updates to sustain effectiveness.

## Predictive Analytics Tools and its Significance in Strategic Management

Predictive analytics is becoming increasingly essential in strategic management for making complex business decisions. These tools empower management accountants to accomplish and expand their strategic goals (Savla, 2023) also predictive analytics has the potential to enhance strategic decision-making in several industries by transforming unprocessed data into practical insights (Olaniyi et al., 2023). Predictive models transform data into practical knowledge, allowing decision-makers to assess information based on their experience in a certain field (Iscaro et al., 2022). Using descriptive, predictive, and prescriptive analytics in a decision intelligence framework improves strategic decisions, operational efficiency, and customer happiness (Sharma et al., 2022). Hence Predictive Analytics is playing as ignificant role in business and strategic management because analytics in strategic management are vital for high profit and sales as organizations get more complex and seek competitive advantages (Sharma et al., 2022). Implementing strategic management and deploying an AI tool necessitates the careful planning and execution of various components, including task design, infrastructure setup, staff training, implementation, and performance monitoring (Ukrainian Engineering Pedagogics Academy et al., 2024) and Artificial intelligence (AI) has the ability to improve decision-making, increase operational efficiency, and foster creativity within organizations (Peoples' Friendship University of Russia et al., 2024). Therefore, Strategy implementation involves growing capabilities, organizing the organization, distributing finances, creating policies, implementing support systems, and reviewing strategies. Strategic management AI solutions can be implemented and evaluated using these strategies (Thompson, n.d.).

The use of Artificial Intelligence has been increased in the business environment because they significantly outperform human beings in monitoring and predicting operational performance metrics. Both medium and large-sized firms can significantly increase their credit worthiness through the use of AI. Both medium and large-sized firms for which accurate relationships in the financial statements were not available, could reveal a much lower risk of bankruptcy. The predictive performance of the AI models of discriminant analysis, neural networks, and DNN outperforms the bachelor-level financial analysis. The findings show that using AI and standard financial assessments may coexist. AI and standard techniques have divergent strengths as well as comparative restrictions, and together they can construct powerful analytical resources for business. Industries having an interest in strategic decision-making and the performance evaluation of companies can apply the current strategy based on the collection of large volumes of standardized data from a non-representative period of trading. Due to current technological advances, it is possible to enhance the quality, amplification, and simplification of trade data. As a result of an evidence-based approach visual inspections came to support some common beliefs about domestic economies. Developing visual inspection tools and applying them to national data can be advisable because interpretation and exploration of AI models is complex (Patra et al., 2024).

Table 2 offers a comprehensive look at various AI-based tools and their importance in strategic management. It emphasises their descriptions, strengths, weaknesses, and suitability for specific applications. This table is a valuable resource for understanding the strategic implementation of different AI technologies in organizations. It aids in enhancing decision-making processes, optimising operations, and fostering innovation. Machine learning algorithms have a remarkable versatility and wide applicability, which makes them incredibly effective in handling large datasets. They have a unique talent for adjusting and improving tasks based on their extensive experience. However, smaller or resource-constrained organizations may encounter challenges in using these tools because they require large datasets and powerful computational resources. They demonstrate exceptional proficiency in predictive maintenance, customer segmentation, and demand forecasting, showcasing their expertise in these areas. In utilizing the

**Table 2** Predictive Analytics Tools and its Significance in Strategic Management.

| *S.No* | *AI-based Tool* | *Description* | *Strengths* | *Weaknesses* | *Suitability for Strategic Management Applications* |
|---|---|---|---|---|---|
| 1 | Machine Learning Algorithms | Algorithms that use statistical methods to enable machines to improve tasks with experience. | Versatile, widely applicable, and capable of handling large datasets. | Requires large datasets and significant computational power. | Suitable for predictive maintenance, customer segmentation, and demand forecasting. |
| 2 | Deep Learning Models | A subset of ML algorithms that use neural networks with many layers to model complex patterns. | Capable of capturing complex patterns and relationships in data. | Computationally intensive and requires a large amount of data and time for training. | Ideal for image and speech recognition, natural language processing, and complex pattern recognition. |
| 3 | Natural Language Processing (NLP) | Techniques for analyzing and synthesizing natural language data. | Effective in understanding and generating human language. | Complex to implement and may require large computational resources. | Useful for sentiment analysis, chatbots, and market analysis. |
| 4 | Decision Trees | A non-parametric supervized learning method used for classification and regression. | Simple to understand and interpret, suitable for small datasets. | Prone to overfitting and can become complex with large datasets. | Applicable for decision support systems, customer relationship management, and risk assessment. |
| 5 | Random Forests | An ensemble learning method that operates by constructing multiple decision trees. | Reduces overfitting, handles large datasets well, and provides better accuracy. | Complex to implement and interpret, computationally expensive. | Suitable for market analysis, credit scoring, and customer segmentation. |
| 6 | Support Vector Machines (SVM) | A supervized learning model that analyzes data for classification and regression. | Effective in high-dimensional spaces and used for both classification and regression. | Requires careful tuning of parameters and significant computational resources. | Ideal for anomaly detection, predictive maintenance, and market trend analysis. |

*Contd.*

**Table 2** *Contd.*

| *S.No* | *AI-based Tool* | *Description* | *Strengths* | *Weaknesses* | *Suitability for Strategic Management Applications* |
|---|---|---|---|---|---|
| 7 | Neural Networks | Computing systems inspired by biological neural networks to perform various tasks. | Highly flexible and can model any form of data pattern. | Can be prone to overfitting and requires large datasets for training. | Applicable for risk management, fraud detection, and customer relationship management. |
| 8 | Gradient Boosting Machines | A machine learning technique for regression and classification that produces a prediction model. | Effective in improving prediction accuracy by combining weak models. | Complex and time-consuming to train, requires large datasets. | Suitable for customer churn prediction, sales forecasting, and risk management. |
| 9 | Reinforcement Learning | An area of ML where an agent learns to make decisions by taking actions in an environment. | Can learn optimal actions through trial and error, suitable for dynamic environments. | Requires significant computational resources and time to train. | Ideal for dynamic pricing, supply chain management, and adaptive marketing strategies. |

expertise of data analysis and predictive analytics, strategic management becomes a formidable asset for organizations to analyse past data, forecast results, and make informed choices. Deep Learning Models, a subset of machine learning, are widely respected for their ability to uncover complex patterns in data through the use of multiple layers of neural networks. These models are highly proficient in image and speech recognition, natural language processing, and complex pattern recognition. However, the demanding computational requirements and the necessity for extensive data and time for training present significant challenges. When it comes to strategic management, deep learning models can be incredibly valuable for tackling complex tasks that require a deep understanding of intricate data. For example, they can be used to analyze customer behaviour and develop personalized marketing strategies.

Having a strong grasp of Natural Language Processing (NLP) is essential for effectively analyzing and synthesising human language data. It greatly enhances our ability to understand and generate natural language. This system has some drawbacks, including its complexity and the significant computational resources it demands. In a similar vein, NLP is highly valuable in strategic management for tasks like sentiment analysis, chatbots, and market analysis. It enables organizations to derive valuable insights from textual data, such as customer reviews and social media, to inform strategic decisions related to brand management and customer engagement. Similarly, decision trees are renowned for their simplicity and ease of interpretation, making them an excellent option for analysing small datasets. They have immense value in decision support systems, customer relationship management, and risk assessment. However, their tendency to overfit and become complex with larger datasets limits their effectiveness in broader data environments. Decision trees are an invaluable tool in strategic management, enabling clear and transparent decision-making. They are particularly valuable in scenarios where understanding the results is crucial. Furthermore, it would approach the problem, ensemble learning methods like Random Forests are designed to overcome the limitations of decision trees. They accomplish this by reducing overfitting and efficiently handling large datasets. These tools provide exceptional accuracy and are highly effective for analysing markets, scoring credit, and segmenting customers. However, their complexity and computational cost are recogniz ed as drawbacks. Applying Random Forests in strategic management can greatly improve the precision of predictive models, leading to more dependable strategic forecasts and decisions. Support Vector Machines (SVM) are renowned for their exceptional performance in high-dimensional spaces and their versatility in handling both classification and regression tasks. Additionally, they encounter challenges that involve fine-tuning parameters and having access to powerful computational resources. SVMs are a great choice for tasks like anomaly detection, predictive maintenance, and market trend analysis. Also, SVMs can be used in strategic management to identify anomalies or patterns that could affect business strategy. Organizations can now be proactive in addressing potential concerns. Neural Networks have gained significant recognition for their remarkable capacity to capture diverse data patterns, taking cues from the intricate workings of biological neural networks. However, overfitting can be a concern and extensive datasets are necessary for optimal training. Neural networks are widely used in strategic management for a range of applications such as risk management, fraud detection, and customer relationship management. Organizations and individuals are able to skilfully analyze data in order to reveal concealed patterns and valuable insights. With the expertise organizations are able to make more informed decisions, reducing risks and capitalising on opportunities. Gradient Boosting Machines are incredibly powerful when it comes to improving prediction accuracy by combining weaker models. These models can handle complex tasks like customer churn prediction, sales forecasting, and risk management, but they do require extensive training and time investment, Organizations can harness the power of Gradient Boosting Machines to obtain accurate predictive insights, With this knowledge, they can fine-tune their strategies and stay one step ahead of any changes in the market. Reinforcement Learning is truly remarkable as it has the ability to learn optimal actions through experimentation and adaptation, making it highly suitable for dynamic environments. One downside that is quite noticeable is the significant number of computational resources and time required for training. However, in the field of strategic management, reinforcement learning can be highly beneficial. It has wide applications in dynamic pricing, supply chain management, and adaptive marketing strategies, where continuous learning and adaptation are crucial. Every tool mentioned in the table serves a unique purpose in enhancing strategic management. With a strong grasp of these tools, organizations can develop effective strategies that are adaptable and customized to the demands of the current business environment. AI-driven tools are essential in shaping the future of strategic management. They contribute to enhancing predictive accuracy, improving customer engagement, and optimising operational efficiency.

**The aspects AI implementation in the organizations such as resource needs, barriers and enablers at different stages of strategic management**

A majority of "how do I implement AI/X in my organization" discussions provide insight on process-level, single-function, and maturity-driven approaches. This chapter seeks to contend with these discussions by addressing three common depth approach questions. Firstly, AI implementation should be used as an overarching framework. Secondly, efforts should be made to document the specifics of AI implementation. Thirdly, that deeper insight into the resources required, barriers, and enablers at different stages (of strategic management) would be illuminating. An implementation framework should align with strategic management. AI implementation can guide one through the daily operations of AI initiatives from problem identification to preparedness. This effort is the response to understanding of particular nuances useful in beginning, understanding, and operating such models. Efforts to implement these only in the third phase of strategic management. Broadly, these are diagnosed then, ABMS IRPRs called for the conduct of activities related to long-term strategic goals such as those generally found in the Cloud marketplace, teasing apart specifics of AI implementation strategy. Main components consist of a task (the results of which may consist of reports, roadmaps, and methods tools furthering alignment), which aims to describe and assess AI readiness and potential for strategic alignment with more targeted AI initiative development. Sub-tasks involved include E-STAF

Part 1: Identify Data Sets, E-STAF

Part 2: Collect Model Benchmarks, and E-STAF

Part 3: Compile AI Policy. Broadly, these encompass an analysis of the problem domain in efforts to apply artificial intelligence (AI) to create effectively tailored models (Teemu Thero Artificial Intelligence Transformation and Implementation Frameworks Semantic Scholar, n.d.).

## Findings, Result and Discussion

The study suggests that the use of AI-powered predictive analytics has the potential to revolutionize strategic management. Artificial intelligence (AI) assists companies in efficiently allocating resources, making informed decisions, and reducing risk. Strategic concerns are addressed by marketing, operations, finance, and risk management through the use of predictive analytics. The empirical research, literature reviews, and case studies in this chapter provide evidence that AI contributes to strategic decision-making and Artificial intelligence has the capability to simulate and assist with initial, disorganized strategic decision-making (Spangler, 1991). Qualitative interviews conducted with industry experts and practitioners demonstrate that the utilization of AI-powered predictive analytics enhances organizational performance and competitiveness. Quantitative research indicates that AI enhances strategic outcomes. The research outlines that AI in strategic management encompasses various stages, such as data gathering, preprocessing, feature engineering, model development, evaluation, deployment, and constant monitoring. AI resources connected to strategy encompass a range of advanced approaches such as machine learning, deep learning models, natural language processing, decision trees, random forests, support vector machines, neural networks, gradient boosting machines, and reinforcement learning. Strategic managers can select the optimal AI solutions for their firms by evaluating the technological capabilities, limitations, and suitability. More research is needed on strategic marketing decision-making as AI progresses from operational to strategic (Stone et al., 2020). The study addresses issues pertaining to the quality of data used in AI deployment, privacy concerns, biases, and the need for technical expertise. The chapter presents pragmatic strategies for surmounting these obstacles and employing AI in strategic management in a responsible manner.

### Limitations

1. Predictive analytics in AI-driven strategic management may overlook natural language processing, machine learning, and autonomous systems that might improve strategic outcomes. The chapter understates AI's strategic management impact.

2. Industry Specific Applicability: The chapter addresses several topics, but not all. AI strategic application may be less relevant to other firms owing to different criteria or limits.
3. Strategic management predictive analytics accuracy and efficacy rely on data quality and availability. This chapter presupposes massive, high-quality datasets, which many firms struggle to get or manage. Thus, the results may not apply to all organizations, especially those with insufficient data.
4. AI technology advances fast, therefore the chapter's conclusions and concepts may be obsolete. New AI and predictive analytics technologies, methods, and applications may make the provided notions outdated.

### *Ethical Considerations and Data Privacy*

The global, exponential growth of data, the evolution of machine learning algorithms and the proliferation of internet of things (IoT) devices have endowed Artificial Intelligence (AI) with capabilities that might eventually exceed those of human intelligence by 2050. These transformative potential nurtures a contention that AI presents unique opportunities to address problems relevant for different economic sectors, impacting the global trajectory. Given the ongoing transition of Indian firms to Industry 4.0, AI's potential as an economic disruptor could be especially salient in this context (Radanliev et al., 2024) Currently, firms in industrializ ed countries like the UK and Germany adopt AI in narrowly focused areas, prioritising acquisitions and in-house development of AI technology. However, it's not yet clear how these developments in the Global North will diffuse to firms in the Global South, specifically from a theoretical and practical perspective. That said, it seems plausible that the patterns of AI utilisation and diffusion between these countries differ, sparking a number of research questions. How does the utilization of AI for strategic management vary with the economic sector and how do predictive analytics tools and methods differ between and within firms in the UK, Germany, and India? Given the present patterns of AI technology diffusion and adoption in the industrialised countries, how does the diffusion of AI in the strategic management domain affect economic sectors in the UK, Germany, and India differently?

## Conclusion

This chapter discussed the incorporation of artificial intelligence into strategic management through the utilization of predictive analytics tools, methods, and applications. The study suggests that AI has the potential to enhance strategic decision-making, risk management, and competitive advantage in several businesses. The entire perspective on the current and future directions of AI-driven predictive analytics in strategic management is achieved through a multidisciplinary approach that includes literature reviews, empirical research, and case studies. The chapter about strategic management with artificial intelligence (AI) in India was focused on predictive analytics tools, methods, and applications. It encompassed an integral state of the art survey about AI and predictive analytics in the context of strategic management. Analysis of the current literature has shown wide-spread application and significance of predictive analytics in different areas of strategic management. Therefore, the chapter aimed to fill a gap in the existing research by providing an analysis targeted on the market with very specific conditions and potentials, such as India. The literature evaluated for the preparation of this paper is mostly based on the predictive analytics tools, methods, and applications that enable strategic management. This chapter's distinctive combination of theoretical and practical insights is advantageous for researchers and practitioners and a conceptual framework for integrating artificial intelligence and machine learning into corporate strategy with the aim of generating business value (Kitsios and Kamariotou, 2021). The study demonstrates the necessity for managers and policymakers to utilize sophisticated artificial intelligence in their strategic planning. Also the deliberate implementation of artificial intelligence (AI) has a significant impact on the effectiveness, creativity, and environmental responsibility of enterprises, while also giving rise to ethical concerns (Lucknow and Dixit, 2024) because Artificial intelligence (AI) can profoundly transform company strategy by enhancing decision-making, minimizing risks, and delivering a competitive advantage (Kaggwa et al., 2024). And hence, AI and Predictive analytics are dedicated to addressing strategic management concerns, with a specific focus on innovation and advanced artificial intelligence (AI).

### *Future Scope of the Study*

The field of strategic management is experiencing tremendous growth in the application of artificial intelligence, with a wide range of fascinating study topics. Researchers are currently studying artificial intelligence methods that are capable of managing the increasing complexity and volume of commercial data. Another area of study examines the ethical and appropriate utilization of artificial intelligence in strategic management for the mutual benefit of all involved parties. Subsequent investigations may integrate artificial intelligence (AI) with blockchain and Internet of Things (IoT) technologies to develop stronger and innovative strategic management systems. Extensive research is necessary to ascertain the impact of AI on strategic management and organizational effectiveness over a prolonged period. Exploring these unexplored areas enables us to understand the groundbreaking strategic management abilities of AI. This will enhance the profitability and long-term viability of firms in the AI era.

## References

Aldoseri, A., Al-Khalifa, K.N. and Hamouda, A.M. (2023). Re-Thinking Data Strategy and Integration for Artificial Intelligence: Concepts, Opportunities, and Challenges. *Applied Sciences*, *13*(12), 7082. https://doi.org/10.3390/app13127082

Alerasoul, S.A., Afeltra, G., Hakala, H., Minelli, E. and Strozzi, F. (2022). Organisational learning, learning organisation, and learning orientation: An integrative review and framework. *Human Resource Management Review*, *32*(3), 100854. https://doi.org/10.1016/j.hrmr.2021.100854

Assistant Professor, Shri Jai Narain Mishra PG College, Lucknow, and Dixit, A. (2024). Navigating the Future: Exploring the Strategic Integration of Artificial Intelligence in Contemporary Management Practices. *Shodh Sari-An International Multidisciplinary Journal*, *03*(02), 295–303. https://doi.org/10.59231/SARI7705

Attaran, M. and Attaran, S. (2018). Opportunities and Challenges of Implementing Predictive Analytics for Competitive Advantage: *International Journal of Business Intelligence Research*, *9*(2), 1–26. https://doi.org/10.4018/IJBIR.2018070101

Breese, J.S., Heckerman, D. and Kadie, C. (n.d.). *Empirical Analysis of Predictive Algorithms for Collaborative Filtering.*

Carvalho, I. and Ivanov, S. (2024). ChatGPT for tourism: Applications, benefits and risks. *Tourism Review*, *79*(2), 290–303. https://doi.org/10.1108/TR-02-2023-0088

C.V. Asuzu, O.F., Olorunsogo, T., Elufioye, O.A., Nduubuisi, N.L., and Daraojimba, A.I. (2024). Business analytics and decision science: A review of techniques in strategic business decision making. *World Journal of Advanced Research and Reviews*, *21*(2), 1761–1769. https://doi.org/10.30574/wjarr.2024.21.2.0247

Dewitte, S., Cornelis, J.P., Müller, R. and Munteanu, A. (2021). Artificial Intelligence Revolutionises Weather Forecast, Climate Monitoring and Decadal Prediction. *Remote Sensing*, *13*(16), 3209. https://doi.org/10.3390/rs13163209

Dimitrieska, S., Stankovska, A. and Efremova, T. (2018). Artificial Intelligence and Marketing. *Entrepreneurship*, *6*(2), 298–304.

Dwivedi, Y.K., Hughes, L., Wang, Y., Alalwan, A.A., Ahn, S.J. (Grace), Balakrishnan, J., Barta, S., Belk, R., Buhalis, D., Dutot, V., Felix, R., Filieri, R., Flavián, C., Gustafsson, A., Hinsch, C., Hollensen, S., Jain, V., Kim, J., Krishen, A.S., … Wirtz, J. (2023). Metaverse marketing: How the metaverse will shape the future of consumer research and practice. *Psychology & Marketing*, *40*(4), 750–776. https://doi.org/10.1002/mar.21767

Dwivedi, Y.K., Kshetri, N., Hughes, L., Slade, E.L., Jeyaraj, A., Kar, A.K., Baabdullah, A.M., Koohang, A., Raghavan, V., Ahuja, M., Albanna, H., Albashrawi, M.A., Al-Busaidi, A.S., Balakrishnan, J., Barlette, Y., Basu, S., Bose, I., Brooks, L., Buhalis, D., … Wright, R. (2023). Opinion Paper: "So what if ChatGPT wrote it?" Multidisciplinary perspectives on opportunities, challenges and implications of generative conversational AI for research, practice and policy. *International Journal of Information Management*, *71*, 102642. https://doi.org/10.1016/j.ijinfomgt.2023.102642

He, W., Shen, J., Tian, X., Li, Y., Akula, V., Yan, G. and Tao, R. (2015). Gaining competitive intelligence from social media data: Evidence from two largest retail chains in the world. *Industrial Management & Data Systems*, *115*(9), 1622–1636. https://doi.org/10.1108/IMDS-03-2015-0098

Hu, C., Tam, S.C., Hsu, F-C., Ko, P-K., Chan, T-Y. and Terrill, K.W. (1985). Hot-electron-induced MOSFET degradation—Model, monitor, and improvement. IEEE Transactions on Electron Devices, 32(2), 375–385. https://doi.org/10.1109/T-ED.1985.21952

*Hill and Jones—2008—Strategic management theory an integrated approac.pdf*. (n.d.). Retrieved August 1, 2024, from http://librodigital.sangregorio.edu.ec/librosusgp/00851.pdf

Holloway, C. (1983). Strategic management and artificial intelligence. *Long Range Planning*, *16*(5), 89–93. https://doi.org/10.1016/0024-6301(83)90082-1

Hong, S.J. and Weiss, S.M. (1999). Advances in Predictive Data Mining Methods. In P. Perner & M. Petrou (Eds.), *Machine Learning and Data Mining in Pattern Recognition* (pp. 13–20). Springer. https://doi.org/10.1007/3-540-48097-8_2

Ibeh, C.V., Onyeka Franca Asuzu, O.F., Olorunsogo, T., Elufioye, O.A., Nduubuisi, N.L. and Andrew Ifesinachi Daraojimba. (2024). Business analytics and decision science: A review of techniques in strategic business decision making. *World Journal of Advanced Research and Reviews*, *21*(2), 1761–1769. https://doi.org/10.30574/wjarr.2024.21.2.0247

Iscaro, V., Castaldi, L., Maresca, P. and Mazzoni, C. (2022). Digital transformation in the economics of complexity: The role of predictive models in strategic management. *Journal of Strategy and Management*, *15*(3), 450–467. https://doi.org/10.1108/JSMA-02-2021-0059

Jackson, S. and Brownie, J. (1992). AI-based decision support tool for strategic decision making in the factory of the future. *Computer Integrated Manufacturing Systems*, *5*(2), 83–90. https://doi.org/10.1016/0951-5240(92)90002-T

Jan, Z., Ahamed, F., Mayer, W., Patel, N., Grossmann, G., Stumptner, M. and Kuusk, A. (2023). Artificial intelligence for industry 4.0: Systematic review of applications, challenges, and opportunities. *Expert Systems with Applications*, *216*, 119456. https://doi.org/10.1016/j.eswa.2022.119456

Jiakui, C., Abbas, J., Najam, H., Liu, J. and Abbas, J. (2023). Green technological innovation, green finance, and financial development and their role in green total factor productivity: Empirical insights from China. *Journal of Cleaner Production*, *382*, 135131. https://doi.org/10.1016/j.jclepro.2022.135131

Joshi, A.P. and Patel, B.V. (2021). Data Preprocessing: The Techniques for Preparing Clean and Quality Data for Data Analytics Process. *Oriental Journal of Computer Science and Technology*, *13*(0203), 78–81. https://doi.org/10.13005/ojcst13.0203.03

Kaggwa, S., Eleogu, T.F., Okonkwo, F., Farayola, O.A., Uwaoma, P.U. and Akinoso, A. (2024). AI in Decision Making: Transforming Business Strategies. *International Journal of Research and Scientific Innovation*, *X*(XII), 423–444. https://doi.org/10.51244/IJRSI.2023.1012032

Kitsios, F. and Kamariotou, M. (2021). Artificial Intelligence and Business Strategy towards Digital Transformation: A Research Agenda. *Sustainability*, *13*(4), 2025. https://doi.org/10.3390/su13042025

Kobbacy, K.A.H. and Vadera, S. (2011). A survey of AI in operations management from 2005 to 2009. *Journal of Manufacturing Technology Management*, *22*(6), 706–733. https://doi.org/10.1108/17410381111149602

Kopalle, P.K., Gangwar, M., Kaplan, A., Ramachandran, D., Reinartz, W. and Rindfleisch, A. (2022). Examining artificial intelligence (AI) technologies in marketing via a global lens: Current trends and future research opportunities. *International Journal of Research in Marketing*, *39*(2), 522–540. https://doi.org/10.1016/j.ijresmar.2021.11.002

Li, X., Ang, C. L. and Gay, R. (1997). An intelligent scenario generator for strategic business planning. *Computers in Industry*, *34*(3), 261–269. https://doi.org/10.1016/S0166-3615(97)00062-6

Miller, R. (2023). The Role of Machine Learning and Artificial Intelligence in Strategic Management. *SSRN Electronic Journal*. https://doi.org/10.2139/ssrn.4392353

Nargesian, F., Samulowitz, H., Khurana, U., Khalil, E.B. and Turaga, D. (2017). Learning Feature Engineering for Classification. *Proceedings of the Twenty-Sixth International Joint Conference on Artificial Intelligence*, 2529–2535. https://doi.org/10.24963/ijcai.2017/352

Olaniyi, F.G., Olaniyi, O.O., Adigwe, C.S., Abalaka, A.I. and Shah, N.H. (2023). Harnessing Predictive Analytics for Strategic Foresight: A Comprehensive Review of Techniques and Applications in Transforming Raw Data to Actionable Insights. *Asian Journal of Economics, Business and Accounting*, *23*(22), 441–459. https://doi.org/10.9734/ajeba/2023/v23i221164

Patra, A.K., Praharaj, A., Sudarshan, D. and Chhatoi, B.P. (2024). AI and business management: Tracking future research agenda through bibliometric network analysis. *Heliyon*, *10*(1), e23902. https://doi.org/10.1016/j.heliyon.2023.e23902

Peoples' Friendship University of Russia named after Patrice Lumumba, Moscow, Russian Federation, Pchelincev, A.S., Gil`manov, M.M., Naberezhnye Chelny Institute, branch of the Kazan (Volga region) Federal University, Naberezhnye Chelny, Russian Federation, Musina, L.F., and Kazan

State Energy University, Kazan, Russian Federation. (2024). Implementation of Artificial Intelligence in Management. *Ekonomika I Upravlenie: Problemy, Resheniya*, *4/9*(145), 101–107. https://doi.org/10.36871/ek.up.p.r.2024.04.09.016

Radanliev, P., Santos, O., Brandon-Jones, A. and Joinson, A. (2024). Ethics and responsible AI deployment. *Frontiers in Artificial Intelligence*, *7*, 1377011. https://doi.org/10.3389/frai.2024.1377011

Raschka, S. (2020). *Model Evaluation, Model Selection, and Algorithm Selection in Machine Learning* (arXiv:1811.12808). arXiv. https://doi.org/10.48550/arXiv.1811.12808

Sargent, R.G. (2015). Model Verification and Validation. In M.L. Loper (Ed.), *Modeling and Simulation in the Systems Engineering Life Cycle* (pp. 57–65). Springer London. https://doi.org/10.1007/978-1-4471-5634-5_6

Savla, N.A. (2023). Predictive Analytics and the Enhanced Strategic Role of Management Accountants. *The Management Accountant Journal*, *58*(9), 93. https://doi.org/10.33516/maj.v58i9.93-95p

Sharma, A.K., Sharma, D.M., Purohit, N., Rout, S.K. and Sharma, S.A. (2022). Analytics Techniques: Descriptive Analytics, Predictive Analytics, and Prescriptive Analytics. In P. M. Jeyanthi, T. Choudhury, D. Hack-Polay, T.P. Singh and S. Abujar (Eds.), *Decision Intelligence Analytics and the Implementation of Strategic Business Management* (pp. 1–14). Springer International Publishing. https://doi.org/10.1007/978-3-030-82763-2_1

Shrivastava, P., and Grant, J.H. (1985). Empirically derived models of strategic decision-making processes. *Strategic Management Journal*, *6*(2), 97–113. https://doi.org/10.1002/smj.4250060202

Spangler, W.E. (1991). The role of artificial intelligence in understanding the strategic decision-making process. *IEEE Transactions on Knowledge and Data Engineering*, *3*(2), 149–159. https://doi.org/10.1109/69.87995

Stone, M., Aravopoulou, E., Ekinci, Y., Evans, G., Hobbs, M., Labib, A., Laughlin, P., Machtynger, J. and Machtynger, L. (2020). Artificial intelligence (AI) in strategic marketing decision-making: A research agenda. *The Bottom Line*, *33*(2), 183–200. https://doi.org/10.1108/BL-03-2020-0022

*Strategic management by Arthur A. Thompson | Open Library*. (n.d.). Retrieved August 1, 2024, from https://openlibrary.org/works/OL2000302W/Strategic_management

Taylor, J.M.G., Ankerst, D.P. and Andridge, R.R. (2008). Validation of Biomarker-Based Risk Prediction Models. *Clinical Cancer Research*, *14*(19), 5977–5983. https://doi.org/10.1158/1078-0432.CCR-07-4534

Teemu Terho Artificial Intelligence Transformation and Imple-Mentation Frameworks | *Semantic Scholar*. (n.d.). Retrieved January 13, 2025, from https://www.semanticscholar.org/paper/Teemu-Terho-Artificial-Intelligence-Transformation-Pekkola/18ee38b4a059e168efc8f611b7c8c1c2e2ea66d5

Tettamanzi, A.G.B., Carlesi, M., Pannese, L. and Santalmasi, M. (2007). Business Intelligence for Strategic Marketing: Predictive Modelling of Customer Behaviour Using Fuzzy Logic and Evolutionary Algorithms. In M. Giacobini (Ed.), *Applications of Evolutinary Computing* (Vol. 4448, pp. 233–240). Springer Berlin Heidelberg. https://doi.org/10.1007/978-3-540-71805-5_26

*Tools and Algorithms for the Construction and Analysis of Systems: 15th International Conference, TACAS 2009, Held as Part of the Joint European Conferences on Theory and Practice of Software, ETAPS 2009, York, UK, March 22-29, 2009, Proceedings | SpringerLink*. (n.d.). Retrieved July 28, 2024, from https://link.springer.com/book/10.1007/978-3-642-00768-2

Tuarob, S. and Tucker, C.S. (2015). Quantifying Product Favorability and Extracting Notable Product Features Using Large Scale Social Media Data. *Journal of Computing and Information Science in Engineering*, *15*(3), 031003. https://doi.org/10.1115/1.4029562

Ukrainian Engineering Pedagogics Academy, Klymenko, V., Polova, T., and Ukrainian Engineering Pedagogics Academy. (2024). Implementation of Artificial Intelligence Tools in Enterprise Management Processes. *Business Navigator*, *2(75)*. https://doi.org/10.32782/business-navigator.75-44

Wang, S., Abbas, J., Sial, M.S., Álvarez-Otero, S. and Cioca, L.-I. (2022). Achieving green innovation and sustainable development goals through green knowledge management: Moderating role of organizational green culture. *Journal of Innovation & Knowledge*, *7*(4), 100272. https://doi.org/10.1016/j.jik.2022.100272

# 4 Collaborative Robots in Manufacturing MSMEs: An Illustrative Discussion on Extending AI to Sustainable Shop Floor Operations

Pulok Ranjan Mohanta[1*] and Biswajit Mahanty[2]

With proliferation of Industry 4.0 technologies and the wider penetration of the notion of Society 5.0, the manufacturing industry is recently observing a trend to enhance the inclusivity in various production operations. To attain this objective of social sustainability, deployment of collaborative robots (COBOTs) to assist their human counterparts on the shop floor operations is recently being considered as one of the promising strategies. This chapter critically explores the application of AI in attaining sustainability in the shop floor operations through COBOT deployment. The objective is to offer a review of the typical applications and propose potential research avenues. Accordingly, illustrations of use cases from the manufacturing industry are presented in this chapter. Further, considering the economic importance of the MSMEs in the sector and to illustrate the wide scope of COBOT deployment, this chapter also presents the contextual enablers and the barriers to such deployment. Towards the end, a framework for sustainable deployment of COBOTs is provided. The chapter is useful as a reference material for researchers, technologists, consultants, and policy makers to drive a successful COBOT deployment project in the manufacturing MSMEs and also to extend AI for the attainment of social sustainability.

## Introduction

In the era of rapid technological advancements, achieving social sustainability in the manufacturing industry increasingly involves the integration of collaborative robots, also known as "COBOTs," into different value creation stages (Mohanta and Mahanty, 2023). COBOTs, unlike their traditional counterparts, that usually operate in isolation, are specially developed to share the workspace alongside the workers.. Their deployment in manufacturing is targeted at enhancing capabilities, improving productivity, and ensuring safety. COBOTs are built to interact directly with human workers, facilitating a harmonious and efficient working environment.

[1] RCG School of Infrastructure Design and Management, IIT Kharagpur.
[2] Department of Industrial and Systems Engineering, IIT Kharagpur.
* Corresponding author: pulok@iitkgp.ac.in

DOI: 10.1201/9781003559849-4

The deployment of COBOTs can significantly contribute to social sustainability in several keyways such as (1) enhancing workplace safety, (2) promoting inclusive workplaces, (3) improving job quality and satisfaction, (4) supporting lifelong learning and skills development, (5) enhancing productivity and economic stability, and (6) enabling work-life balance. While the deployment of COBOTs has the potential to offer a transformative approach to achieving social sustainability in the manufacturing sector by improving the Industry 4.0 maturity (Mohanta and Mahanty, 2024a), they can also play an important role in creating a more sustainable and equitable future for all. In this chapter, a detailed discussion on COBOT deployment in manufacturing MSMEs (i.e. Micro Small and Medium Enterprises), is presented with a special emphasis on social sustainability.

The rest of the chapter is organized as follows. Section 2 describes the overview of the COBOT deployment in the manufacturing MSMEs. The aspect of AI integration with some illustrations are included in section 3. Section 4 illustrates the COBOT deployment for different shop floor applications. In section 5, an elaboration on achieving social sustainability through COBOT deployment is included. Section 6 summarizes the barriers and enablers to COBOT deployment in MSMEs. A deliberation on social and ethical concerns associated with the COBOT deployment in MSMEs is included in section 7, followed by the proposal of a framework for sustainable COBOT deployment in section 8. Section 9 delineates the potential research avenues and section 10 concludes the chapter.

## COBOTs in Manufacturing MSMEs

In manufacturing MSMEs, the production processes often involve manual assembly of a large number of parts of different variants. Further, the production processes witness frequent disruptions due to short cycle time needs. However, in today's mass customization scenario, such traditional labor-intensive processes without automation are finding it increasingly difficult to address different challenges (Malik and Bilberg, 2019). As a solution, the practitioners and decision makers are considering creating a shared work environment by deploying industrial automation alongside manual work (Bauer et al., 2016).

The proliferation of Industry 4.0 technologies augmented the research and development directed at the development of a new variation of robots that can share the workplace with human workers. These are popularly known as "Collaborative robots" or "COBOTs". Differing to their typical counterparts, COBOTs are recognized to improve the shop floor operations by making them more flexible, versatile, and safe.They are typically developed to provide necessary support to their human counterpart and to improve productivity while managing unpredictability (El Zaatari et al., 2019). The idea is to amalgamate the capabilities of humans and machines (Fig. 1). This new paradigm is getting wider acceptance for two prime technological progressions: (1) the inclusion of improved safety features and (2) the deployment of high-tech user interfaces so that the interaction with COBOTs is more insightful and safer (Villani, et al., 2018; Ajoudani et al.,

2018). Additionally, since the COBOTs are now being integrated with AI, they are capable of easy adaptation and perform even when the manufacturing environment is unstructured (Valori et al., 2021). COBOTs are getting wider acceptance in industry. This can be observed from the projection of market growth by Markets and Markets, (2023) from $1.2 bn in 2023 to $6.8 bn by 2029.

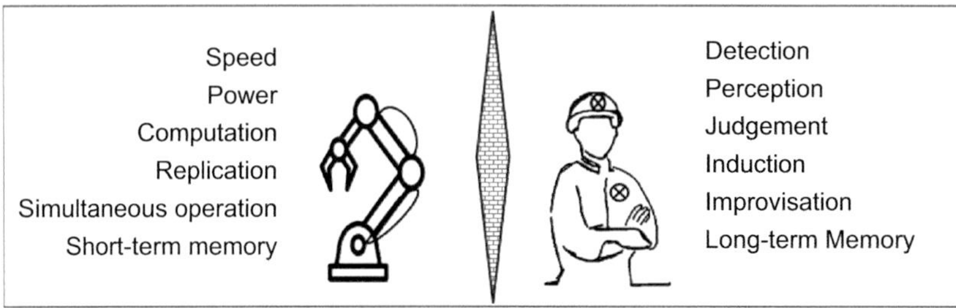


**Fig. 1** Comparison of human capabilities with that of machines.

### *COBOT Deployment on the Shop Floor*

In the manufacturing MSMEs, there are many situations wherein the workers are subjected to repetitive tasks that require high precision or repeatability. Further, some situations involve handling heavy loads and work involving repetitive, burdensome and stressful activities that distress the workers. Several existing studies discussed such situations in the work environment and proposed the deployment of COBOTs as a potential solution to address the associated problems. Dimeas et al., (2019) exemplified the COBOT deployment to perform the assigned task of repetitively lifting and placing the components. Aliev et al., (2019) reviewed the situation wherein the COBOTs execute the assembly jobs while having the human operators as co-workers. In a similar context, Michalos et al., (2018) devised a multi criteria decision making (MCDM) technique for development of the plan for collaboratively assembling the components of the final product. The research by Aliev et al., (2019) discussed a method to perform the pick and place tasks with the application of a camera mounted on a COBOT to augment the job identification process. To reduce the risk of getting biomechanical injuries due to recurring jobs in awkward positions and handling heavy weights, Ranavolo et al., (2022) discussed the role of wearable COBOTs. Describing the working scenario of a welding station in a shop floor, Müller et al., (2017) elaborated the application of COBOTs and classified the scenarios of collaboration between the human and COBOTs. The generalized scenarios are: (1) co-existence without any interactions, (2) synchronized to work in a sequence, (3) coexistence in the same workspace but, working simultaneously on different jobs, and (4) simultaneous execution of the same task with proper collaboration.

Whatever the type of interactions, it is important to have proper coordination between the worker and the COBOTs (Ajoudani et al., 2020). In this regard the proper integration of technologies such as wearable haptic systems (Bianchi, 2016) and augmented reality systems (Andaluz et al., 2016) are found to be of significant help. To summarize, the rationale for COBOT deployment in the MSMEs can be:

1. The capability of COBOTs to collaboratively work with the human operators to improve productivity.
2. Relieving the operator from strenuous and repetitive jobs so that they can focus on other important activities.
3. Working for extended duration to enhance the production output.
4. Deployment of COBOTs in unsafe work environments (such as high pollution, loud noise and high temperature etc.) thereby reducing health hazards to human workers.

## AI Integration in COBOTs

Integration of Artificial intelligence (AI) into the COBOTs has identified the creative answers to various problems encountered during the deployment for shop floor activities. AI integration enables the COBOTs to perceive the work environment (Taesi et al., 2023). With the help of AI, operation of COBOTs in shared environments ensured the safety of human workers (Semeraro et al., 2022). In addition, they could work independently to execute complicated tasks such as metal cutting, deburring, buffing, welding, and inspection. By leveraging Machine Learning, the COBOTs got the ability to learn and improve their performance over time. Also, they created new approaches to learn through experience as well as real-time data and enhance their competency. This further made COBOTs useful to address novel and unusual issues.

To ensure the COBOT operations are safe and simple, techniques that utilize multisensory interfaces and advanced motion control tools together with augmented reality can be effectively deployed (Pierson and Gashler, 2017). Further, COBOTs working with such techniques can also be utilized to lower the training expenditure and facilitate rapid prototyping. In addition to machine learning techniques, the COBOTs are also being integrated with computer vision and superior gripping techniques to expand their application to complex operating environments such as medical surgery, assembly operations, research laboratories and silicon wafer handling. Some typical illustrations of AI integration in COBOTs to achieve aided functionality/ application are listed here. In the subsequent section, we illustrate the COBOT deployment for specific manufacturing functions.

- Liu et al., (2024) proposed a novel approach to manage data in the COBOT deployment scenario, integrated to a digital twin system by deploying blockchain. This approach helps in devising implementation strategies, carry out process simulations, and ensure workplace safety in a collaborative work environment.
- Li et al., (2024) proposed a COBOT integrated with augmented reality for deployment in a power battery dismantling system to address the challenges of source complexity, large variations in design, differences in the process of manufacturing and varied operating conditions.

- Zhang, et al., (2024) contribute to the assembly line balancing problem addressing the requirement for uncertain environments that consider the collaborative interaction between human and COBOT.
- Pickard and Elkington (2024) illustrated the COBOT application in assisting the laminators in the fibre-reinforced composites manufacturing, to reduce the health hazard risks of the human operators.
- Dik, Emmanouilidis, and Duqueroie (2024) used a spatiotemporal graph neural network approach to address the problem of identifying the path for the robots in a shared environment with the human workers.
- Katsampiris-Salgado et al., (2024) described an innovative approach to detect the current location of the operator and predict the future trajectory. Along with the infrared-thermal imaging, they used depth cameras and a multi-layer Long Short-Term Memory (LSTM) neural network to detect and predict the trajectory so as to avoid possible collisions.
- Park, et al., (2024) presented a framework to link an exoskeleton-type robotic system with the digital twin of a COBOT deployed in a manufacturing process. The framework explores the interactions between (1) the COBOT and the digital twin, (2) COBOT and the operator as well as (3) operator and the digital twin to develop the learnings that can be used to improve the task execution by the COBOTs.
- Levratti et al., (2016) presented a discussion on COBOT deployment as a workshop assistant used for lifting and transferring heavy loads. The COBOT can either take instructions by capturing gestures of the operator using RGB-D camera or can be remotely controlled using a haptic interface capable of returning force feedback. Additionally, the COBOT is programmed to operate autonomously to accomplish the given task after getting instructions from a manager.
- Peternel et al., (2016) and Cherubini et al., (2016) discussed the working of the intelligent system that considers the estimated human motor fatigue for auto-activation of the COBOT to assist the operator upon requirement. The system automatically deploys the COBOT particularly in the case when the estimated fatigue exceeds a specified threshold.
- Donner and Buss (2016), in their research related to COBOT deployment for material handling application, illustrated the dampening of unwanted oscillations from the pendulum-like objects that occur when an object is suspended while transporting. In the same vein, Dimeas et al., (2016) researched the detection and stabilization of the instabilities, and devised a technique that reliably eliminates the negative effects from oscillatory behavior.
- Kruse et al., (2015) contributed to developing the mechanism for a COBOT to handle a highly deformable material. The COBOT had the capability to sense the contact force via coupled action of torque sensors and RGBD sensors to maintain the desired tension of the sheet, and subsequently act conforming to human motion.

- For the quality and process inspection deployments of COBOTs, as described by Magalhaes and Ferreira, (2022) and Weiss, Wortmeier and Kubicek, (2021), they are equipped with either 2-D or 3-D vision sensors to meet all the inspection requirements of the production stage.
- Kruger et al., (2009) described the deployment of COBOT as an intelligent assistant for the complex assembly process in a flexible manufacturing environment. The COBOT deployment improved the efficiency of the assembly process and offered the desired level of changeability.

## Illustrative Applications of COBOTs in Manufacturing Functions

In the manufacturing sector, the common functions that occur in the shop floor of a typical MSME are related to material handling, part assembly, fabrication and maintenance activities. In the traditional setup, all these activities were executed by human workers. But as the technology associated with COBOTs matured, they are increasingly being deployed to assist their human counterparts. Ample discussions can be found in the literature that describe aspects of sharing workspace, collaborating and cooperating to execute tasks, control programming, and human-COBOT interaction mechanisms. Taesi et al., (2023) described four possibilities of deploying COBOTs for manufacturing operations:

1. *Coexistence:* The scenario in which the operator and the COBOT perform the assigned activities independently without having to share the work environment.
2. *Synchronization:* The scenario in which the operator and the COBOT perform the assigned activities with independent tasks in a shared work environment.
3. *Cooperation:* The operator and the robot share the work environment to sequentially perform the assigned tasks in a step-by-step manner.
4. *Collaboration:* The operator and robot concurrently work on the assigned tasks while sharing the work environment.

This section explores some typical applications of COBOTs in manufacturing operations. The discussion highlights the different context in which AI is enabling COBOTs to perform.

## COBOTs for Material Handling

Material handling, in a manufacturing organization, is often a complex process that involves several types of equipment working in multiple stages. It is always a challenging task to ensure proper coordination among different stages and executing the assigned task accurately. The deployment of COBOTs for the material handling operations brings in several significant benefits such as: (1) increased efficiency and productivity, (2) improved precision and consistency, (3) more adaptability and flexibility and (4) improved workplace safety (Faccio et al., 2022). Along with these benefits, the ability of the COBOTs to work alongside human workers makes them an asset in modern manufacturing environments. Here is an overview of how COBOTs are used for material handling in manufacturing:

#### *Loading and Unloading Machines*

COBOTs can be programmed for efficient loading of the raw materials into machines and unloading the finished products. This lowers the requirement of executing the repetitive tasks by the human workers, making them available for more complex and value-added activities. Further, this reduces fatigue and risk of potential hazards. This task is common in CNC machining, where the precision and consistency of COBOTs improve productivity and reduce downtime.

#### *Handling Hazardous Materials*

COBOTs can be deployed to safely handle hazardous or toxic materials, reducing the risk to human workers. This is crucial in industries such as chemicals or pharmaceuticals, where exposure to dangerous substances must be minimized.

#### *Picking and Placing*

COBOTs can pick up items from one location and place them in another, such as moving parts from a conveyor belt to an assembly line or packing items into boxes. Their precision and consistency improve the overall quality and speed of the production process. This ensures a smooth and efficient production flow, especially in electronics and automotive manufacturing.

#### *Sorting and Organizing*

COBOTs can sort materials based on size, shape, or other criteria, and organize them accordingly. This is particularly useful in industries where various parts need to be separated and organized for further processing. This is essential in industries such as recycling, and auto component manufacturing processes that require the separation of different types of materials.

### Palletizing and Depalletizing

COBOTs can stack products onto pallets (palletizing) or remove them from pallets (depalletizing). This is a common task in warehouses and distribution centers where large volumes of goods need to be moved efficiently. They are particularly useful in packaging and logistics, where large volumes of goods need to be handled quickly and accurately.

### Assembly Line Assistance

COBOTs can assist human workers in the assembly line by handling parts and components, so that the human workers are set free to perform more intricate assembly tasks such as screwing, welding, or gluing, enhancing the speed and efficiency of the assembly process. They can work at a consistent pace, ensuring a steady flow of materials through the production process.

## Material Feeding

Material feeding is a crucial process in manufacturing that involves supplying raw materials, parts, or components to production lines or machines. COBOTs can be programmed to continuously feed materials into production lines or machines. This helps maintain a steady flow of materials, preventing interruptions and ensuring that production processes run smoothly. This is particularly important in high-speed manufacturing environments where continuous operation is critical in maintaining productivity.

## Quality Control and Inspection

Some COBOTs are equipped with sensors and cameras to inspect products for defects or inconsistencies. They handle items in a consistent manner, ensuring thorough and repeatable inspection processes. They can handle and position materials in a way that makes it easier to perform quality checks, ensuring that only high-quality products move forward in the production line.

## Ergonomic Assistance

In the context of material handling in manufacturing, COBOTs significantly enhance ergonomics by taking over tasks that are physically demanding, repetitive, or hazardous. By handling heavy or awkward materials, COBOTs help reduce the physical strain on human workers. They can handle heavy loads effortlessly and repeatedly, thereby preventing repetitive strain injuries (RSIs) and the injuries related to overexertion and improper lifting techniques. They can position materials at ergonomic heights and angles, allowing workers to maintain better posture and reducing the need for awkward movements. Further, COBOTs can be deployed to operate safely in hazardous conditions, handling dangerous materials and working near risky machinery, so that the human workers are protected from these hazards. COBOTs can also be used to assist the workers with physical limitations or disabilities by taking over tasks that are difficult for them to perform, enabling a more inclusive and accessible workplace.

## Transporting Materials within Facilities

COBOTs can play a crucial role in transporting materials within manufacturing facilities by efficiently moving parts, components, and finished products between different production stages. They handle tasks such as fetching materials from storage, delivering them to assembly lines, and transferring items between workstations. AI applications significantly enhance the role of COBOTs in transporting materials within manufacturing facilities by improving navigation, handling, maintenance, learning, and task optimization. This integration of AI ensures that COBOTs operate efficiently, adaptively, and reliably, contributing to a more streamlined and productive manufacturing process. In an example scenario from a typical automotive manufacturing plant, AI-powered COBOTs can transport various parts from storage to various points of assembly. Using AI for navigation, they avoid crowded paths and deliver the parts precisely when needed. Object recognition allows them to handle different components appropriately, while predictive maintenance ensures they remain operational without unexpected breakdowns. Task scheduling algorithms optimize their workload, coordinating with human workers and other robots to maintain a seamless production flow.

## COBOTs for Assembly Operations

As industries continue to evolve with the adoption of Industry 4.0 technologies, the role of COBOTs in assembly operations is expanding. COBOTs are particularly valuable in assembly operations, where they can be deployed for a range of tasks, from handling small, delicate components to performing complex assembly sequences (Mohanta and Mahanty. 2024b). Their flexibility and ease of programming make them ideal for environments that require frequent product changes or small-batch production. Additionally, COBOTs can relieve workers from monotonous tasks, allowing them to focus on more complex and creative aspects of the assembly process. Their ability to seamlessly integrate with existing processes, work safely alongside humans, and adapt to varying production needs makes them a powerful tool for manufacturers aiming to improve efficiency, quality, and safety on the assembly line. Here are some typical applications of COBOTs from the assembly operations point of view.

## Precision Component Placement

COBOTs can be effectively deployed for assembly operations that involve placing small, delicate components with high precision, reducing human error. For example, in electronics assembly, COBOTs can handle microchips or circuit boards, ensuring exact placement without damaging sensitive parts. Their ability to continuously repeat the assigned assembly work with high accuracy helps in enhancing quality while minimizing waste. Such performance can be observed even when the assembly process is executed at high speed. Further, COBOTs can be reprogrammed quickly for different tasks, making them ideal for small-batch production with frequent product changes.

## Screwdriving and Fastening

COBOTs are increasingly being used in screwdriving and fastening applications in manufacturing due to their ability to execute assemblies with (1) precision and consistency, (2) programming flexibility, (3) ability to work safely alongside human operators, and (4) ability to reduce errors. They can be equipped with torque-controlled screwdrivers for consistent and precise screwdriving tasks. This application is crucial in automotive or electronic assembly, where precise torque is necessary to avoid over-tightening or under-tightening screws.

## Part Feeding and Sorting

In assembly lines, COBOTs can be deployed to automate the process of feeding and sorting parts. For such operations, COBOTs are often equipped with computer vision systems that can identify and pick up different components from bins, trays, or conveyors, and deliver them to specific assembly stations. This application is especially useful in industries such as electronics, where a wide variety of small parts need to be assembled quickly and accurately.

## Packaging and Palletizing

After the assembly process, COBOTs can be used for automating the end-of-line processes such as packaging, labelling, tagging and palletizing. COBOTs can efficiently pack assembled products into boxes, ensuring that each item is placed correctly to minimize damage during shipping. They can also palletize boxes, stacking them in a stable and organized manner. This application is particularly beneficial in industries such as consumer electronics, where speed and precision in packaging are crucial in achieving high production volumes.

## Quality Inspection

In industries such as automotive manufacturing, where quality and safety are paramount, COBOTs can inspect every assembled component for defects, ensuring that only products that meet strict quality standards move forward. For this activity, COBOTs can be integrated with computer vision systems for real-time quality inspection during the assembly process. They can be programmed to check for defects, measure dimensions, and ensure that parts are assembled correctly. This not only improves product quality but also reduces the need for manual inspection, allowing for faster production cycles.

## Surface Finishing and Polishing

COBOTs can be employed for surface finishing and polishing tasks, where consistent pressure and movement are essential for achieving high-quality finishes. In industries such as consumer electronics or automotive manufacturing, where appearance and surface quality are critical, COBOTs can execute jobs such as sanding, buffing, and polishing with a level of precision and consistency that is difficult to achieve manually. Through the automation of these tasks, manufacturers can improve the final product's aesthetic quality and reduce the time required for manual finishing processes.

## Custom Assembly Processes

COBOTs are ideal for custom or low-volume assembly processes where flexibility is crucial. In industries such as custom electronics or luxury goods, where each product may require a slightly different assembly process, COBOTs can be quickly reprogrammed to handle specific tasks such as inserting components, applying adhesives, or performing detailed inspections. This adaptability allows manufacturers to maintain high levels of customization and quality without sacrificing efficiency. The ability to easily switch between different tasks makes COBOTs particularly valuable in environments where product designs frequently change.

## Collaborative Material Handling

COBOTs can assist in material handling tasks, such as loading and unloading of parts or products on the assembly line. In a collaborative setting, COBOTs can work alongside human operators, lifting and positioning heavy or awkward components that would otherwise require significant physical effort. This not only reduces the risk of injury for workers but also speeds up the assembly process by allowing COBOTs to handle the physical demands of material handling while human workers focus on more skilled tasks. The integration of COBOTs into the material handling processes can lead to an efficient and ergonomic production environment.

### *COBOTs for Fabrication Operations*

Fabrication involves a range of complex processes such as cutting, bending, and assembling metal components, which demand high precision and efficiency. COBOTs are engineered to work closely with human operators, enhancing the quality and speed of these tasks. They excel in repetitive, dangerous, or delicate operations where consistency is key, significantly reducing human error and physical strain. Thus, COBOTs have become a pivotal force in the manufacturing industry, particularly in fabrication operations, offering precision, consistency, and safety that are essential in high-stake manufacturing environments. By integrating COBOTs, manufacturers can streamline workflows, minimize downtime, and ensure the highest standards of quality, all the while maintaining a safer working environment. Some typical instances of COBOT deployment for fabrication operations are discussed here.

## Sheet Metal Bending

In fabrication, the bending of sheet metal is a critical task that demands precision and consistency. COBOTs are employed to handle this process with a high degree of accuracy. They are even capable of executing complex bends in various geometries. Their ability to control force and angle ensures that each bend meets exact specifications thus reducing waste due to errors. This is particularly valuable in industries where precise metal forms are crucial, such as automotive and aerospace sectors. By automating the bending process, COBOTs also reduce the physical strain on human workers.

### Automated Welding of Intricate Joints

Welding is a core operation in fabrication, especially when dealing with intricate joints that require precise and consistent welds. COBOTs are equipped with advanced sensors and programming capabilities that allow them to execute complex welding paths with high accuracy. They can adapt to dissimilar materials and thicknesses, ensuring strong and reliable joints. This not only improves the structural integrity of the fabricated parts but also speeds up the welding process by eliminating the need for manual adjustments. Moreover, COBOTs can work in environments that are hazardous to humans, such as areas with high heat or toxic fumes, enhancing overall safety.

### Plasma and Laser Cutting Operations

COBOTs play a vital role in plasma and laser cutting, where precision is paramount. They can hold materials securely and guide the cutting process to ensure that the cuts are made exactly according to the design specifications. This is particularly important in custom fabrication, where unique or intricate shapes are often required. By automating the cutting process, COBOTs reduce material waste and ensure a higher level of consistency across production runs. Additionally, COBOTs can operate continuously without fatigue, allowing for increased throughput and efficiency in cutting operations.

### Robotic Deburring

Deburring, the process of removing sharp edges or excess material from fabricated parts, is essential for both safety and quality. COBOTs are increasingly used for this task, where they provide consistent pressure and movement, resulting in a smooth and uniform finish. This precision is especially important in industries such as aerospace and medical device manufacturing, where even the smallest imperfection can lead to significant issues. By automating the deburring process, COBOTs reduce the risk of injury to human workers and ensure that each part meets stringent quality standards. COBOTs can also work continuously, handling high volumes of parts with the same level of precision.

### Tube Bending and Forming

In fabrication processes that involve tube bending, such as in the production of automotive exhaust systems or structural frameworks, COBOTs provide high precision. They can control the bending angle, radius, and orientation of the tube with great accuracy, ensuring that each piece meets the required specifications. This is crucial in industries where exact tolerances are essential for the performance and safety of the final product. The use of COBOTs in tube bending also reduces the likelihood of material deformation or damage, which can occur if the process is done manually. Furthermore, COBOTs can be programmed to handle different tube sizes and shapes, making them highly versatile in fabrication operations.

### End-to-End Material Flow Management

COBOTs enhance the efficiency of material flow in fabrication environments by seamlessly transporting parts between different workstations. They can be automated to handle specific tasks, such as moving raw materials to the cutting station, then transferring cut parts to the welding or assembly areas. This automation reduces the time and effort required for manual handling, minimizes the risk of damage during transport, and ensures that each part is correctly positioned for subsequent operations. By managing the material flow, COBOTs help to streamline the entire fabrication process, reducing bottlenecks and improving overall production efficiency.

### Structural Steel Assembly

COBOTs are instrumental in the assembly of large structural steel components, such as those used in construction or heavy machinery. They can precisely position and hold heavy parts in place while they are welded or bolted together, improving both the safety and accuracy of the assembly process. This is particularly valuable in projects where exact alignment is critical to the structural integrity of the final product. COBOTs can also be programmed to execute repetitive assembly tasks, so that the physical strain on human workers is minimized. Thus the workers can have more time to carry out the other important aspects of the project.

### CNC Machining Assistance

In CNC machining, COBOTs assist by loading raw materials into the machine and unloading finished parts, a process that would otherwise require significant manual labor. This automation not only speeds up the machining process but also reduces the risk of errors that can occur when handling complex or delicate parts. COBOTs can be automated to work with a wide range of materials and shapes, making them highly adaptable to different machining tasks. By handling the repetitive aspects of CNC machining, COBOTs free up human operators to focus on programming and quality control, further enhancing the efficiency and precision of the fabrication process.

### Automated Riveting

Riveting is a common process in metal fabrication, used to join sheets or components together. COBOTs are increasingly used for automated riveting, where they can apply consistent force and ensure that each rivet is placed accurately. This is especially important in industries such as aerospace or automotive manufacturing, where the strength and reliability of riveted joints are critical to safety. By automating the riveting process, COBOTs not only improve the consistency and quality of the joints but also reduce the time required for assembly. This leads to faster production cycles and higher throughput without compromising on quality.

## Precision Grinding and Polishing

Grinding and polishing are essential finishing processes in metal fabrication, ensuring that parts have smooth surfaces and meet precise dimensional tolerances. COBOTs excel in these tasks by providing consistent pressure and movement, resulting in high-quality finishes. They can be programmed to handle different materials and surface requirements, making them ideal for industries where surface quality is critical. By automating grinding and polishing, COBOTs not only improve the quality and consistency of the finished parts but also reduce the physical strain on workers, who would otherwise need to perform these repetitive tasks manually.

### *COBOTs for Machine Maintenance*

The deployment of COBOTs across various industries to perform machine maintenance tasks is transforming the way industries manage their equipment. By automating the maintenance related tasks that are repetitive, strenuous, dangerous, or require high precision, COBOTs can be credited for enhancing efficiency, reducing downtime, and improving the overall reliability of machinery. As the associated technologies advance, the role of COBOTs in maintenance will expand, offering even greater benefits to industries that rely on well-maintained equipment for their operations. In this section, we shall explore some instances where COBOTs have been effectively utilized for machine maintenance, highlighting the specific tasks they perform, the benefits they bring, and their impact on overall operational efficiency.

## Predictive Maintenance through Automated Inspections

COBOTs are being used to perform routine inspections of machinery, ensuring that the potential issues are identified before they lead to unplanned shutdowns or breakdowns. For this, COBOTs are appropriately equipped with sensors to detect anomalies such as unusual vibrations, temperature fluctuations, or misalignments. These COBOTs follow a pre-programmed path around the machine, capturing data in real-time, which are then analyzed to predict when maintenance should be scheduled. This predictive maintenance approach reduces unplanned downtime, increases the lifespan of the machinery, and enhances overall operational efficiency.

### Lubrication and Fluid Replenishment

Routine lubrication and fluid checks are critical for the smooth operation of various machinery. COBOTs can be programmed to autonomously carry out these tasks with precision, ensuring that the right amount of lubricant is applied to the right parts at the appropriate time intervals. This reduces the risk of related human errors and ensures that machinery operates at optimal efficiency. COBOTs can also monitor fluid levels and automatically top them up when necessary, preventing wear and tear that could result from insufficient lubrication.

### Tightening and Torque Management

Maintaining the correct torque on bolts and screws is essential to ensure that machinery remains secure and operational. COBOTs are increasingly used to perform torque management tasks, particularly in environments where precision is critical. These robots can be equipped with torque sensors to apply the exact amount of force required, reducing the likelihood of over-tightening or under-tightening. This not only enhances the safety and reliability of the machinery but also speeds up the maintenance process.

### Component Replacement and Assembly

In machine maintenance, replacing worn-out components is a frequent task. COBOTs can be deployed to remove old parts and install new ones, especially in cases where the process is repetitive or requires high precision. For example, in an automotive assembly line, COBOTs can replace parts such as filters, belts, or bearings with minimal disruption to the production flow. Their ability to work continuously without fatigue allows for faster and more consistent maintenance, leading to reduced downtime and increased machine availability.

### Calibration of Sensitive Equipment

Some machines require regular calibration to maintain accuracy, such as CNC machines or robotic arms used in manufacturing. COBOTs can be employed to calibrate these machines automatically, ensuring that they operate within the required tolerances. This task requires precision and consistency, making COBOTs an ideal solution. By automating the calibration process, companies can ensure that their machines produce high-quality outputs without the variability that human intervention might introduce.

### Cleaning and Decontamination

COBOTs can be used for cleaning and decontaminating machinery, especially in environments where cleanliness is critical, such as in pharmaceutical or food processing industries. These robots can be programmed to clean hard-to-reach areas, ensuring that machines remain free from contaminants that could affect their operation or the quality of the products they produce. By automating the cleaning process, companies can reduce the risk of contamination, enhance hygiene standards, and ensure compliance with industry regulations.

## Data Logging and Reporting

In modern maintenance strategies, data plays a crucial role in decision-making. COBOTs can be integrated into machine maintenance routines to collect and log data on machine performance, wear patterns, and maintenance activities. This data can then be used to generate reports that help maintenance teams make informed decisions. By providing accurate and up-to-date information, COBOTs contribute to more effective maintenance planning, helping avoid unnecessary repairs and ensuring that resources are used efficiently.

## Emergency Shutdown and Safety Protocols

In situations where a machine's operation poses a risk to human workers or other equipment, COBOTs can be programmed to perform emergency shutdowns. These COBOTs are equipped with sensors that detect hazardous conditions, such as overheating or a sudden spike in vibration. When such conditions are detected, the COBOT can initiate safety protocols, including shutting down the machine, alerting maintenance personnel, and isolating the affected area. This capability not only enhances workplace safety but also prevents potential damage to machinery and reduces the likelihood of costly repairs.

### *Social Sustainability through COBOT Deployment*

The deployment of COBOTs, in manufacturing MSMEs, represents a significant technological advancement, considering their design to work alongside human workers, enhancing efficiency, safety, and productivity. Their integration into manufacturing processes not only revolutionizes the production landscape but also contributes to social sustainability, which focuses on the well-being of individuals and communities. It is an important pillar of sustainable development. The introduction of COBOTs in manufacturing MSMEs aligns with several Sustainable Development Goals (SDGs), promoting decent work, economic growth, and reduced inequalities, among others (See Fig. 2).

#### *Promoting Inclusive and Equitable Education (SDG 4)*

The deployment of COBOTs in small manufacturing enterprises can also indirectly support inclusive and equitable education (SDG 4). As small enterprises adopt COBOTs, there is a growing need for workers who are skilled in robotics, programming, and automation. This demand can drive educational institutions and vocational training centers to offer courses and programs related to these fields, thereby expanding access to technical education. Further, MSMEs can

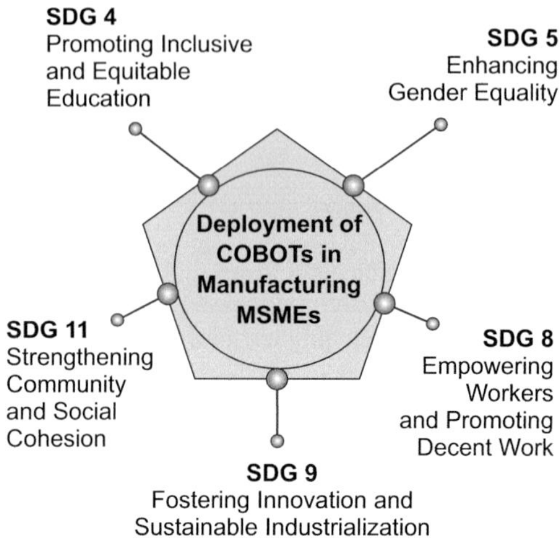


**Fig. 2** COBOT Deployment and Sustainable Development Goals.

partner with local educational institutions to create training programs that provide students with hands-on experience in operating and maintaining COBOTs. These opportunities can help the students gain practical skills and be better prepared for the emerging job scenarios. By promoting education and skills development, COBOT deployment can contribute to the broader goal of inclusive and equitable education for all.

### *Enhancing Gender Equality (SDG 5)*

Gender equality (SDG 5) is an important aspect of social sustainability that can be positively impacted by the deployment of COBOTs in manufacturing MSMEs. In many traditional manufacturing settings, certain tasks are gendered, with men often assigned to physically demanding roles while women are relegated to less physically intensive tasks, which may also be less paying. COBOTs can help break down these gender-based labor divisions by taking over physically demanding tasks, allowing all workers, regardless of gender, to engage in a wider range of activities within the enterprise. Moreover, the implementation of COBOTs can create opportunities for women in technical roles, such as programming and robot maintenance. These roles are typically higher-paying and provide greater opportunities for career advancement. By facilitating equal access to these opportunities, COBOT deployment can contribute to reducing gender disparities in the workplace and promoting gender equality in MSMEs.

### *Empowering Workers and Promoting Decent Work (SDG 8)*

COBOTs play a pivotal role in promoting decent work and economic growth (SDG 8) within small enterprises. Unlike the traditional counterparts, COBOTs are designed to work safely alongside human workers. This collaboration allows workers to focus on more complex and creative tasks while COBOTs handle repetitive, mundane, or physically demanding activities. By reducing the physical strain and risk of injury associated with such tasks, COBOTs contribute to a safer and healthier work environment. Furthermore, the deployment of COBOTs can lead to the upskilling of the workforce. Workers are trained to operate, program, and maintain these robots, which not only enhances their skill set but also increases their employability in an increasingly automated world. This upskilling fosters a sense of job security and satisfaction among employees, as they are not merely displaced by automation but are instead empowered to work alongside advanced technology. This approach aligns with the concept of decent work, where workers have access to opportunities for personal and professional development within a safe and dignified environment.

### *Fostering Innovation and Sustainable Industrialization (SDG 9)*

COBOT deployment also aligns with SDG 9, emphasizing on (1) resilient infrastructure, (2) inclusive and sustainable industrialization, and (3) promoting innovation. In small manufacturing enterprises, COBOTs can serve as catalysts for innovation by enabling more efficient and flexible production processes. They can be quickly re-programmed and adapted to execute different tasks. This enables MSMEs to respond more rapidly to changes in market demand and experiment with new products and production methods. This flexibility and adaptability are crucial for the survival and growth of small enterprises in competitive markets. By fostering innovation, COBOTs help MSMEs maintain their relevance in a rapidly changing industrial landscape, contributing to the sustainability of these businesses. Additionally, the use of COBOTs can lead to more sustainable production practices, as they can be appropriately programmed to minimize waste and energy consumption, aligning with broader environmental sustainability goals.

### *Strengthening Community and Social Cohesion (SDG 11)*

As small manufacturing businesses grow and become more efficient, they can provide stable employment opportunities within local communities, contributing to economic stability and social cohesion. COBOTs can help MSMEs remain competitive and profitable, ensuring they can continue to operate profitably and generate job opportunities. Furthermore, the presence of technologically advanced small enterprises can attract additional investment and development to the locality, contributing to the economic and social growth of the community. Thus, by contributing to the stability and growth of MSMEs, COBOTs help strengthen the resilience of local economies and communities, making them more sustainable in the long term.

The deployment of COBOTs in small manufacturing enterprises is not just a technological advancement; it is a significant contributor to social sustainability. By promoting decent work, reducing inequalities, fostering innovation, enhancing gender equality, strengthening community cohesion, and supporting education,

COBOTs align with several Sustainable Development Goals. As small enterprises embrace COBOTs, they not only enhance their competitiveness but also contribute to the well-being of their workers and communities, laying the foundation for a more sustainable and inclusive future.

## Enablers and Barriers to COBOT Deployment in MSMEs

In the planning process of deploying collaborative robots (COBOTs) in manufacturing MSMEs, it is essential to understand the enablers and barriers that influence the deployment projects. On one hand, barriers are the challenges and obstacles that can impede the deployment projects. On the other hand, enablers are the positive forces that support and drive the adoption of COBOTs, thereby helping MSMEs to enhance productivity, improve quality, and remain competitive. Understanding both enablers and barriers is essential for MSMEs as they navigate the complexities of COBOT deployment (Mohanta and Mahanty, 2021). This would ensure that they can leverage the benefits of automation while addressing potential challenges effectively. By identifying and addressing these factors, MSMEs can create a strategic roadmap for sustainable and successful COBOT integration into their manufacturing processes. In Table 1, important barriers and enablers are grouped and tabulated.

**Table 1** Barriers and Enablers to COBOT Deployment

| *Barriers to COBOT deployment* | *Enablers to COBOT deployment* |
|---|---|
| ***Financial*** | |
| • High Initial Investment for procurement<br>• Uncertain Return on Investment (ROI)<br>• Increased Maintenance and Operation Costs<br>• Additional expenses related to integrating COBOTs with existing systems and processes<br>• Limited access to financial instruments | • Financial incentives through Government Grants and Subsidies<br>• Leasing Options through servitization models<br>• Cost Efficiency and financial benefits in the long run<br>• Tax Incentives for investments in automation technology<br>• Partnerships or shared investment models that reduce the financial risk |
| ***Technological*** | |
| • Complexity in Integration to existing system<br>• Inconsistencies in technology standards across different COBOT manufacturers<br>• Lack of in-house technical expertise required<br>• Compatibility issues with existing machinery and software<br>• Data security concerns | • User-friendly interfaces to reduce the complexity<br>• Use of advances in technology that improve interoperability<br>• Access to comprehensive technical support and training programs<br>• Adoption of cloud platforms for easier management, monitoring, and updates of COBOT systems<br>• Availability of advanced and sophisticated cyber security measures |

*Contd.*

**Table 1** *Contd.*

| | |
|---|---|
| ***Organizational*** | |
| • Resistance to Change<br>• Existing skill gap<br>• Lack of proper management support<br>• Change management challenges<br>• Operational disruption during the initial phase of implementation | • Fostering a culture of innovation<br>• Investment in upskilling programs<br>• Strong commitment from management<br>• Fostering a culture to encourage human and robots' collaboration<br>• Employee involvement in the deployment process |
| ***Regulatory and Safety*** | |
| • complex regulations related to safety, data security, and labor laws<br>• Safety concerns related to integrating COBOTs into a human-centric work environment<br>• Labor law related challenges<br>• Standardization and certification requirements | • Government initiatives that streamline the regulatory process<br>• Availability of comprehensive safety standards and guidelines<br>• Advanced safety features in COBOTs<br>• Risk management tools and protocols for effectively managing and mitigating safety risks |
| ***Market and Competition*** | |
| • Volatility in market demand<br>• Competitive pressure from larger companies<br>• Concerns associated with customer acceptance for products made with significant automation<br>• Constraints from the suppliers to support COBOT-enabled processes | • Enhancement of competitive position through market differentiation<br>• Scalability to gradually increase the automation level in response to market demands<br>• Achieving competitive advantage through increased efficiency and reduced costs<br>• Leveraging COBOTs to improve customer service and responsiveness<br>• Improved agility and flexibility |
| ***Environmental and Sustainability*** | |
| • Increased energy consumption<br>• Managing electronic waste generated due to COBOTs that are at the end of their lifecycle<br>• Difficulty in sourcing environment-friendly COBOT components or materials<br>• Concerns that increased automation could lead to overuse of natural resources<br>• Challenges associated with environmental compliance | • Advances in energy-efficient technologies for COBOTs<br>• Availability of recycling programs for COBOT components<br>• Aligning COBOT deployment with broader sustainability goals, such as reducing waste and improving precision<br>• Green certifications that validate the environment-friendliness of COBOT-powered operations<br>• Adopting circular economy principles to designing COBOTs and processes that maximize resource efficiency and minimize waste |

*Contd.*

**Table 1** *Contd.*

| *Social and Ethical* | |
|---|---|
| • Concerns about job losses<br>• Ethical concerns about the impact of automation on employment and social equity<br>• Potential negative impact on employee morale if COBOTs are perceived as a threat to job security<br>• Challenges in gaining social acceptance | • Job creation potential in new roles<br>• Resulting improvements in workplace safety<br>• Strategies that ensure automation benefits to be fairly distributed across the workforce<br>• Active employee engagement in the transition process<br>• Incorporating COBOT deployment into broader CSR initiatives that focus on community development and employee welfare |

## *MSME-specific Challenges in COBOT Deployment*

The deployment of COBOTs in manufacturing MSMEs are often subjected to several challenges that are unique to their scale and resource capacity. Some of these challenges are stated here:

*a.* ***Initial costs and ROI concerns:*** Since the MSMEs operate with tighter financial margins, the higher cost of COBOTs, associated with purchase, installation, and maintenance can make it difficult to justify the long-term ROI, when compared to immediate operational costs.

*b.* ***Inadequate technical expertise:*** The deployment of COBOTs and their operations require sound technical know-how related to troubleshooting, programming and maintaining. MSMEs often operate with smaller, less specialized teams, and may lack operators with the necessary technical skills. This can lead to increase in expenses corresponding to training the operators or outsource the required technical support.

*c.* ***Customization and flexibility requirements:*** Off-the-shelf COBOTs might not provide flexibility requirements to fit their unique production needs, leading to integration challenges and the need for expensive custom configurations.

*d.* ***Integration with legacy systems:*** Usually, the MSMEs operate with the older equipment and legacy systems that may not be compatible with newer COBOT technologies. The integration of COBOTs into these existing systems can be complex and costly. Upgrading or retrofitting older machinery to work with COBOTs can further add to the expense and technical difficulty.

*e.* ***Safety and regulatory compliance:*** Although COBOTs are designed to work safely alongside humans, ensuring compliance with workplace safety regulations can be challenging. MSMEs may lack the resources to conduct extensive safety assessments, and the cost of modifying workspaces to meet safety requirements could be a deterrent. Furthermore, understanding and navigating the regulatory landscape can be more difficult for smaller organizations.

f. ***Cultural and workforce resistance:*** In MSMEs, employees usually have diverse roles and are integral to daily operations. The introduction of automation in the form of COBOTs can create concerns about job displacement or reduced job security among employees. There might be stronger resistance to change due to fears that automation will make human workers redundant, making adaptation slower and difficult.

g. ***Uncertainty around maintenance and downtime:*** COBOTs, like any machinery, require proactive maintenance to avoid downtime. A malfunctioning COBOT in an MSME could have a disproportionate impact on production activities, since they often lack redundancy in their operations. They possess limited ability to quickly repair or replace malfunctioning robots.

### *Social and Ethical Concerns of COBOT Deployment*

The deployment of COBOTs in manufacturing MSMEs is revolutionizing the industry by offering increased efficiency, productivity, and enhanced workplace safety. However, while COBOTs bring numerous advantages, their introduction also raises significant social and ethical concerns. As these robots are programmed to take over the repetitive and hazardous tasks, concerns about job displacement, deskilling of the workforce, and worker morale emerge. The concerns are typical for the case of MSMEs where employees are fewer and more vulnerable. Additionally, the unequal access to advanced technology and privacy issues arising from data collection are pressing ethical challenges. These concerns are amplified in smaller organizations with limited resources for robust safety protocols and employee upskilling. To successfully integrate COBOTs, the MSMEs must strike a balance between technological advancement and maintaining a fair, safe, and ethical work environment. In this section some prominent social and ethical concerns are highlighted.

## Job Displacement and Unemployment Risks

One of the major social concerns surrounding COBOT deployment is the potential for job displacement. COBOTs are designed to work alongside humans, automating repetitive or dangerous tasks. However, in small manufacturing companies, where jobs may already be scarce, the fear of unemployment arises as some tasks performed by humans could be replaced by robots. The displacement of low-skilled workers raises ethical questions about the role of businesses in preserving livelihoods and ensuring a just transition i.e. the transition which is both fair and inclusive. Companies may need to consider strategies for upskilling their workforce rather than directly replacing workers with robots.

## Worker Deskilling and Associated Resistance

While COBOTs are intended to augment human labour, there is a concern that workers might become overly reliant on automated systems, leading to a reduction in skill levels over time. Additionally, workers may resist learning to work with these robots out of fear of eventual obsolescence. This presents an ethical dilemma about the responsibility of companies to ensure continuous skill development for their employees, ensuring they remain relevant in an increasingly automated world.

## Workplace Safety and Liability Issues

COBOTs are designed to interact with humans, but concerns arise regarding workplace safety if a robot malfunctions or behaves unpredictably. This is especially sensitive in smaller manufacturing environments with less robust safety oversight compared to larger factories. Questions arise regarding who bears the responsibility if an accident involving a COBOT occurs. Employers must carefully consider the legal and moral obligations to ensure worker safety and address potential liability concerns.

## Impact on Worker Morale and Social Dynamics

The introduction of COBOTs into the workplace can have a significant impact on worker morale. Employees may feel devalued or perceive that their contributions are less important, especially if they see robots performing tasks they once managed. This could lead to increased stress, anxiety, or hostility towards automation, creating a negative work culture. MSMEs must ethically balance the use of COBOTs while maintaining a supportive and inclusive work environment.

### *Privacy and Data Security*

COBOTs and associated technologies often rely on sensors, cameras, and data collection to operate efficiently. In MSME settings, this can raise concerns about the privacy of workers, as they may feel constantly monitored. Companies must be transparent about how data collected from COBOTs is used, stored, and protected. Workers have the right to know how their personal information and performance data are being handled.

### *Ethical use of COBOTs in Hazardous Tasks*

COBOTs are often used in hazardous environments to perform tasks that might be too dangerous for humans. However, there is a moral question about whether the company is prioritizing profitability by reducing human involvement in these tasks without fully addressing the underlying dangers of the work environment. While using COBOTs to reduce human exposure to hazards is positive, it's crucial that companies do not simply rely on robots to mitigate risks while neglecting standard practices to improve overall workplace safety.

### *Environmental Concerns*

While COBOTs can increase efficiency and reduce waste, their production, energy consumption, and eventual disposal raise environmental concerns. For MSMEs, this adds to the ethical debate about sustainability. Companies must evaluate the environmental footprint of adopting COBOT technology, considering long-term sustainability goals and responsible usage.

### *Human-robot Collaboration and Ethical Boundaries*

There may be concerns about the extent to which human workers are expected to collaborate with robots, especially in high-stress or physically demanding jobs. The balance between automation and human dignity can become blurred. Companies must ensure that workers are not reduced to mere extensions of automated systems, and that human autonomy and decision-making remains central to the workplace.

### *Economic Pressures and Ethical Decision-Making*

Small manufacturing companies face pressure to remain competitive, and this might lead them to prioritize cost-saving measures, such as automation, over ethical labour practices. Companies must consider the broader social impact of their decisions and the ethical obligation to contribute positively to the community and workforce while staying competitive.

In summary, the deployment of COBOTs in small manufacturing companies presents several social and ethical concerns that must be addressed through thoughtful decision-making, transparent communication, and a commitment to workforce and community well-being.

## Sustainable COBOT Deployment Framework

The initiation of COBOTs has revolutionized manufacturing, offering unprecedented opportunities for efficiency, precision, and flexibility. However, the successful and sustainable deployment of COBOTs in these environments requires a strategic and holistic approach, one that not only considers immediate operational benefits but also long-term impacts on the business, workforce, and environment. The concept of a sustainable COBOT deployment framework emerges as a crucial guide for MSMEs, ensuring that the integration of these advanced technologies is both effective and responsible. The proposed framework is presented in Fig. 3. Each stage of this sustainable COBOT deployment framework is briefly described in the following paragraphs.

This framework begins with a thorough requirement assessment and feasibility study, where MSMEs identify specific areas within their operations that could benefit from automation. This initial stage is critical as it helps businesses align COBOT capabilities with their unique operational needs. This ensures that the deployment will address real operational challenges rather than introduce unnecessary complexities. Beyond technical feasibility, this stage also involves a comprehensive cost-benefit analysis, where financial, environmental, and social factors are weighed to ensure that the investment in COBOTs will be sustainable in the long term.

Following the assessment, the selection of appropriate COBOTs is vital. This step involves identification of COBOTs that match the specific tasks and operational environments of the MSME. The factors that should be considered in decision making are related to payload capacity, precision, and integration capabilities. It is important that the selection process must consider the sustainability of the technology itself, including energy efficiency, ease of maintenance, and lifecycle management. Sustainable deployment is not just about choosing the right technology but also ensuring that this technology can be supported and scaled within the business without causing undue strain on resources or the environment.

Once selected, a pilot testing phase allows MSMEs to implement COBOTs on a smaller scale, closely monitoring their performance and making adjustments as necessary. This iterative approach helps identify potential issues early, allowing businesses to refine their processes before full-scale deployment. It also provides an opportunity to engage employees, gathering feedback and building a culture of collaboration between human workers and robots, which is essential for long-term success. Safety and regulatory compliance then becomes a crucial stage in the deployment framework. Given that COBOTs work closely with human operators, ensuring their safety is paramount. This stage involves adhering to national and international safety standards, conducting risk assessments, and implementing robust safety protocols. Compliance with regulatory requirements not only safeguards workers but also helps MSMEs avoid legal penalties and reputational damage. This stage also includes obtaining necessary certifications and ensuring that COBOTs are equipped with the latest safety features, such as sensors and emergency stop functions, to prevent accidents and injuries.

Further, scaling up the deployment involves careful planning to ensure that the increased use of COBOTs does not lead to unforeseen challenges. This includes ongoing training for employees, process optimization, and continuous monitoring of both operational performance and environmental impact. The framework emphasizes the need for a feedback loop, where data from COBOT operations are regularly reviewed to identify areas for improvement. Ahead of scaling, the framework emphasizes process optimization and integration, ensuring that the COBOTs are not just added elements but are integral parts of the manufacturing workflow. This stage involves fine-tuning the interactions between COBOTs and human workers, optimizing the entire process to achieve maximum efficiency and productivity. Integration also includes ensuring that the COBOTs work seamlessly with existing systems, software, and machinery.

Next critical stage is continuous improvement and innovation, where MSMEs regularly evaluate the performance of COBOTs and explore new technological advancements that could further enhance their operations. This stage encourages

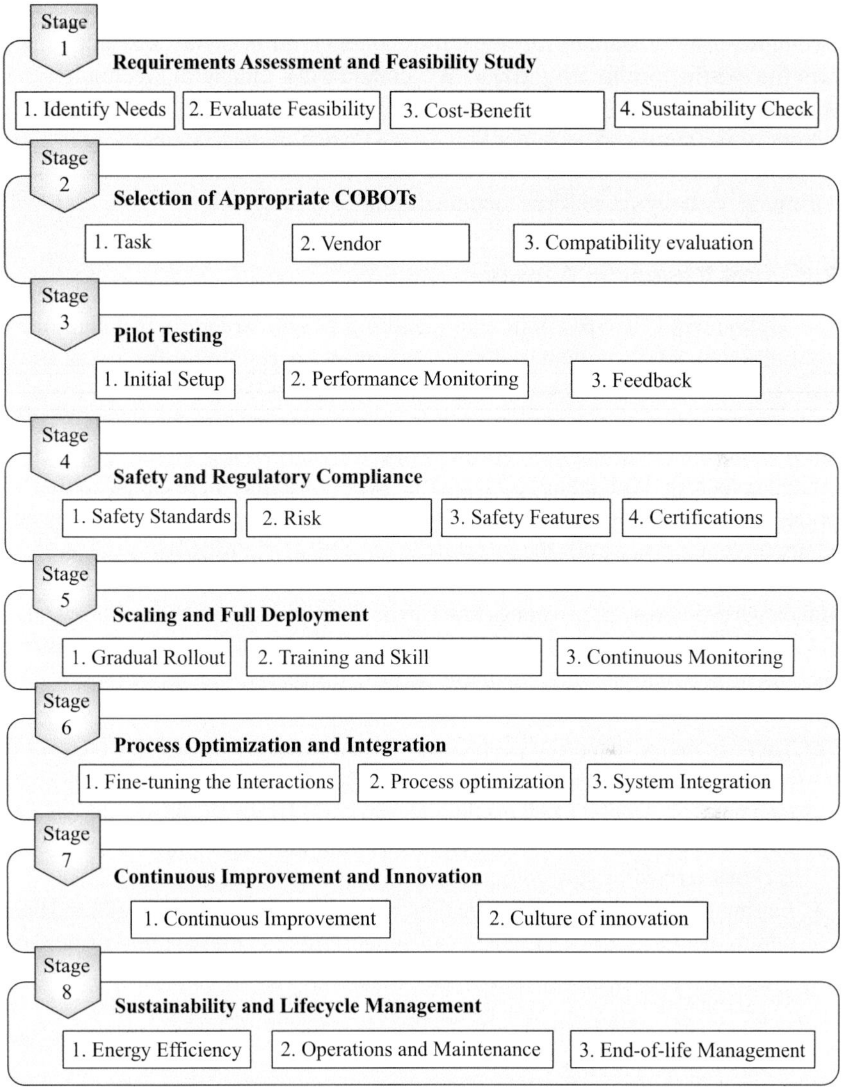


**Fig. 3** A sustainable COBOT deployment framework for MSMEs.

a culture of innovation, where businesses continually seek to improve their automation strategies, keeping pace with technological trends and market demands.

Finally, the framework includes sustainability and lifecycle management, which ensures that the deployment of COBOTs aligns with broader environmental goals. This stage focuses on the energy efficiency of the robots, their maintenance requirements, and their end-of-life management, including recycling and disposal. Sustainable lifecycle management ensures that the COBOTs contribute positively to the business's environmental footprint over their entire lifespan.

This sustainable COBOT deployment framework provides MSMEs with a comprehensive roadmap for integrating automation in a way that maximizes benefits while minimizing risks. By considering financial, technological, organizational, safety-related, regulatory-related, environmental, and innovative factors, this framework ensures that COBOT deployment supports long-term business goals, workforce development, and environmental stewardship, making it a crucial strategy for modern manufacturing enterprises.

## Potential Research Avenues

The deployment of COBOTs in manufacturing MSMEs represents a significant technological advancement with the potential to revolutionize small-scale manufacturing. Unlike the conventional robots, COBOTs are designed to share the workspace alongside human operators, enhancing productivity, flexibility, and safety in production processes. For MSMEs, which often face challenges such as limited resources, high labor costs, and the need for agility in response to market demands, COBOTs offer a viable solution to improve operational efficiency and competitiveness. However, the integration of COBOTs in MSMEs is presently at a nascent stage having several research fronts yet to be explored. Here are some of the interesting research avenues that can be furthered to enable the full potential of COBOT deployment in MSMEs, ensuring that these enterprises can harness the benefits of automation while maintaining their distinct advantages in innovation and adaptability.

- There is much scope for exploration of the ways to customize COBOTs to handle the unique tasks and workflows found in MSMEs, including mass customization, small batch production and varied tasks. Typically, the optimal COBOT deployment should be customized for the scenario where production is characterized by low volumes and high product variety.
- Further investigations can also be directed at developing the COBOTs and their deployment strategies so that it can support agile manufacturing principles, allowing MSMEs to respond quickly to market changes and customer demands. Research also can be extended to explore COBOT integration into the broader supply chain of MSMEs, improving logistics, inventory management, and production scheduling.
- Investigations can be done on integration of COBOTs into (1) quality control processes, ensuring consistent product quality in small-scale production. (2) facilitating rapid prototyping and iterative product design in MSMEs, enhancing innovation capacity.
- There are a limited number of studies available that explore the aspects of the interaction between workers and COBOTs in small-scale manufacturing environments, focusing on safety, ergonomics, and productivity. The related research should also focus on how COBOT adoption affects employment patterns, job roles, and the overall workforce structure in MSMEs. Attention should also be focused on developing training programs to equip MSME

workers with the skills needed to operate and collaborate with COBOTs effectively.

- Potential for research also exists in the development of simplified programming interfaces that allow MSME operators with limited technical skills to configure and deploy COBOTs. Further, safety protocols can be researched by considering the MSME settings, where space constraints and worker proximity to COBOTs are significant factors.
- The frameworks for reliability analysis of COBOTs in MSMEs are scant in the existing literature. Related studies can also include the aspects of energy efficiency of COBOTs in MSME manufacturing processes and develop improvement strategies. Considering the sustainability aspect, environmental footprint of COBOTs in MSMEs, including waste reduction, energy use, and material efficiency can also be explored. Researchers and practitioners can also explore how COBOTs can support lean manufacturing practices to reduce waste and improve operational efficiency.

## Conclusion

The deployment of COBOTs on the shop floors of manufacturing MSMEs represents a pivotal shift toward modernization and efficiency. By integrating these advanced technologies, MSMEs can significantly enhance productivity, reduce operational costs, and maintain competitiveness in a rapidly evolving market. COBOTs not only offer the flexibility and precision needed in manufacturing processes but also foster a safer and more ergonomic working environment for employees. As the adoption of COBOTs grows, MSMEs stand to benefit from increased operational resilience and the ability to scale their operations sustainably. Embracing this technology is not just an investment in machinery but a strategic move toward a future-ready manufacturing ecosystem.

## References

Ajoudani, A., Albrecht, P., Bianchi, M., Cherubini, A., Del Ferraro, S., Fraisse, P., Fritzsche, L., Garabini, M., Ranavolo, A., Rosen, P.H. and Sartori, M. (2020). Smart collaborative systems for enabling flexible and ergonomic work practices [industry activities]. *IEEE Robotics & Automation Magazine*, *27*(2), pp. 169–176.

Ajoudani, A., Zanchettin, A.M., Ivaldi, S., Albu-Scha ffer, A., Kosuge, K. and Khatib, O. (2018). Progress and prospects of the human–robot collaboration. *Autonomous Robots*, *42*, pp. 957–975.

Aliev, K., Antonelli, D. and Bruno, G. (2019). Task-based programming and sequence planning for human-robot collaborative assembly. *IFAC-PapersOnLine*, *52*(13), pp. 1638–1643.

Andaluz, V.H., Quevedo, W.X., Chicaiza, F.A., Varela, J., Gallardo, C., Sánchez, J.S. and Arteaga, O. (2016). Transparency of a bilateral tele-operation scheme of a mobile manipulator robot. In *Augmented Reality, Virtual Reality, and Computer Graphics: Third International Conference, AVR 2016, Lecce, Italy, June 15-18, 2016. Proceedings, Part I 3* (pp. 228–245). Springer International Publishing.

Bauer, W., Bender, M., Braun, M., Rally, P.E.T.E.R. and Scholtz, O. (2016). Lightweight robots in manual assembly–best to start simply. *Frauenhofer-Institut für Arbeitswirtschaft und Organisation IAO, Stuttgart*, *1*.

Bianchi, M. (2016). A fabric-based approach for wearable haptics. *Electronics*, *5*(3), p. 44.

Cherubini, A., Passama, R., Crosnier, A., Lasnier, A. and Fraisse, P. (2016). Collaborative manufacturing with physical human–robot interaction. *Robotics and Computer-Integrated Manufacturing*, *40*, pp. 1–13.

Dik, C., Emmanouilidis, C. and Duqueroie, B. (2024). Graph network-based human movement prediction for socially-aware robot navigation in shared workspaces. *Neural Computing and Applications*, 1–17.

Dimeas, F. and Aspragathos, N. 2016. Online stability in human-robot cooperation with admittance control. *IEEE Transactions on Haptics*, *9*(2), pp. 267–278.

Dimeas, F., Fotiadis, F., Papageorgiou, D., Sidiropoulos, A. and Doulgeri, Z. 2019. Towards progressive automation of repetitive tasks through physical human-robot interaction. In *Human Friendly Robotics: 10th International Workshop* (pp. 151–163). Springer International Publishing.

Donner, P. and Buss, M. (2016). Cooperative swinging of complex pendulum-like objects: Experimental evaluation. *IEEE Transactions on Robotics*, *32*(3), pp. 744–753.

El Zaatari, S., Marei, M., Li, W. and Usman, Z. 2019. Cobot programming for collaborative industrial tasks: An overview. *Robotics and Autonomous Systems*, *116*, pp. 162–180.

Faccio, M., Granata, I., Menini, A., Milanese, M., Rossato, C., Bottin, M., Minto, R., Pluchino, P., Gamberini, L., Boschetti, G. and Rosati, G. (2023). Human factors in cobot era: a review of modern production systems features. *Journal of Intelligent Manufacturing*, *34*(1), pp. 85–106.

Katsampiris-Salgado, K., Dimitropoulos, N., Gkrizis, C., Michalos, G. and Makris, S., (2024). Advancing human-robot collaboration: Predicting operator trajectories through AI and infrared imaging. *Journal of Manufacturing Systems*, *74*, pp. 980–994.

Kru ger, J., Lien, T.K. and Verl, A. (2009). Cooperation of human and machines in assembly lines. *CIRP annals*, *58*(2), pp. 628–646.

Kruse, D., Radke, R.J. and Wen, J.T. (2015) May. Collaborative human-robot manipulation of highly deformable materials. In *2015 IEEE International Conference on Robotics and Automation (ICRA)* (pp. 3782–3787). IEEE.

Levratti, A., De Vuono, A., Fantuzzi, C. and Secchi, C. (2016). TIREBOT: A novel tire workshop assistant robot. In *2016 IEEE International Conference on Advanced Intelligent Mechatronics (AIM)* (pp. 733–738). IEEE.

Li, J., Duan, L., Qu, W., and Zheng, H. (2024). A knowledge transfer method for human-robot collaborative disassembly of end-of-life power batteries based on augmented reality. *AI EDAM*, *38*, e9.

Liu, X., Li, G., Xiang, F., Tao, B., and Jiang, G. (2024). Blockchain-based cloud-edge collaborative data management for human-robot collaboration digital twin system. *Journal of Manufacturing Systems*, *77*, 228–245.

Magalhaes, P. and Ferreira, N., 2022. Inspection application in an industrial environment with collaborative robots. *Automation*, *3*(2), pp. 258–268.

Malik, A.A. and Bilberg, A. (2019). Complexity-based task allocation in human-robot collaborative assembly. *Industrial Robot: The International Journal of Robotics Research and Application*, *46*(4), pp. 471–480.

Markets and Markets, https://www.marketsandmarkets.com/Market-Reports/collaborative-robot-market-194541294.html, last accessed 2023/08/1.

Michalos, G., Spiliotopoulos, J., Makris, S. and Chryssolouris, G. (2018). A method for planning human robot shared tasks. *CIRP Journal of Manufacturing Science and Technology*, *22*, pp.76–90.

Mohanta, P.R. and Mahanty, B., 2021. Modelling critical success factors for the implementation of industry 4.0 in Indian manufacturing MSMEs. In *IFIP International Conference on Advances in Production Management Systems* (pp. 89–97). Cham: Springer International Publishing.

Mohanta, P.R. and Mahanty, B. (2023). Collaborative Robots in Manufacturing MSMEs: Identification and Operationalization of Enablers and Barriers. In *International Working Conference on Transfer and Diffusion of IT* (pp. 237–250). Cham: Springer Nature Switzerland.

Mohanta, P. R., and Mahanty, B. (2024 (a). Assessing Industry 4.0 implementation maturity in manufacturing MSMEs–a graph theory and matrix-based approach. *The TQM Journal*.

Mohanta, P. R., and Mahanty, B. (2024 b). Exploring the performance improvement and skill set transformations in sheet metal operations through digital technology. In *Artificial Intelligence and Internet of Things based Augmented Trends for Data Driven Systems* (pp. 239–261). CRC Press.

Müller, R., Vette, M. and Geenen, A. (2017). Skill-based dynamic task allocation in human-robot-cooperation with the example of welding application. *Procedia Manufacturing*, *11*, pp.13–21.

Park, H., Shin, M., Choi, G., Sim, Y., Lee, J., Yun, H., Jun, M.B.G., Kim, G., Jeong, Y. and Yi, H. (2024). Integration of an exoskeleton robotic system into a digital twin for industrial manufacturing applications. *Robotics and Computer-Integrated Manufacturing*, *89*, p.102746.

Peternel, L., Tsagarakis, N., Caldwell, D. and Ajoudani, A. (2016), November. Adaptation of robot physical behaviour to human fatigue in human-robot co-manipulation. In *2016 IEEE-RAS 16th International Conference on Humanoid Robots (Humanoids)* (pp. 489–494). IEEE.

Pickard, L. R., and Elkington, M. (2024). Laminator trust in human–robot collaboration for manufacturing fibre-reinforced composites. *IET Collaborative Intelligent Manufacturing*, *6*(4), e12123.

Pierson, H.A. and Gashler, M.S. ( 2017). Deep learning in robotics: a review of recent research. *Advanced Robotics*, *31*(16), pp.821–835.

Ranavolo, A. , Chini, G., Draicchio, F., Silvetti, A., Varrecchia, T., Fiori, L., Tatarelli, A. et al. (2022). "Human-robot collaboration (HRC) technologies for reducing work-related musculoskeletal diseases in industry 4.0." In *Proceedings of the 21st Congress of the International Ergonomics Association (IEA 2021) Volume V: Methods & Approaches 21*, pp. 335–342. Springer International Publishing .

Semeraro, F., Griffiths, A. and Cangelosi, A. (2023). Human–robot collaboration and machine learning: A systematic review of recent research. *Robotics and Computer-Integrated Manufacturing*, *79*, p.102432.

Taesi, C., Aggogeri, F. and Pellegrini, N. (2023). COBOT applications—recent advances and challenges. *Robotics*, *12*(3), p. 79.

Valori, M., Scibilia, A., Fassi, I., Saenz, J., Behrens, R., Herbster, S., Bidard, C., Lucet, E., Magisson, A., Schaake, L. and Bessler, J. (2021). Validating safety in human–robot collaboration: Standards and new perspectives. *Robotics*, *10*(2), p. 65.

Villani, V., Pini, F., Leali, F. and Secchi, C. (2018). Survey on human–robot collaboration in industrial settings: Safety, intuitive interfaces and applications. *Mechatronics*, *55*, pp.248–266.

Weiss, A., Wortmeier, A.K. and Kubicek, B. (2021). Cobots in industry 4.0: A roadmap for future practice studies on human–robot collaboration. *IEEE Transactions on Human-Machine Systems*, *51*(4), pp. 335–345.

Zhang, X., Fathollahi-Fard, A. M., Tian, G., Yaseen, Z. M., Pham, D. T., Zhao, Q., and Wu, J. (2024). Human-Robot Collaboration in Mixed-Flow Assembly Line Balancing under Uncertainty: An Efficient Discrete Bees Algorithm. *Journal of Industrial Information Integration*, *41*, 100676.

# 5 Chatbot-based AI: A Catalyst for Sustainable Competitive Advantages to Gen Z and Beyond

Dr Rashmi Singel[1*], Dr Kulbir Kaur Bhatti[2], Dr Utpala Das[3], Dr Richa Nangia[4] and Dr Alka Agnihotri[5]

## Introduction

### *Background*

AI is one of the most significant breakthrough technologies in practically every field. The introduction of this technology has completely altered the regular routines of industries and people's relationships with technology. The different AI applications have piqued our interest, but it is generative models that we find most interesting. This is because generative technologies allow us to develop designs, compose content, and gain insights that would otherwise be impossible for humans to do. One AI (Artificial Intelligence) has already arrived, together with a group of various and advanced technologies. OpenAI, GPT, DeepArt, and Runway ML are examples of such technologies. Text, photographs, videos, and other media can also be employed as creative and analytical tools in the democratization process.

For India, one of the world's largest countries with one of the youngest populations, AI generative tools are not just a faraway dream. They imply majority success. Generation Z, aka Gen Z, the generation mainly born between the mid-1990s and early 2010s, is at the center of the digital age. They were raised at a time when the technology was easily installed and part of their day-to-day life, which is a reason behind their natural aptitude for it. Gen Z represents the group that was home-schooled with digital technology. Their great adaptability to digital tools, along with the innate creative impulse they have, makes them an especially attractive demographic to engage in innovative learning and to have a competitive advantage in the field of labour, besides education.

AI generative models have broken the threshold of mere facility and are causing major changes in the sector of education, creative designs, and the labour market (Newman, Mintrom, & O'Neill, 2022). There are several benefits of AI tools

1-3 Associate Professor, Manav Rachna International Institute of Research and Studies, Sector 43, Faridabad, Haryana, India.
4 Associate Professor, Sushant University, Sector 55, Gurugram, Haryana, India.
5 Associate Professor, Galgotias University, Greater Noida, Uttar Pradesh, India.
* Corresponding author: rashmicharujain@gmail.com

DOI: 10.1201/9781003559849-5

in the domain of education that include highly personalized learning environments and enabling students to engage with content through interaction and feedback. At the same time, in the creative sector, AI tools help with graphic design, composing music, and writing scripts, thereby increasing productivity and creativity. Along with their professional backgrounds, being skilled in AI tools is like having an ace up your sleeve at a time when recruiters hunt for people who are capable of using new technologies to bring change and also increase efficiency (Nguyen & Malik, 2022). The labor market is experiencing increased competency demands, which represent a constant process of innovation for workers.

### *Problem Statement*

In recent years, artificial intelligence instruments have captured attention in various fields. However, the lack of solid research related to Gen Z in India and the factors that help them make maximum use of these resources at the expense of others is still to be found. Whereas the issue of technology adoption has been covered in a lot of studies, little is known about the determinants of a fruitful combination of AI generative tools with this age group. In developing cities such as India, digital illiteracy and social-economics conditions are one of the factors that may lead to the discrepancy between technology adoption and usage (Rymarczyk, 2020).

Recognizing the forces that create the competitive advantage given by AI generative tools is not just for one group of stakeholders. Teachers can develop a more experiential approach that combines the social and technical skills of the students to meet the labor market needs. Regulation makers can come up with plans that will improve the situation in the network infrastructure, ensuring everyone has a chance to join the transformation. Telecom companies can offer innovative intelligence tools to this group that adopts the most, and thus, it would be possible to create the desired customer satisfaction (Belanche et al., 2012).

### *Research Questions*

This research is driven by the following research questions:

1. What are the main reasons for AI generative tools that help Gen Z youth in India to be competitive with their peers?
2. In this manner , how do those determinants regulate the competitive standing of Indian Generation Z in the job industry and education system?

These questions aim at discovering the factors that reinforce the provision and utilization of AI generative tools by Gen Z as well as appraising how the tools substantially contribute to their competence on the job and environment accordingly.

### *Objectives*

The main aims of this study are:

1. To identify the main factors responsible for AI generative technology that is creating a competitive edge for Gen Z in India.
2. To evaluate the impact of different factors on the utilization and effectiveness of AI generative tools by Gen Z.
3. To give suggestions on policy and education per the results to increase the acceptance and usefulness of AI generative tools for generation Z in India.

## Significance of the Study

The study's significance lies in its potential to fill in the existing research vacuum that concerns the factors of AI generative tools that enable Gen Z in India. As the global economy progressively puts itself in a new direction of a knowledge-based framework, the ability to deploy AI technologies becomes a crucial success factor. For Gen Z, learning AI generative tools is not only about keeping updated with the latest technological innovations but also about acquiring a leading-edge position that will help them be more employable in a highly competitive job market.

### For Educators

The prior knowledge gained as a result of this research might be used to develop the curriculum, allowing educational institutions to introduce AI generative tools in a way that fosters students' critical thinking and creativity while also preparing them for their future careers. By grasping the essentials that make learning possible with such instruments, teachers can then come up with more suitable lessons that conform to the technical behaviour of Gen Z.

### For Policymakers

The results are valuable in outlining the existence of policies and measures designed to promote digital literacy and guarantee fair access to AI technologies. This is particularly important in a diverse and populous country like India, where regional disparities can have a major impact on technology adoption rates. Speaking of e.g. the following affordability and accessibility are the aspects of an initiative that can help to reduce the differences of income, hence making digital inclusion a reality.

### For Technology Providers

The knowledge of the factors that influence the adoption and the use of AI generative tools properly by AI machine learning can help technology companies create more user-driven products (Wheeler & Buckley, 2021). Areas like simplicity, ease of use, and cost should be the focal points for technology outfits trying to make their products more satisfying to the users, thus enabling user ring to the grand level.

### *For Gen Z Individuals*

On an interpersonal scale, the study can help Gen Zers by outlining the underlying factors that contribute to their competitive advantage. As a result, knowledge interlegibility is the issue of the use of digital assistive tools as a strategic competitive by generation Z throughout its growth period (Holendova et al., 2024).

### *For Researchers*

Through the analysis of four factors of technology adoption, i.e., positive attitude, self-use/enjoyment, subjective norm and perceived usefulness and competitive advantage, this chapter not only fills the gap in the general literature but also in the specific case of the context of a developing country. As a consequence, it paves the way for further studies to focus on other determinants in different contexts or among different demographic groups.

## Literature Review

### *AI Generative Tools: An Overview*

Generative tools that use Artificial Intelligence (AI) are growing in their relevance in the digital world as they bring huge changes to various industries. They can make use of machine learning algorithms, and in such a way, they can create content, designs or data-driven insights almost with no human intervention (Kumar, Kar, & Ilavarasan, 2021). To clarify, some of the most well-known GPT OpenAI models provided an introduction to coherent and contextually appropriate language, while the others are conventional deep art models capable of drawing visual renderings of iconic art styles. Non-technical persons can now use these tools to design or create the texts they want. The evolution of natural language processing, computer vision, and other AI subfields has witnessed expansion (Walter, 2024).

### *Adoption of AI by Gen Z*

Generation Z (Gen Z) is a group of people born between the mid-1990s and early 2010s who are defined by their use of the internet, technology, and access to digital information. Unlike earlier generations, Gen Z has grown up in a world where the internet and cellphones are omnipresent, which has resulted in a greater openness to technology breakthroughs, such as AI generative tools. According to studies, Generation Z is more interested in technology that improves company innovation and productivity (Turner, 2015). This generation's technological expertise (Colbert et al., 2016) and preference for a traditional, user-friendly style make AI generative tools an ideal alternative for them.

But the use of AI generative tools varies from one individual to another within Gen Z. The terms of access, costs and instruction impact the extent to which AI tools are used. For example, research shows that while urban youth in India have greater access to AI tools, those in rural areas have problems due to limited internet connectivity and a deficiency of resources (Sindakis and Showkat, 2024). These inequalities underpin the importance of considering socio-economic factors in the study of the participants' adoption of AI solutions and technologies.

### *Educational Integration of AI Tools*

AI tools that are used in teaching methods are seen as one of the essential elements of the training of students for work environments of the future. Now, educational institutions all over the world are realizing the significance of AI in the curriculum. Their focus is changing, and not only do they use it as a subject to study, but a means by which the quality of learning is increased. The Indian innovation initiatives, such as Atal Tinkering Labs, are among some of the major programs under the Atal Innovation Mission, aside from AI and other sophisticated technology, this is one of the important resources for encouraging student innovation (Ziemba, Eisenbardt, Mullins, & Dettmer, 2022).

The work done by Walter in 2024 confirms the results of a program that showed when students are exposed to AI tools as part of their education, they demonstrate the ability to improve their thinking and solution of problems that are the key requirements in today's job market. In addition, AI tools can individualize learning experiences such that students can easily learn according to their own pace and needs. This approach is particularly effective for Gen Z, who is known for trying on different things and demanding flexibility and personalization in their educational settings.

### *Competitive Edge through Technology*

The concept of technology has been widely discussed in the corporate world. Knowing how to use AI generative tools will considerably motivate Gen Z's professional development and job prospects. As organizations seek personnel who can unleash AI for improved production and efficiency, digitally skilled staff are likely to hold their own in a competitive environment (Monteiro & Adler, 2022). A study on redesigned AI literacy courses showed that students that come from various backgrounds could understand AI better and feel more empowered, setting them up for broader AI usage (Kong et al., 2022).

Moreover, AI facilities also support users in producing not only high-quality outputs but also creative and original ones. The potential of AI to become a chance for ingenious professionals is very appealing to employers, who are currently seeking to resolve problems in an out-of-the-box manner. The literature cites that the competitive edge from the use of AI tools is not only limited to technical professions; it is also available in areas such as marketing, design, and liberal arts, where AI-generated insights can direct innovative creative strategies and help discover solutions (Anantrasirichai and Bull, 2022).

### *Gaps in Existing Research*

Though researchers and professionals are becoming increasingly concerned about the widespread use of AI and its implications, there has been little research on the AI generating tool adoption factors prevalent among Gen Z in developing nations, particularly India. Current study focuses on artificial intelligence (AI) and its adoption in general, without focusing on any specific technology or taking into consideration the unique difficulties and abundance of opportunities that Generation Z encounters in the Indian environment (Mustak, Salminen, Plé, & Wirtz, 2021). This research aims to bridge this gap by examining the factors that influence Gen Z's proper use of AI generating tools in India.

## Research Methodology

### *Research Design*

This study follows a descriptive and analytical research design to explore the determinants of AI generative tools that are responsible for the competitive edge of Gen Z in India. The descriptive part is devoted to presenting the usage patterns and the opinion of the AI generative tools of Generation Z (Gen Z) that are under study. In the explanatory part, the analysis was conducted on the number of possible connections between the identified determinants—accessibility, ease of use, affordability, educational integration, creative and innovative applications, and technological literacy—and the perceived competitive edge. This approach helps in the form of understanding the interaction of the identified factors with the adoption of AI and the resulting position of Gen Z in the competitive field.

### *Population and Sample*

The target population of this research consists of Gen Z members in India, particularly those in higher education institutions and graduates who are entering the workforce. This population is chosen due to its being more likely to interact with AI and its aggregation of digital economy. A sample of 415 respondents has been established based on the decision that this would give a statistically reliable and generalizable figure. In the current study, stratified random sampling method is used to ensure representation across different regions of India, educational backgrounds, and socio-economic statuses.

### *Data Collection*

Primary data was collected through a structured questionnaire that was aimed at obtaining detailed information about the factors influencing the adoption and use of AI generating tools among Gen Z. The questionnaire was prepared based on the conclusions made from the literature review and was pilot-tested with a small number of the target population to ensure the clarity, the relevance, and the reliability of the questions.

The outline of the questionnaire was as follows:

- Demographic Information: Including age, gender, education level, and place of residence.

- Usage Patterns: Questions related to the frequency of AI tool usage, types of tools used, and specific applications (e.g., content creation, design, coding).
- Perception of AI Tools: Respondents were asked to rate their agreement with various statements related to the accessibility, ease of use, and affordability of AI generative tools on a Likert scale (1 = Strongly Disagree to 5 = Strongly Agree).
- Impact on Competitive Edge: Questions measuring the perceived impact of AI tools on respondents' academic and professional success, using a composite score derived from multiple indicators.

Data was collected using both online questionnaires and personal interviews to ensure that even the most remote and isolated places were covered, particularly in the countryside where internet connectivity may be unavailable. The questionnaires were sent by an online survey sample of institutions, the digital platform processed them, and email lists were managed, whereas interviews were conducted in a limited area to obtain a variety of perspectives.

### *Variables*

This work presents the gaming over to AI generative tools that enhance the students' competitiveness via training and consequently the development of fully functional Gen Z AI creative minds. The mean of this is a score combining the respondents' reviews of AI tools in the contribution of their academic performance, creativity, job readiness, and innovation capabilities.

The independent variables are the six determinants extracted from the reviewed reference materials are listed as:

1. Accessibility (X1): The AI generative tools respondents use at their will.
2. Ease of Use (X2): The tools that are friendly users and require only a few efforts to learn and use them.
3. Affordability (X3): The total amount of money included in the purchase and the use of artificial intelligent tools, including the initial and continuous expenses.
4. Educational Integration (X4): The possibility to which AI tools are part of the curricula and learning systems in schools.
5. Creative and Innovative Applications (X5): The applications that are: AI tools creativity skills development and learning various techniques.
6. Technological Literacy (X6): The degree of the respondent's familiarity as well as their know-how about the computers and AI equipment.

### *Data Analysis Techniques*

The analysis of the collected data is performed through the Statistical Package for the Social Sciences (SPSS) software. Following this, the analysis was done through the two-step approach.

Firstly, factor analysis was used to identify the underlying structure of the data and confirm the key determinants of AI generative tool adoption using based on the literature review insights from the literature review. This way we can reduce the data into meaningful factors by pairing related variables, considering their correlations.

Secondly, utilizing multiple regression analysis to examine the relationship between the identified determinants (independent variables) and the competitive edge (dependent variable). Regression analysis was employed to get a measure of the impact of each determinant on the competitive edge, therefore enabling the detection of the most predominant faculties.

## Results

### *Descriptive Statistics*

The research team started with getting 350 respondents across various areas of India, a widespread mix of Generation Z(Gen Z). The profile of the respondents included students and graduates from urban and rural areas, with almost equal numbers of males and females. The age group of the respondents mainly turned out to be between 18 and 25, having different background information, from undergraduate to postgraduate students. The descriptive statistics revealed interesting patterns in the usage of AI generative tools among the respondents. Approximately 68% of the respondents reported using AI tools frequently, with 32% using them occasionally. The most commonly used tools included text generation software like OpenAI's GPT models, image editing tools like Adobe Photoshop, and coding platforms that incorporate AI-based features. The primary applications of these tools were found in content creation (45%), design (30%), and coding or data analysis (25%).

In terms of perceived impact, 74% of respondents agreed that AI tools significantly enhanced their productivity, while 65% believed that these tools provided them with a creative edge in their academic and professional work. Interestingly, 58% of the respondents from rural areas indicated that they faced challenges related to the accessibility and affordability of AI tools, highlighting the digital divide that still exists in parts of India.

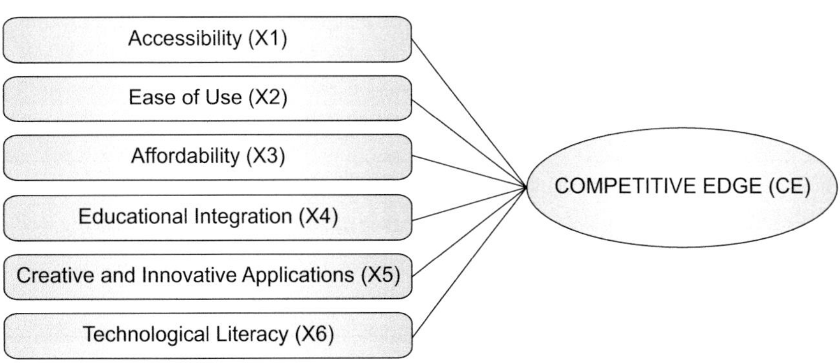


**Fig. 1** Proposed Research Model.
(*Source:* Compiled by Authors)

## *Factor Analysis*

**Table 1** Variable Description in Research Model

| *VARIABLES* | | *EXPLANATION* |
|---|---|---|
| Accessibility | ST 4 | AI generative tools are easily accessible on my preferred devices (e.g., smartphone, laptop, tablet). |
| | ST 8 | I can access AI tools without needing to purchase expensive hardware or software. |
| | ST 13 | AI generative tools are available in multiple languages or formats that I understand. |
| | ST 14 | I can access AI tools both online and offline, making them more versatile for my needs. |
| Ease of Use | ST 1 | AI generative tools have intuitive interfaces that are easy to navigate. |
| | ST 12 | I can quickly learn how to use AI tools without needing extensive training or prior knowledge. |
| | ST 15 | The tutorials and help resources for AI tools are clear and helpful. |
| | ST 16 | AI tools allow me to accomplish tasks more easily than traditional methods. |
| Affordability | ST 2 | AI generative tools are affordable and fit within my budget. |
| | ST 5 | The cost of using AI tools is justified by the benefits I receive. |
| | ST 6 | I can access free or low-cost versions of AI tools that meet my needs. |
| | ST 9 | The ongoing costs (subscriptions, updates) for AI tools are manageable for me. |
| Educational Integration | ST 7 | AI generative tools are part of the curriculum in my educational institution. |
| | ST 10 | I have received formal training or instruction on how to use AI tools in my studies. |
| | ST 11 | AI tools are used in my coursework or projects to enhance learning outcomes. |
| | ST 12 | My educational institution encourages the use of AI tools for assignments and research. |
| Creative and Innovative Applications | ST 18 | AI generative tools enable me to create content that would be difficult to produce manually. |
| | ST 21 | Using AI tools has sparked new ideas and innovations in my work. |
| | ST 23 | AI tools help me explore creative solutions to problems that I would not have considered otherwise. |
| | ST 28 | The outputs from AI tools enhance the quality and originality of my work. |

*Contd.*

**Table 1** *Contd.*

| *VARIABLES* | | *EXPLANATION* |
|---|---|---|
| Technological Literacy | ST 19 | I am confident in my ability to learn and use new AI generative tools. |
| | ST 22 | I keep up with the latest developments in AI technology and tools. |
| | ST 27 | I find it easy to adapt to updates or new versions of AI tools. |
| | ST30 | My previous experience with technology helps me use AI tools more effectively. |

*Source:* Author

To identify the key determinants of AI generative tool adoption, a factor analysis was conducted. This statistical method helped in reducing the data by identifying the underlying relationships between observed variables and grouping them into meaningful factors. Six factors were extracted, each representing a distinct determinant that influences the adoption and use of AI tools by Gen Z in India.

**Table 2** Exploratory factor analysis (EFA)

| *Variables* | | *Cronbach Alpha* | *Factor Loading* | | | | | |
|---|---|---|---|---|---|---|---|---|
| | | | *1* | *2* | *3* | *4* | *5* | *6* |
| Ease of Use | ST 4 | 0.902 | 0.891 | | | | | |
| | ST 8 | | 0.868 | | | | | |
| | ST 13 | | 0.773 | | | | | |
| | ST 14 | | 0.656 | | | | | |
| Accessibility | ST 1 | 0.884 | | 0.866 | | | | |
| | ST 12 | | | 0.892 | | | | |
| | ST 15 | | | 0.780 | | | | |
| | ST 16 | | | 0.535 | | | | |
| Affordability | ST 2 | 0.853 | | | 0.875 | | | |
| | ST 5 | | | | 0.798 | | | |
| | ST 6 | | | | 0.691 | | | |
| | ST 9 | | | | 0.545 | | | |
| Educational Integration | ST 7 | 0.781 | | | | 0.821 | | |
| | ST 10 | | | | | 0.698 | | |
| | ST 11 | | | | | 0.651 | | |
| | ST 12 | | | | | 0.578 | | |
| Creative and Innovative Applications | ST 18 | 0.752 | | | | | 0.836 | |
| | ST 21 | | | | | | 0.738 | |
| | ST 23 | | | | | | 0.714 | |
| | ST 28 | | | | | | 0.626 | |

*Contd.*

**Table 2** *Contd.*

| *Variables* | | *Cronbach Alpha* | *Factor Loading* | | | | | |
|---|---|---|---|---|---|---|---|---|
| | | | *1* | *2* | *3* | *4* | *5* | *6* |
| Technological Literacy | ST 19 | 0.657 | | | | | | 0.761 |
| | ST 22 | | | | | | | 0.721 |
| | ST 27 | | | | | | | 0.7014 |
| | ST30 | | | | | | | 0.636 |

*Source:* Author

### *Ease of Use*

This was the most significant factor, accounting for 15% of the total variance. Respondents who indicated their user-friendliness, intuitive interfaces and minimal learning curves had high factor loadings (above 0.9) on this item, suggesting that ease of use is the deciding factor for AI tool adoption among Gen Z. The participants who found these tools easy to handle stated that they would be most likely to employ them in their studies or jobs regardless of their objectives.

### *Accessibility*

Exclusively talking about the second factor, which accounted for 13% of the variance, it dealt with the variables which were connected to different AI tools being widely present, ease of access to them, and internet connectivity. The very high factor loadings were above 0.8 and were on items like the presence of AI tools on different platforms, easy access, and internet connectivity. According to the data, those respondents who were better connected with the internet and had the more current versions of devices were seen as the ones who frequently used AI tools (Raisch & Krakowski, 2021).

### *Affordability*

This component was the way to explain 12% of the Rather flexible and had to do with the cost of procurement and the use of Al devices. Some interviewees underlined that AI tools are not only free, but also there are low-cost versions of the same, and the cost of the best hardware is the obstacle for some. With the high factor loadings (for all the items above 0.8) these items showed that in the perimeter when the AI tools are more affordable it is often the case that students from less privileged families will begin the use of the technology.

### *Educational Integration*

The fourth factor, which accounts for 11% of the variance, deals with things related to the inclusion of AI tools into the curricula and learning environments. Those people who had been given access to AI tools as part of their formal education were more likely to regard them as useful and to use them regularly. It was noticed that the factor loadings (above 0.7) that were being derived from education integration are prominently responsible for the widespread adoption of AI technology and in fact, that makes them comfortable with the use.

### *Creative and Innovative Applications*

The 11% of the variation was contributed by this factor which considered the tools' proficiency in terms of affected creativity and innovation. It dominates with high acceptable factor loadings on items such as "AI tools can be my personal assistant and give my ideas the form that I could never dream of without its help" that is desired by the researchers who appreciate the predicted aspect of AI (Votto, Valecha, Najafirad, & Rao, 2021). This factor is actually very crucial for people mainly concerned with the creative fields such as design, writing, and media.

### *Technological Literacy*

The final factor, explaining 10% of the variance, measured the respondents' skill and comfort in using AI and other advanced technologies. High factor loadings of items measuring this factor suggested people with more knowledge of technology were more likely to take up and efficiently learn and use AI generative tools. This learning emphasizes the significance of digital skills in gaining the benefits of AI.

## *Regression Analysis*

After the first phase, multiple regression analysis was made precisely to evaluate the impact of these listed factors on the achievement of the competitive advantage Gen Z got through the use of AI generative tools. Multiple Regression analysis has been applied to check the impact and setup a research Model.

$$Y = \beta0 + \beta1X1 + \beta2X2 + \beta3X3 + \beta4X4 + \beta5X5 + \beta6X6 + \epsilon Y$$

Where:

- $Y$ represents the competitive edge
- $X1$ to $X6$ represent the six factors (Ease of Use, Accessibility, Affordability, Educational Integration, Creative and Innovative Applications, Technological Literacy),
- β1 to β6 are the coefficients indicating the impact of each factor,
- $\epsilon$ is the error term.

The regression analysis has resulted in the R-squared value of 0.68, which tells us that 68% of the deviation in the competitive edge could be explained by the six factors mentioned above. A strong relationship is illustrated between these variables and the competitive edge received by Gen Z by using Artificial Intelligence tools.

All coefficients for the factors were positive and statistically significant, with Ease of Use ($\beta1 = 0.28$) and Accessibility ($\beta2 = 0.25$) being the most impactful.

These results, as such, indicate that AI is easily usable and easily accessible, vital to its overall acceptance as well as its usefulness. The Affordability of products and Educational Integration ($\beta 3 = 0.20$) ($\beta 4 = 0.18$) were also positive and strong. They point out that the AI tools must be cost-effective and their application must be into the education sector.

Creative and Innovative Application of AI ($\beta 5 = 0.15$) and Technological Literacy ($\beta 6 = 0.14$) were also significant, and were less expressive than the others. The results clearly demonstrate that AI-based systems, in general, may have different components and arise from different historical contexts.

### *Summary of Findings*

The outcomes revealed by both factor and regression analyses brings light to the interaction of different inciting factors that give rise to the adoption and effective use of AI generative tools by Gen Z in India (Silva, Corbo, Vlacic, & Fernandes, 2020). The results show that ease of use and accessibility are the most dominant influences, followed by affordability and educational integration. In addition, creativity, innovative applications, and technological literacy play a significant role nevertheless to a lesser extent than the previous mentioned factors.

The pieces of information are helpful in understanding the ways in which generative artificial intelligence tools affect the competitiveness of Generation Z. They give suggestions for the development of training to educators, policymakers and technology providers. Additionally, they help to promote AI acceptance among this generation.

## Discussion

### *Interpretation of Results*

In this study, the results exhibit a deeper understanding of reasons for Indian Gen Z adopting AI tools and how they shape the competitive edge of Generation Z (Gen Z) in India. As reflected in the regression analysis, by their high factor loadings and the strong coefficients, Ease of Use and Accessibility were the most significant factors that drove the adoption of these tools among Gen Z. Most significantly, AI tools must be both user-friendly and easy to access in order to get the young people to use them. So, it naturally follows that the easy movable capacity of the very tools (the AI ones) allows the new generation of digital natives to incorporate them into their daily academic work as well as business life, without a break in their productivity and creativity (Sieja & Wach, 2019). The significance of the Affordability aspect as a determinant might not be as high as the other two aspects; however, it should not be ignored. The result of regression analysis was the price as a significant factor of AI tools adoption; the students and recent graduates mentioned that their financial situations might confine their procurement of these tools. These results are in agreement with the earlier study in which it was observed that technological expenses are a significant problem in emerging markets, e.g.

India (Mikalef and Gupta, 2021). AI tools with a free or low-cost option, having brevity in a more substantial part of Gen Z are gaining access to the technologies and benefits backed by the same.

Educational Integration, too, was first witnessed as an essential factor. Using AI tools in educational settings showed up as highly significant, which means that this approach is the future for accelerating wider use. The participants who had the likelihood to use AI tools as a part of their curriculum were more eager to consider these tools as useful utilities. Firstly, it shows that schools are the biggest drivers of AI technologies among students, and secondly, students are encouraged to use them. The outcomes of this study make the claim that the integration of AI in educational settings develop not only students' technological literacy but also prepares them for the rapid changes in the labor market.

Creations and technological literacy are important, but their effect was less notable compared to the other aspects. AI applications that assist in creativity and innovation are received enthusiastically, especially in such disciplines such as design, content writing, and marketing (Silva, Corbo, Vlacic, & Fernandes, 2020). Teenagers from Gen Z credited AI tools in forming ideas that often are-artistic and one-of-the-kind, which can otherwise be virtually unattainable. Nevertheless, the influence of technological literacy is such that although these teenagers generally believe that technology is comfortable, there is still the need for training and ability development to fully make use of AI creative tools.

### *Implications for Educators and Policymakers*

The findings of this study have several important implications for educators and policymakers. First, the strong influence of Ease of Use and Accessibility on AI tool adoption underscores the need for technology providers to prioritize user-friendly design and broad accessibility. This includes ensuring that AI tools are available on multiple platforms, compatible with a wide range of devices, and easy to learn and use without extensive technical training. Educational institutions should collaborate with technology providers to integrate such tools into their curricula, ensuring that students are not only exposed to AI technologies but also trained in their effective use.

Affordability also emerged as a critical factor, particularly for students from lower-income backgrounds. Policymakers should consider initiatives that subsidize the cost of AI tools or provide grants and scholarships to students for purchasing necessary technology. Additionally, there should be a focus on expanding access to high-speed internet and modern digital infrastructure, especially in rural areas, to bridge the digital divide that still exists in parts of India.

The significance of Educational Integration highlights the need for curriculum reform that incorporates AI tools and technologies into all levels of education. This includes not only higher education but also secondary and vocational training, where students can develop the skills needed to thrive in a tech-driven economy. Educators should be equipped with the necessary resources and training to effectively teach

AI-related content, and institutions should invest in the infrastructure required to support AI-based learning.

Finally, the impact of Creative and Innovative Applications along with Technological Literacy suggests that there is still room for improvement in how AI tools are used to enhance creativity and innovation among Gen Z. Educational programs should emphasize the creative potential of AI, encouraging students to experiment with these tools in ways that go beyond traditional applications. This could involve integrating AI into arts, humanities, and social sciences curricula, where the potential for innovation is beginning to be explored.

### *Limitations of the Study*

Even though this study unequips operable "darts" for the promotion of AI tool use among Generation Z in India, one can say functioning conjoints are essential. The given sample for data is suitable for this target only, but it can't completely identify the diversity of experiences in this age group across regions and socio-economic backgrounds. Besides, the study is confined to a specific set of participants in a certain country, which means that findings might not be applied to other environmental settings or the exploration of other age groups.

Along with the above, the fact that self-reported data are the basis for finding the links between such behaviours and technology cannot be overlooked. This data comes from the memory of the participants, so they may perceive them differently or sometimes forget some details. The researchers tried not to overemphasize subjects and these biases, but they could not be completely excluded. Analysis of deficiencies which could be done in the randomized control trials might include more but larger and diverse samples and the design of longitudinal studies regarding the changes in AI adoption and use over time.

### *Future Research Directions*

The findings of this study open several avenues for future research. One potential area of exploration is the long-term impact of AI tool adoption on career success and professional development among Gen Z. Longitudinal studies could provide insights into how early exposure to AI tools influences career trajectories and job satisfaction. Additionally, research could examine the specific barriers to AI adoption in rural and underserved areas, providing a more nuanced understanding of the digital divide in India. Another area of interest is the exploration of AI tool adoption among other demographic groups, such as older generations or different cultural contexts. Comparing the determinants of AI adoption across these groups could provide valuable insights into how technology adoption varies and what factors are universally important. Furthermore, research could investigate the ethical implications of AI tool usage, especially in education, where the issues of data privacy and algorithmic bias are only getting worse.

## Conclusion and Recommendations

### *Conclusion*

This research identified the critical aspects that led to the adoption and proper use of AI generative tools by Generation Z (Gen Z) in India. It aimed to unveil the pronounced role of the items that source the attractiveness of employability of these devices in toleration in a competitive scenario proffered in academic and career spheres. The discovery is that ease of use and accessibility are the most important components, leading to the conclusion that the crucial factor is an AI tool that can be used by youngsters who have not yet learned to read. Educational system also points to the fact that the—as a crucial factor. Especially in poor countries like India where the poor cannot access computer technologies the project was designed to make them network add-ons. The role of Institutional Synergy (IIS) has also emerged, which suggests that AI tools should be seen as part of the educational curriculum and hence students will be more likely to adopt their use and use them effectively. Creativity and innovation continue to play important roles, and technology literacy is also a significant factor, but they are less important than the other two, contributing to the fact that AI tools have additional benefits beyond the primary benefits that drove their initial adoption. Overall, the study indicated that AI generative tools among Gen Z students are unlikely to be embraced and used effectively, with several potential metrics relevant to institutions, policymakers, and technology developers. All of these concerned parties must work together to ensure easy access and affordability of AI tools, as well as their smooth integration into educational systems, so that Generation Z has the skills needed to compete in the ever-changing digital economy.

### *Recommendations*

#### *Prioritize User-Friendly Design*

Technology providers ought to concentrate on AI tools which can be used with a minimal learning curve because they are user-friendly and generally easy to use. For example, simple interfaces and assistive resources, robust tutorials, and FAQs will make these tools more accessible for people with lower technical abilities.

#### *Enhance Accessibility Across Platforms*

AI tools ought to be developed on different platforms (e.g. Mobile, desktop) so that the new generation will be able to use them no matter which device they have. Additionally, companies should also focus on making offline versions or lightweight versions of websites that can easily be accessed in areas with slow or no network connectivity. This way, people in underserved areas will have the capability to use smart tools and make well-informed decisions.

### *Address Affordability Barriers*

Authorities and technology providers need to work together to decrease the AI tool adoption cost hurdles. Inclusion of such activities as providing subsidies, grants, or discounts for students, especially those from lower-income backgrounds, and promoting affordable AI solutions which would meet the requirements of the Indian market would be the most appropriate way to improve affordability.

### *Integrate AI Tools into Educational Curricula*

AI should be an incorporated subject in all levels of educational institutions from secondary to higher education, which could be done through utilization of AI generative tools in teaching. Meanwhile, teachers should not focus only on showing learners how to use the AI tools but they should also teach them how to be critical thinkers, how to be creative, and how to solve problems. Teacher preparation programs should as well be reformed to make sure that teachers have the necessary knowledge and skills to include AI-related materials.

### *Promote Digital Literacy and Skills Development*

However, there should be a common effort to technological literacy for Gen Z, aiming at the rural and underprivileged areas in particular. This can be done through the development of focused digital literacy programs that will teach the students how to use AI tools efficiently and be aware of the various real-world applications of this technology. Both the public and private sectors should set aside monies for infrastructure strengthening in support of digital education, which implies that every student will have such learning materials to aid in acquiring these important skills.

### *Foster Creative and Innovative Use of AI Tools*

Educational institutions and educators should encourage students to explore the creative and innovative potential of AI tools. This might involve introducing AI into projects that require creative thinking, such as in the arts, humanities, and social sciences. By creating an environment in which AI experimentation is actively encouraged, children are more likely to acknowledge the defectiveness of such machines automatically.

## References

Anantrasirichai, N. and Bull, D. (2022). Artificial intelligence in the creative industries: A review. Artificial Intelligence Review 55: 589–656. https://doi.org/10.1007/s10462-021-10024-4

Belanche, D., Casal´o, L.V. and Guinal´ıu, M. (2012). Website usability, consumer satisfaction and the intention to use a website: The moderating effect of perceived risk. *Journal of Retailing and Consumer Services 19*(1): 124–132.

Colbert, A., Yee, N. and George, G. 2016. The digital workforce and the workplace of the future. *Academy of Management Journal*, *53*:731–739.

Holendova , J., Svoboda, D. and eriC, N. (2024). The impact of chatbots on the buying behaviors of Generation Z toward brands. *E+M Ekonomie a Management 27*: 201–214.

Kong, S.C., Cheung, W.M.-Y. and Zhang, G. (2022). Evaluating artificial intelligence literacy courses for fostering conceptual learning, literacy, and empowerment in university students: Refocusing to conceptual building. *Computers in Human Behaviour Reports 7*:100223.

Kumar, S., A. Kar, K. and Ilavarasan, P.V. (2021). Applications of text mining in services management: A systematic literature review. *International Journal of Information Management Data Insights 1*(1):8.

Mikalef, P. and Gupta, M. (2021). Artificial intelligence capability: Conceptualization, measurement calibration, and empirical study on its impact on organizational creativity and firm performance. *Information and Management*, *58*(3): 103434.

Monteiro, P. and Adler, P.S. (2022). Bureaucracy for the 21st century: Clarifying and expanding our view of bureaucratic organization. *Academy of Management Annals 16*(2): 427–475.

Mustak, M., Salminen. L. Pl´e, J. and Wirtz, J. (2021). Artificial intelligence in marketing: Topic modeling, scientometric analysis, and research agenda. *Journal of Business Research 124*: 389–404.

Newman, J., M. Mintrom, M. and O'Neill, D. (2022). Digital technologies, artificial intelligence and bureaucratic transformation. *Futures 136*: 102886.

Nguyen, T. -M. and Malik, M. (2022). Impact of knowledge sharing on employees' service quality: The moderating role of artificial intelligence. *International Marketing Review 39*(3): 482–508.

Raisch, S. and Krakowski, S. (2021). Artificial intelligence and management: The automation–augmentation paradox. *Academy of Management Review 46*(1): 192–210.

Rymarczyk, J. (2020). Technologies, opportunities and challenges of the industrial revolution 4.0: Theoretical considerations. *Entrepreneurial Business and Economics Review 8*(1): 185–198.

Sieja, M. and Wach, K. (2019). The use of evolutionary algorithms for optimization in the modern entrepreneurial economy: Interdisciplinary perspective. *Entrepreneurial Business and Economics Review 7*(4): 117–130.

Silva, S., Corbo, L., Vlacic, B. and Fernandes, M. (2020). Marketing accountability and marketing automation: An empirical analysis of Portuguese companies. *EuroMed Journal of Business 18*(1): 145–164.

Sindakis, S. and Showkat, G. (2024). The digital revolution in India: Bridging the gap in rural technology adoption. *Journal of Innovation and Entrepreneurship 13*: 29.

Sung, E. C., Bae, S., Han, D.-I.D. and Kwon, O. (2021). Consumer engagement via interactive artificial intelligence and mixed reality. *International Journal of Information Management*, *60*:102382.

Turner, A. (2015). Generation Z: Technology and social interest. *The Journal of Individual Psychology 71*(2): 103–113.

Votto, A. M., Valecha, R., Najafirad, P. and Rao, H.R. (2021). Artificial intelligence in tactical human resource management: A systematic literature review. *International Journal of Information Management Data Insights 1*(2): 100047.

Walter, Y. (2024). Embracing the future of artificial intelligence in the classroom: The relevance of AI literacy, prompt engineering, and critical thinking in modern education. *International Journal of Educational Technology in Higher Education 21*:15.

Wheeler, A.R. and Buckley, M.R. (2021). The current state of HRM with automation, artificial intelligence, and machine learning. *HR without People*? Emerald Publishing, 45–67.

Ziemba, E., Eisenbardt, M., Mullins, R. and Dettmer, S. 2022. Consumer engagement in business process innovation–ICT companies cases from Poland and UK. *Journal of Computer Information Systems 62*(2): 302–315.

# 6 Understanding Blockchain and Its Foundations: The Evolution Towards Decentralized Systems

Priyanka Desai [1*], Karthik P[3*], D Loganathan[2†], Preethi S[4†], Bharani B R[5†] and Jayanthi MG[6†]

In the age of big data with expanding web utilization, the requirement for a decentralized information storage and transmission system is becoming critical. Traditional centralized systems, though successful for small-scale organizations, face critical difficulties in larger, more mind-boggling conditions. Blockchain technology, a progressive decentralized system, has changed the financial sector through secure transactions especially through digital currencies like Bitcoin. A brief implementation of Bitcoin is explained in this chapter. The gaps in the existing data structures are mentioned as follows:

- Flat Lists: While simple, a flat list requires checking each transaction individually, leading to linear time complexity for verification and updates.
- Simple Binary Trees: Although better than flat lists, simple binary trees still do not provide the logarithmic scalability and efficient update capabilities of Merkle trees.
- Radix Trees: While efficient for certain types of data, radix trees are not as optimized for hashing and secure verification as Merkle trees.
- Skip Lists: Skip lists offer logarithmic time complexity but are more complex and do not provide the same level of security and tamper-evidence as Merkle trees.

Hence, Merkel tree data structure is used to efficiently and securely verify the integrity and consistency of data. A Merkle tree is a binary tree where each leaf node contains the hash of a data block, and each non-leaf node contains the hash of its child nodes. This structure ensures that any modification in the data can be detected quickly and efficiently. This section dives into the essentials of blockchain innovation, compares it with Centralized vs. Decentralized vs. Distributed Systems, and investigates how Bitcoin influences the blockchain for secure, straightforward, and decentralized transactions.

[1-5] Department of Information Science and Engineering, Cambridge Institute of Technology, Bangalore, India.

[6] Department of Computer Science and Engineering, Cambridge Institute of Technology, Bangalore, India.

Email: loganathan.ise@cambridge.edu.in[2]; preethi.ise@cambridge.edu.in[4]; bharani.ise@cambridge.edu.in[4]; jayanthi.cse@cambridge.edu.in[5]

* Corresponding author: priyankadesai.ise@cambridge.edu.in; karthik.ise@cambridge.edu.in

DOI: 10.1201/9781003559849-6

## Introduction

In an era where big data and the internet are integral to our daily lives, the need for robust, efficient, and secure data storage and transmission systems is paramount. Traditional centralized systems, which have been the backbone of many organizations, are increasingly inadequate for the demands of larger, more complex environments. These systems, while manageable for small-scale operations such as educational institutions and startups, face significant limitations, including single points of failure, bandwidth constraints, and data corruption risks.

The evolution of technology has given rise to decentralized and distributed systems, which offer solutions to the inherent problems of centralized architectures. Decentralized systems distribute control among multiple nodes, reducing the risk of a single point of failure and enhancing system resilience. However, they can still struggle with network-wide failures and coordination complexities. Distributed systems take these concepts further by ensuring all nodes communicate and share data, maintaining local copies that are consistently updated across the network. This architecture enhances fault tolerance, security, and scalability.

Blockchain technology epitomizes the principles of distributed systems. Initially popularized by cryptocurrencies like Bitcoin, blockchain provides a decentralized ledger that records transactions across multiple computers. This ensures data security, transparency, and immutability. Each node in a blockchain network holds a copy of the entire ledger, continually updated through consensus mechanisms that validate and synchronize transactions across the network.

This chapter explores the transition from centralized to decentralized and distributed systems, emphasizing the role of blockchain technology in this shift. We will compare centralized, decentralized, and distributed systems, highlighting their respective advantages and challenges. Additionally, we will examine how Bitcoin leverages blockchain to provide a secure, transparent, and decentralized platform for digital transactions. Understanding these foundational concepts is crucial as we delve deeper into the applications and implications of blockchain technology in subsequent chapters.

## Literature Survey

The Bitcoin basis, blockchain, has drawn a lot of attention lately. Blockchain acts as an unchangeable ledger that permits decentralized transaction processing. Applications built on blockchain are proliferating and spanning a wide range of industries, such as financial services, reputation management, Internet of Things (IoT), and more. Blockchain technology still faces a number of obstacles, though, including issues with scalability and security that need to be resolved. An extensive description of blockchain technology is provided in this paper. First, we give a summary of blockchain architecture and then we analyze many common consensus techniques across several blockchains. A brief summary of current developments and technological difficulties is also provided. We also outline potential blockchain developments for the future (Zheng et al., 2017).

The blockchain, a public ledger used by the Bitcoin cryptocurrency, keeps track of all of its transactions. The blockchain's distributed protocol, which is managed by users known as miners, is vital to its security. An attack may have serious repercussions for Bitcoin. The Bitcoin system is no longer a decentralized currency at this moment. Selfish mining could be possible for any coalition size of conspiring miners, unless certain assumptions are met. We suggest a workable addition to the Bitcoin protocol that, in most cases, safeguards Bitcoin. It forbids a coalition in control of less than 25% of the resources from engaging in self-serving mining. This threshold is better than the current situation, where any size coalition can undermine the system, but it is lower than the incorrectly believed 1/2 bound (Eyal and GünSirer, 2018).

An organization or society that follows rules, values, and group consensus can be described as a decentralized autonomous organization (DAO), with its processes, operational tasks, and design encoded as agreements or smart contracts. SmartPLS was used to provide empirical study findings (perhaps the first empirical research paper) on the application of blockchain DAO in organization design using an online survey of 262 blockchain DAO practitioners and scholars. Understanding the role of blockchain DAO in organization design and innovation, as well as how users may take advantage of the technology, its alternatives, readiness for deployment, and its effects on organizations, are the main goals of the study (Saurabh et al., 2024).

In contrast to traditional apps, decentralized applications built on the Ethereum blockchain employ smart contract algorithms to automate decision-making and policy execution. The execution of DAO and non-DAO-based applications, as well as an adaptive resource choreography scheme, were not examined in previous studies. For both DAO and non-DAO-based application execution over blockchain and MEC-enabled 6G networks, this study provides a street smart multi-platform coordination, application scheduling, and low-latency-aware resource choreography scheme by taking into account heterogeneous DAO and non-DAO application count, application requirements, physical worker, virtual worker, and communication resource status. The findings confirmed that, in comparison to the analyzed schemes, the suggested kaizen scheme yields at least 11.26% app task completion delay gain, 7.2% user energy overhead gain, 6.55% user economic charge gain, and 21% service provider profit (Chowdhury, 2024a).

It is challenging for a user to judge the reliability of other users in a permissionless social network. As a result, maintaining trust becomes essential to maintaining social interactions. The traditional approach to evaluating trust entails the use of an authority to spot fraud. Furthermore, contemporary social networks are growing more varied and flatter. Developing a proper blockchain consensus for decentralized trust management is a pressing matter. Rather than requiring social network users to expend excessive computing resources on solving a hash puzzle, this study suggests a verifiable and lightweight blockchain consensus proof of trust for decentralized trust management. Moreover, simulation and performance analysis findings demonstrate the validity and flexibility of our model for artificial and actual social networks (Huang and Si, 2024).

The development of Mobile Crowd-Sensing (MCS) is made feasible by the increasing variety of sensors carried by mobile intelligent devices. This development lowers the price as well for consumers. Nonetheless, the majority of common MCS in use today have a centralized structure. Because of this, the edge node becomes extremely dependent on the central node, which presents challenges including high costs and vulnerability to malicious attacks. In actuality, there isn't a single central service provider that can be completely trusted. The center will have unthinkable consequences once it starts putting people in jeopardy. In this regard, it is no longer necessary for a third party to monitor the transaction. Simply put, each node on the blockchain acts as a transaction supervisor (Hao et al., 2024).

Prior to making a final decision, Decision-Makers (DMs) engage in a consensus reaching process (CRP) as part of group decision making (GDM). The Group Decision Support Systems (GDSS) are computer-based decision support systems that are used to assist in decision-making. We provide a novel concept of a decentralized group decision-making structure based on blockchain technology to overcome these problems. We suggested a consensus approach that works well with the blockchain. We use the Ethereum blockchain to implement the proposed work for validation. The suggested work decreases the gas cost by minimizing the feedback cost, as indicated by the potential trials. To the best of our knowledge, this work represents the idea's introduction, and the more sophisticated techniques will naturally follow (Singh et al., 2023).

Three smart contracts are presented here that enable a briber to equitably trade bribes with miners who follow a mining strategy that suits the briber. The first contract, CensorshipCon, demonstrates how the uncle block reward scheme of Ethereum can effectively offset the expense of paying miners to bribe. Reversing transactions or imposing a new state of another contract pays miners an in-band payment through the second contract, HistoryRevisionCon. In the third contract, known as GoldfingerCon, miners of one cryptocurrency receive rewards for decreasing the usefulness of another (McCorry et al., 2018). The desire to comprehend how much smart contracts can affect the incentive mechanisms in consensus methods a la Nakamoto inspires this work (Doe, 2020).

This study looks into how profitable US stocks are and Bitcoin. More specifically, we compare the returns and volatilities of the S&P 500 index and Bitcoin to examine their respective performances. Consequently, we get the following important conclusions. First, our regression study makes it clear that there was only a minimal correlation between the returns of Bitcoin and the S&P 500 index during the time after the unexpected emergence of COVID-19. Furthermore, our return and the return spread research shows that, on average, Bitcoin returns throughout this time period were significantly greater than the returns of the S&P 500 index. Furthermore, our examination of volatility and volatility spread shows that, on average, during this time period, Bitcoin returns had substantially higher volatilities than the returns of the S&P 500 index (Roussou, 2019).

Bitcoin faces a network effects problem: although its widespread adoption is related to an increase in the number of users, its price volatility lowers consumption. Given the low consumption, a low number of merchants accepting bitcoins would also be expected. However, an increasing number of venues (i.e. merchants) are observed. The results indicate that the number of merchants is unaffected by a shock of the market capitalization, while it is only initially affected by a shock of the price and then stabilizes. Our study contributes to a better understanding of the network effects' phenomena appearing in the Bitcoin's market and has significant implications for e-commerce practitioners concerning their decision-making process about Bitcoin adoption (Maghrebi and Abid, 2018).

The market-based economy taken into consideration in this study is made up of two asset classes: physical, gold, and digital, or cryptocurrency. The process of the cryptocurrency is called Jump-diffusion. We computed the ideal percentage invested in each of the two asset classes at each point during the holding period using the secant approach. In a dangerous environment, digital currency appears to be emerging as a new type of safe-haven value, despite the fact that gold is still considered the conventional safe-haven asset (Sahoo and Chaurasiya, 2024).

Device authentication is the first problem, particularly in light of the vast array of variously linked devices (such as cars, drones, sensors, and other gadgets). Attackers may use this vulnerability to get access to IoT networks. To get around these restrictions, we create a novel decentralized system that makes use of a hybridization of the public and local blockchains. This hybrid system guarantees object authentication prior to enabling device-to-device connection and information exchange. To develop our approach, we use the public and local versions of the Ethereum blockchain, and we compare its performance to the body of current literature. The acquired results validated its efficacy using the same criteria as the most recent works: execution time and energy consumption (Chowdhury, 2024b).

With the BIoTope H2020 project, it is the first Perun-based plan to exchange IoT data and address the scalability issue with current blockchain models. By suppressing the platform service provider with incentives, the proposed model offers: (i) a novel algorithm to integrate Ethereum virtual payment with the Internet of Things ecosystem and IoT data trading between client and supplier; (ii) a payment model free from flood and loot attacks that secures payment without compromising privacy with intermediaries in virtual payment; and (iii) guarantees that there is no single point of failure and penalties for malicious participants and contract violators. Compared to other blockchain models now in use, the resulting approach guarantees speedier payment, taking 99 fewer seconds. The Interplanetary File System (IPFS) and the SHA3 algorithm, which makes use of cryptographic tokens, enable efficient data storage (Ametrano, 2016).

One of the greatest forms of private money ever is Bitcoin, the most popular kind of cryptocurrency. The distributed consensus aspect of the blockchain technology that powers bitcoin is highlighted, facilitating a thorough comprehension of its quirks. The only relevant non-monetary blockchain applications that are being described are notarization and trust anchoring. In the end, the hype surrounding distributed ledger technology is evaluated, revealing its true potential and applicability: it is revealed as an evolutionary database technology that is scarcely revolutionary. Rather, bitcoin may be seen as the digital version of gold, and as such, it has the potential to influence how money is used in the future as well as the development of our digital society (Anoop and Goldston, 2022).

A Single Sign-On method called OAuth2.0 enables users to log into several apps without having to re-enter their login information. Here, identity theft and third-party fraud may result from the central repository under the control of the OAuth service provider. We require a distributed framework to authenticate and authorize the user without the assistance of a third party to get around this issue. We put our suggested structure into practice on the Ethereum TestNet (permissionless blockchain) and Hyperledger Fabric (permissioned blockchain). According to our performance investigation, the production and verification of a combination of shares for secret sharing-based authentication require very little time. Furthermore, security research demonstrates the robustness, end-to-end security, and Universal Composability Framework compliance of our approach (Conti et al., 2018).

All transactions pertaining to the well-known cryptocurrency known as “Bitcoin” are kept on a distributed, append-only public ledger called “Blockchain.” The blockchain is mostly maintained honestly by network nodes known as “miners,” who execute a distributed consensus process based on proof-of-work (PoW) in exchange for rewards. The regular functioning of Bitcoin can be compromised by a variety of security concerns because of these weaknesses. We also discuss the threats to users’ privacy that are tied to Bitcoin, the existing issues with anonymity in Bitcoin, and an analysis of the privacy-preserving solutions that are now accessible. Finally, we present a summary of the important unresolved problems and suggestions for further study to tackle these problems (Yli-Huumo et al., 2016).

Blockchain is gaining popularity due to its key features, which include security, anonymity, and data integrity without requiring a third party to manage transactions. As a result, it opens up new research areas, particularly when considering technical difficulties and constraints. To compile all pertinent studies on Blockchain technology, we have carried out a methodical mapping investigation in this study. Our goal is to comprehend, from a technical standpoint, the current research subjects, issues, and future directions related to Blockchain technology. The bulk of research focuses on identifying and addressing Blockchain’s privacy and security flaws, although many of the suggested fixes haven’t had their efficacy well tested (Reyna et al., 2018).

One important technology that is poised to revolutionize information sharing is blockchain. One technical advancement that has the potential to transform many industries, including the Internet of Things, is the ability to build trust in distributed systems without the need for authority. Since its inception, IoT has used disruptive technologies like big data and cloud computing to overcome its limits, and we believe blockchain will be the next one. To examine how blockchain could potentially enhance the Internet of Things, this article examines this link, looks into issues with blockchain IoT applications, and reviews the most pertinent research (Xu et al., 2019).

A decentralized environment powers the backend of a distributed application. This is not the same as the backend of typical programs, which run on a single server. Similar to regular apps, dapps can have user interfaces and frontend programs that communicate with their backends via APIs. On a central server, the frontend can be served as a webpage. Like a regular app, a dapp might also t ake advantage of decentralized data storage like IPFS.Six An Ethereum-based directory of dapps is called State of the Dapps7. Additionally, this directory is documented on the Ethereum blockchain (More et al., 2023).

These days, dynamic big data—a term used to describe the real-time signals and variable types of digital data derived from numerous IoT sensors—operates on a decentralized basis in our daily lives. Non Fungible Token (NFT), a novel transaction paradigm, is becoming more and more well-liked. It has a high market value in sectors like the arts and intellectual property rights. However, a secure system policy is needed for the NFT trading system. High availability and security are essential for P-to-P node transfer and confirmation policies in the NFT exchange marketplace system. The creation of a smart contract technique to validate blockchain transactions on an autonomous, decentralized, layer one voting blockchain system is proposed in this work. The architecture of the blockchain voting system is displayed (Zhou et al., 2023).

The capacity of blockchain technology to offer a transparent and decentralized platform for a wide range of applications has led to a significant surge in its popularity. A decentralized trust management and voting system that utilizes blockchain technology is suggested as a solution to the shortcomings of current systems. To guarantee the security and integrity of voting and trust data, the system makes use of the decentralization, transparency, and immutability of blockchain technology. The method lowers expenses and increases efficiency by using smart contracts to automate the verification process and do away with the need for middlemen. The system also includes decentralized consensus techniques, which allow for fair and dependable voting procedures. Participants' confidentiality and privacy are protected by the use of encryption (Bajoudah et al., 2019).

As the sectors that use personal data have grown in recent years, security and digital identification solutions have emerged to coincide with the expansion of the digital ecosystem. Nonetheless, the issue of personal data exposure resulting from the usage of malicious codes and applications with inadequate protection never goes away. Owning and maintaining your own personal data can help address the significant issue of financial losses caused by unlawful theft of exposed personal information and situations of abuse of sensitive privacy data, such as medical data. A promising technological solution for this is garnering interest. This paper explains the self-sovereign identity card that is suggested as a solution to the problems with the identity authentication system that is now in use by businesses and institutions, as well as its history and drawbacks. Subsequently, we provide a decentralized architecture that safeguards personal data by employing blockchain technology to store identification and medical data on individual devices and within IPFS (Ballal et al., 2023).

It's becoming obvious that data streams produced by Internet of Things (IoT) devices have value for prospective third-party customers as data marketplaces proliferate. By enabling any pair of data providers and consumers to engage in data exchange transactions without any prior assumption of mutual confidence, we foresee an IoT data stream marketplace that may unlock such potential value in a scalable manner. We describe a marketplace concept and architecture to facilitate data trading, including data asset advertising, trade agreements that are legally binding, trade fulfillment, and payment settlement. Most importantly, we demonstrate how we may provide users with a choice between the expense of exchanging transactional data and the possibility of data loss when interacting with unreliable third parties by utilizing blockchain technology in general and Smart Contracts in particular. We evaluate these trade-offs through experimentation on an Ethereum Smart Contract testbed (Al-Sumaidaee et al., 2023).

Because they enable healthcare practitioners to digitally capture, store, and communicate patient health information (PHI), electronic health records, or EHRs, have become more important in the healthcare sector. This makes it possible for patient data to be exchanged more effectively and helps to ensure that healthcare services are delivered smoothly. Nevertheless, there are security, privacy, interoperability, and data integrity issues with the present EHR systems. Blockchain technology has the ability to overcome these restrictions by offering a transparent and safe platform for transferring and storing PHI because of its decentralized and unchangeable nature. The blockchain technology presented in this paper can be used to enhance the security, privacy, and interoperability of electronic health records. We go over the planned system's architecture and execution, including how smart contracts are used to regulate access and consent. We also evaluate the recommended system's scalability and performance, contrasting it with more established EHR systems. Our findings show that the suggested system offers a safe and effective platform for handling electronic health records, which can enhance patient outcomes and healthcare quality. Security and accessibility are the two main criteria used to assess the performance of the suggested solution (Jha et al., 2023).

For blockchain applications to function, the blockchain ledger's metadata must be connected. Because metadata is frequently kept on centralized cloud servers, the blockchain's decentralization is constrained. As an alternative, distributed storage systems can incorporate metadata to fully decentralized blockchain networks. On the other hand, assessing distributed storage systems' performance is frequently overlooked. We offer a framework with a number of technical indicators to close this gap. In particular, we take the InterPlanetary File System (IPFS) as an example of a distributed storage system and present a real-world use case to show how our framework may be applied (Kshetri, 2017).

The current certification systems have a number of issues, including being vulnerable to fraud, requiring lengthy verification processes, taking a long time to obtain certificates, limiting access due to geographical restrictions, being expensive, having outdated content, being rigid, having problems with credibility, having problems with quality control, having technical difficulties, limiting interaction, providing little feedback, and creating barriers to access. We suggest Certifier Dapp, a decentralized application developed on the Ethereum blockchain, as a solution to these issues. The Certifier Dapp provides features including issuing new certificates, changing issued certificates, confirming certificates, and tracking change history, and it uses the MetaMask wallet for authentication and communication with the blockchain. The Certifier Dapp uses blockchain technology to guarantee data security, immutability, integrity, and transparency. By addressing the shortcomings of the present certification systems and improving accessibility and credibility for users, the suggested solution seeks to offer a smooth and effective certification procedure (Takahashi and Lakhani, 2023).

The study makes the case that blockchain's decentralized nature is probably going to lead to a low susceptibility to manipulation and fabrication by bad players using real-world examples and practical applications. It covers and assesses industry, interorganizational network, and organizational actions on this front. Many policy ramifications are examined. First, regulators can compel companies to use blockchain in supply chains, particularly in mission-critical systems that offer significant benefits to national security and the economy. This will reinforce the Internet of Things. Second, training important players and boosting investment in this technology should be the main goals of public policy initiatives aimed at leveraging blockchain to preserve privacy. Third, focusing on public-private collaborations would be one method to improve the blockchain ecosystem (Takahashi and Lakhani, 2023).

From an engineering standpoint, the advent of Renewable Energy Sources (RES) has presented a number of issues, mostly because of their unpredictable nature. A decentralized architecture has replaced the monolithic architecture of the traditional power system to increase energy production, distribution, transmission, and consolidation. Decentralized Control Systems, sometimes referred to as Distributed Control Systems (DCS), frequently use edge computing to handle data locally near to where it is generated. The purpose of this paper is to examine Blockchain technology and the benefits and drawbacks of applying Blockchain technology to a decentralized solution in the rapidly changing Cloud and IOT markets (Reddaiah et al., 2024).

As technology has developed, cybercrime has also grown more commonplace. Conventional identification systems will eventually become obsolete as Web3 technology advances, with the goal of decentralizing the internet and establishing a trustless network of smart contracts. Because blockchain technology fosters confidence among end users, it alleviates security issues. In this project, SoulBound Tokens will be used to create a blockchain-based identity system. After minting, these NFT-like tokens become immutable and secure since they cannot be transferred. Users' credentials are available to third parties upon request, and the blockchain's transparent chain of custody makes verification simple. This strategy shields user assets and data from nefarious actors by establishing a trustworthy and secure identification system. This idea encompasses government, healthcare, and financial services (Huang and Si, 2024).

One of the most significant technological innovations of the last several years is blockchain. Blockchain is an open platform for exchanging money that has revolutionized the way businesses operate. Businesses and internet behemoths have begun making large investments in the blockchain space, which is predicted to have a valuation of over $3 trillion within the next five years. Its unquestionable security and capacity to offer a comprehensive solution to problems with digital identity have led to its increasing popularity. It is a peer-to-peer network's digital ledger. This essay gives an overview of blockchain technology, including its origin, history, architecture, operation, benefits, drawbacks, and applications across several industries (Krishna, 2023).

During the COVID-19 pandemic, the Cognitive Internet of Medical Things (CIoMT) emerged, and its impact has been revolutionary. By tracking and monitoring vital signs including blood pressure, heart rate, and temperature, the CIoMT can give healthcare professionals up-to-date patient health information. Nonetheless, the issue of privacy during data processing or sharing still exists in these systems. Federated learning (FL) thus plays a key role in the Cognitive Internet of Medical Things (CIoMT) by enabling safe, dispersed, and privacy-preserving collaboration amongst several medical devices. However, there are a number of drawbacks to traditional centralized FL architectures, including rogue servers and single points of failure. This study provides a federated learning system based on blockchain that enhances the current DASS-CARE 2.0 platform. In a multi-organizational setting, the suggested solution offers a dependable and safe distributed learning platform for medical data analytics and sharing. The federated learning framework built on blockchain provides a novel way to get over the problems with conventional FL. Additionally, while taking into account the previously described security challenges, we offer a thorough evaluation of the benefits of the suggested architecture through a comparative study between our DASS-CARE 2.0 and the conventional centralized FL approach. Overall, the suggested framework's performance outperforms conventional techniques by a wide margin (Watanabe, 2022).

As a result, the special connection between a memory chip and a logical node may hold the key to solving the Internet of Things' root-of-trust issue. We suggest a memory chip-based challenge-response system to achieve this goal. In terms of central management, a central node restricts access to the network for electronic appliances equipped with memory chips and keeps a spoofing entity or other fake node out of the network it oversees. Merkle's tree for decentralized communications turns out to be made up of memory chips that the logical nodes are uniquely connected to, correspondingly. The memory chip that holds the most recent data transaction record turns out to be the foundation of Merkle. This memory chip can be registered as a new block if the proof-of-consensus criteria is met. Even the central node finds it more difficult to alter the transaction record between memory chips after blocks are linked. This allows for the coexistence of the central management and the decentralized system (like blockchain). There is also a brief discussion of a novel concept of security state (Watanabe, 2022, Ballal et al., 2023).

To improve security and privacy in peer-to-peer (P2P) communication, we use Be-Mutual, a blockchain-based identity management and mutual authentication system. To prevent unwanted access, it uses mutual authentication based on asymmetric encryption and offers user-centric identity management based on blockchain addresses. By integrating the Blockchain-enabled Domain Name System (Be-DNS) into BeMutual, we solve the complexity of blockchain addresses, a significant challenge in real-world applications like Decentralized Physical Infrastructure (DePIN) and Decentralized Wireless (DeWi). BeDNS enhances user experience without compromising security by translating difficult-to-remember domain names into complex blockchain addresses. The BeMutual system, which combines mutual authentication, blockchain-based identity management, and domain name resolution, presents a novel approach to safe and intuitive peer-to-peer (P2P) communication in decentralized settings (Gabriel et al., 2019).

With the use of smart contracts—a collection of self-executing code made possible by a blockchain—traditional components of a centralized financial system may be replaced by decentralized finance. The idea behind a decentralized method like this is to do away with middlemen by establishing an environment that is transparent, open-source, and trust-free. Late in 2020, there was a surge in the popularity of decentralized finance thanks to platforms like Uniswap, Maker DAO, Aave, and Curve. As of May 9, 2021, the total market capitalization of Decentralized Finance had surpassed USD $87 billion in locked value. The realm of decentralized finance has expanded rapidly, encompassing stablecoins, tokenized Bitcoin, money lending, and borrowing platforms. Although decentralized finance provides numerous benefits over the centralized financial system, it also has several drawbacks, including unpredictable, occasionally exorbitant transaction charges and poor transaction speeds. As a result, hybrid finance has been introduced. It is run by verified companies via a public blockchain system and is supposed to have low transaction costs, fast transaction rates, and compliance with Know Your Customer laws. This case study describes the partnership between Current, a challenger bank based in New York that specializes in online banking, mobile payments, and financial services, and Acala, a decentralized finance platform built on the Polkadot blockchain, as they created a new category in the financial technology industry with hybrid finance (Beck et al., 2017).

The blockchain is a distributed ledger system that takes the shape of a dispersed transactional database. It is controlled by a consensus process and encrypted for security. This is because the blockchain is extraordinarily tamper-resistant due to its distributed transaction data and cryptographic logic at its foundation. The ramifications for how we structure interpersonal and interorganizational relationships may be profound when developing a dependable, trustworthy distributed record system, or ledger. Important documents that are crucial to our social, professional, or health lives are frequently created or kept up by outside parties. Such third-party record repositories may be susceptible to corruption due to human error or storage system malfunction, but this risk may be reduced by impartial and impervious blockchain-based digital systems.

Having understood the foundational aspects of blockchain as a distributed ledger system, we now explore its methodology through a comparison of centralized, decentralized, and distributed architectures.

## Methodology

### *Centralized vs. Decentralized vs. Distributed Systems*

As the internet evolves towards handling big data, the limitations of centralized systems become increasingly apparent. Centralized systems, such as those used in small educational institutions or start-ups, involve a single point of control, which can lead to inefficiencies and vulnerabilities. In contrast, decentralized systems, epitomized by blockchain technology, offer a robust solution by distributing control and ensuring data integrity.

### *Centralized Systems*

In a centralized system, all data and control are managed by a single entity or server. While this approach simplifies management and coordination, it introduces a single point of failure. For example, if a server crashes or bandwidth is insufficient, the entire system can be disrupted.

### *Decentralized Systems*

Decentralized systems distribute control among multiple nodes or coordinators. This approach mitigates the risk of a single point of failure, as each node operates independently and can function even if other nodes fail. However, decentralized systems can still face challenges if the overall network fails.

### *Distributed Systems*

Distributed systems take decentralization further by ensuring that all nodes communicate and share data among themselves. Each node maintains a local copy of the data, which is consistently updated across the network. This architecture, embodied by blockchain technology, ensures data integrity and availability even in the face of individual node failures.

### *Centralized Systems and Their Limitations*

In a centralized system, a single server acts as the coordinator for all nodes connected to it. This configuration works well in small-scale environments, where data transactions are limited and manageable. For instance, in educational institutes or startup companies, the centralized approach ensures efficient communication and data sharing. However, this system has inherent drawbacks:

1. Single Point of Failure: If the central server fails, all connected nodes lose the ability to communicate and access data.
2. Bandwidth Limitations: High data traffic can overwhelm the server, causing delays and potential data loss.
3. Data Corruption: If the server's data gets corrupted, all connected nodes are affected.

## Decentralization in Data Storage: An Intermediate Solution

As the internet evolves into an era of big data, the need for efficient and reliable data storage systems becomes paramount. Traditionally, centralized systems have been effective in smaller organizations like educational institutions and startups. However, as data demands grow, these centralized systems reveal significant limitations, especially in larger, more complex environments. This chapter explores the shift from centralized to decentralized and distributed systems, emphasizing the role of blockchain technology in this transition.

Decentralization offers a solution to some of the problems inherent in centralized systems. In a decentralized environment, multiple coordinators manage the nodes. If one coordinator or node fails, the others can continue to function, ensuring a more robust and resilient network. However, decentralization is not without its challenges:

1. Network Dependency: If the entire network fails, the system cannot function.
2. Complex Coordination: Managing multiple coordinators and ensuring consistent data updates across nodes can be complex.

## Distributed Systems: The Optimal Approach

Distributed systems further enhance the robustness and reliability of data storage and management. In these systems, all nodes communicate directly with each other, eliminating the dependency on a single or multiple central coordinators. This approach offers several advantages:

1. High Fault Tolerance: Since every node holds a copy of the data, the failure of one or more nodes does not affect the system's overall functionality.
2. Enhanced Security: The distributed nature of data storage makes it more challenging for malicious entities to corrupt or alter data.
3. Scalability: Distributed systems can easily scale by adding more nodes without overloading a central server.

## The Role of Blockchain in Distributed Systems

Blockchain technology epitomizes the principles of distributed systems. Each node in a blockchain network maintains a local copy of the data, which is synchronized across the network through a consensus mechanism. This architecture offers several key benefits:

1. Data Consistency: Blockchain ensures that all copies of the data are consistent across the network.
2. Security and Privacy: Transactions are encrypted and validated through complex cryptographic algorithms, ensuring data integrity and privacy.
3. Immutability: Once data is added to the blockchain, it cannot be altered or deleted, providing a permanent record of all transactions.

## Security in Blockchain within Distributed Systems

Blockchain technology is crucial in enhancing security in distributed systems, primarily through cryptographic techniques and consensus mechanisms. Below is a breakdown of key security elements in blockchain:

### *Consensus Mechanisms*

Consensus mechanisms are essential to ensure that all participants in a distributed network agree on a single version of the truth. Key consensus mechanisms include:

**Proof of Work (PoW):** This mechanism requires participants (miners) to solve complex mathematical puzzles to add new blocks to the blockchain. It ensures security by making it computationally expensive to alter transaction history.

- Process: In PoW, miners compete to solve a complex cryptographic puzzle. The first one to solve it gets the right to add a new block to the blockchain and is rewarded with cryptocurrency.
- Security Aspect: The difficulty of the puzzle ensures that it requires significant computational power to solve. This makes it extremely hard for any single entity to dominate the mining process and alter the blockchain history (e.g., 51% attack). Altering any block would require re-mining all subsequent blocks, which is computationally impractical.
- Example: Bitcoin uses PoW, where miners solve SHA-256 hash puzzles. The network adjusts the difficulty of the puzzle every two weeks to ensure that blocks are mined approximately every 10 minutes.

**Proof of Stake (PoS):** PoS selects validators based on the number of coins they hold and are willing to "stake" as collateral. It is more energy-efficient than PoW and secures the network by aligning the interests of validators with the network's integrity.

- Process: In PoS, validators are chosen to create new blocks based on the number of coins they hold and are willing to "stake" as collateral. The more coins a validator holds, the higher their chances of being selected to add the next block.
- Security Aspect: PoS aligns the validators' interests with the network's security. Validators who act maliciously or attempt to manipulate the blockchain risk

losing their staked coins. This economic incentive discourages attacks and ensures that only those with a vested interest in the network's integrity are allowed to validate transactions.

- Example: Ethereum 2.0 is transitioning from PoW to PoS, where validators are selected based on the amount of ETH they hold and are willing to stake.

**Delegated Proof of Stake (DPoS):** In DPoS, stakeholders vote for delegates who are responsible for validating transactions and maintaining the blockchain. This mechanism provides scalability and security by decentralizing the selection of validators.

- Process: In DPoS, coin holders vote for a small number of delegates who are responsible for validating transactions and maintaining the blockchain. This system is more democratic and scalable, as it allows for quicker block creation and transaction validation.
- Security Aspect: DPoS enhances security by decentralizing the selection of validators. The voting mechanism ensures that only trusted and reputable delegates are selected. If a delegate acts maliciously, they can be voted out by the community.
- Example: EOS uses DPoS, where 21 delegates are elected by the community to validate transactions and maintain the network.

## Cryptographic Security

Cryptography plays a critical role in securing transactions and ensuring data integrity within blockchain networks. Key cryptographic elements include:

**Hash Functions:** These are used to create a unique digital fingerprint of data. In blockchain, hash functions ensure that any change in transaction data will alter the hash, making tampering easily detectable.

- Definition: A hash function takes an input (or 'message') and returns a fixed-size string of bytes. The output, known as a hash or digest, is unique to each input.
- Role in Blockchain: In blockchain, each block contains a hash of the previous block, linking them together in a chain. If any part of a block's data is altered, the hash changes, breaking the chain and signaling tampering. This ensures the immutability of the blockchain.
- Security Aspect: Hash functions like SHA-256 used in Bitcoin are designed to be one-way functions, meaning it's computationally infeasible to reverse-engineer the input from the output. This ensures data integrity and prevents unauthorized modifications.

**Digital Signatures:** Digital signatures ensure that transactions are authenticated and originate from the rightful sender. They use the sender's private key to create a signature that can be verified with the corresponding public key.

- Definition: A digital signature is a cryptographic technique that allows a person to prove ownership or approval of a document or message in a secure way.

- Role in Blockchain: When a transaction is made, the sender signs it with their private key, creating a digital signature. This signature is unique to both the transaction and the sender's private key. Anyone with the sender's public key can verify the signature, ensuring the transaction is legitimate.
- Security Aspect: Digital signatures provide authentication, ensuring that the transaction was indeed made by the legitimate owner of the cryptocurrency. They also provide non-repudiation, meaning the sender cannot deny the transaction since only they have access to their private key.

**Elliptic Curve Cryptography (ECC):** ECC provides the basis for digital signatures in blockchain. It offers strong security with smaller key sizes, making it efficient for use in resource-constrained environments.

- Definition: ECC is a type of public-key cryptography based on the algebraic structure of elliptic curves over finite fields.
- Role in Blockchain: ECC is used to generate the private-public key pairs in most blockchain systems, including Bitcoin and Ethereum. It allows for strong security with smaller key sizes compared to other cryptographic systems like RSA.
- Security Aspect: ECC provides robust encryption and digital signature capabilities while using less computational power. This efficiency is crucial for the decentralized and resource-constrained environments in which blockchains often operate.

The diagram visually represents these security components and their interactions within a blockchain-based distributed system.

Figure 1 visually represents the interaction between these three layers within a blockchain system:

1. **Consensus Layer**:
    - Shows miners or validators working to agree on the next block to add to the blockchain.
    - Illustrates how the network achieves decentralized consensus, whether through solving cryptographic puzzles (PoW) or selecting validators based on stakes (PoS).
2. **Cryptographic Layer**:
    - Displays how hash functions and digital signatures secure transactions.
    - Shows the process of creating a transaction, signing it, and adding it to a block, ensuring that all data is authenticated and unaltered.
3. **Data Integrity**:
    - Highlights the importance of the linked structure of blocks (using hashes) in maintaining the integrity of the blockchain.
    - Demonstrates how any attempt to alter the data would break the chain and immediately signal a breach in the blockchain's integrity.

This combination of consensus mechanisms, cryptographic techniques, and data integrity measures makes blockchain technology a robust solution for securing distributed systems. The integration of these layers ensures that blockchains are

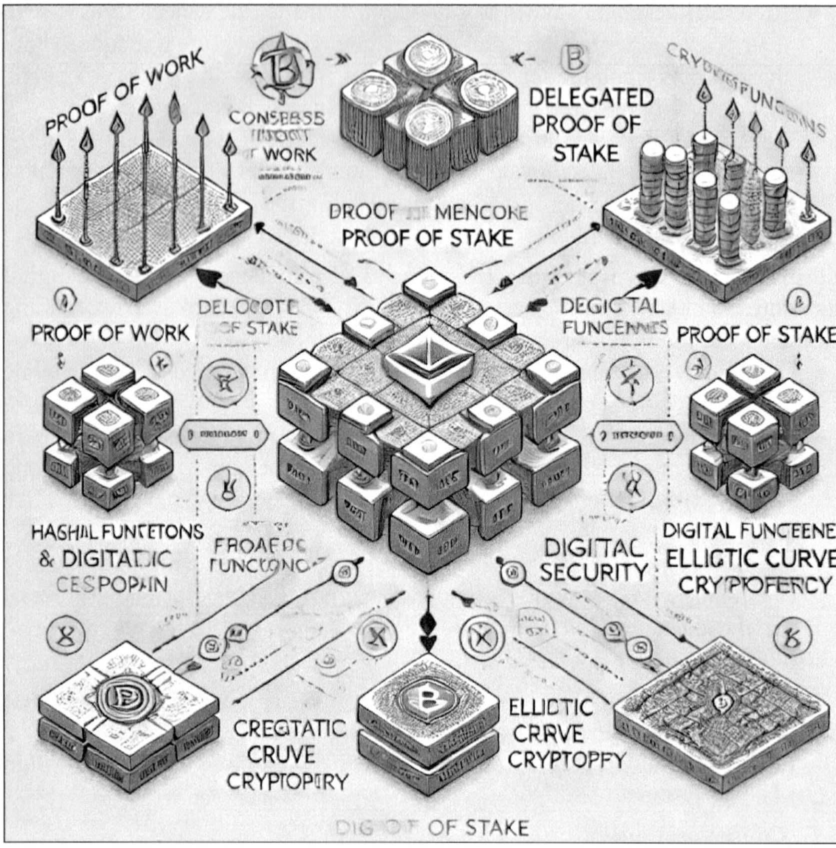


**Fig. 1** Interaction Between Layers in Blockchain.

resistant to tampering, fraud, and unauthorized access, maintaining trust and reliability in decentralized environments.

This comprehensive approach ensures that blockchain technology remains secure, transparent, and resistant to tampering, making it a reliable framework for distributed systems.

## Bitcoin in Blockchain

Bitcoin is the pioneering digital currency that introduced the concept of decentralized finance, challenging traditional financial systems. Since its inception in 2009 by the pseudonymous Satoshi Nakamoto, Bitcoin has paved the way for a broader movement towards decentralization in various sectors, including finance, technology, and governance.

## The Birth of Bitcoin

Bitcoin emerged in response to the 2008 financial crisis, which exposed vulnerabilities in centralized financial institutions. Satoshi Nakamoto proposed a new system, free from central authority, where users could directly exchange value. Bitcoin is powered by blockchain technology, a decentralized ledger that records all transactions transparently and securely.

### *Core Concepts of Bitcoin*

1. Decentralization: Bitcoin operates on a peer-to-peer network without a central authority, making it resistant to censorship and control. This decentralization is a key feature that distinguishes Bitcoin from traditional currencies and financial systems.
2. Blockchain Technology: The blockchain is the backbone of Bitcoin, serving as a public ledger that records all transactions. It ensures transparency, security, and immutability, with each block linked to the previous one through cryptographic hashes.
3. Consensus Mechanism: Proof of Work: Bitcoin uses a consensus mechanism called Proof of Work (PoW) to validate transactions. Miners solve complex mathematical puzzles to add new blocks to the blockchain, ensuring the network's security and integrity.
4. Limited Supply: Bitcoin has a maximum supply of 21 million coins, making it a deflationary asset. This scarcity is built into its code, distinguishing it from fiat currencies that can be printed in unlimited quantities.
5. Pseudonymity and Privacy: Bitcoin transactions are pseudonymous, with users identified by alphanumeric addresses rather than personal information. While all transactions are publicly visible on the blockchain, the identities of the participants remain hidden.

### *Technical Details of Bitcoin*

- Transaction Process: Bitcoin transactions involve transferring value from one address to another. These transactions are broadcast to the network, verified by miners, and added to the blockchain once confirmed. A transaction typically includes inputs (the source of the coins), outputs (the destination addresses), and a digital signature for verification.
- Mining and Block Creation: Miners compete to solve cryptographic puzzles in a process called mining. The first miner to solve the puzzle adds the new block of transactions to the blockchain and is rewarded with newly minted bitcoins and transaction fees. This process also introduces new bitcoins into circulation.
- Difficulty Adjustment: The Bitcoin network automatically adjusts the difficulty of the puzzles every 2016 blocks (approximately every two weeks)

to maintain a consistent block creation time of about 10 minutes. This mechanism ensures a stable and predictable supply of new bitcoins.

- Security through Cryptography: Bitcoin relies on cryptographic techniques to secure transactions. The SHA-256 hash function is used to create a unique identifier for each block, while public and private keys ensure that only the rightful owner can spend bitcoins associated with a given address.
- Scalability Challenges: Bitcoin's scalability has been a topic of debate due to its limited transaction throughput. Currently, the Bitcoin network can process approximately 7 transactions per second. Solutions like the Lightning Network, which enables off-chain transactions, have been proposed to address these limitations.

## Bitcoin and the Broader Movement towards Decentralization

Bitcoin's success has inspired a broader movement towards decentralized systems across various industries. Decentralization offers several benefits, including enhanced security, transparency, and resistance to censorship. However, it also presents challenges, such as scalability, governance, and regulatory concerns.

- Decentralized Finance (DeFi): Bitcoin laid the foundation for Decentralized Finance (DeFi), a movement that aims to recreate traditional financial systems using blockchain technology. DeFi platforms offer services like lending, borrowing, and trading without intermediaries, empowering users with greater control over their assets.
- Smart Contracts and Ethereum: While Bitcoin focuses primarily on value transfer, the Ethereum blockchain introduced smart contracts, self-executing contracts with the terms of the agreement directly written into code. This innovation has enabled the creation of decentralized applications (dApps) that can operate autonomously.
- Decentralized Autonomous Organizations (DAOs): DAOs are organizations governed by code rather than traditional hierarchical structures. They operate on blockchain networks, allowing participants to make decisions collectively and transparently. Bitcoin's decentralized nature has been a precursor to the development of DAOs.
- Decentralized Identity and Data Ownership: Decentralized systems also extend to identity management and data ownership. Projects are emerging that aim to give individuals control over their digital identities and personal data, reducing reliance on centralized platforms that often exploit user information.
- Challenges in Decentralization: While decentralization offers numerous advantages, it also comes with challenges. Governance in decentralized systems can be complex, as decision-making processes often require consensus among a large number of participants. Additionally, regulatory frameworks for decentralized systems are still evolving, leading to uncertainty and potential legal challenges.

Bitcoin has not only revolutionized the concept of money but has also catalysed a global shift towards decentralized systems. By removing intermediaries and central authorities, Bitcoin and other decentralized technologies offer greater autonomy, security, and transparency.

## Smart Contracts and Ethereum

The introduction of Ethereum in 2015 by VitalikButerin marked a significant evolution in blockchain technology, expanding beyond the financial transactions of Bitcoin to include programmable contracts known as smart contracts. These self-executing contracts, which automatically enforce and execute the terms of an agreement, have been a driving force behind the rise of decentralized applications (dApps) and the broader movement towards decentralized systems.

- Ethereum and the Birth of Smart Contracts: Ethereum was designed to be a decentralized platform that supports a Turing-complete programming language, allowing developers to create and deploy smart contracts. Unlike Bitcoin, which was primarily conceived as a digital currency, Ethereum was envisioned as a "world computer" where any application could run without downtime, censorship, or third-party interference.
- Smart Contracts Defined: A smart contract is a piece of code that automatically executes, enforces, or facilitates an agreement based on predefined conditions. Once deployed on the Ethereum blockchain, a smart contract cannot be altered, ensuring that the terms are transparent and immutable.
- Ethereum Virtual Machine (EVM): The EVM is the decentralized computer that runs smart contracts on Ethereum. It allows any developer to create dApps, which are decentralized applications that operate autonomously, often without any human intervention after deployment.

### *Key Features and Technical Details of Ethereum*

- Decentralized Computation: Ethereum's decentralized nature means that smart contracts are executed across a global network of nodes. This eliminates the need for a central server or authority, ensuring that the application remains available and tamper-proof.
- Gas Fees: To prevent misuse and to allocate resources on the network, Ethereum requires gas fees for executing operations. Gas fees are paid in Ether (ETH), the native cryptocurrency of the Ethereum network. The more complex the operation (e.g., running a smart contract), the higher the gas fee.
- Solidity Programming Language: Solidity is the primary programming language used to write smart contracts on Ethereum. It is a high-level, contract-oriented language designed specifically for implementing smart contracts on the EVM.
- Decentralized Applications (dApps): dApps are software applications that run on a decentralized network rather than a centralized server. They leverage

smart contracts to function without intermediaries, providing services like decentralized finance (DeFi), gaming, supply chain management, and more.

## Smart Contracts: Enabling Decentralization

Smart contracts are integral to the concept of decentralization, as they remove the need for intermediaries, reducing costs and increasing efficiency. Here are some key areas where smart contracts are making a significant impact:

- Decentralized Finance (DeFi): DeFi platforms use smart contracts to offer traditional financial services like lending, borrowing, and trading without relying on banks or financial institutions. Users can interact with these platforms directly through their wallets, retaining control over their assets.
- Tokenization and Initial Coin Offerings (ICOs): Ethereum's ERC-20 token standard has enabled the creation of a vast array of tokens, which represent various assets, rights, or utilities. ICOs, which are a method of raising capital by issuing tokens, have become a popular means for startups to fund their projects.
- Non-Fungible Tokens (NFTs): NFTs, built on Ethereum's ERC-721 and ERC-1155 standards, represent unique digital assets like art, collectibles, and virtual real estate. Smart contracts manage the ownership and transfer of these assets, ensuring authenticity and provenance.
- Supply Chain Management: Smart contracts are used to automate and secure the supply chain, ensuring that each step of the process is recorded on the blockchain. This transparency helps in tracking goods, verifying authenticity, and reducing fraud.
- Decentralized Autonomous Organizations (DAOs): DAOs are organizations governed by smart contracts, where decisions are made collectively by token holders rather than a central authority. This structure promotes transparency and democratizes decision-making processes.

## Challenges and Limitations

While smart contracts and Ethereum have opened up new possibilities for decentralization, they also come with challenges that need to be addressed:

- Scalability Issues: Ethereum's current infrastructure faces scalability problems, as the network can become congested with high transaction volumes, leading to increased gas fees and slower processing times. Solutions like Ethereum 2.0 and Layer 2 scaling solutions (e.g., Optimistic Rollups, zk-Rollups) are being developed to address these challenges.
- Security Concerns: Smart contracts, once deployed, cannot be altered, making them vulnerable to bugs or vulnerabilities in the code. High-profile incidents, like the DAO hack in 2016, have highlighted the importance of rigorous security audits and testing before deployment.

- Regulatory Uncertainty: The decentralized nature of smart contracts poses challenges for regulators, as these contracts operate across borders and without a central authority. Legal frameworks for smart contracts are still evolving, leading to uncertainties in their enforceability in traditional legal systems.
- Complexity and User Experience: Interacting with dApps and smart contracts can be complex for users, especially those unfamiliar with blockchain technology. Improving the user experience and making the technology more accessible is crucial for broader adoption.

## The Future of Ethereum and Smart Contracts

Ethereum's ongoing development, including the transition to Ethereum 2.0, aims to address current limitations and enhance the network's scalability, security, and sustainability. As the ecosystem matures, Ethereum is likely to remain a central platform for innovation in decentralized systems, driving the adoption of smart contracts across various industries.

- Ethereum 2.0 and Proof of Stake (PoS): Ethereum 2.0 is a major upgrade that aims to transition the network from Proof of Work (PoW) to Proof of Stake (PoS). This shift is expected to reduce energy consumption, increase scalability through shard chains, and improve security.
- Interoperability: The future of decentralized systems will likely involve greater interoperability between different blockchains. Cross-chain solutions are being developed to enable smart contracts on Ethereum to interact with other blockchain networks, enhancing the versatility and reach of decentralized applications.
- Expanding Use Cases: Beyond finance and digital assets, smart contracts have the potential to revolutionize areas such as healthcare, legal services, and governance. As the technology evolves, we can expect to see more innovative applications that leverage the power of decentralized systems.

Smart contracts and Ethereum have been pivotal in advancing the movement towards decentralized systems. By enabling trustless and automated agreements, they have the potential to disrupt traditional industries and create new opportunities for innovation. Results and discussion will be done in the next section.

## Results and Discussion

The graph produced from the code shows the time taken to mine each block. As more blocks are mined, the difficulty in solving the cryptographic puzzle increases, leading to varying times required for each block's mining process. This demonstrates the Proof of Work (PoW) consensus mechanism, where computational effort is required to secure the blockchain.

**Security Features Summary**

- **Consensus Layer:** Ensures agreement among network participants without a central authority.

- **Cryptographic Layer:** Provides security through hash functions and digital signatures.
- **Data Integrity:** Maintains the immutability and consistency of the blockchain data.

This implementation and analysis showcase how blockchain technology secures data and ensures trust in decentralized systems like Bitcoin and shown in Fig. 2.

New Block Mined: 1
BlockHash:
0000126d086b15548d90b93f319e187dec3077a3e926170946939064e472f29b
Transactions: 41

New Block Mined: 2
BlockHash:
00002899a4edf3b138d2f7e06b89267bb3f48e0e13750bd48b5d005e7640d39b
Transactions: 41

New Block Mined: 3
Block Hash:
0000e1612bd9524568f326ef10ed094f07ca00c051fcf1d57f235329012770a2
Transactions: 21

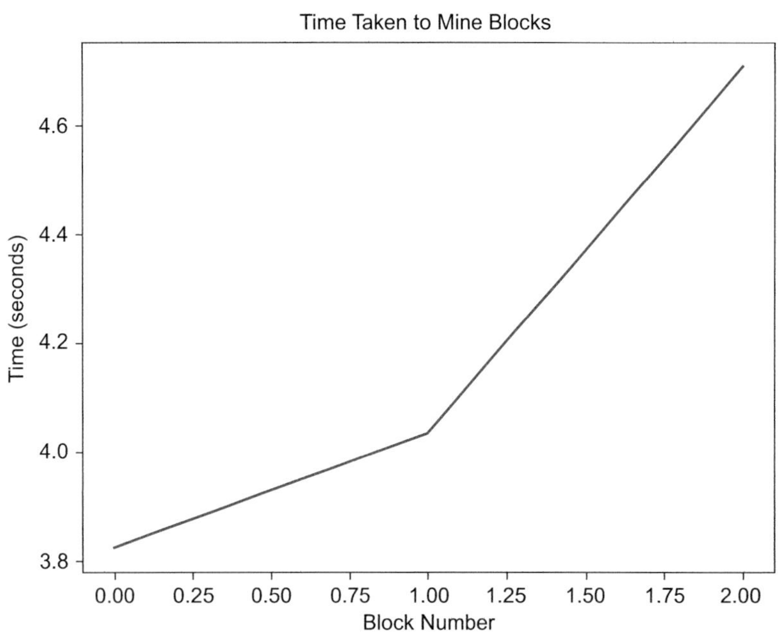


**Fig. 2** Implementation of Decentralized using Hash Function

## The Advent of Blockchain

Blockchain technology provides a decentralized manner to maintain a secure, immutable ledger across multiple nodes. This ensures data integrity and transparency without relying on a central authority.

**Key Components of Blockchain**

1. **Distributed Ledger:** Each node in the blockchain network holds a synchronized copy of the ledger, ensuring that transactions are public and validated by consensus.
2. **Blocks:** Each block contains a set of transactions and is linked to the previous block through cryptographic hashes, forming a secure chain.
3. **Consensus Mechanisms:** Mechanisms like Proof of Work (PoW) or Proof of Stake (PoS) ensure that all nodes agree on the blockchain's state, preventing tampering or fraud.

## Case Study: Document Sharing

In a traditional document-sharing system, updates are sequential and can lead to conflicts or errors. Google Docs allows simultaneous updates but still relies on a central server. Blockchain enhances this by allowing decentralized, real-time updates across a network, ensuring consistency and security.

**Blockchain Mechanisms**

1. **Public Ledger:** Every node maintains a copy of the blockchain, validating new transactions against the public ledger.
2. **Consensus Protocols:** Ensure that all nodes agree on the state of the blockchain without a central authority.
3. **Security Protocols:** Data is secured using cryptographic techniques, making unauthorized changes virtually impossible.
4. **Protocols for Commit:** Transactions are validated and committed in a timely manner, ensuring that the blockchain remains up-to-date.

## Discussion

### *Blockchain in Action: Bitcoin*

Bitcoin, a decentralized cryptocurrency, operates on a peer-to-peer network using blockchain. Transactions are secure, transparent, and immutable.

**How Bitcoin Transactions Work**

- **Transaction Creation:** A sender initiates a Bitcoin transaction using their wallet.
- **Signing the Transaction:** The sender's private key signs the transaction to ensure authenticity.

- **Broadcasting the Transaction:** The transaction is broadcast to the Bitcoin network for verification.
- **Mining:** Miners validate transactions, add them to a block, and append the block to the blockchain.
- **Updating the Blockchain:** The updated blockchain is propagated across the network, ensuring all nodes have the latest version.

**Key Features of Bitcoin:**

- **Decentralization:** Operates without a central authority, leveraging a peer-to-peer network.
- **Security:** Cryptographic techniques ensure that transactions are secure and tamper-proof.
- **Transparency:** All transactions are recorded on a public ledger, ensuring transparency.
- **Immutability:** Once added to the blockchain, transactions cannot be altered.

## Conclusion

Blockchain technology addresses the limitations of centralized systems by providing a decentralized, secure, and transparent method for recording transactions. Bitcoin exemplifies the potential of blockchain, offering a peer-to-peer, decentralized digital currency that operates without a central authority. As the internet continues to handle increasingly large volumes of data, blockchain's distributed architecture offers a promising solution for ensuring data integrity and availability.

The transition from centralized to decentralized and ultimately distributed systems marks a significant advancement in data storage and management. Blockchain technology, with its decentralized and distributed architecture, addresses many of the limitations of traditional systems, offering enhanced security, reliability, and efficiency. This chapter sets the foundation for understanding the intricate details of blockchain technology and its application in various sectors, which will be explored in subsequent chapters.

## References

Al-Sumaidaee, G., Alkhudary, R., Zilic, Z. and Swidan, A. (2023) "An Evaluation Framework for Assessing IPFS Performance within a Blockchain-Based Healthcare System," 2023 IEEE International Conference on Blockchain (Blockchain), Danzhou, China, 2023, pp. 100–104, doi: 10.1109/Blockchain60715.2023.00025.

Ametrano, F.M. (2016) Bitcoin, Blockchain, and Distributed Ledgers: Between Hype and Reality (August 30, 2016). Available at SSRN: https://ssrn.com/abstract=2832249 or http://dx.doi.org/10.2139/ssrn.2832249.

Anoop, V.S. and Goldston, J. (2022). Decentralized finance to hybrid finance through blockchain: a case-study of acala and current. *J Bank Financ Technol* 6, 109–115. https://doi.org/10.1007/s42786-022-00041-0.

Bajoudah, S., Dong, C. and Missier, P. (2019). "Toward a Decentralized, Trust-Less Marketplace for Brokered IoT Data Trading Using Blockchain," 2019 *IEEE International Conference on Blockchain (Blockchain)*, Atlanta, GA, USA, 2019, pp. 339–346, doi: 10.1109/Blockchain.2019.00053.

Ballal, S., Chandre, Y., Pise, R., Sonare, B. and Patil, S. (2023). "Blockchain-Based Decentralized Platform for Electronic Health Records Management," *2023 IEEE International Conference on Blockchain and Distributed Systems Security (ICBDS)*, New Raipur, India, 2023, pp. 1–5, doi: 10.1109/ICBDS58040.2023.10346392.

Beck, R., Avital, M., Rossi, M. et al. (2017) Blockchain Technology in Business and Information Systems Research. *Bus InfSystEng* 59, 381–384. https://doi.org/10.1007/s12599-017-0505-1

Chowdhury, M. (2024a) Kaizen: A Street Smart Low Latency-Aware Resource Choreography Scheme for Decentralized Autonomous Organization (DAO) and Non-DAO Based Application Execution Over Blockchain and MEC Empowered 6 G Network. *Int J Netw Distrib Comput* (2024). https://doi.org/10.1007/s44227-024-00033-0.

Chowdhury, M. (2024b) Kaizen: A Street Smart Low Latency-Aware Resource Choreography Scheme for Decentralized Autonomous Organization (DAO) and Non-DAO Based Application Execution Over Blockchain and MEC Empowered 6 G Network. *Int J Netw Distrib Comput* (2024). https://doi.org/10.1007/s44227-024-00033-0.

Conti, M., Sandeep Kumar, E., Lal, C. and Ruj, S. (2018) "A Survey on Security and Privacy Issues of Bitcoin," in *IEEE Communications Surveys & Tutorials*, vol. 20, no. 4, pp. 3416–3452, Fourthquarter 2018, doi: 10.1109/COMST.2018.2842460.

Doe, J., Smith, J. and Brown, E. (2020). Quantum-Assisted Attacks on Blockchain Consensus Mechanisms. In *Proceedings of the IEEE International Conference on Quantum Computing and Engineering (QCE)*, Denver, CO, USA, October 12–16, 2020 Chikashi Tsuji, " Bitcoin and Stock Returns: An Empirical Study", ibusines, vol 15, pp. 147–153.

Eyal, I. and GunSirer, E. (2018). Majority is not enough: bitcoin mining is vulnerable. *Commun. ACM* 61, 7 (July 2018), 95–102. https://doi.org/10.1145/3212998

Gabriel, T., Cornel-Cristian, A., Arhip-Calin, M. and A. Zamfirescu, A. (2019) "Cloud Storage. A comparison between centralized solutions versus decentralized cloud storage solutions using Blockchain technology," 2019 *54th International Universities Power Engineering Conference (UPEC)*, Bucharest, Romania, 2019, pp. 1–5, doi: 10.1109/UPEC.2019.8893440.

Huang, Q.A. and Si, Y.W. (2024) Blockchain-based autonomous decentralized trust management for social network. *J Supercomput* 80, 14725–14751 (2024). https://doi.org/10.1007/s11227-024-06024-w

Hao, D., Wang, E., Liu, W. et al. (2024) Blockchain-based decentralized model for mobile crowd-sensing. CCF Trans. *Pervasive Comp. Interact.* 6, 68–81 (2024). https://doi.org/10.1007/s42486-023-00140-x

Jha, S., Modak, A., Pise, R. and S. Patil, S. (2023) "Certifier Dapp - Decentralized and Secured Certification System Using Blockchain," 2023 *IEEE International Conference on Blockchain and Distributed Systems Security (ICBDS),* New Raipur, India, 2023, pp. 1–6, doi: 10.1109/ICBDS58040.2023.10346509.

Krishna, D.P., Ramaguru, R., Praveen, K. et al. (2023). SSH-DAuth: secret sharing based decentralized OAuth using decentralized identifier. *Sci Rep* 13, 18335 (2023). https://doi.org/10.1038/s41598-023-44586-6.

Kshetri, N. (2017) *Blockchain's roles in strengthening cybersecurity and protecting privacy, Telecommunications Policy*, Volume 41, Issue 10, 2017, Pages 1027–1038, ISSN 0308-5961, https://doi.org/10.1016/j.telpol.2017.09.003.

Maghrebi, A. and Abid, F. (2018). "The Investors' Behavior towards the Relationship Between Bitcoin, Litcoin, Dash Coins, and Gold: A Portfolio Modeling Approach",

McCorry, P., Hicks, A. and Meiklejohn, S. (2018). Smart Contracts for Bribing Miners. In Financial Cryptography and Data Security: FC 2018 International Workshops, BITCOIN, VOTING, and

WTSC, Nieuwpoort, Curaçao, March 2, 2018, Revised Selected Papers. Springer-Verlag, Berlin, Heidelberg, 3–18. https://doi.org/10.1007/978-3-662-58820-8_1

More, A., Poddar, V. and Sarda, S. (2023) "Blockchain-Based Decentralized Identification System Using SoulBound Tokens," *2023 International Conference on Integration of Computational Intelligent System (ICICIS)*, Pune, India, 2023, pp. 1–6, doi: 10.1109/ICICIS56802.2023.10430319.

Reddaiah, S., Subramanyam, R., Refonaa, J., Jany Shabu, S.L., Maheswari and S. Praveen, S. (2024) "Blockchain-Enabled Decentralized Trust Management and Secure Voting system," *2024 4th International Conference on Pervasive Computing and Social Networking (ICPCSN)*, Salem, India, 2024, pp. 554–559, doi: 10.1109/ICPCSN62568.2024.00093.

Reyna, A., Martín, C., Chen, J., Soler, E. and Díaz, M. (2018) On blockchain and its integration with IoT. Challenges and opportunities, *Future Generation Computer Systems*, Volume 88, 2018, Pages 173–190, ISSN 0167-739X, https://doi.org/10.1016/j.future.2018.05.046.

Roussou, I., Dritsaki, C., and Stiakakis, E. (2019) " The Bitcoin's Network Effects Paradox – A Time Series Analysis" *Theoretical Economics Letters*, Vol. 9, pp. 1981–2001.

Sahoo, S.S. and Chaurasiya, V.K. (2024) VIBE: Blockchain-based Virtual Payment in IoT Ecosystem: A Secure Decentralized Marketplace. Multimed Tools Appl 83, 16869–16894. https://doi.org/10.1007/s11042-023-15634-0

Saurabh, K., Upadhyay, P. and Rani, N. (2024)Towards Blockchain Decentralized Autonomous Organizations (DAO) Design. *Inf Syst Front* (2024). https://doi.org/10.1007/s10796-023-10455-w

Simanta, S. S. (2018) "Understanding Blockchain Technology", *Computer Science and Engineering*, vol.2, Issue 3, pp 23–29.

Singh, M., Baranwal, G. and Tripathi, A.K. (2023) Decentralized group decision making using blockchain. *J Supercomput* 79, 20141–20178 (2023). https://doi.org/10.1007/s11227-023-05426-6

Takahashi, H. and Lakhani, U. (2023)."Implementation of Smart Contract on Autonomous Decentralized Voting Blockchain," *2023 IEEE 15th International Symposium on Autonomous Decentralized System (ISADS)*, Mexico City, Mexico, 2023, pp. 1–7, doi: 10.1109/ISADS56919.2023.10092152.

Watanabe, H. 2022. "On coexistence of decentralized system (blockchain) and central management in Internet-of-Things," *2022 IEEE 1st Global Emerging Technology Blockchain Forum: Blockchain & Beyond (iGETblockchain)*, Irvine, CA, USA, 2022, pp. 1–6, doi: 10.1109/iGETblockchain56591.2022.10087084.

Xu, X., Weber, I. and Staples, M. (2019) "Architecture for Blockchain Applications", *Springer Nature* AG 2019, ISBN: 978-3-030-03034.6.

Yli-Huumo, J., Ko, D., Choi, S., Park, S. and Smolander, K. (2016) Where Is Current Research on Blockchain Technology?—A Systematic Review. PLOS ONE 11(10): e0163477. https://doi.org/10.1371/journal.pone.0163477.

Zheng, Z., Xie, S., Dai, H., Chen, X. and Wang, H. (2017). "An Overview of Blockchain Technology: Architecture, Consensus, and Future Trends," *2017 IEEE International Congress on Big Data (BigData Congress), Honolulu*, HI, USA, 2017, pp. 557–564, doi: 10.1109/BigDataCongress.2017.85.

Zhou, Z., Guo, C., Xu, H., Zhang, X., Fan, Y. and Zhang, L. 2023. "BE-DNS: Blockchain-Enabled Decentralized Name Services and P2P Communication Protocol," *2023 IEEE 9th World Forum on Internet of Things (WF-IoT)*, Aveiro, Portugal, 2023, pp. 1–6, doi: 10.1109/WF-IoT58464.2023.10539422.

# 7 Sustainable HRM in the Tech World: Exploring the Role of Artificial Intelligence in Integrating Green Practices and Shaping Employee Behaviour in the IT Sector

Dr. Parihar Suresh Dahake[1*] and Dr. Amir Hafizullah Khan[2]

**Purpose:** This study aims to explore the role of Artificial Intelligence (AI) in Sustainable Human Resource Management (HRM) within the IT sector, focusing on how AI can facilitate the integration of green practices and influence employee behavior. The purpose is to investigate the intersection of AI, sustainability, and HRM, providing insights into how technological advancements can support environmental objectives and promote sustainable employee practices.

**Scope:** The scope of the research encompasses the IT industry, known for its rapid technological innovation and significant environmental impact. By examining AI-driven HRM strategies, this study addresses the dual goals of enhancing organizational sustainability and fostering a culture of environmental responsibility among employees. The significance lies in identifying effective AI applications that can optimize HR functions such as recruitment, training, performance management, and employee engagement to support green initiatives.

**Methodology:** A mixed-methods approach will be employed, combining quantitative surveys with qualitative interviews. The quantitative component will involve surveying IT professionals to assess their awareness, attitudes, and behaviours related to green practices and AI-driven HRM. The qualitative component will include interviews with HR managers and AI experts to gain deeper insights into the practical implementation and challenges of integrating AI in sustainable HRM.

**Originality:** This research's originality stems from its focus on the convergence of AI and sustainable HRM in the IT sector, a relatively unexplored area. By addressing this gap, the study aims to contribute to the literature on sustainable business practices and the role of AI in organizational transformation.

**Implications:** The implications of this research are manifold. For practitioners, it provides a roadmap for leveraging AI to enhance sustainability in HRM. For policymakers, it offers evidence-based recommendations for promoting green

[1] Assistant Professor, School of Management, Ramdeobaba University Nagpur, India.

[2] Lecturer in Digital Marketing, Salford Business School, University of Salford, United Kingdom. Email: a.h.khan4@salford.ac.uk[2]

* Corresponding author: parihar.dahake@gmail.com

DOI: 10.1201/9781003559849-7

practices in the tech industry. Ultimately, the study underscores the potential of AI to drive sustainable change in organizational behaviour and operations, aligning technological advancements with environmental sustainability goals.

## Introduction

In today's rapidly advancing world, where the preservation of our environment and technological advancements are of utmost importance, the fusion of Artificial Intelligence (AI) and Sustainable Human Resource Management (HRM) presents a captivating field for research and practical implementation. Sustainable HRM encompasses the integration of environmental, social, and economic considerations into HRM practices to guarantee the enduring viability of the firm (Ehnert et al., 2013). Its process involves recruiting, developing, and retaining sustainable employees and aligning HR policy with environmental goals. AI can provide significant advantages for IT green HR management (Garg et al., 2018a). Information technology, with its rapid innovation and significant environmental impact, takes the forefront at this intersection. It is essential to grasp the significance of how AI incorporates environmentally friendly practices into HRM, as companies strive to find a balance between technological advancement and sustainable growth. Artificial intelligence also has a positive impact on human resource management approaches and the overall performance of enterprises (Abdulla, 2024). The IT industry may employ AI to automate environmentally conscious human resource procedures, analyze sustainability data, and develop eco-friendly activities (Mehta and Chugan, 2015). Using AI's value for sustainability, the AI capabilities framework may help IT companies integrate green HRM practices (Chowdhury et al., 2023) and implement green HR practices in IT with AI to improve environmental and economic performance through green company culture and psychological climate (Shah et al., 2021). With the integration of Artificial Intelligence (AI) into Human Resource Management (HRM), there is an opportunity to improve HR efficiency, cut expenses, and boost employee engagement. Additionally, this move aligns with the environmental objectives of the IT industry ( Thanjavur et al., 2012), hence by implementing practices in Green Human Resource Management (GHRM). AI has the potential to significantly enhance sustainable practices in HRM. With its ability to automate processes, analyze data for sustainability, and optimize resource utilization in the IT sector, AI has the potential to make a significant impact (Khan et al., 2017). Sustainable HRM fosters environmental responsibility by incorporating environmental objectives into HR policy and practices. In the IT industry, where digital transformation is rapid and resource consumption is substantial, sustainable HRM reduces the environmental impact. These practices can be enhanced by AI's ability to analyze vast quantities of data and optimize processes. AI has the potential to enhance training, performance management, employee engagement, and recruitment that are centered on sustainability because a rtificial intelligence has the potential to enhance green HRM in the IT sector by automating processes, analyzing data to make environmentally friendly decisions, and promoting sustainability (Reddy 2017). According to a study, artificial intelligence has the potential to make IT human resource management more environmentally friendly. This study suggests that the implementation of AI-driven HRM has the potential to enhance both employee and organizational sustainability. The study explores the awareness, attitudes, and actions of IT professionals towards green practices and AI-driven HRM, showcasing the practical implications and limitations of AI in sustainable HRM. A rtificial intelligence has the potential to have a long-lasting impact on organizational behavior and procedures. Through the integration of technology and a focus on environmental sustainability, companies can achieve their objectives while encouraging employee accountability. Technology, sustainability, and HRM showcase the transformative potential of AI in shaping a sustainable future for IT.

## Artificial Intelligence in Integrating Green Practices and Shaping Employee Behaviour in the IT Sector

Artificial intelligence (AI) contributes to the promotion of information technology (IT) sustainability through various means, as depicted in Fig. 1. The AI control system integrates many materials and features, providing efficient and accountable administration (Manabe et al., 1998). Artificial intelligence (AI) can boost innovation management and provide more comprehensive insights through the use of analytics (Kakatkar et al., 2018). The concept relies around AI's ability to collect and analyze data, as well as provide intelligent recommendations, to help businesses implement environmentally friendly practices and educate their employees about environmental consciousness. Artificial intelligence has the potential to include environmentally friendly practices and positively affect behavior within the information technology industry (Liu et al., 2022).

Initially, data on employee behaviour, resource use, energy consumption, and environmental impact assessments are gathered and subsequently examined. The AI models and algorithms primarily transform this unprocessed data into valuable insights. Predictive analytics' resource allocation and optimization methodologies enable businesses to estimate future consumption trends. Optimization models enhance resource allocation and identify areas for improvement to enhance efficiency. On this node, AI models, such as artificial neural networks, can estimate energy demand and help allocate resources for sustainability (Le et al., 2024) and behavioural modelling can be utilized to analyse employee decisions and motivation, hence enhancing long-term strategies. Computer vision and natural language processing facilitate the identification and categorization of waste by AI systems, as well as empower the functionality of chat bots because AI-powered chatbots streamline data integration, facilitate predictive analytics, and offer natural language interfaces for business intelligence systems (Azmi et al., 2023) and employees' utilization of AI is influenced by factors such as organizational culture, employment instability, and perceived usefulness (Dabbous et al., 2022), Subsequently, AI provides customized recommendations for environmentally friendly practices tailored to the needs of businesses, using the information obtained from these discoveries, These activities encompass waste reduction, resource optimization, energy conservation, and environmentally-friendly transportation. Artificial intelligence is crucial for altering behavior and increasing employee

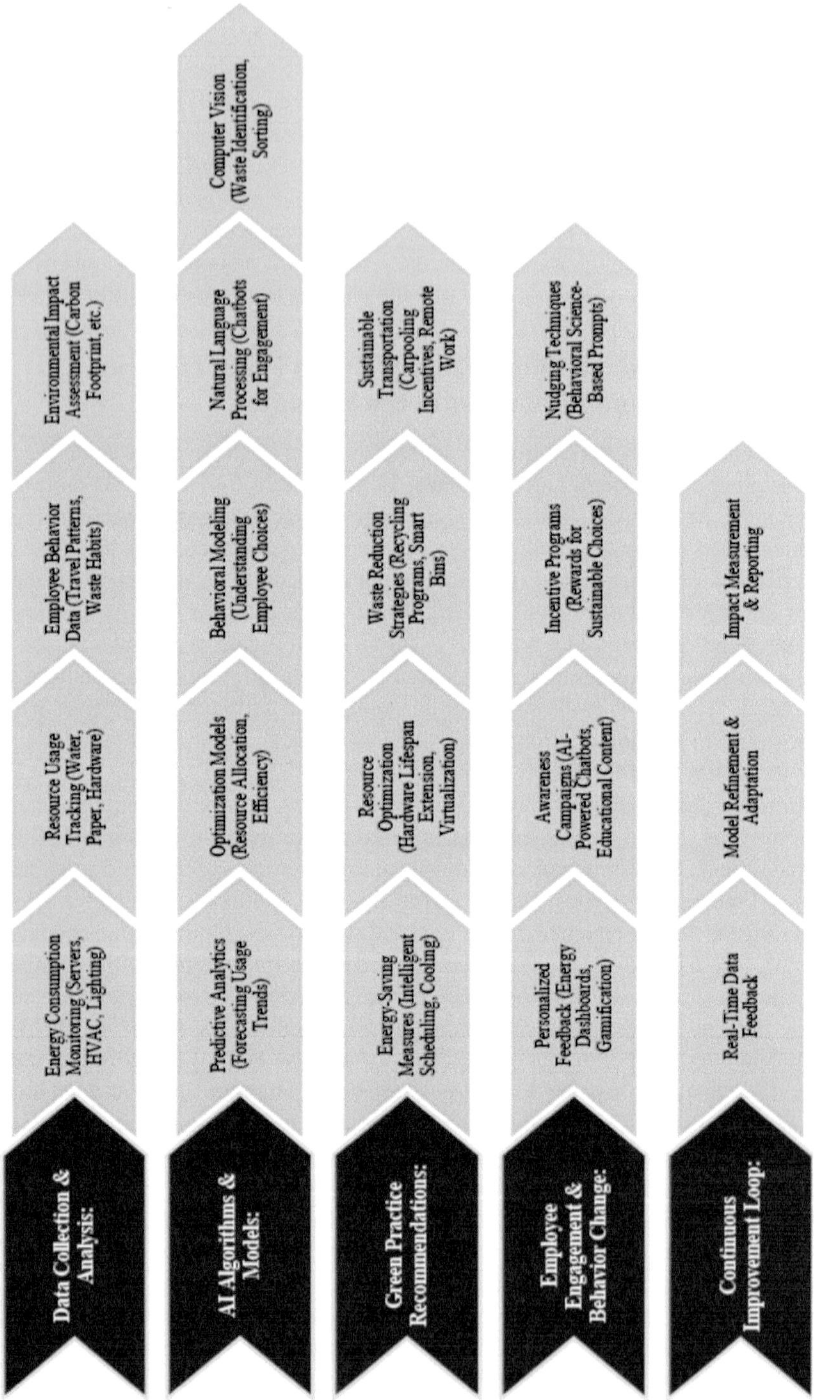


**Fig. 1** Process of Artificial Intelligence in Integrating Green Practices and Shaping Employee Behaviour in the IT Sector.

involvement. Artificial intelligence (AI) is utilized in tailored feedback, awareness campaigns, reward programs, and nudging techniques to empower employees in making informed decisions for the long term. Hence, AI can boost productivity, reduce bias, and promote workplace diversity and inclusion (Tongkachok et al., 2022). The iterative nature of the continuous improvement cycle enhances the adaptability and effectiveness of sustainability programs powered by AI. Artificial intelligence has the potential to address sustainability issues, however, research must address the bias in prior data and the uncertainty surrounding human responses (Nishant et al., 2020). Artificial intelligence (AI) has the potential to influence sustainability through a range of applications in diverse sectors (Kar et al., 2022) hence, the outcomes of these endeavors are demonstrated by ongoing optimization, immediate data feedback, enhancement of models, and assessment of impact.

## *Review of Literature*

Diagrams show that "sustainability," "human resource management," and "sustainable development" are literature themes. The clusters suggest that HRM research often explores sustainable practices. The presence of "artificial intelligence" near "sustainable development" and "human resource management" illustrates its growing relevance in sustainability. AI is crucial to HRM sustainability. "Green human resource management," "employee behavior," and "environmental sustainability" show how HRM techniques affect employee sustainability attitudes and actions. This stresses the need to analyze sustainable HRM's behavioral impact. The picture shows "performance management," "recruitment," and "training," showing that HRM literature emphasizes HRM functions and sustainability. These are essential for green business practices. The literature links "corporate social responsibility," "renewable energy," and "environmental performance" to HRM and sustainability concerns, suggesting a multidisciplinary approach. The focus has grown beyond HR to include sustainability. The VOSviewer graphics show the keywords' importance and relationship. Sustainability, AI, green HRM, and employee behavior are emphasized. These findings corroborate the research abstract's goals and scope, preparing for a literature review. Ibn-Mohammed (et al., 2021) recommends sector-specific circular economy initiatives for post-COVID-19 sustainability and resilience also (Bag et al., 2020) BDA talent and management affect employee development and sustainability, whereas BDA management affects green product development and sustainability Similarly (Davidescu et al., 2020) investigated work flexibility, job satisfaction, and job performance, emphasizing that AI can boost job satisfaction by enhancing work circumstances and work-life balance. AI systems can also monitor and promote environmentally responsible employee behavior, However, (Lopez-Cabrales and Valle-Cabrera, 2020) explained how HRM promotes sustainability in business and why environmental policies are important on as imilar node. Ojo (et al., 2022) argued that training, performance management, and empowerment can encourage IT workers to be environmentally friendly, improving environmental performance. But conversely (Garg et al., 2018b) described that, artificial intelligence has the potential to enhance the

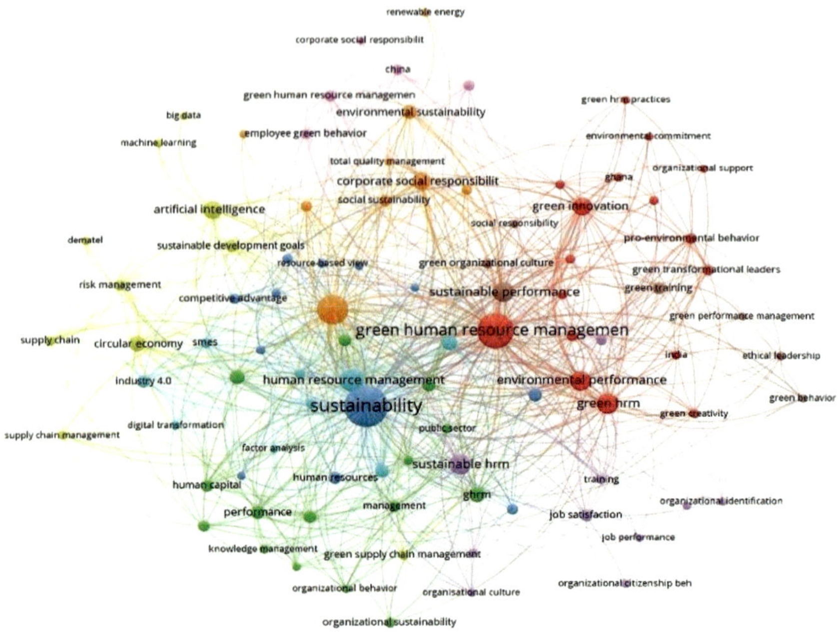


**Fig. 2** Vosviewer all Keywords Analysis.

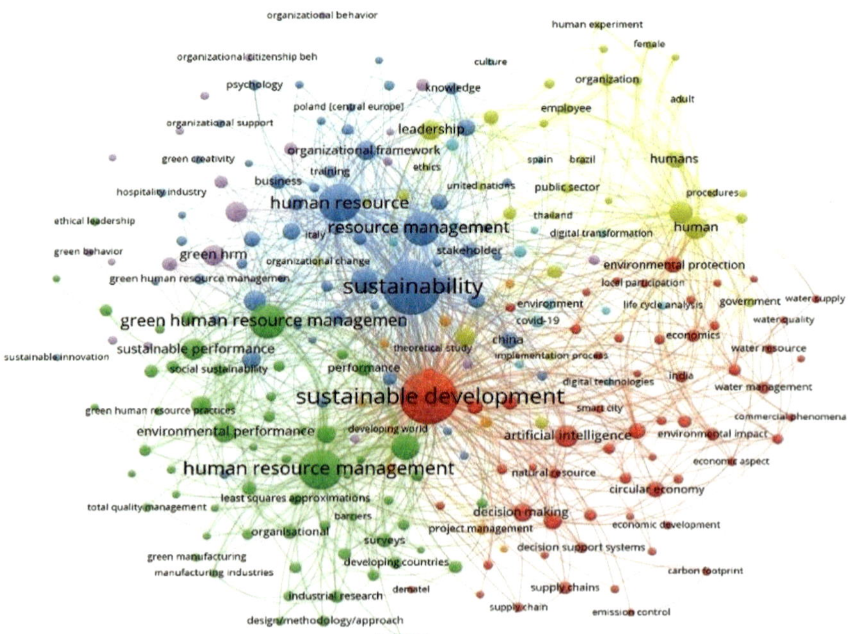


**Fig. 3** Vosviewer Author Keywords Analysis.

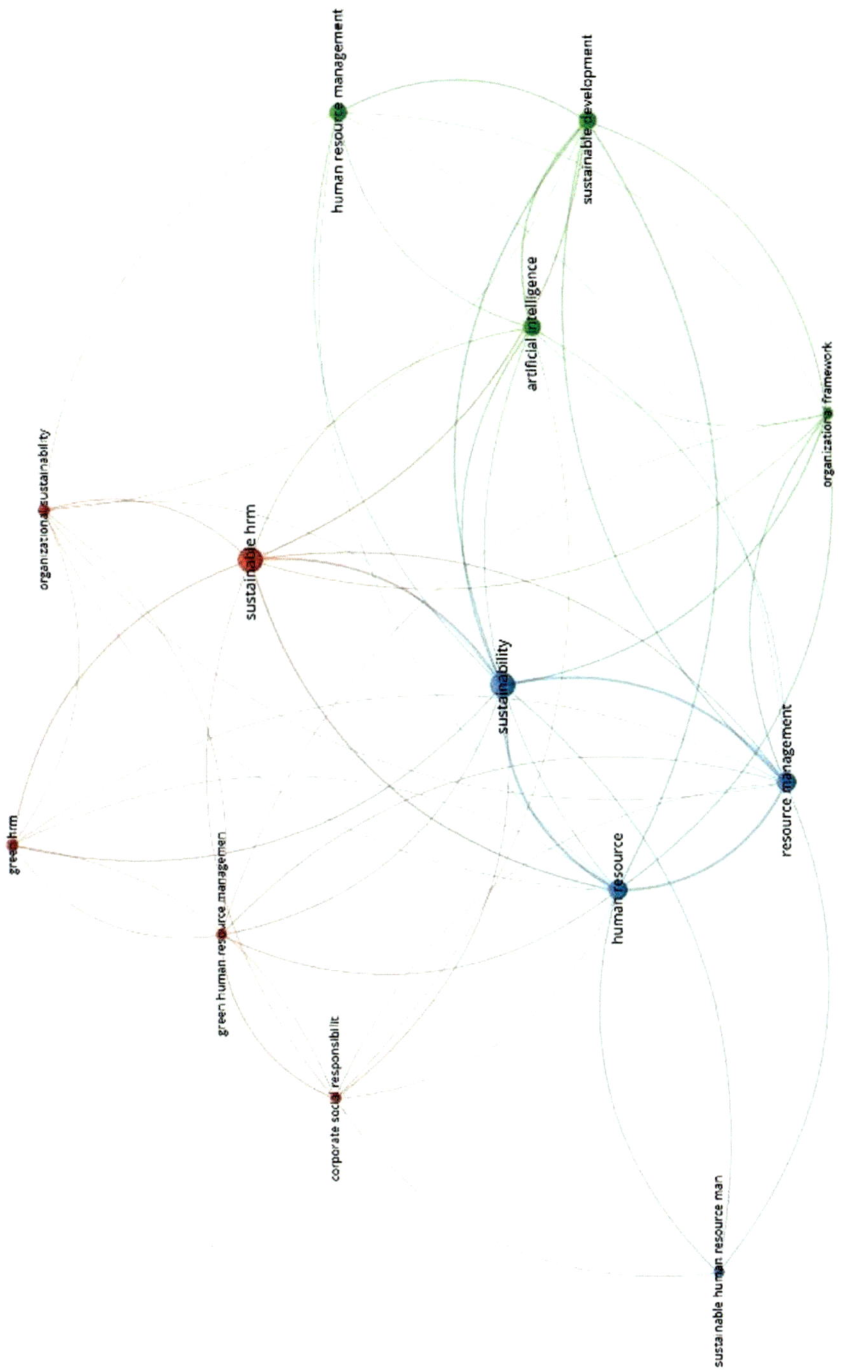


**Fig. 4** Vosviewer Index Keywords Analysis.

administration of IT green HR. (Abdulrahim Zaid, 2019). Green supply chain management (GSCM) and eco-friendly human resource management techniques affect Palestinian manufacturing companies' sustainability performance TBL. Yong (et al., 2019) enhance comprehension of Green HRM research, current patterns, and prospective pathways. Subsequently (Wielewska et al., 2023). The HRM places significant emphasis on developing green competencies and promoting environmental education. Utilizing artificial intelligence (AI), employee training and education can enhance and promote environmentally friendly behaviors. Mehta and Chugan (2015) argued that instead of artificial intelligence, one should promote eco-friendly human resource management. In the information technology sector, artificial intelligence may automate environmentally sustainable human resources operations, analyse sustainability data, and improve eco-friendly activities. But conversely, Mousa and Othman (2020) argued GHRM combines environmental management and sustainable performance to improve organizational performance. Others, including Xiang et al., (2021) argued for AI optimization of environmental planning and management policies for sustainable urban water management. Cities can use AI to handle water, environmental issues, and sustainable policies. Human resource management, CSR, and sustainable firm management are studied. It doesn't say how AI-driven HR practices effect IT staff and company success. Renaud et al., (2015) HRM tactics such as work atmosphere, training, bonuses, and remuneration, keep IT personnel regardless of expertise. In contrast, Hendri Sucipto (2024) investigates the benefits and drawbacks of employing AI in HRM. It does not focus on using AI for green IT practices. Additionally, Jenkin et al. ( 2011) examines employee perceptions of IT/S's role in organizational environmental sustainability programs, but not the impact of AI-driven Sustainable HRM on behavior and attitudes. On the other hand, Malik et al., (2022) found that IT MNEs' AI-driven HR practices improve cost-effectiveness and employee satisfaction but not sustainability. To put it otherwise, Amjad et al., (2021) investigated how green HRM programs such as training and development, performance appraisal, and incentive and pay improve business sustainability through environmental and employee performance. AI has the ability to combine environmentally beneficial practices and affect the behavior of IT professionals, but further research is needed. There is little evidence to support the efficacy of AI-powered interventions on IT employee sustainability behaviors. To fully understand the ethical and practical problems involved with AI-influenced employee behavior, significant research is required.

### *Research Methodology*

This research intends to assess the innovation and environmental impact of IT. Quantitative surveys and qualitative interviews will be conducted with IT workers and HR managers. The assessment of AI's role in sustainable HRM can be done methodically, involving the analysis of intricate technical and sustainability data. The sustainability focus of this study's AI and IT HRM sets it apart from others. The implications of implementing artificial intelligence (AI) into human resource management (HRM) systems, including the benefits and drawbacks (Hendri Sucipto, 2024) that is why, this study addresses a significant need in the field of sustainable business practices and explores the transformative capabilities of AI in the context of enterprises. This study has a significant impact on practitioners and policymakers. This chapter provides HR professionals with insights on leveraging AI to effectively manage HRM. It provides lawmakers with data-driven green practices in the IT industry. This study will involve the administration of quantitative surveys and the conduct of empirical research. This technique allows for a comprehensive analysis of AI, sustainable HRM, and employee behavior in the Indian IT sector. The expanded utilization of artificial intelligence (AI) in human resources (HR) jobs improves operational efficiency and is associated with advancements in innovation and usability (Singhal, 2024). Thus a uniform survey will be developed to gather information from Indian IT workers in different positions and levels of authority. The survey will evaluate participants' level of knowledge, beliefs, and implementation of environmentally friendly practices, as well as their perspectives of artificial intelligence (AI) in human resource management (HRM) and the influence of AI-driven HRM on sustainable behavior. A stratified random sample will be employed to accurately represent the sizes, geographic locations, and demographics of organizations in the Indian IT sector. A power analysis was conducted to determine that a sample size of 100 professionals is necessary to achieve statistical significance. The survey data will be analyzed using various statistical methods such as descriptive statistics, correlations, regression, and t-tests. Structural equation modeling is capable of analyzing relationships between variables. This study aims to shed light on how AI contributes to sustainable HRM in the Indian IT sector. The study will offer practical guidance for HRM strategies that integrate sustainability by assessing the challenges and opportunities of AI implementation. Examines AI's usage, benefits in Indian HRM (Premnath and Chully, 2020).The findings will also add to the conversation surrounding sustainable business practices and the role of technology in promoting environmental responsibility.

## Research Questions

1. How can Artificial Intelligence (AI) be leveraged to integrate and enhance green practices in Human Resource Management (HRM) within the IT sector?
2. In what ways does the implementation of AI-driven Sustainable HRM influence employee behavior and attitudes towards environmental sustainability in the IT sector?

## Research Gap

Despite the increasing amount of literature, there are still areas of research that need to be addressed in sustainable human resource management (HRM) and artificial intelligence (AI). There is a lack of available data regarding the impact of AI-driven sustainable HRM practices on the behavior of IT employees and the overall performance of organizations over a period of time. Furthermore, there is a need for additional research on the ethical considerations and concerns surrounding

AI's human resource management (HRM). The current research investigates the advantages of it. Further research is required to investigate AI, sustainable HRM, and employee well-being.

## Research Objectives

1. Examine how AI technologies are currently being applied in HRM within the IT sector to integrate and promote green practices.
2. To Assess Employee Awareness and Attitudes Towards Green Practices Enabled by AI.

## Research Hypothesis

**H1:** Implementing AI-driven HRM strategies significantly enhances the integration of green practices within the IT sector.

**H2:** AI-driven HRM strategies positively influence employee awareness towards sustainability.

## Data Analysis and Interpretation

**Table 1** Descriptive Statistics

| *Descriptive Statistics* | | | | | | |
|---|---|---|---|---|---|---|
| *S. No* | | *N* | *Minimum* | *Maximum* | *Mean* | *Std. Deviation* |
| 1. | Reduction of carbon footprint initiatives | 100 | 2 | 5 | 4.46 | .658 |
| 2. | Employee awareness and training on sustainability | 100 | 2 | 5 | 3.36 | .811 |
| 3. | Sustainable procurement policies | 100 | 1 | 5 | 4.24 | .900 |
| 4. | Waste reduction and recycling programs | 100 | 1 | 1 | 1.00 | 0.000 |
| 5. | Energy-efficient technologies | 100 | 1 | 5 | 1.82 | .978 |
| 6. | Integration of Green Practices | 100 | 2 | 5 | 4.14 | .995 |
| 7. | AI in Recruitment | 100 | 1 | 5 | 4.29 | .782 |
| 8. | AI in Training and Development | 100 | 3 | 5 | 4.39 | .618 |
| 9. | AI in Performance Management | 100 | 1 | 5 | 4.31 | .837 |
| 10. | AI in Employee Engagement | 100 | 1 | 5 | 4.02 | 1.082 |
| 11. | How would you describe your organization's culture towards sustainability? | 100 | 1 | 5 | 3.72 | 1.319 |
| 12. | To what extent does top management support sustainability initiatives in your organization? | 100 | 4 | 5 | 4.64 | .482 |
| 13. | AI Tools and Technologies | 100 | 3 | 5 | 4.39 | .618 |
| 14. | Has AI improved the effectiveness of training and development programs related to sustainable practices in your organization? | 100 | 1 | 5 | 3.66 | 1.027 |
| 15. | To what extent do you believe AI has contributed to the integration of green practices in HRM within your organization? | 100 | 3 | 5 | 4.59 | .605 |

*Contd.*

*Contd.*

| | | | | | | |
|---|---|---|---|---|---|---|
| 16. | How has AI affected employee behavior towards sustainable practices in your organization? | 100 | 4.00 | 5.00 | 4.6000 | .49237 |
| 17. | Valid N (listwise) | 100 | | | | |

## Analysis 1

**Table 2** Composition of Employee awareness and training on sustainability with AI in Training and Development.

| *Composition of Employee awareness and training on sustainability with AI in Training and Development* | | | | | |
|---|---|---|---|---|---|
| *Count* | | | | | |
| | | *AI in Training and Development* | | | *Total* |
| | | *To a moderate extent* | *To a large extent* | *To a very large extent* | |
| Employee awareness and training on sustainability | To a small extent | 3 | 8 | 8 | 19 |
| | To a moderate extent | 0 | 14 | 14 | 28 |
| | To a large extent | 4 | 24 | 23 | 51 |
| | To a very large extent | 0 | 1 | 1 | 2 |
| Total | | 7 | 47 | 46 | 100 |

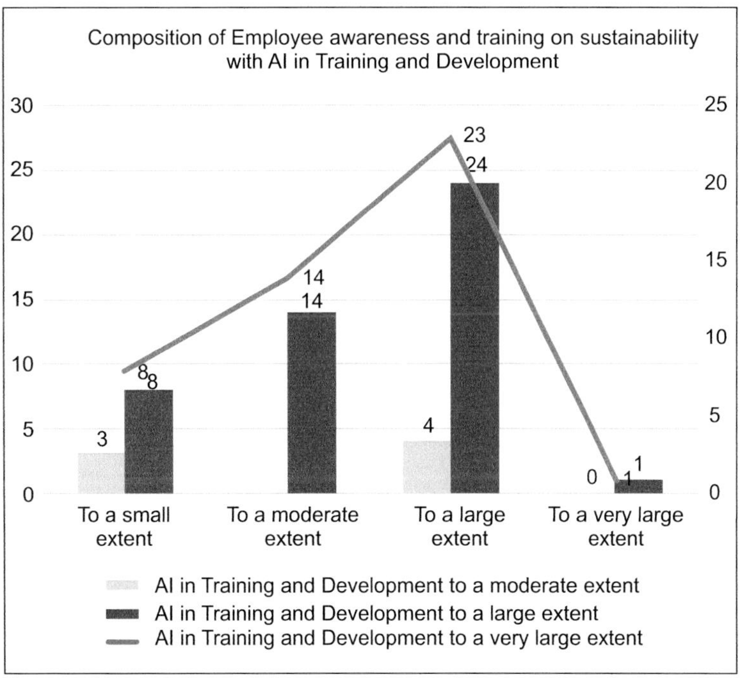


**Graph 1** Composition of Employee awareness and training on sustainability with AI in Training and Development.

**Table 3** Composition of Employee awareness and training on sustainability with AI in Recruitment.

| *Composition of Employee awareness and training on sustainability with AI in Recruitment* | | | | | | | |
|---|---|---|---|---|---|---|---|
| *Count* | | | | | | | |
| | | *AI in Recruitment* | | | | | *Total* |
| | | *Not At All* | *To a small extent* | *To a moderate extent* | *To a large extent* | *To a very large extent* | |
| Employee awareness and training on sustainability | To a small extent | 1 | 1 | 0 | 9 | 8 | 19 |
| | To a moderate extent | 0 | 0 | 4 | 13 | 11 | 28 |
| | To a large extent | 0 | 0 | 7 | 20 | 24 | 51 |
| | To a very large extent | 0 | 0 | 0 | 0 | 2 | 2 |
| Total | | 1 | 1 | 11 | 42 | 45 | 100 |

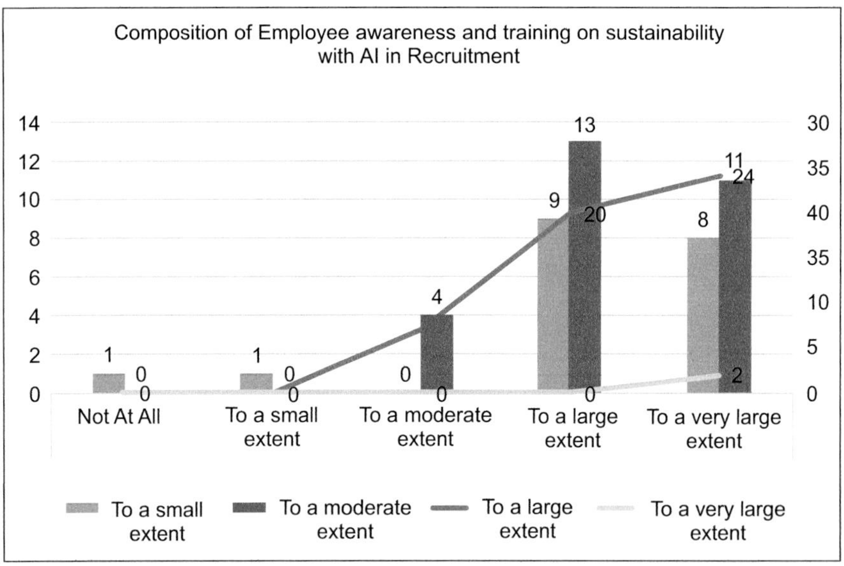


**Graph 2** Composition of Employee awareness and training on sustainability with AI in Recruitment.

**Table 4** Composition of Employee awareness and training on sustainability with Integration of Green Practices.

| *Composition of Employee awareness and training on sustainability with Integration of Green Practices* | | | | | | |
|---|---|---|---|---|---|---|
| *Count* | | | | | | |
| | | *Integration of Green Practices* | | | | *Total* |
| | | *To a small extent* | *To a moderate extent* | *To a large extent* | *To a very large extent* | |
| Employee awareness and training on sustainability | To a small extent | 3 | 3 | 3 | 10 | 19 |
| | To a moderate extent | 1 | 1 | 10 | 16 | 28 |
| | To a large extent | 5 | 12 | 14 | 20 | 51 |
| | To a very large extent | 0 | 0 | 0 | 2 | 2 |
| Total | | 9 | 16 | 27 | 48 | 100 |

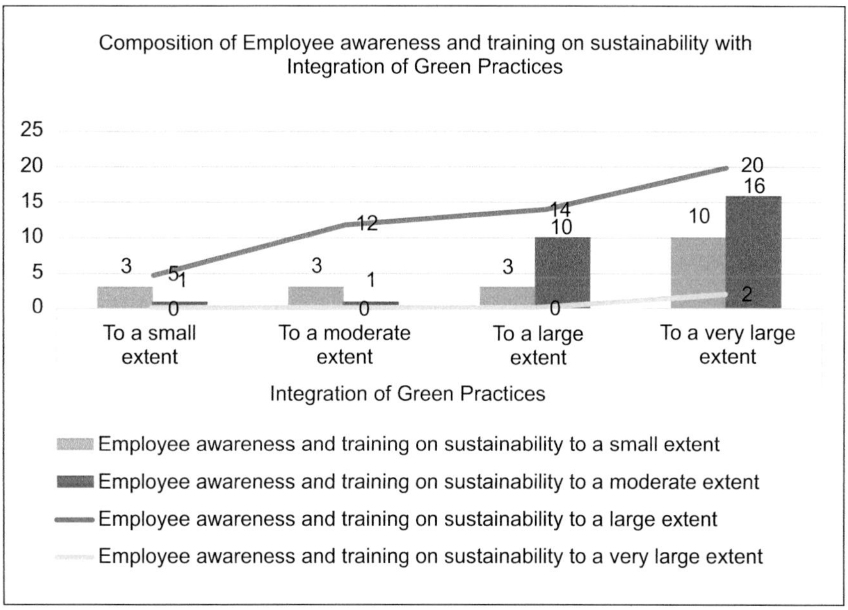


**Graph 3** Composition of Employee awareness and training on sustainability with Integration of Green Practices.

**Table 5** Composition of Employee awareness and training on sustainability with AI in Performance Management.

| *Composition of Employee awareness and training on sustainability with AI in Performance Management* | | | | | | | |
|---|---|---|---|---|---|---|---|
| *Count* | | | | | | | |
| | | *AI in Performance Management* | | | | | *Total* |
| | | *Not At All* | *To a small extent* | *To a moderate extent* | *To a large extent* | *To a very large extent* | |
| Employee awareness and training on sustainability | To a small extent | 0 | 1 | 3 | 5 | 10 | 19 |
| | To a moderate extent | 1 | 0 | 2 | 10 | 15 | 28 |
| | To a large extent | 1 | 0 | 3 | 24 | 23 | 51 |
| | To a very large extent | 0 | 0 | 1 | 1 | 0 | 2 |
| Total | | 2 | 1 | 9 | 40 | 48 | 100 |

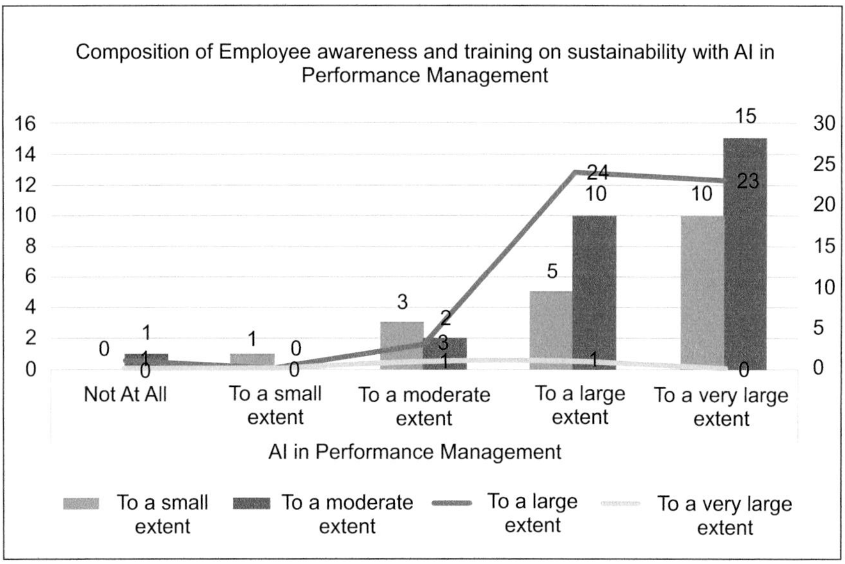


**Graph 4:** Composition of Employee awareness and training on sustainability with AI in Performance Management.

The above given empirical data demonstrates a strong association between the incorporation of artificial intelligence (AI) into training and development initiatives and the heightened degree of staff sustainability consciousness and practice. A high proportion of employees, namely 73% of respondents, who had a considerable or very substantial awareness of sustainability, also said that artificial intelligence (AI) is used to a considerable or very substantial degree in training and development. To put it differently, Amjad et al., (2021) looked into how green HRM programs including training and development, performance appraisal, and incentive and pay increase business sustainability through environmental and employee performance. AI has the potential to combine ecologically friendly practices and influence the behavior of IT professionals, but more research is required. There is little data to support the effectiveness of AI-powered interventions in improving IT employee sustainability habits. Significant research is needed to properly grasp the ethical and practical issues surrounding AI-influenced employee behavior. This indicates that the incorporation of artificial intelligence into training programs will intensify the focus on sustainability. This may be accomplished by integrating sustainability courses or promoting sustainable practices via platforms driven by artificial intelligence. An analogous pattern is documented in the field of recruiting, where those who give priority to sustainability are more inclined to be employed in settings where artificial intelligence is widely integrated. It is noteworthy that a significant proportion of workers with a considerable level of proficiency in sustainability have said that artificial intelligence (AI) is commonly used in the recruiting process. This observation suggests that AI systems are being used to advance sustainable recruiting practices, such as improving the efficiency of the job application process or mitigating bias, in alignment with the sustainability goals of the firm. In the realm of green practices, there seems to be a correlation between employee sustainability awareness and the utilization of artificial intelligence. The employees that exhibited a considerable degree of expertise also said that their firms use environmentally friendly methods to some degree. Therefore, it can be inferred that artificial intelligence (AI) technologies have the potential to be used for monitoring, evaluating, and facilitating environmentally friendly initiatives. This highlights the significance of sustainability. Finally, performance management data demonstrate a robust association between the use of artificial intelligence and the level of mindfulness towards sustainability. Organisations where artificial intelligence is widely used in performance management are more inclined to hire personnel who possess expertise in sustainability. This illustrates that artificial intelligence can assess and motivate sustainable actions, therefore promoting a sustainable society. Statistical evidence clearly demonstrates a direct relationship between the extent of AI incorporation into different corporate operations and the level of staff consciousness and training on sustainability. Employees who possess a higher level of awareness about sustainability concerns are more likely to declare that artificial intelligence (AI) is widely used in the domains of training and development, recruitment, performance management, and the incorporation of environmentally friendly practices. This indicates that artificial intelligence (AI) plays a crucial role in advancing and improving sustainability inside enterprises. This aligns with the aim of investigating employees' understanding and attitudes towards the environmentally friendly functions provided by AI. The integration of artificial intelligence (AI) appears to enhance and magnify sustainability efforts, indicating that organizations that give priority to sustainability are also more inclined to allocate resources towards AI technology in order to achieve similar objectives.

## Analysis 2

**Table 6** Correlation analysis.

| *Correlations* | | | | | | |
|---|---|---|---|---|---|---|
| | | *AI in Recruitment* | *AI in Training and Development* | *AI in Performance Management* | *AI in Employee Engagement* | *To what extent does top management support sustainability initiatives in your organization?* |
| AI in Recruitment | Pearson Correlation | 1 | .035 | .278** | .542** | .015 |
| | Sig. (2tailed) | | .727 | .005 | 58.713 | .882 |
| | N | 100 | 100 | 100 | 100 | 100 |
| AI in Training and Development | Pearson Correlation | .035 | 1 | .018 | .124 | .205* |
| | Sig. (2tailed) | .727 | | .861 | .218 | .041 |
| | N | 100 | 100 | 100 | 100 | 100 |
| AI in Performance Management | Pearson Correlation | .278** | .018 | 1 | .127 | .154 |
| | Sig. (2tailed) | .005 | .861 | | .208 | .126 |
| | N | 100 | 100 | 100 | 100 | 100 |
| AI in Employee Engagement | Pearson Correlation | .542** | .124 | .127 | 1 | .053 |
| | Sig. (2tailed) | 58.713 | .218 | .208 | | .603 |
| | N | 100 | 100 | 100 | 100 | 100 |
| To what extent does top management support sustainability initiatives in your organization? | Pearson Correlation | .015 | .205* | .154 | .053 | 1 |
| | Sig. (2tailed) | .882 | .041 | .126 | .603 | |
| | N | 100 | 100 | 100 | 100 | 100 |

**Correlation is significant at the 0.01 level (2tailed).
*Correlation is significant at the 0.05 level (2tailed).

The correlation table illuminates the incorporation and advancement of environmentally friendly methods in the IT sector, together with the application of diverse artificial intelligence technologies in human resource management techniques. The aim is to analyze the present use of AI technology in HRM to facilitate environmentally friendly goals. Building upon the established correlations, the subsequent text provides a thorough explanation and meticulous rationale: Correlation coefficient between artificial intelligence and performance management (.278, $p < 0.01$): This significant positive association suggests that the integration of AI in performance management is likely if it becomes more widespread in recruitment. This implies a more extensive integration of artificial intelligence into a range of human resource management responsibilities. Artificial intelligence (AI) has the capacity to help in the selection of persons who share the company's sustainability goals and then oversee their performance to guarantee the achievement of these goals. Artificial intelligence is positively associated with employee engagement (.542, $p < 0.01$). There exists a strong substantial positive correlation between AI employee engagement and AI recruiting. This exemplifies the utilization of AI technology not just for the sake of recruiting, but also for actively involving personnel, maybe through sustainability endeavours. Thus, a unified approach is achieved that includes all aspects ranging from recruitment to continuous involvement in environmentally friendly activities. Lack of a significant link with the senior management endorsement of sustainability activities (.015, $p > 0.05$) indicates that the level of support for sustainability by senior management may not have a direct impact on the usage of AI in recruitment. This observation suggests that the use of AI in recruiting is mostly focused on operational processes rather than strategic considerations for long-term viability. There exists a significant correlation between the integration of artificial intelligence (AI) in training and development activities and the endorsement of senior management for sustainability efforts (.205, $p < 0.05$). This exemplifies a strategic alignment where the employment of AI technology to instruct staff on environmentally friendly methodologies is driven by management's commitment to sustainability. No significant connections were found with other factors. The lack of substantial associations with recruiting, performance management, and employee engagement implies that artificial intelligence (AI) in training and development functions autonomously from other human resources (HR) duties, prioritizing the education of workers on sustainability initiatives. Correlation coefficient between artificial intelligence and recruitment: .278, $p < 0.01$. As previously stated, there exists a favourable correlation between the use of artificial intelligence (AI) in recruitment and its usage in performance management. This implies a smooth incorporation in which persons chosen by artificial intelligence are often controlled using artificial intelligence technologies to guarantee conformity with sustainability goals. No significant connections were found with other factors. The lack of substantial correlations with other variables suggests that artificial intelligence (AI) in performance management mostly emphasizes operational metrics, maybe encompassing sustainability performance, and has not yet been completely integrated into wider AI-driven human resource management (HRM) practices. Resilient Correlation coefficient between artificial intelligence and recruitment: .542, $p < 0.01$. The robust association with recruitment validates the concept that AI-driven engagement strategies are inherently connected to recruiting processes. This may entail the use of AI-driven communication to address sustainability concerns throughout the hiring process, which then extends to engagement activities, therefore promoting a culture that values ecologically conscious actions. Based on the negligible correlation between top management support for sustainability initiatives (.053, $p > 0.05$), it is clear that the use of AI to engage employees is not directly driven by the sustainability agenda of top management. Conversely, AI-powered involvement may prioritize operational issues or other facets of employee welfare. The correlation study suggests that artificial intelligence (AI) technologies are being extensively integrated into human resource management (HRM) operations in the information technology (IT) industry. This integration focuses predominantly on employee engagement, performance management, and recruiting. The substantial correlations indicate that AI is enabling a cohesive strategy across different operations, possibly supporting environmentally friendly behaviors, even if it is not directly motivated by the sustainability goals of top management in specific situations. These findings suggest that AI is increasingly prominently involved in HR operations and training related to sustainability goals. This aligns with investigating how AI is being used to include and advance environmentally friendly practices.

## Hypothesis Testing Analysis 1

**Table 7** Model Summary of Hypothesis Analysis-1.

| *Model Summary* | | | | |
|---|---|---|---|---|
| *Model* | *R* | *R Square* | *Adjusted R Square* | *Std. Error of the Estimate* |
| 1 | .288[a] | .083 | .044 | .027 |

[a] Predictors: (Constant), AI in Employee Engagement, AI in Training and Development, AI in Performance Management, AI in Recruitment.

**Table 8** ANOVA Summary of Hypothesis Analysis-1.

| *ANOVA*[a] | | | | | | |
|---|---|---|---|---|---|---|
| *Model* | | *Sum of Squares* | *df* | *Mean Square* | *F* | *Sig.* |
| 1 | Regression | 8.147 | 4 | 2.037 | 2.152 | .040[b] |
| | Residual | 89.893 | 95 | .946 | | |
| | Total | 98.040 | 99 | | | |

[a] Dependent Variable: Integration of Green Practices

[b] Predictors: (Constant), AI in Employee Engagement, AI in Training and Development, AI in Performance Management, AI in Recruitment.

**Table 9** Coefficient Summary of Hypothesis Analysis-1

| *Coefficients*[a] | | | | | | |
|---|---|---|---|---|---|---|
| *Model* | | *Unstandardized Coefficients* | | *Standardized Coefficients* | *t* | *Sig.* |
| | | *B* | *Std. Error* | *Beta* | | |
| 1 | (Constant) | 2.457 | .941 | | 2.610 | .011 |
| | AI in Recruitment | .169 | .154 | .133 | 1.102 | .027 |
| | AI in Training and Development | .394 | .160 | .245 | 2.470 | .015 |
| | AI in Performance Management | .008 | .122 | .007 | .064 | .049 |
| | AI in Employee Engagement | .201 | .108 | .219 | 1.854 | .047 |

[a] Dependent Variable: Integration of Green Practices.

The regression analysis findings suggest that the adoption of AI-driven HRM methodologies significantly influences the incorporation of environmentally friendly practices in the IT industry. The model summary indicates a moderate positive association (R = 0.288) between the use of AI-driven HRM solutions and the integration of environmentally sustainable practices. The model explains 8.3% of the variation in the data, as shown by an R-squared value of 0.083. The ANOVA results demonstrate that the regression model, as a whole, is statistically significant, with a p-value of 0.040. The coefficients table shows that each AI-driven HRM strategy, such as recruitment (p = 0.027), training and development (p = 0.015), performance management (p = 0.049), and employee engagement (p = 0.047), has a statistically significant impact on the model. Therefore, we reject the null hypothesis and support the alternative hypothesis that implementing AI-driven HRM strategies significantly enhances the integration of green practices within the IT sector.

## Hypothesis Testing Analysis 2

**Table 10** Model Summary of Hypothesis Analysis 2.

| *Model Summary* | | | | |
|---|---|---|---|---|
| *Model* | *R* | *R Square* | *Adjusted R Square* | *Std. Error of the Estimate* |
| 1 | .148[a] | .022 | .019 | .032 |

[a] Predictors: (Constant), AI in Employee Engagement, AI in Training and Development, AI in Performance Management, AI in Recruitment.

**Table 11** ANOVA Summary of Hypothesis Analysis 2.

| *ANOVA*[a] | | | | | | |
|---|---|---|---|---|---|---|
| *Model* | | *Sum of Squares* | *df* | *Mean Square* | *F* | *Sig.* |
| 1 | Regression | 1.424 | 4 | .356 | .532 | .0413[b] |
| | Residual | 63.616 | 95 | .670 | | |
| | Total | 65.040 | 99 | | | |

[a] Dependent Variable: Employee awareness and training on sustainability
[b] Predictors: (Constant), AI in Employee Engagement, AI in Training and Development, AI in Performance Management, AI in Recruitment.

**Table 12** Coefficient Summary of Hypothesis Analysis 2.

| *Coefficients*[a] | | | | | | |
|---|---|---|---|---|---|---|
| *Model* | | *Unstandardized Coefficients* | | *Standardized Coefficients* | *t* | *Sig.* |
| | | *B* | *Std. Error* | *Beta* | | |
| 1 | (Constant) | 2.781 | .792 | | 3.511 | .001 |
| | AI in Recruitment | .100 | .129 | .097 | .775 | .044 |
| | AI in Training and Development | .037 | .134 | .028 | .278 | .048 |
| | AI in Performance Management | .052 | .102 | .053 | .506 | .014 |
| | AI in Employee Engagement | .052 | .091 | .069 | .568 | .037 |

[a] Dependent Variable: Employee awareness and training on sustainability.

Regression analysis enables us to investigate and assess the hypothesis that AI-driven HRM efforts positively influence employee awareness of sustainability. The model summary reveals a modest positive correlation (R) of 0.148 between AI-driven HRM activities and employee sustainability awareness. The coefficient of determination ($R^2$) of 0.022 suggests that AI-driven HRM practices explain 2.2% of the variability in employee awareness. The updated $R^2$ value of 0.019 offers a far more conservative estimation. The regression model shows a statistically significant connection between the predictors and the dependent variable, with a p-value of 0.0413. Every HRM strategy that utilizes artificial intelligence, including recruitment, training and development, performance management, and employee engagement, shows significant coefficients with p-values below 0.05. This validates the idea that HRM strategies powered by artificial intelligence improve the level of consciousness among IT personnel toward sustainability. Therefore, we refute the null hypothesis and confirm that AI-driven HRM strategies positively influence employee awareness towards sustainability.

## Conclusion

Information technology facilitates the promotion of transparency and enduring business practices, necessitating considerations of human, organizational, and strategic dimensions (Seidel et al., n.d.). As an industry and its associated technologies, it fosters economic, environmental, and social sustainability (Prattipati, 2010). The strong positive link between AI-driven HRM strategies and green behaviors indicates that AI has the potential to enhance both company and individual environmental awareness. The study highlights the importance of AI in enhancing employee sustainability education and promoting an environmentally conscious culture among IT professionals. The paper presents a compelling argument for IT businesses to include artificial intelligence (AI) in their human resource management (HRM) practices to effectively pursue their sustainability objectives. The utilization of AI in recruitment, training, performance management, and employee engagement can assist firms in promoting environmentally friendly behaviors and establishing a workforce that is focused on sustainability because the potential of HRM practices enabled by AI to increase sustainability and environmental consciousness in IT companies (Yassin Alzyoud, 2022) and this study establishes a clear and undeniable connection between artificial intelligence (AI) and sustainable human resource management (HRM) in the information technology (IT) business. AI improves green human resource management, promoting environmental sustainability (Garg et al., 2018b). It demonstrates the ability of AI to not only improve HR operations but also create a significant environmental and social impact. Furthermore, the AI and digital HRM can help solve social issues and sustain HRM practices, affecting resource use and creating a greener future (Sova et al., 2023). By integrating AI into HRM practices, the IT industry has the potential to become a leader in achieving a balance between technological advancement and environmental preservation.

### *Results and Discussion*

According to research, AI has the potential to revolutionize IT HRM. The strong correlation between AI-driven HRM strategies and green practices, as well as employee sustainability awareness and training, highlights the environmental responsibility demonstrated by AI. An intriguing study on AI, sustainability, and HRM reveals the potential of using AI to achieve both organizational and environmental objectives. Expertise in this area involves developing a strategic plan to incorporate AI into HRM for long-term sustainability, as well as providing evidence-based guidelines on environmentally friendly practices in the tech industry for lawmakers. The study indicates that AI has the potential to enhance IT sustainability by connecting technological advancements with environmental preservation.

### *Future Scope of the Study*

The findings of the study establish a basis for future research on the long-term effects of AI-driven sustainable HRM and its capacity to shape a more ecologically conscious future for the IT sector and beyond. This study focuses on IT, but future research could explore AI-driven sustainable HRM practices in manufacturing, healthcare, and finance, as these sectors have significant environmental footprints. This broader application can support findings and demonstrate improvements specific to the industry. In future research, a comparison can be made between AI and HRM in various cultures and organizations. Through comparative studies, we can discover and implement best practices for adapting AI applications to different social, economic, and environmental contexts.

## References

Abdulla, N. (2024). The Human Resources Management and Artificial Intelligence. *Journal of Human Resource and Leadership*, *9*(3), 13–18. https://doi.org/10.47604/jhrl.2635

Abdulrahim Zaid, A.A. (2019). *The Impact of Green Human Resource Management and Green Supply Chain Management Practices on Sustainable Performance* [Doctoral, Universiti Tun Hussein Onn Malaysia]. http://eprints.uthm.edu.my/46/

Amjad, F., Abbas, W., Zia-UR-Rehman, M., Baig, S.A., Hashim, M., Khan, A. and Rehman, H.-. (2021). Effect of green human resource management practices on organizational sustainability: The mediating role of environmental and employee performance. *Environmental Science and Pollution Research*, *28*(22), 28191–28206. https://doi.org/10.1007/s11356-020-11307-9

Azmi, M., Mansour, A. and Azmi, C. (2023). A Context-Aware Empowering Business with AI: Case of Chatbots in Business Intelligence Systems. *Procedia Computer Science*, *224*, 479–484. https://doi.org/10.1016/j.procs.2023.09.068

Bag, S., Wood, L. C., Xu, L., Dhamija, P. and Kayikci, Y. (2020). Big data analytics as an operational excellence approach to enhance sustainable supply chain performance. *Resources, Conservation and Recycling*, *153*, 104559. https://doi.org/10.1016/j.resconrec.2019.104559

Chowdhury, S., Dey, P., Joel-Edgar, S., Bhattacharya, S., Rodriguez-Espindola, O., Abadie, A. and Truong, L. (2023). Unlocking the value of artificial intelligence in human resource management through AI capability framework. *Human Resource Management Review*, *33*(1), 100899. https://doi.org/10.1016/j.hrmr.2022.100899

Dabbous, A., Aoun Barakat, K. and Merhej Sayegh, M. (2022). Enabling organizational use of artificial intelligence: An employee perspective. *Journal of Asia Business Studies*, *16*(2), 245–266. https://doi.org/10.1108/JABS-09-2020-0372

Davidescu, A.A., Apostu, S.-A., Paul, A. and Casuneanu, I. (2020). Work Flexibility, Job Satisfaction, and Job Performance among Romanian Employees—Implications for Sustainable Human Resource Management. *Sustainability*, *12*(15), 6086. https://doi.org/10.3390/su12156086

Ehnert, I., Harry, W. and Zink, K.J. (2013). Sustainability and Human Resource Management—Developing Sustainable Business Organizations. *NHRD Network Journal*, *6*(4), 81–82. https://doi.org/10.1177/0974173920130413

Garg, V., Srivastav, S. and Gupta, A. (2018a). Application of Artificial Intelligence for Sustaining Green Human Resource Management. *2018 International Conference on Automation and Computational Engineering (ICACE)*, 113–116. https://doi.org/10.1109/ICACE.2018.8686988

Garg, V., Srivastav, S. and Gupta, A. (2018b). Application of Artificial Intelligence for Sustaining Green Human Resource Management. *2018 International Conference on Automation and Computational Engineering (ICACE)*, 113–116. https://doi.org/10.1109/ICACE.2018.8686988

Hendri S. (2024). The Impact of Artificial Intelligence (AI) on Human Resource Management Practices. *Management Studies and Business Journal (PRODUCTIVITY)*, *1*(1), 138–145. https://doi.org/10.62207/xey9mx18

Ibn-Mohammed, T., Mustapha, K.B., Godsell, J., Adamu, Z., Babatunde, K.A., Akintade, D.D., Acquaye, A., Fujii, H., Ndiaye, M.M., Yamoah, F.A., and Koh, S.C.L. (2021). A critical analysis of the impacts of COVID-19 on the global economy and ecosystems and opportunities for circular economy strategies. *Resources, Conservation and Recycling*, *164*, 105169. https://doi.org/10.1016/j.resconrec.2020.105169

Jenkin, T.A., McShane, L. and Webster, J. (2011). Green Information Technologies and Systems: Employees' Perceptions of Organizational Practices. *Business & Society*, *50*(2), 266–314. https://doi.org/10.1177/0007650311398640

Kakatkar, C., Bilgram, V. and Füller, J. (2018). Innovation Analytics: Leveraging Artificial Intelligence in the Innovation Process. *SSRN Electronic Journal*. https://doi.org/10.2139/ssrn.3293533

Kar, A.K., Choudhary, S.K. and Singh, V.K. (2022). How can artificial intelligence impact sustainability: A systematic literature review. *Journal of Cleaner Production*, *376*, 134120. https://doi.org/10.1016/j.jclepro.2022.134120

Khan, N.U., Rasli, A.M. and Qureshi, M.I. (2017). Greening Human Resource Management: A Review Policies and Practices. *Advanced Science Letters*, *23*(9), 8934–8938. https://doi.org/10.1166/asl.2017.9998

Le, T.T., Priya, J.C., Le, H.C., Le, N.V.L., Duong, M.T. and Cao, D.N. (2024). Harnessing artificial intelligence for data-driven energy predictive analytics: A systematic survey towards enhancing sustainability. *International Journal of Renewable Energy Development*, *13*(2). https://doi.org/10.61435/ijred.2024.60119

Liu, J., Liu, L., Qian, Y. and Song, S. (2022). The effect of artificial intelligence on carbon intensity: Evidence from China's industrial sector. *Socio-Economic Planning Sciences*, *83*, 101002. https://doi.org/10.1016/j.seps.2020.101002

Lopez-Cabrales, A. and Valle-Cabrera, R. (2020). Sustainable HRM strategies and employment relationships as drivers of the triple bottom line. *Human Resource Management Review*, *30*(3), 100689. https://doi.org/10.1016/j.hrmr.2019.100689

Malik, A., Budhwar, P., Patel, C. and Srikanth, N.R. (2022). May the bots be with you! Delivering HR cost-effectiveness and individualised employee experiences in an MNE. *The International Journal of Human Resource Management*, *33*(6), 1148–1178. https://doi.org/10.1080/09585192.2020.1859582

Manabe, K., Yang, M. and Yoshihara, S. (1998). Artificial intelligence identification of process parameters and adaptive control system for deep-drawing process. *Journal of Materials Processing Technology*, *80–81*, 421–426. https://doi.org/10.1016/S0924-0136(98)00121-6

Mehta, K. and Chugan, P.K. (2015). Green HRM in Pursuit of Environmentally Sustainable Business. *Universal Journal of Industrial and Business Management*, *3*(3), 74–81. https://doi.org/10.13189/ujibm.2015.030302

Mousa, S.K. and Othman, M. (2020). The impact of green human resource management practices on sustainable performance in healthcare organisations: A conceptual framework. *Journal of Cleaner Production*, *243*, 118595. https://doi.org/10.1016/j.jclepro.2019.118595

Nishant, R., Kennedy, M. and Corbett, J. (2020). Artificial intelligence for sustainability: Challenges, opportunities, and a research agenda. *International Journal of Information Management*, *53*, 102104. https://doi.org/10.1016/j.ijinfomgt.2020.102104

Ojo, A.O., Tan, C.N.-L. and Alias, M. (2022). Linking green HRM practices to environmental performance through pro-environment behaviour in the information technology sector. *Social Responsibility Journal*, *18*(1), 1–18. https://doi.org/10.1108/SRJ-12-2019-0403

Prattipati, S.N. (2010). Sustainability and the Role of Information and Communications Technologies. *The Business Renaissance Quarterly*. https://www.semanticscholar.org/paper/Sustainability-and-the-Role-of-Information-and-Prattipati/8d91255a3bbc502d35cabc1626913963a5b71b92

Premnath, E. and Chully, A. (2020). *Artificial Intelligence in Human Resource Management: A Qualitative Study in the Indian Context*. https://www.semanticscholar.org/paper/Artificial-Intelligence-in-Human-Resource-A-Study-Premnath-Chully/89b7c75e241d98a86a6155fe8cf53448d129acf2

Reddy, Y.V.P. (2017). Green HRM Initiatives: Practices and Strategic Implementation within the Organization. *Abhinav-National Monthly Refereed Journal of Research in Commerce & Management*. https://www.semanticscholar.org/paper/GREEN-HRM-INITIATIVES%3A-PRACTICES-AND-STRATEGIC-THE-Reddy/198cc424941f36f6d0d0f22142c799301d926c5c

Renaud, S., Morin, L., Saulquin, J.-Y. and Abraham, J. (2015). What are the best HRM practices for retaining experts? A longitudinal study in the Canadian information technology sector. *International Journal of Manpower*, *36*(3), 416–432. https://doi.org/10.1108/IJM-03-2014-0078

Sathyapriya J, S.J., Kanimozhi R, K.R., and Adhilakshmi V, A.V. (2012). Green HRM - Delivering High Performance HR Systems. *International Journal of Scientific Research*, *3*(4), 31–34. https://doi.org/10.15373/22778179/APR2014/223

Seidel, S., Recker, J., Pimmer, C. and vom Brocke, J. (n.d.). *Enablers and barriers to the organizational adoption of sustainable business practices*. Retrieved August 4, 2024, from https://core.ac.uk/outputs/10897659/?source=2

Shah, A.V., Srivastava, V.K., Mohanty, S.S. and Varjani, S. (2021). Municipal solid waste as a sustainable resource for energy production: State-of-the-art review. *Journal of Environmental Chemical Engineering*, *9*(4), 105717. https://doi.org/10.1016/j.jece.2021.105717

Singhal, R.K., Dr. S.P., Garg, A. and Pandey, T.R. (2024). Unveiling the Transformative Influence of Artificial Intelligence on Human Resource Management. *European Economic Letters (EEL)*, *14*(1), 1733–1739. https://doi.org/10.52783/eel.v14i1.1240

Sova, O., Bieliaieva, N., Antypenko, N. and Drozd, N. (2023). Impact of artificial intelligence and digital HRM on the resource consumption within sustainable development perspective. *E3S Web of Conferences*, *408*, 01006. https://doi.org/10.1051/e3sconf/202340801006

Tongkachok, K., Garg, S., Vemuri, V.P., Chaudhary, V., Vitthal Koli, P. and Suresh Kumar, K. (2022). The Role of Artificial Intelligence on Organisational support Programmes to Enhance work outcome and Employees Behaviour. *Materials Today: Proceedings*, *56*, 2383–2387. https://doi.org/10.1016/j.matpr.2021.12.205

Wielewska, I., Kacprzak, M., Król, A., Czech, A., Zuzek, D.K., Gralak, K. and Marks-Bielska, R. (2023). Green human resource management. *Ekonomia i Środowisko - Economics and Environment*, *83*(4), 276–302. https://doi.org/10.34659/eis.2022.83.4.496

Xiang, X., Li, Q., Khan, S. and Khalaf, O.I. (2021). Urban water resource management for sustainable environment planning using artificial intelligence techniques. *Environmental Impact Assessment Review*, *86*, 106515. https://doi.org/10.1016/j.eiar.2020.106515

Yassin Alzyoud, A.A. (2022). Artificial Intelligence for Sustaining Green Human Resource Management: A Literature Review. *2022 ASU International Conference in Emerging Technologies for Sustainability and Intelligent Systems (ICETSIS)*, 321–326. https://doi.org/10.1109/ICETSIS55481.2022.9888840

Yong, J.Y., Yusliza, M.-Y., and Fawehinmi, O.O. (2019). Green human resource management: A systematic literature review from 2007 to 2019. *Benchmarking: An International Journal*, *27*(7), 2005–2027. https://doi.org/10.1108/BIJ-12-2018-0438

# 8 Harnessing Artificial Intelligence for Marketing Strategies and Business Innovation

Dr. Ganesan Muruganantham[1] and Mr. Dharun Krishna K B[2*]

Artificial Intelligence (AI) is revolutionizing marketing strategies and business, offering unprecedented opportunities for innovation, efficiency, and customer engagement. AI helps to reshape business practices, enabling hyper-personalization, real-time optimization, and decision-making driven by data. The future of business management and marketing lies in the synergy between AI capabilities and human insight, creating a new paradigm of technology-driven, customer-centric approaches. This chapter explores the role of AI in marketing, AI tools and platforms for effective marketing, AI applications across various marketing functions and the future of AI in marketing strategy. It also addresses challenges and the resulting ethical issues associated with the adoption of AI in business with case studies on successful AI implementations. This book chapter offers valuable insights for marketers, business leaders, and researchers navigating the rapidly evolving landscape for better digital customer experience.

## Introduction

Artificial Intelligence (AI) is transforming business operations and decision-making processes across various industries. The integration of AI technologies enables organizations to enhance efficiency, accuracy, and overall performance, driving unprecedented levels of innovation and competitive advantage. De Cremer (2024) states that "Successful AI implementation requires cross-functional collaboration and continuous human interaction. Leaders must model inclusive behaviour, guide employees in understanding AI, and ensure they feel valued alongside AI technologies". This human-centric approach is essential for fostering adaptability and innovation, which are critical for the effective adoption of AI.

Deloitte's research reveals that organizations are increasingly prioritizing Generative AI initiatives for value creation. While financial Return on Investment is a key metric, factors like competitive differentiation, strategic positioning and innovation are often considered more significant, especially in cases where the

[1] Professor, Department of Management Studies, National Institute of Technology, Tiruchirappalli.
[2] Researcher, Department of Computer Science, SASTRA Deemed University, Thanjavur.
Email: murugan@nitt.edu.[1]
* Corresponding author: kbdharunkrishna@gmail.com.

DOI: 10.1201/9781003559849-8

technology's potential impact is strategic (Mittal et al., 2024). Generative AI can create new content, designs, and solutions, transforming traditional business models and opening up new avenues for growth. For instance, AI-driven analytics facilitates businesses to anticipate future market trends and customer preferences with better accuracy, enabling more informed decision-making and strategic planning.

Furthermore, AI enhances customer experiences through hyper-personalization, where marketing strategies are tailored to individual customer needs and behaviours. This level of personalization is achieved by examining extensive datasets gathered through a multitude of sources, such as online browsing, purchase histories and social media activities.

Chatbots and virtual assistants allow real-time customer support using AI, enhancing both engagement and satisfaction. However, there are several difficulties and moral issues with algorithmic bias and data privacy when integrating AI with corporate processes, which must be resolved to ensure responsible AI adoption. Furthermore, because technology is changing so quickly, leaders and employees must constantly learn new skills and adapt. To fully realize the benefits of AI, businesses must cultivate a culture of creativity and adaptability. This chapter examines AI's revolutionary potential in marketing strategies and commercial innovation, focusing on its primary applications, benefits, problems, and future directions.

## Scope of AI

"Artificial Intelligence (AI) involves developing computer systems capable of performing tasks that typically require human intelligence. These tasks include problem-solving, decision-making, language understanding, and visual perception" (Geeks for Geeks, 2024). AI mimics human behaviours and seeks to train computers for tasks requiring intelligence, such as learning and understanding (Zhang et al., 2021). This capability extends AI's potential applications across various domains, from simple task automation to complex problem-solving scenarios (Haton, 2006).

"Artificial Intelligence is a vast field that encompasses several subfields and technologies, such as robotics, machine learning, and natural language processing. A kind of artificial intelligence called machine learning allows systems to learn from their experiences and become better without needing to be explicitly programmed" (Chintalapati and Pandey, 2021). Algorithms that can recognize patterns in massive datasets, anticipate outcomes, and adjust to new information are all part of this learning process. "Natural language processing enables computers to understand, interpret, and produce human language which is another crucial area of artificial intelligence" (Haleem et al., 2022). "Another essential component of AI is neural networks, which are modelled after the structure of the human brain and can recognize patterns and carry out tasks like voice and picture recognition" (Haleem et al., 2022). Artificial intelligence (AI) is revolutionizing a number of industries, including banking, healthcare and marketing with its capacity to evaluate vast amounts of data and make defensible conclusions (Mariani, 2021). The potential of AI to boost efficiency, accuracy, and overall performance in these sectors highlights its growing importance and widespread adoption.

## History of AI

The concept of intelligent machines originated in early 20th-century science fiction, however concrete explorations began mid-century with Vannevar Bush's 1945 proposal for knowledge enhancement systems marking an early interest in machine intelligence (Smith, 2006). Distributed AI and multi-agent systems, first developed in the 1950s, have significantly impacted areas such as diagnosis and process control. In the near future, artificial intelligence is anticipated to make major advancements in computer vision, natural language processing, and autonomous systems (Chennupati, 2024). As AI technologies become more advanced, they are being increasingly integrated into various facets of everyday life and business operations, influencing the future trajectory of technology and society.

The initial phase of AI development, known as the classic AI period, "focused on symbolic reasoning and problem-solving". During the 1960s and 1970s, researchers developed algorithms and programs capable of solving mathematical problems, playing chess, and proving theorems (Chintalapati and Pandey, 2021). These early programs, such as ELIZA, a natural language processing program developed in 1966, showcased AI's ability to mimic human conversation.

However, the limitations of these early AI systems, including their inability to handle ambiguous or incomplete information, "led to a period of reduced funding and interest, known as the 'AI winter' in the late 1970s and 1980s" (Mariani, 2021). The advent of areas like machine learning, which moved the emphasis from explicit programming to systems that can self-learn from the available data, was what spurred the rebirth in the development of AI in the 1990s and 2000s. An important development during this time was neural networks, which gave AI systems the ability to identify patterns and generate data-driven predictions. The application of these techniques began to be used in diverse areas from financial modelling to medical diagnosis, demonstrating the practical utility of AI and rekindling interest and investment in the field (Haleem et al., 2022).

Alan Turing's 1950 publication on the Turing Test is one of the seminal works in the history of artificial intelligence (AI), as are more recent developments like OpenAI's ChatGPT 4o and o1 in 2024. John McCarthy's 1956 coining of the phrase "Artificial Intelligence," IBM's Deep Blue's 1997 victory over Garry Kasparov, and Google's AlphaGo's 2016 victory against Lee Sedol are among notable contributions. The capabilities of AI have grown dramatically, resulting in sophisticated language models and innovations across a range of industries.

AI's evolution is also marked by its growing integration into everyday applications and industries. For example, recommendation systems using AI are now ubiquitous in online commerce and streaming platforms, guiding consumer choices on platforms like Amazon and Netflix. They are utilized in healthcare to diagnose conditions, predict patient outcomes, and personalize treatment plans. AI is also utilized in finance for fraud detection, risk management and algorithmic trading (Chintalapati and Pandey, 2021).

When combined with other cutting-edge technologies like big data analytics, blockchain, and the Internet of Things (IoT), AI's potential is further enhanced. For example, companies can get real-time data from linked devices by combining AI and IoT, which improves consumer experiences and enables more accurate targeting in marketing efforts. AI-powered Internet of Things (IoT) systems in retail use smart devices to track customer preferences and habits, providing tailored recommendations and encouraging greater interaction.

The development of AI has seen cycles of rapid progress and occasional setbacks, highlighting the intricate challenges of creating intelligent systems. From its early days focused on theoretical concepts and basic rule-based models, the field has evolved into one with highly advanced and complex systems capable of handling diverse tasks. AI has the ability to significantly enhance human capabilities and bring about revolutionary changes in a number of areas as it continues to advance.

## Categorization of AI

Research on artificial intelligence (AI) crosses several fields, such as computer science, logic, linguistics, and cognitive sciences, enabling it to tackle challenging issues ranging from AGI to different approaches and perspectives (Haton, 2006). Chennupati (2024) categorizes artificial intelligence into three categories: "artificial narrow intelligence (ANI), artificial general intelligence (AGI), and artificial superintelligence". ANI (weak AI) is made to effectively and precisely carry out particular tasks like speech recognition and chess play. They are widely used today in advanced technological applications like recommendation engines, autonomous vehicles, and virtual assistants (Amazing Technology, 2024).

Strong AI, or artificial general intelligence (AGI), can carry out any intellectual work that a human can. In contrast to ANI, which is restricted to particular tasks, AGI can comprehend, acquire, and use knowledge in a variety of disciplines. AGI seeks to imitate human cognitive functions so that machines can autonomously think, plan, and solve problems (Amazing Technology, 2024). Developing AGI presents a major challenge because of the intricate complexity involved in replicating human intelligence in machines.

Artificial superintelligence, which goes beyond artificial general intelligence (AGI), is the concept of AI systems that are more advanced than people in all domains, such as creativity, problem-solving, and emotional intelligence. These systems present significant ethical and existential hazards in addition to the ability to propel extraordinary improvements. Conversations about artificial superintelligence highlight the necessity for ethical guidelines and stringent safety measures to oversee its development and societal integration (Chennupati, 2024).

AI's categorization is further detailed by examining its subdomains. "Machine learning, a subset of AI, allows systems to learn and improve from experience without explicit programming" (Chintalapati and Pandey, 2021). This calls for algorithms that can recognize patterns in huge datasets, forecast outcomes, and adjust to fresh data. Neural networks with multiple layers are used in deep learning, an advanced type of machine learning, to obtain greater accuracy in tasks like speech and image recognition (Haleem et al., 2022).

Another essential AI subsystem is natural language processing (NLP) focusing on how computers and humans (natural language) interact. Chatbots, machine translation, and sentiment analysis are examples of NLP applications that enable more intuitive and natural human-computer interactions (Jarek and Mazurek, 2019). The interdisciplinary nature of AI research and its categorization into ANI, AGI, and artificial superintelligence highlights the complexity and potential of AI technologies.

## Methodology

This book chapter adopts a comprehensive methodology that investigates the intersection of artificial intelligence with marketing strategies, and business innovation. Our research draws on an extensive array of sources published between 2021 and 2024, capturing the latest developments and trends in this rapidly evolving field. We utilized high-quality, peer-reviewed publications from reputable journals such as the "International Journal of Management & Entrepreneurship Research, Journal of Business Research, and Discover Artificial Intelligence", in addition to relevant book chapters and industry reports.

We conducted a thorough literature review, analyzing a broad spectrum of theoretical frameworks and empirical studies. This review includes a diverse range of sources from various countries, covering multiple papers and publications to provide a global perspective. Our analysis places a strong emphasis on case studies and real-world applications to show how AI is being used in marketing and business innovation. By adopting an interdisciplinary approach, we integrate insights from marketing, computer science, business strategy, and ethics. This holistic perspective enables us to assess the transformative potential of AI comprehensively. Our methodology involves critical analysis that evaluates the effectiveness and challenges with ethical implications of marketing strategies and innovations using AI.

We conducted a review of empirical articles from leading journals and industry reports, ensuring that our findings are grounded in robust and reliable data. Additionally, we included case studies to gain in-depth insights from real-world implementations and industry practices. This qualitative data complements the quantitative findings from our literature review, offering a comprehensive view of AI's implementation in various business contexts.

## Literature Review

Artificial intelligence (AI) continues to revolutionize marketing and related business functions, with recent literature revealing its transformative impact across various domains Numerous studies have examined how AI may be integrated into marketing strategies, operations, and stakeholder relations, providing important insights into the benefits, problems, and applications of this technology.

Kim Oanh, (2024) thoroughly examines AI's transformative impact on digital marketing, emphasizing its pivotal role in personalizing customer interactions, enhancing content creation, and optimizing marketing strategies. Chatbots, virtual assistants, and recommendation systems are examples of AI-driven technologies that allow for dynamic, customized interactions between customers and brands. By analyzing vast amounts of data, AI allows for precise audience targeting and more efficient advertising campaigns. Nonetheless, ethical issues surrounding AI in marketing must be addressed, including data privacy issues, algorithmic bias mitigation, and the possibility of job displacement due to automation. This comprehensive analysis provides essential insights for marketers navigating the evolving AI-driven landscape responsibly.

The concept of generative AI is accelerating and transforming marketing content creation. Heitmann (2024) investigates this phenomenon, discussing how generative AI can produce high-quality, customized marketing content efficiently, thereby transforming the traditional trade-off between content quantity and quality. Similarly, Kshetri et al., (2024) conducted a study in India with a sample size of 400 marketers, exploring the transformative impacts of generative AI on marketing activities. Their research underscores the effectiveness of AI in generating personalized content and offerings, suggesting that AI-driven marketing content is more likely to resonate on a personal level compared to previous digital technologies, representing a significant leap forward in marketing capabilities.

In the realm of marketing analytics, Syam and Kaul, (2021) explore the application of Support Vector Machines (SVM), a specific AI technique, in marketing and sales. Their work highlights the potential of this advanced AI method for improved decision-making and predictive analytics, offering marketers powerful tools for data-driven strategies. AI integration in marketing has a substantial impact on business-to-business scenarios in addition to consumer-facing applications. Leszkiewicz et al., (2022) explore this in their study "Smart Business and the Social Value of AI". Their research clarifies the benefits and also the drawbacks of applying AI for various stakeholders, such as companies, supply chain partners, organizations, and the general public. It provides a comprehensive view of AI's impact, focusing on both economic and social dimensions. It emphasizes how crucial it is to take legal and ethical issues into account and makes the case that as adoption barriers to AI fall and technological prices rise, AI's social worth will eventually rise. This all-encompassing strategy advances our knowledge of ethical AI applications in commercial settings.

## Consumer Engagement

AI's impact on consumer engagement can be understood through the application of the "Uses and Gratifications Theory". A study conducted in China with

540 participants examined how AI, particularly chatbots, enhances consumer interaction. The research discovered that personalized messages, crafted by AI, resonate deeply with consumers, promoting greater collaboration and engagement (Marjerison et al., 2022).

The study found that consumers' positive sentiments toward AI-driven chatbots are influenced by both pleasurable factors, like perceived pleasure and practical ones like ease and authenticity of communication. This personalization fosters brand loyalty and addresses consumers' specific needs and preferences, creating a more engaging user experience. However, issues like privacy concerns and the nascent state of technology can negatively impact acceptance. The study highlights the importance of understanding AI-driven platforms' effectiveness in gathering customer insights and crafting personalized experiences.

The focus of current research has been on using AI to improve consumer experience and engagement. Armutcu et al., (2024) conducted a study in Turkey involving 398 banking sector consumers. Utilizing the stimulus-organism-response (SOR) model, their study provides valuable insights into how AI-driven marketing initiatives influence brand experience, brand preference, and ultimately, consumer purchase intentions. They found that customers' brand experiences are positively impacted by information delivery, interaction, accessibility, and customisation in AI marketing. This study has important ramifications for the banking sector and AI marketing tactics in addition to furthering our knowledge of the psychological mechanisms by which AI influences consumer decision-making processes.

Artificial intelligence (AI) greatly enhances customer relationship management (CRM) by applying machine learning and predictive analytics to improve client retention. CRM systems with AI capabilities evaluate consumer interactions, forecast behaviour, and tailor outreach campaigns. A study highlighted that these systems significantly boost customer retention rates by enabling timely and relevant actions based on predictive insights (Ledro et al., 2023). Artificial Intelligence has revolutionized the marketing balance by being integrated with product, pricing, place, and promotion. AI's capabilities in data analysis and predictive modelling allow companies to develop products closely aligned with consumer preferences and trends. AI algorithms, for example, may forecast future product trends by analyzing market data and customer input, enabling businesses to stay ahead of the curve (Alchemi.AI, 2023, Broadhurst Digital, 2024).

Artificially intelligent chatbots and virtual assistants are revolutionizing customer service by providing personalized product recommendations and immediate assistance. These technologies improve customer happiness and engagement by handling a large volume of regular inquiries, offering round-the-clock help, and speeding up response times. Artificial intelligence (AI) chatbots are engineered to emulate human communication, generating a feeling of social presence and customization that enhances the user experience (Adam et al., 2021). Additionally, AI solutions assist companies in maintaining high service quality and efficiency by automating answers and analyzing customer data, which eventually improves customer relationships and spurs corporate growth (Cheng and Jiang, 2020).

In B2B marketing, AI's role in supporting buyer-seller exchanges and contract negotiations has been well-documented. AI assists negotiators by assessing risks associated with different contract clauses and ensuring compliance with legal and regulatory requirements, thus streamlining the negotiation process and achieving more efficient and favourable agreements. But there could also be negative consequences, such worsened power disparities and increased organizational inertia (Gligor et al., 2021).

AI's integration into Human Resource Management (HRM) is an important area of study, encompassing various applications such as performance evaluation, employee selection, turnover prediction, and employee assignment. These AI applications enhance recruitment by enabling unbiased candidate evaluations and informed selection decisions. Predictive analytics are crucial in anticipating employee turnover, thus aiding in the development of effective retention strategies. Additionally, AI-driven tools facilitate real-time performance management and improve overall organizational efficiency (Budhwar et al., 2022, Nankervis et al., 2021). Even with these broad benefits, there are still important obstacles to overcome, like the possibility of bias in AI systems and the ongoing need for audits and monitoring to guarantee inclusivity and justice. An AI system's bias may produce unfair and discriminating results, which in turn may lead to societal inequality. To address these biases and improve fairness and transparency in AI systems, frequent audits and ongoing evaluations are necessary (Bertino, Kundu, and Sura 2019; Chaudhuri and Mohanty, 2023; IFACET, 2023).

Research on the nexus between AI and HRM is becoming increasingly important, with implications for marketing and overall corporate strategy. Through a thorough assessment of the subject, Qamar et al., (2021) built a study strategy for future investigations and obtained the most recent information on AI applications in HRM. They present a thorough picture of how AI is changing different HRM activities and how that is affecting marketing skills and organizational performance. Their research draws from a meta-analysis of fifty papers.

Successful adoption of AI depends on ensuring that its implementation is in line with company objectives and human values (Fenwick et al., 2024). This viewpoint is crucial for creating an innovative and flexible culture, both of which are necessary for the successful integration of AI in marketing and other business functions. This study advances our knowledge of how businesses might take a human-centric approach, which has profound effects on marketing tactics and customer interactions, by going beyond the simple application of AI.

The usefulness of AI in companies is further examined by Azeem et al., (2024), who pay close attention to how AI affects employee retention. The results of the study demonstrate how AI methods like machine learning and big data analysis can improve hiring procedures and increase employee satisfaction. These findings are relevant to marketing as they suggest ways in which AI can enhance organizational stability and performance, indirectly supporting marketing efforts.

Artificial Intelligence is going to play a bigger part in marketing strategies in the future. An example of this is the great degree of precision with which

AI-powered predictive analytics can estimate consumer behaviour and industry trends. Companies utilizing AI-driven predictive analytics can significantly enhance customer engagement and operational efficiency. Personalized shopping experiences, focused advertising campaigns, dynamic pricing, and inventory optimization are some of these innovations that enhance forecasting precision and strategic decision-making (Ajiga et al., 2024).

AI's capabilities in sentiment analysis are transforming how businesses understand and respond to consumer feedback. Massive volumes of social media data can be analyzed by AI algorithms to determine how the public feels about a product or brand.

Studies have shown that companies using AI for sentiment analysis can significantly enhance their ability to respond to customer feedback quickly and accurately. For instance, AI-driven sentiment analysis enables businesses to track real-time changes in public opinion, allowing them to address customer concerns promptly and improve their overall brand perception (Krugmann and Hartmann, 2023; Tan et al., 2023).

Due to studies demonstrating AI's revolutionary potential, this application in marketing research is receiving a lot of attention. AI-powered tools enhance the efficiency and accuracy of data analysis by processing vast amounts of data rapidly, which would be challenging to achieve manually. According to Smith Hanley (2024), AI-driven technologies improve data analysis speed and accuracy, enabling researchers to handle larger sample sizes and obtain more reliable insights. These advanced tools allow researchers to concentrate on interpreting the results and formulating strategies based on their findings. Moreover, AI-driven market research solutions can automate various tasks, such as sentiment analysis and customer journey analysis, enabling more efficient and accurate data collection and analysis (Greenbook, 2024)

AI can improve marketing effectiveness, but there are drawbacks as well. The ethical usage of AI in particular is one of the main problems about algorithmic transparency and data privacy. Research like those conducted by Kim Oanh, (2024) and Leszkiewicz et al., (2022) highlights how crucial it is to create frameworks and ethical standards to guarantee that AI technologies are applied ethically. To keep customers' trust, AI systems must be transparent and users must understand how their data is being used. Resolving algorithmic bias presents a substantial additional hurdle. Unintentionally, biases in the data used to train AI systems may be reinforced by them. For AI systems to detect and reduce biases, research by Fenwick et al., (2024) emphasizes the necessity of ongoing monitoring and assessment. This is especially crucial in marketing since discriminatory algorithms can result in unfair targeting and prejudice against specific customer groups.

The rapid pace of AI development presents significant challenges for businesses, particularly in keeping up with the latest technologies. Continuous education and training for marketing professionals are crucial to effectively leverage AI tools. For example, a study highlighted by McKinsey Report (2023) revealed that companies integrating advanced AI tools into their marketing strategies saw substantial improvements in performance and productivity. The potential advantages of AI in marketing are enormous, despite these difficulties. It is anticipated that as AI technologies advance, they will greatly improve marketing tactics and spur corporate expansion. Future research will be essential in addressing ethical and practical challenges in order to enable the responsible and successful implementation of AI in marketing and other commercial operations.

Many studies show how artificial intelligence (AI) is revolutionizing digital marketing, especially in the areas of personalization, content creation, and strategy optimization; how generative AI creates high-quality, customized content; how AI is integrated into advanced methods like Support Vector Machines (SVM) for predictive analytics and decision-making; how AI affects consumer engagement through chatbots and personalized messages; how AI is applied in marketing analytics and B2B contexts; and how AI raises ethical issues. These findings highlight AI's enormous potential to transform company operations, including marketing, and to spur major innovation.

## AI in Marketing Strategies

AI is revolutionizing the field of marketing strategies with applications offering innovative solutions across various domains, including product development, pricing strategies, distribution channels, and promotional activities. This section discusses the specific applications and impacts of AI in these areas.

### *AI in Product Development*

AI technology has brought about a significant shift in product development by enabling companies to leverage data-driven insights to create products that more effectively meet consumer needs. Artificial intelligence (AI) systems can foresee client preferences and identify industry trends by analyzing large data sets. Haleem et al., (2022), for instance, emphasize how AI may improve customer value propositions through data-driven and insight-driven marketing initiatives. By combining their products with more intelligent technologies, organizations have been able to get greater marketing results.

Technologies driven by AI facilitate innovations in product development and trend predictions. These allow analyzing social media data, customer reviews, and market research reports to provide insights into consumer sentiment and emerging trends, thereby guiding companies in developing products that align with current market demands (Chintalapati and Pandey, 2021).

### *AI in Pricing Strategies*

AI's ability to analyze and spot patterns in massive datasets has completely changed pricing strategies. With the use of AI in dynamic pricing models, companies can quickly adapt and modify prices in response to a variety of factors, such as demand, competition, and customer behaviour. Research has shown that retail businesses employing AI-driven dynamic pricing experienced notable revenue increases (BCG, 2024, McKinsey, 2024). These models use machine learning algorithms to estimate the optimum rates and offer customized discounts, which boosts sales and customer happiness. AI tools can dynamically optimize prices by factoring in supply, demand, and competitive actions, enabling businesses to maximize profitability while staying competitive (BCG, 2024; McKinsey, 2024).

Beyond revenue optimization, AI also improves sales forecasting and demand prediction, allowing businesses to set prices that enhance profitability. Syam and Kaul (2021) explain the integration of AI techniques like Support Vector Machines (SVM) in marketing and sales to enhance decision-making and predictive analytics, equipping marketers with robust tools for data-driven strategies.

## AI in Distribution Channels

Artificial Intelligence (AI) is revolutionizing distribution networks by improving several facets of logistics and supply chain management. Among distribution's notable uses of AI is inventory management. AI-powered solutions give businesses accurate real-time visibility into stock levels, enabling them to track inventory and forecast demand trends. Ensuring ideal stock levels reduces the likelihood of stockouts and excess inventory. For example, AI-driven predictive analytics, which estimates demand based on historical data, market trends, and external variables, enables better inventory planning and management (Shatat and Shatat, 2022).

Additionally, AI enhances the efficiency and accuracy of order fulfilment processes by analyzing order history, customer preferences, and inventory levels to streamline the picking, packing, and shipping tasks. Predictive maintenance using AI further helps in spotting any equipment problems before they happen, averting expensive downtime (Shu and Xing, 2021).

AI significantly improves route optimization and quality control within distribution channels. Artificial intelligence (AI) algorithms examine traffic patterns, delivery schedules, and vehicle capacity to recommend the most cost-effective delivery routes, thereby increasing delivery efficiency and decreasing transportation expenses. AI tools contribute to workforce management by analyzing employee performance data, predicting staffing requirements based on demand fluctuations, and optimizing shift schedules. These advancements collectively enhance the overall efficiency and responsiveness of distribution channels, making them more agile and capable of meeting dynamic market demands (Shatat and Shatat, 2022; Shu and Xing, 2021).

## AI in Promotional Activities

Promotional strategies have been significantly enhanced by AI technologies, which enable personalized and targeted marketing campaigns. AI systems examine client data to determine preferences and behaviours, enabling marketers to craft customized advertisements that appeal to specific consumers. According to Kim

Oanh (2024), AI personalizes marketing emails according to the preferences and behaviours of the consumer, resulting in higher engagement and conversion rates.

AI-driven platforms enhance promotional message effectiveness by using advanced data analytics to identify optimal times for engagement, significantly improving conversion rates. Additionally, generative AI technologies, such as ChatGPT and Jasper.ai, create high-quality, tailored marketing content like blog posts, social media updates, and video scripts, automating the process to save time and resources while ensuring relevance and engagement. This comprehensive approach includes analyzing vast data to personalize content and automate testing, leading to more precise marketing strategies. Generative AI revolutionizes content creation by producing high-quality materials across various modalities, breaking traditional trade-offs between content quantity and quality, allowing businesses to maintain a robust online presence and quickly adapt to changing consumer behaviours (Heitmann, 2024; Nosto, 2023; Landingi, 2023).

Additionally, AI dramatically changes the way that products are branded by using behavioural patterns and consumer data to produce more individualized brand experiences. Machine learning models can evaluate large volumes of customer data collected from several touchpoints, including social media, website interactions, and online reviews. This allows brands to instantly gain insights into the preferences of their target audience. This data allows organizations to fine-tune their branding messaging, ensuring they correspond with consumer expectations and desires. AI also makes it feasible for branding strategies to be dynamically adjusted, giving firms the flexibility to swiftly pivot and stay relevant in a market that is evolving at a rapid pace. Brands may better foresee future trends with predictive analytics, which keeps their branding initiatives competitive and forward-thinking. (Haleem et al., 2022).

Therefore, AI is crucial for marketing strategies as it revolutionizes key areas such as product development, pricing strategies, distribution channels, and promotional activities. By leveraging data-driven insights and automation, AI enhances personalization, optimizes efficiency, and significantly boosts consumer engagement.

## Business Innovation with AI

The way businesses function and compete in the global market has changed significantly as a result of the integration of AI into business processes. This section explores how AI is implemented by companies, how it leverages technology and the benefits it provides to multiple stakeholders.

### *Implementing AI in Business*

Successful AI implementation in business requires a strategic approach that addresses employee concerns and fosters a sense of community. De Cremer (2024) emphasizes the importance of a human-centric approach, which is crucial for overcoming resistance and ensuring the long-term success of AI initiatives. This approach involves engaging employees in the AI integration process, providing training, and creating an environment where humans and AI systems can collaborate effectively (De Cremer, 2024).

AI technologies like machine learning enable businesses to transition from descriptive analytics to predictive and prescriptive analytics, significantly enhancing decision-making processes. Apte (2010) notes that this shift allows companies to move from reactive to proactive strategies, enabling more accurate forecasting and better resource allocation. AI may be used by businesses to examine petabytes of data and identify patterns and trends, providing them with crucial information to support strategic decision-making. Bob Suh (2021) argues that the rise of AI has exposed flaws in traditional decision-making traits. He suggests that executives must disrupt their decision-making styles to effectively leverage AI's capabilities, balancing intuition with data-driven insights (Bob Suh, 2021). This entails incorporating AI into decision-making to improve corporate strategy accuracy and efficacy.

### *Leveraging AI Technologies in Business*

AI technologies provide a variety of tools that companies can utilize to innovate and enhance their processes. Predictive analytics driven by AI, for instance, can assist businesses in forecasting consumer behaviour and market changes so they can modify their approach appropriately. This proactive strategy can result in lower expenses, more efficiency, and higher customer satisfaction (Chintalapati and Pandey, 2021). AI is also necessary for automating repetitive tasks so that employees can focus on more strategic work. AI-powered automation technologies can handle jobs like data input, customer support, and inventory management, lowering the potential for human error and boosting efficiency (Haleem et al., 2022). Additionally, AI-driven tools can obtain and summarize information quickly and accurately, providing insights which would be difficult or impossible to obtain manually.

### *Benefits of AI to Business Stakeholders*

The benefits of AI in business innovation extend to various stakeholders, including employees, customers, and shareholders.

*Employees*: AI can increase worker productivity and job satisfaction by enabling more strategic work through the automation of repetitive tasks. Learning how to collaborate with AI systems can help workers advance their careers and acquire new abilities (Haleem et al., 2022).

*Customers*: AI-driven personalization and predictive analytics can significantly improve customer experiences. It can analyze customer information to offer personalized recommendations, predict customer needs, and provide timely customer support through chatbots and virtual assistants which results in higher brand loyalty and satisfaction from customers (Chintalapati and Pandey, 2021).

*Shareholders*: The increased efficiency and cost savings resulting from AI integration can lead to higher profitability, benefiting shareholders. AI can spur innovation, creating new sources of income and strengthening a business's position as a market leader. For instance, by boosting productivity and streamlining several commercial procedures, AI has the potential to boost corporate earnings by up to $4.4 trillion yearly (Chui and Yee, 2023). Additionally, AI helps businesses innovate and stay competitive by sharpening predictions, boosting efficiencies, and optimizing real-time decision-making processes (Townson, 2021).

Table 1 showcases the adoption of AI tools and platforms by major international corporations across diverse industries. It highlights how these global leaders are integrating various AI solutions to drive business innovation and optimize specific aspects of their operations.

The list includes companies from sectors such as industrial manufacturing, aerospace, finance, consumer goods, technology, and retail. Each entry details the company name, its chosen AI platform, the business function it supports, and a primary application. The AI implementations span crucial business areas such as strategic decision-making, production optimization, financial risk management, talent acquisition, targeted marketing, IT services, resource planning, innovation, and customer insights. This selection highlights the versatility and wide-ranging effects of AI technology in promoting innovation, improving operational efficiency, and preserving a competitive edge in several global economic sectors.

**Table 1** Applications of AI in Business Management in various companies globally

| *No* | *Company* | *AI Tool Name/ Platform* | *Application Type* | *Key Use Case* |
|---|---|---|---|---|
| 1 | Humana (Healthcare Insurance) | IBM Watson | Customer Service | Automate and enhance provider calls and support |
| 2 | Airbus (Aerospace) | Google Cloud | Operations Management | Optimize aircraft production |
| 3 | Wells Fargo (Banking) | H2O.ai | Financial Management | Improve fraud detection |
| 4 | Unilever (Consumer Goods) | Pymetrics | Human Resource Management | Streamline recruitment |
| 5 | Coca-Cola (Beverages) | OpenAI GPT-4 and DALL-E | Marketing Management | Personalize marketing campaigns |
| 6 | Siemens (Technology) | ServiceNow AI | IT Management | Automate IT service management |
| 7 | IKEA (Retail) | Demand Sensing AI | Product Management | Optimize resource allocation |

*Contd.*

**Table 1** *Contd.*

| *No* | *Company* | *AI Tool Name/ Platform* | *Application Type* | *Key Use Case* |
|---|---|---|---|---|
| 8 | HSBC (Banking) | Ayasdi | Risk Management | Enhance financial crime detection |
| 9 | PepsiCo (Food and Beverages) | SparkBeyond | Innovation Management | Identify new product opportunities |
| 10 | Adidas (Sportswear) | Salesforce Einstein Content Selection | Customer Relationship Management | Enhance customer segmentation |

(*Source:* Compiled by the authors 2024)

Table 2 presents an overview of AI tool adoption across various prominent Indian companies, spanning different industries and business functions. The table highlights the various ways artificial intelligence is fostering business innovation.

The table illustrates how companies from different sectors, including conglomerates, manufacturing, banking, automotive, e-commerce, IT services, and engineering, are leveraging AI tools from various providers to enhance specific aspects of their operations. These applications range from strategic planning and financial management to human resources, marketing, IT services, project management, risk assessment, innovation, and customer relationship management. This highlights the broad influence of AI on various business domains in the Indian corporate environment, improving operational effectiveness, stimulating creativity, and preserving competitive advantage.

**Table 2** Applications of AI in Business Innovation in Various Companies in India.

| *No* | *Company* | *AI Tool Name/ Platform* | *Application Type* | *Key Use Case* |
|---|---|---|---|---|
| 1 | Reliance Industries (Conglomerate) | Microsoft Azure AI | Strategic Planning | Analyze market trends |
| 2 | Wipro Limited (Conglomerate) | SAP Leonardo | Operations Management | Digital transformation initiatives. |
| 3 | HDFC Bank (Banking) | Oracle AI | Financial Management | Enhance credit scoring |
| 4 | Mahindra Logistics (Supply Chain) | Darwinbox | Human Resource Management | Streamline performance management |
| 5 | Flipkart (E-commerce) | Flippi | Customer Shopping Assistant | Personalize product discovery via chat |
| 6 | Infosys (IT Services) | BMC Helix | IT Management | Enhance service delivery |

*Contd.*

**Table 2** *Contd.*

| *No* | *Company* | *AI Tool Name/ Platform* | *Application Type* | *Key Use Case* |
|---|---|---|---|---|
| 7 | Larsen & Toubro (Engineering) | Azure, OpenAI and Google Cloud AI | Operations Management | Streamline operations and improve project planning |
| 8 | Tech Mahindra (IT Services) | Tech Mahindra AI | Customer Service | Improve customer engagement |
| 9 | BYJU'S (Education) | BYJU'S Wiz | Learning Management | Personalize student learning |
| 10 | Zomato (E-commerce) | Zomato AI | Customer Experience | Enhance product recommendations and customer assistance |

(*Source:* Compiled by the authors 2024)

AI's integration into business processes fosters innovation, enhances efficiency, and provides significant benefits to employees, customers, and shareholders, ultimately driving competitive advantage and transforming industries.

## Opportunities of AI in India

India has significant opportunities to leverage AI for economic growth and social development. By 2035, AI might increase India's yearly growth rate by 1.3%, adding US$957 billion to the economy (Accenture, 2024). Key opportunities include pursuing an "AI for all" approach to enhance financial inclusion, personalized healthcare, and other public services, contrasting with the Western focus on private enterprise applications (Ernst & Young LLP 2024; Tyagi, 2024).

AI technologies, particularly generative AI, are poised to contribute immensely to the global economy. According to McKinsey (2024), generative AI might boost GDP by $2.6 to $4.4 trillion a year, having a big effect on the media, telecommunications, and technology industries. Invest India (2023) projects that the AI market in India will reach $7.8 billion by 2025, driven by the industrial, automotive, healthcare, retail, and agricultural sectors. In the next seven years, India's GDP might grow by $1.2– 1.5 trillion just from generative AI, with business services, financial services, education, retail, and healthcare accounting for 69% of the increase (Ernst & Young LLP, 2024).

AI's ability to automate tasks and processes is a key driver of economic impact. AI can automate 60–70% of work activities, accelerating the technical potential for automation (McKinsey Report, 2024). Better operational performance, cost savings, and enhanced production can result from this increased efficiency. AI-driven analytics help businesses make quick, well-informed decisions by giving them real-time insights into customer behaviour, market trends, and operational performance (Kavanagh, 2019).

**India AI Initiative: Catalyzing AI Adoption and Innovation in India**

The India AI initiative is a strategic program that the Indian government has undertaken intending to accelerate AI development and promote creativity throughout the country. With a substantial allocation of ₹10,372 crore, this initiative aims to cultivate a robust AI ecosystem through strategic public-private partnerships. The program includes several important components, such as the creation of a unified platform for high-quality datasets, the promotion of AI applications in vital industries like healthcare, agriculture, and education, and the development of scalable AI computing infrastructure with over 10,000 GPUs. The plan also prioritizes deep-tech AI startup support and streamlined finance availability, with a focus on growing AI education and training programs to develop a qualified workforce. By prioritizing responsible AI development and nurturing innovation, the IndiaAI initiative positions India as an emerging global leader in AI, poised to drive socio-economic transformation across diverse sectors.

*Source:*
https://indiaai.gov.in/article/global-indiaai-summit-2024-concludes-paving-way-for-india-s-leadership-in-ai-innovation, https://www.pmindia.gov.in/en/news_updates/cabinet-approves-ambitious-indiaai-mission-to-strengthen-the-ai-innovation-ecosystem/, https://nanobits.beehiiv.com/p/global-indiaai-summit-2024-key-highlights

**Indian Government's "AI for All" Program**

The Indian government's "AI for All" program, which was introduced in partnership with Intel and CBSE, aims to raise the awareness and literacy of AI among its citizens. In its initial year, the effort was intended to benefit one million students. A 4–hour self-paced course in 11 Indian languages is offered by the program, making it accessible to a diverse group of individuals such as professionals, older residents, and students. The course is broken up into two sections: AI Appreciation, which looks at applications and societal advantages, and AI Awareness, which covers basic AI ideas. Participants get digital badges after they finish. This program complements India's goal of inclusive growth through artificial intelligence (AI) and is in line with the National Education Policy 2020, hence advancing the nation's aspiration to lead the world in emerging technologies.

*Source:*
https://www.intel.com, https://ai-for-all.in, https://indiaai.gov.in

## Challenges of AI

Acquiring high-quality training data is a significant challenge for businesses implementing AI. This encompasses issues of data creation, procurement, and addressing privacy concerns (Chintalapati and Pandey, 2021). Building reliable, thorough, and representative data is essential to creating AI models that work. To preserve the accuracy and calibre of their datasets, businesses need to make significant investments in solid data management procedures. Ensuring compliance with data protection regulations when training AI models is another critical challenge (Rajmohan, 2024). This includes conducting timely legal reviews to assess the lawfulness of collected data for machine-learning purposes. Respecting laws like GDPR and other data privacy legislation contributes to the security of user data and fosters confidence among stakeholders and customers.

Concerns over the reliability of large language model prompts, especially when confronted with unconventional queries and reasoning tasks, highlight the need for robust testing and validation processes in AI development (Genkina, 2024).

Ensuring that AI systems perform reliably across a wide range of scenarios is essential for their successful deployment in real-world applications. Moreover, it might be difficult and resource-intensive to integrate AI into current business processes. Organizations must carefully plan and execute AI implementation strategies to ensure smooth integration with minimal disruption to operations. This calls for constant tuning and monitoring to adjust to evolving business requirements and technology breakthroughs. To successfully implement and operate AI systems, addressing these issues calls for cooperation across several disciplines, including data science, legal, and IT teams (Haleem et al., 2022).

## Emerging AI Technologies

Van der Made (2023) notes that neural networks, the backbone of AI, have exponentially increased in complexity, demanding substantial computing resources and enabling feats like defeating humans in strategic games and generating sophisticated content. In the business and marketing sectors, neural networks are leveraged for predictive analytics, customer segmentation, and personalized marketing strategies, driving enhanced customer engagement and operational efficiency (Chintalapati and Pandey, 2021).

Efforts to reduce large language model sizes are crucial for enhancing computational efficiency and accessibility. Gent (2024) and Hutson (2024) report that shrinking large language models (LLMs) to 1-bit can enhance energy efficiency, accessibility, and computational performance while addressing concerns over the high energy consumption of AI systems. These advancements allow businesses to deploy sophisticated AI tools without incurring prohibitive costs or energy demands, making AI-driven insights more accessible to smaller enterprises (Genkina, 2024).

In addition to developments in neural networks and language models, Van der Made (2023) highlights the potential of neuromorphic computing. This approach is based on the composition and functions of the brain, it offers a feasible route for the development of artificial intelligence. Neuromorphic systems are smaller, quicker, and more energy-efficient, emulating the brain's dynamics. Neuromorphic computing has the potential to greatly improve response times in dynamic markets by facilitating real-time data processing and decision-making in business applications.

Gent (2024) suggests that innovations such as sparsity techniques and hardware optimizations can mitigate the energy demands associated with large AI models. These advancements are crucial for making AI more sustainable and accessible. In marketing, these innovations allow for the deployment of real-time, AI-driven campaigns that can adapt to consumer behaviours instantaneously, enhancing the effectiveness and reach of marketing efforts (Haleem et al., 2022). As artificial intelligence (AI) technologies advance, their incorporation into marketing and business plans will lead to unprecedented levels of creativity and productivity, helping businesses to remain competitive in a market that is becoming more and more digital (Rajmohan, 2024).

## Ethical Considerations of AI

Research on artificial intelligence in marketing continues to place a strong emphasis on ethical issues. The necessity of implementing AI responsibly is emphasized by several studies, including those by Kim Oanh (2024) and Leszkiewicz et al., (2022), which address issues including algorithmic biases, confidentiality of data, and the influence of AI adoption on society.

These studies contribute to the ongoing dialogue about ethical AI use in business contexts, providing frameworks for marketers to consider as they integrate AI into their strategies. The ethical considerations of AI encompass various aspects, including the responsible use of AI technologies, ensuring transparency, and maintaining trust. To reduce the possibility of disruptions brought on by fast AI integration, Tabrizi et al., (2023) and Delaney (2024) stress the importance of clear communication, training, and participation in AI deployment. They highlight the importance of a "human in the loop" approach, which involves employees in the design and testing of AI tools. This strategy guarantees that AI technologies are made to complement human abilities and improve the calibre of work while simultaneously assisting in gaining the trust of employees.

Shah and Patel (2023) discuss the unique challenges India faces in adopting generative AI due to its linguistic and cultural diversity. These challenges include ensuring linguistic freedom and addressing concerns about authenticity and trust. Such challenges present opportunities for research and innovation in AI development, aiming to create AI systems that are inclusive and respectful of India's diverse linguistic landscape. These studies contribute to the ongoing dialogue about ethical AI use in business contexts, providing frameworks for marketers to consider as they integrate AI into their strategies.

Stokel-Walker (2024) brings up some significant issues with AI's application in scientific publications. Scientists have found that AI-generated keywords and phrases are frequently used in scientific publications. This emphasizes how crucial it is to maintain the standard and dependability of research aided by AI. Keeping the integrity of scientific work requires that AI tools employed in research meet strict requirements for authenticity and accuracy. Forging ethical norms and standards for AI is crucial to building confidence and guaranteeing the proper application of these technologies. A growing number of businesses and legislators are focusing on developing frameworks that handle problems like algorithmic transparency, security, and data privacy. Haleem et al., (2022) claim that these frameworks are designed to safeguard user data and guarantee that AI systems are created and applied in a way that upholds moral standards and societal norms.

**Case Study 1: Sivi–Democratizing Design with Generative AI**

Sivi is a pioneering AI-powered design generator startup that is revolutionizing the creation of visual content for businesses. Founded in 2019 and based in Karnataka, India, Sivi has developed advanced generative AI models that can instantly generate high-quality designs for ads, social media posts, banners, and more in over 72 languages (Sivi AI, 2023).

Many small and medium-sized businesses face challenges in creating visually appealing marketing materials due to limited design resources and expertise. Sivi addresses this gap by providing an AI-powered tool that generates custom visuals tailored to the user's content and brand preferences. Unlike template-based design tools, Sivi uses generative AI to understand the user's input and create unique, template-free designs that reflect the brand's identity.

Sivi's technology is built on the Atomic Design methodology and a Human-in-the-Loop approach ensures that users can fine-tune the AI-generated designs to their liking. This collaborative process between human creativity and machine intelligence significantly boosts productivity and allows businesses to create and iterate on visual content quickly, enhancing their marketing efficiency.

Sivi's innovative approach and global impact have earned it significant recognition. Within eight weeks of its official launch in June 2023, users from over 135 countries had generated more than 100,000 designs using Sivi. The startup was named the #1 Product of the Day on Product Hunt and was also selected as one of the top 3 champions of the YOURSTORY Techsparks Tech30 in 2023. Furthermore, Forbes India recognized Sivi as one of the 200 Select Companies with Global Business Potential. By leveraging the power of generative AI, Sivi is making professional-grade design accessible to businesses of all sizes, aligning with its mission to democratize design and empower millions of businesses worldwide.

*Source:*
https://sivi.ai/, https://in.linkedin.com/company/sivi-ai, https://yourstory.com/2024/06/startup-sivi-gen-ai-text-visual-designs, https://news.thenewsuniverse.com/story/469021/sivi-ai-pioneering-the-design-revolution-with-generative-ai.html

**Case Study 2: Hirex.ai–Automating Hiring with AI-Powered Interviews**

Hirex.ai is an innovative recruitment platform redefining the hiring process through the use of cognitive voice-enabled AI bots. Founded in 2019 by Ugendreshwar Kudupudi and Sayyad Nayyaroddeen, the startup was incubated at the International Institute of Information Technology (IIIT) in Hyderabad in the Center for Innovation and Entrepreneurship (CiE).

The platform's mission is to assist HR managers in sourcing, screening, assessing, and onboarding new employees by leveraging advanced AI technology. The voice AI bots from Hirex.ai are capable of conducting level–1 interviews on their own and evaluating candidates' non-technical and technical skills without the need for human participation. The time and resources needed for preliminary screening are greatly reduced by this technology, freeing up HR teams to work on higher-level duties.

Hirex.ai addresses common recruitment challenges, such as limited interview resources, inconsistent selection criteria, and interviewer biases. The platform offers a comprehensive suite of AI-powered talent management solutions, including search and resume parsing, AI-proctored coding and MCQ assessments, remote interviews, WhatsApp chatbots, and ATS automation for recruiters. This versatility makes Hirex.ai a valuable tool for various industries and recruitment needs.

*Contd.*

*Contd.*

The company's unique selling proposition lies in its ability to analyze and score technical answers accurately, a feature for which it has filed a patent. This ensures that the assessment process is both efficient and reliable. Furthermore, Hirex.ai's platform can handle up to 10,000 interviews per day, demonstrating its scalability and effectiveness in large-scale recruitment scenarios.

*Source:*

https://www.hirex.ai, https://t-hub.co/hirex-ai-redefining-the-hr-paradigm-through-ai-technology/, https://www.cioinsiderindia.com/vendor/hirexai-building-a-more-efficient-hiring-system-powered-by-ai-cid-1398.html

## Conclusion

Artificial intelligence is revolutionizing business innovation and marketing strategies by facilitating previously unheard-of levels of efficiency, customisation, and strategic decision-making. Artificial intelligence innovations that are transforming business models and spurring growth include generative AI and predictive analytics. To guarantee responsible AI deployment mitigating ethical issues. Organizations must prioritize the responsible development of AI systems that are equitable and transparent, while also promoting ongoing learning and flexibility. Future research should address information gaps about how AI affects long-term marketing success, analyze how AI is embraced in diverse markets, and investigate how AI is integrated with other cutting-edge technology. By tackling these challenges and leveraging AI's opportunities, businesses can unlock new levels of progress, creating a more sustainable and prosperous future. Embracing innovation, adaptability, and ethical responsibility will be vital in fully realizing AI's disruptive potential in marketing and business.

## References


Adam, M., Wessel, M. and Benlian, A. (2021). AI-based chatbots in customer service and their effects on user compliance. Electronic Markets, 31(2), 427–445.

Ajiga, D.I., Ndubuisi, N.L., Asuzu, O.F., Owolabi, O.R., Tubokirifuruar, T.S. and Adeleye, R.A. (2024). AI-Driven Predictive Analytics in Retail: A Review of Emerging Trends and Customer Engagement Strategies. *International Journal of Management and Entrepreneurship Research.* https://doi.org/10.51594/ijmer.v6i2.772

Alchemi.ai. (2023). Transforming Marketing for the Digital Age: Master the 4Ps with AI-powered Strategies. https://www.alchemi.ai/journals/transforming-marketing-for-the-digital-age-master-the-4ps-with-ai-powered-strategies

Amazing Technology. (2024). *How will AI change your future*? (22nd ed., p. 11).

Apte, C. (2010). The role of machine learning in business optimization. *Proceedings of the 27th International Conference on Machine Learning*, Haifa, Israel.

Armutcu, B., Tan, A., Ho, S.P.S., Chow, M.Y.C. and Gleason, K.C. (2024). The effect of bank artificial intelligence on consumer purchase intentions. Kybernetes. https://doi.org/10.1108/K-01-2024-0145

Azeem, M.M., Febriyanto, U., Nurhadi, F.A. and Halid, H. (2024). Unlocking the Values of Artificial Intelligence (AI) in Human Resource Management (HRM) in Enhancing Employee Retention. 16(2).

Bertino, E., Kundu, A. and Sura, Z. (2019). Data transparency with blockchain and AI ethics. *Journal of Data and Information Quality*, *11*(4), 1–8. https://doi.org/10.1145/3312750

BCG. (2024). Overcoming Retail Complexity with AI-Powered Pricing. https://www.bcg.com/publications/2024/overcoming-retail-complexity-with-ai-powered-pricing

Broadhurst Digital. (2024). How To Use AI Across the 7Ps Extended Marketing Mix. https://broadhurst.digital/blog/how-to-use-ai-in-the-7p-marketing-mix

Budhwar, P., et al., (2022). Artificial intelligence–challenges and opportunities for international HRM: a review and research agenda. *International Journal of Human Resource Management.*

Chaudhuri, S. and Mohanty, I. (2023). The Importance of Bias Mitigation in AI: Strategies for Fair Ethical AI Systems. UXmatters. https://www.uxmatters.com/mt/archives/2023/07/the-importance-of-bias-mitigation-in-ai-strategies-for-fair-ethical-ai-systems.php

Cheng, Y. and Jiang, H. (2020). How do AI-driven chatbots impact user experience? Examining gratifications, perceived privacy risk, satisfaction, loyalty, and continued use. *Journal of Broadcasting & Electronic Media*, *64*(4), 592–614.

Chennupati, A.K. (2024). The evolution of AI: What does the future hold in the next two years. *World Journal of Advanced Engineering Technology and Sciences*, *12*(01), 022–028. https://doi.org/10.30574/wjaets.2024.12.1.0176

Chintalapati, S. and Pandey, S.K. (2021). Artificial intelligence in marketing: A systematic literature review. *International Journal of Market Research*, *64*(1), 38–68. https://doi.org/10.1177/14707853211018428

Chui, M. and Yee, L. (2023). AI could increase corporate profits by $4.4 trillion a year. McKinsey Global Institute. https://www.mckinsey.com/mgi/overview/in-the-news/ai-could-increase-corporate-profits-by-4-trillion-a-year-according-to-new-research

Davenport, T.H., Guha, A. and Grewal, D. (n.d.). How to Design an AI Marketing Strategy.

De Cremer, D. (2024 June). For Success with AI, Bring Everyone on Board. *Harvard Business Review*, 125–131.

Delaney, J. (2024 June 24). As employers embrace AI, workers fret and seek input. TIME.

Ernst & Young LLP. (2024). Realizing "AI for all" in India.

Fenwick, A., Molnar, G. and Frangos, P. (2024). The critical role of HRM in AI-driven digital transformation: A paradigm shift to enable firms to move from AI implementation to human-centric adoption. *Discover Artificial Intelligence*, *4*(1), 34. https://doi.org/10.1007/s44163-024-00125-4.

Geeks for Geeks. (2024). Artificial Intelligence: An Introduction. https://www.geeksforgeeks.org/artificial-intelligence-an-introduction/

Genkina, D. (2024). AI Prompt Engineering is dead. IEEE Spectrum. https://spectrum.ieee.org/prompt-engineering-is-dead

Gent, E. (2024). When AI's Large Language Models Shrink. IEEE Spectrum. https://spectrum.ieee.org/large-language-models-size

Gligor, D.M., Pillai, K.G. and Golgeci, I. (2021). Theorizing the dark side of business-to-business relationships in the era of AI, big data, and blockchain. *Journal of Business Research*, *133*, 79–88. https://doi.org/10.1016/j.jbusres.2021.04.043

Haleem, A., Javaid, M., Asim Qadri, M., Pratap Singh, R. and Suman, R. (2022). Artificial intelligence (AI) applications for marketing: A literature-based study. *International Journal of Intelligent Networks*, *3*, 119–132. https://doi.org/10.1016/j.ijin.2022.08.005

Haton, J. (2006). A brief introduction to artificial intelligence, 1-13. https://www.sciencedirect.com/science/article/pii/S1474667015330226

Heitmann, M. (2024). Generative AI for Marketing Content Creation: New Rules for an Old Game. *NIM Marketing Intelligence Review*, *16*(1), 10–17. https://doi.org/10.2478/nimmir-2024-0002.

Hutson, M. (2024). 1-bit LLMs Could Solve AI's Energy Demands. *IEEE Spectrum*. https://spectrum.ieee.org/1-bit-llm

IFACET. (2023). Understanding Bias in Artificial Intelligence: Challenges, Impacts, and Mitigation Strategies. EICTA. https://eicta.iitk.ac.in/knowledge-hub/artificial-intelligence/understanding-bias-in-artificial-intelligence-challenges-impacts-and-mitigation-strategies/

Jarek, K. and Mazurek, G. (2019). Marketing and artificial intelligence. *Central European Business Review*, *8*(2), 46–55. https://doi.org/10.18267/j.cebr.213

Kavanagh, C. (2019). New Tech, New Threats, and New Governance Challenges: An Opportunity to Craft Smarter Responses? https://www.jstor.org/stable/resrep20978.5

Kim Oanh, V.T. (2024a). Evolving Landscape of E-Commerce Marketing and Customer Service: The Impact of AI Integration. *Journal of Electrical Systems*, 20(3s), 1125–1137. https://doi.org/10.52783/jes.1426.

Kim Oanh, V.T. (2024b). Revolutionizing Engagement: How AI is Transforming the Digital Marketing Landscape. Journal of Electrical Systems, 20(4s), 2504–2514. https://doi.org/10.52783/jes.2914.

Krugmann, J.O. and Hartmann, J. (2024). Sentiment Analysis in the Age of Generative AI. *Customer Needs and Solutions*, *11*(1), 3. https://doi.org/10.1007/s40547-024-00143-4

Kshetri, N., Dwivedi, Y.K., Davenport, T.H. and Panteli, N. (2024). Generative artificial intelligence in marketing: Applications, opportunities, challenges, and research agenda. *International Journal of Information Management*, 75, 102716. https://doi.org/10.1016/j.ijinfomgt.2023.102716

Landingi. (2023). Conversion Rate Optimization with AI in 2023. https://landingi.com/blog/conversion-rate-optimization-with-ai

Ledro, C., Nosella, A. and Vinelli, A. (2022). Artificial intelligence in customer relationship management: literature review and future research directions. *Journal of Business & Industrial Marketing*, *37*(13), 48–63.

Leszkiewicz, A., Hormann, T. and Krafft, M. (2022). Smart Business and the Social Value of AI. In T. Bondarouk and M. R. Olivas-Luján (Eds.), *Advanced Series in Management* (pp. 19–34). Emerald Publishing Limited. https://doi.org/10.1108/S1877-636120220000028004

Mariani, M. M., Perez-Vega, R. and Wirtz, J. (2022). AI in marketing, consumer research, and psychology: A systematic literature review and research agenda. *Psychology & Marketing*, 39(4), 755–776. https://doi.org/10.1002/mar.21619

Marjerison, R.K., Zhang, Y. and Zheng, H. (2022). AI in E-Commerce: Application of the Use and Gratification Model to The Acceptance of Chatbots. *Sustainability*, *14*(21), 14270. https://doi.org/10.3390/su142114270

McKinsey. (2023). AI-powered marketing and sales reach new heights with generative AI, https://www.mckinsey.com/~/media/mckinsey/business%20functions/marketing%20and%20sales/our%20insights/ai%20powered%20marketing%20and%20sales%20reach%20new%20heights%20with%20generative%20ai/ai-powered-marketing-and-sales-reach-new-heights-with-generative-ai.pdf

McKinsey. (2024). How retailers can drive profitable growth through dynamic pricing. https://www.mckinsey.com/industries/retail/our-insights/how-retailers-can-drive-profitable-growth-through-dynamic-pricing

Mittal et al. (2024). State of Generative AI in the Enterprise Quarter Two report. Deloitte.

Nankervis, A., et al. (2021). 'Are we there yet?' Australian HR professionals and the fourth industrial revolution. *Asia Pacific Journal of Human Resources*.

Nosto. (2023). Email Marketing eCommerce Conversion Rate Boosting Best Practices. https://www.nosto.com/blog/email-marketing-ecommerce-conversion-rate

Qamar, S., et al. (2021). AI applications in HRM: A systematic review. *Journal of Business Research*, 123, 1–15. https://doi.org/10.1016/j.jbusres.2020.11.012.

Rajmohan, S. (2024). The Legal Issues to Consider When Adopting AI. IEEE *Spectrum*. https://spectrum.ieee.org/legal-issues-to-consider-ai

Rodriguez, A., et al. (2023). Sentiment analysis using AI: Insights from a study in Brazil. *Journal of AI Research*, *45*(3), 256–278.

Shah, V. and Patel, K. (2023). Generative AI: Challenges and Opportunities in the Context of India. CVPR 2023. https://virajshah.com/assets/genai_indian_context.pdf

Shatat, A. and Shatat, A. (2022). The use of artificial intelligence capabilities in logistics and supply chain management: Major challenges and key benefits. *2022 ASU International Conference in Emerging Technologies for Sustainability and Intelligent Systems (ICETSIS)*. https://doi.org/10.1109/ICETSIS55481.2022.9888901

Shu, S.C. and Xing, T.H. (2021). Application of AI in modern logistics systems. *2021 11th International Conference on Information Technology in Medicine and Education*. https://doi.org/10.1109/ITME53901.2021.00015.

Smith, C. (2006). The History of Artificial Intelligence, *History of Computing*, University of Washington. https://courses.cs.washington.edu/courses/csep590/06au/projects/history-ai.pdf

Smith Hanley Associates. (2024). *AI in Market Research*. https://www.smithhanley.com/2024/03/28/ai-in-market-research/

Stokel-Walker, C. (2024). Chatbot invasion. *Scientific American*, July/August 2024, 16.

Suh, B. (2021). When Should You Use AI to Solve Problems? *Harvard Business Review*. https://hbr.org/2021/02/when-should-you-use-ai-to-solve-problems

Syam, N. and Kaul, R. (2021). Support Vector Machines in Marketing and Sales. In N. Syam and R. Kaul (Eds.), *Machine Learning and Artificial Intelligence in Marketing and Sales* (pp. 85–137). Emerald Publishing Limited. https://doi.org/10.1108/978-1-80043-880-420211005

Tabrizi, B., et al. (2023). Companies That Replace People with AI Will Get Left Behind. *Harvard Business Review*. https://hbr.org/2023/06/companies-that-replace-people-with-ai-will-get-left-behind

Tan, K.L., Lee, C.P. and Lim, K.M. (2023). A Survey of Sentiment Analysis: Approaches, Datasets, and Future Research. *Applied Sciences*, *13*(7), 4550. https://doi.org/10.3390/app13074550

Townson, S. (2021). *Three Areas Where AI Will Boost Your Competitive Advantage*. Oliver Wyman. https://www.oliverwyman.com/our-expertise/insights/2021/dec/three-areas-where-ai-will-boost-your-competitive-advantage.html

Tyagi, S. (2024 January 31). Artificial Intelligence: Transforming India with a Glimpse into the Future. LinkedIn. https://www.linkedin.com/pulse/artificial-intelligence-transforming-india-glimpse-future-tyagi-gdahc/

Van der Made (2023). The Future of Artificial Intelligence. *Forbes*. https://www.forbes.com/sites/forbestechcouncil/2023/04/10/the-future-of-artificial-intelligence/

Zhang, C., et al. (2021). Study on artificial intelligence: The state of the art and future prospects. *Journal of Industrial Information Integration*, 23, 1. https://www.sciencedirect.com/science/article/pii/S2452414X21000248

# 9 The Integration of Artificial Intelligence (AI) in Hospitality Management

Dr. Kaushik Samaddar[1*] and Dr Sanjana Mondal[2]

**This chapter discusses how Artificial Intelligence (AI) is being integrated into Hospitality Management, including how it helps improve customer service, boost operational efficiencies, and stimulates creativity.** It puts these developments in the larger context of the Fourth Industrial Revolution (IR 4.0), which is about using new technologies in all parts of life. It also discusses the obstacles and critical factors to consider when incorporating AI into this area, such as protecting guest information, locating and training the necessary staff, and the expenses of using these technologies. It also examines real-world examples of how hotel organizations in India, such as Taj Hotels, Lemon Tree Hotels, and Oyo Rooms, are utilizing AI to improve guest experiences, smooth operations, and increase efficiency. This chapter provides detailed guidance to hotels and managers on how to use AI to not only improve current operations but also prepare for future growth and sustainability.

## Changing Dynamics in Hospitality Management

**Hospitality Management** (HM) has transformed significantly; partly due to changes in consumer behaviour, technological advancement, economic developments, regulatory changes, and growing consciousness of sustainability (Samaddar and Mondal, 2024). These changing dynamics have pushed the customer's expectations towards better and more personalized service (Law et al., 2024). Initially, the focus was on basic services and manual processes, but since then, the HM industry has embraced smart technologies like mobile apps, AI, IoT, and big data analytics. These developments have revolutionized the way customers interact; from merely checking in with their mobile phones, and controlling their room settings, to house-keeping and service delivery, thanks to AI-powered customization and automation. Using cloud services for managing properties and improving cyber security helps keep operations smooth and keeps data safe. Efforts to use energy and water more wisely show the industry's move towards being more

[1] Assistant Professor (Marketing), Symbiosis Institute of Business Management, Bengaluru.
[2] Associate Professor (Marketing), CMS Business School, JAIN University, Bangalore, India. Email: sanjana.official86@gmail.com[2]
* Corresponding author: samaddar.kaushik@gmail.com

DOI: 10.1201/9781003559849-9

sustainable. As the HM continues to evolve, industry stakeholders eye towards more personalized, efficient, and sustainable guest experiences. This would reflect the ongoing commitment to excellence and adaptation efforts to strive and evolve in the dynamic global landscape. Some dimensions of change in across the HM sector (See Fig. 1) are mentioned below:

## Technological Innovations

Technological advancements have brought about a significant transformation in the HM sector that has, in turn, enhanced guest experiences, streamlined day-to-day operations, and boosted efficiency all across. Advanced mobile technology has ensured maximum convenience and minimizing wait times through mobile check-in/check-out, and mobile keys have revolutionized the process of guest arrival and departure experience (Nam et al., 2021). AI and Machine Learning (ML) have customised service offerings through the help of virtual assistants and chatbots. Moreover, data analytics enabled optimization of prices and initiation of effective marketing strategies. The Internet of Things (IoT) supports controlling smart rooms (lighting, temperature, and entertainment) that not only ensure energy saving but also have enhanced customer experiences throughout (Osei et al., 2020). Additionally, AR and VR-based technologies present visitors and guests with an overall immersive experience through the virtual tours. Hence, these technological advancements have transformed the HM sector toward a more personalised and innovative future.

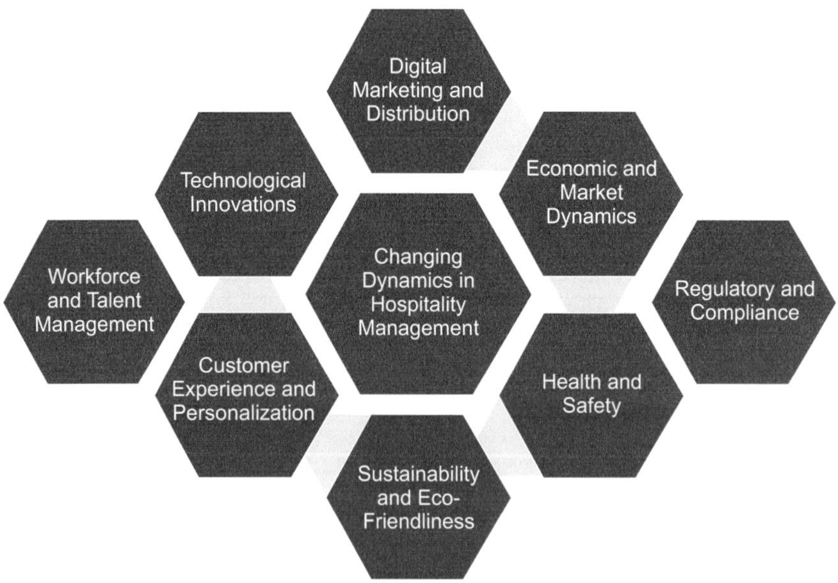


**Fig. 1** Changing Dynamics in HM.
(*Source:* Author')

### Customer Experience and Personalization

The dimensions of "Customer Experience" and "Personalization" have enabled the HM industry to develop innovative service offerings and enhance visitors' experience. Industry stakeholders have been leveraging data-analytics to meet the guests' preferences, drawing increased satisfaction and building loyalty among visitors (Mariani and Borghi, 2021). This customized offerings range from eccentric room settings to curated local cultural experiences and involvement. Recently, the HM industry stakeholders have also been making use of advanced CRM facilities to closely monitor visitors' tastes and preferences, on-site behaviours, and service feedback. This enables them to make an efficient forecast of demand and suitably offer decisional cues. Furthermore, digital concierge services together with smartphone-based applications offer individualized suggestions and real-time guidance, which in turn creates an intriguing and momentous stay (Kong et al., 2024). Zeroing in on the essence of customization, hospitality stakeholders not only improvise the overall guest experience but also leverage a competitive market advantage, fostering long-term association and recurring business .

### Sustainability and Eco-Friendliness

Sustainability and eco-friendliness are increasingly becoming an integral component of HM as the industry promptly responds to increasing consciousness about the environment and responsible consumption (Mondal and Samaddar, 2022). Hotels and resorts are embracing green initiatives like energy-efficient lighting, smart thermostats, and water-saving fixtures to minimize their carbon footprint and check on their operational costs (Buhalis and Moldavska, 2022). To minimize the environmental impact and support local economies, many businesses are also increasingly aiming at sustainable procurement of foods that are eco-friendly and also locally grown (Samaddar and Mondal, 2023). Staff training programs ensured that the staff and guests were well-versed in the new health and safety protocols. This, in turn, builds an environment of trust and instills a sense of confidence among guests and other related stakeholders.

### Economic and Market Dynamics

Economic and market variables have a significant impact on HM strategies, affecting everything from pricing policies to service offerings. The hospitality industry is heavily governed by global economic conditions where disposable income, exchange rates, and evolving tourism patterns and preferences drive demand (Doborjeh et al., 2022). Hotels and restaurants now target specific groups through customized experiences and curated marketing strategies, indicating a more advanced targeting and robust market segmentation process. The advent of alternative lodgings like the shared space concept propounded by Airbnb, has throttled business competition, making traditional players adapt and differentiate themselves through distinct value propositions. With the advent of dynamic pricing concepts, demand and market conditions now decide the product and service prices, and become a critical instrument for increasing revenue in the sector (Talo n-Ballestero et al., 2022). Finally, globalization has expanded the acceptability and demand of hotel brands, resulting in cross-border collaboration and worldwide popularity. Hence, to survive and grow in today's increasingly challenging business environment, hospitality managers should exhibit agility, embrace a data-driven outlook, and adopt a customer-centric attitude.

### *Digital Marketing and Distribution*

Digital marketing and distribution concerning the HM industry have become significant factors, guiding how different stakeholders like hotels and restaurants attract and involve their customers. With the emergence of online travel agencies (OTAs), social media platforms, and search engines, the HM sector has adopted a multi-dimensional approach to target and involve a larger audience. Hotels and restaurants have embraced search engine optimization (SEO) strategy, pay-per-click (PPC) advertising features, and content marketing tactics to develop their online presence and enhance direct reservations, and reduce their dependence on third-party agencies. Marketing through social media platforms and influencers, they connect with key prospects in more personalised and impactful ways, focusing on the unique service offerings and experiences (Kong et al., 2024). Additionally, e-mail marketing promotions through advanced customer relationship management (CRM) systems also provide targeted promotions and individualised communication to foster customer confidence, driving cultural loyalty and boosting repeat business. Furthermore, testimonials and visitors' review mechanisms are also critical in establishing credibility. Through integrating digital marketing with diverse distribution methods, HM industry stakeholders achieve revenue optimization, enhanced brand presence, and develop a competitive business environment.

### *Workforce and Talent Management*

One of the most critical attributes of the HM industry is the talent and workforce management, which has a direct connection with both operational effectiveness and the overall service quality. Hence, the hotel and restaurant businesses put a lot of importance on efficient talent acquisition, developing and retaining important staff members who not only contribute toward enriching guest experiences but also contribute to the economic well-being of the business (Mondal and Samaddar, 2023). Rigorous training and development practices ensure that employees are aware of the most recent health and safety procedures, technology tools, and service standards. Additionally, cultivating an inclusive and diverse workplace fosters creativity and problem-solving skills, which are crucial in a fast-paced HM sector (Odugbesan et al., 2023). The popularity of flexible working environments, such as remote work or work-from-home options for administrative positions and flexible scheduling for front-line employees, boost employee satisfaction and attract a larger talent pool. Performance appraisal and long-term development procedures provide chances for professional advancement, and frequent feedback is crucial for sustaining high levels of motivation and engagement. Businesses in the HM industry can thus create a devoted, competent team that can propel long-term success and provide guests with memorable experiences by investing in their workers.

## Regulatory and Compliance

HM practices are also governed by regulatory and compliance matters, which guarantee that hotels and resorts adhere to industry norms and legal frameworks. Compliance in the form of local, national, and international standards, including environmental sustainability, labour laws, health and safety, data protection, etc. Since the COVID-19 outbreak, strict adherence to health and safety protocols is essential for safeguarding both visitors and employees. Adherence to prevalent labour laws ensures equitable compensation and a suitable working environment. Building trust and protecting guest information are all governed by laws like the GDPR (General Data Protection Regulation) (Yallop et al., 2023). Hence, these critical dimensions together shape today's HM industry, fostering innovation, customer-centricity, and sustainability.

## Artificial Intelligence in Hospitality Management

This section discusses the application of AI and the impact of IR 4.0 on the HM industry.

### *Key Areas of AI Application in Hospitality Management*

Five application areas of AI on HM are discussed in the following sub-sections (See Fig. 2):

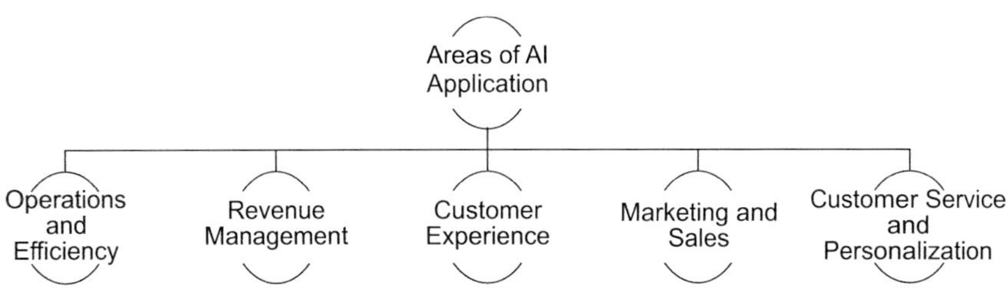


**Fig. 2** Application of AI in HM. (*Source:* Author's Creation)

## Customer Service and Personalization

AI has brought in a revolution in the hotel management industry by improvising and amalgamating two important dimensions of customer service and personalization.

The AI-driven technological advancements in the form of virtual assistants and chatbots provide round the clock guest services in diverse languages, ensuring timely and prompt service,boosting customer satisfaction. Self-check-in and out facilities, enabled by the AI-powered facial recognition system, have decreased wait times and optimized overall customer service processes. Through visitor data analysis, AI-driven mechanisms initiate strategic decision making like dynamic pricing or marketing policies. Tourists can also keep track on their requirements for room settings, food preferences, and other related services. These developments not only have spiked overall efficiency and consistent service delivery but also have drawn maximum customer loyalty through repeat bookings.

### *Operations and Efficiency*

Recent years have witnessed a transformation in the HM industry with the adoption of AI-driven mechanisms that have brought a holistic operational efficiency. From demand forecasting to inventory management processes, functional attributes within hotels and restaurants are now managed by predictive analytics facilitated by AI. Even daily operational chores like housekeeping schedules, floor management, energy maintenance, and repair requirements are automated through AI-driven technologies, resulting in optimum resource utilization while minimizing operational expenses. Additionally, AI-based revenue management mechanisms monitor current market trends and real-time customer information for setting pricing policies, augmenting maximum occupancy and enhancing revenue. Apart from helping in forecasting demand, AI boosts efficient supply chain management functions in timely refiling and restocking and minimizing excess stocking and reducing wastages. Finally, AI also plays a major role in supporting administrative work and presenting data-driven insights in customizing service delivery and maintaining quality across. These processes not only achieve operational efficiency but also augment service quality and holistic customer experience, initiating an inclusive growth, market competitiveness and business profitability.

### *Revenue Management*

An AI-based revenue management system in the HM industry helps to optimize pricing and maximize profits. Here, the volume of customer data that consists of previous booking patterns, market demand, competitor pricing, and even local cultural events are used to forecast future trends precisely. Additionally, AI helps profile and segment its customers based on their past booking behaviours and choices, enabling them to develop curated promotions and packages for each market segment separately (Kong et al., 2023). Moreover, by leveraging machine learning algorithms, hotels can detect ongoing market trends and insights that manual human analysis might overlook, leading to more precise decision-making. Overall, AI in revenue management streamlines the overall pricing strategies, boosts occupancy rates, and enhances overall financial performance, providing a significant advantage in a fiercely competitive market.

### Customer Experience

AI-enabled chatbots and virtual assistants offer 24-hour customer service, answering inquiries, reservations, and special requests quickly and accurately. AI-based systems can forecast future demands and curate interactions by assessing guest data and offering activities, dining choices, and facilities based on the guest's previous behaviour and options (Bulchand-Gidumal et al., 2023). In-room AI gadgets allow visitors to control their room temperature and lighting, and access services with voice commands, deriving pleasure and comfort. Additionally, AI-driven sentiment analysis of customer reviews and comments aids hotel staff in locating key areas for further improvement and addressing pressing issues promptly. Finally, AI augments guest experience by automating repetitive chores and offering personalized attention, while spreading satisfaction and building loyalty.

### Marketing and Sales

The marketing and sales domain in HM is getting transformed under the AI revolution, wherein hotels and restaurants are developing targeted communications and campaigns, resulting in more customer engagement and conversion. Data analytics through AI systems, segmenting consumers based on booking history that includes their choices, tastes, and behaviours, enabling targeted marketing messages and offers that resonate with certain audiences. Future guest forecasting through predictive analytics facilitated by AI-based systems ensures that marketing strategies are relevant and updated. Chatbots and virtual assistants enable a 24/7 online service that answers questions and provides suggestions throughout the booking process, resulting in more direct bookings (Jabeen et al., 2022). AI-driven systems further improve the CRM process by automating follow-ups and personalized messaging, which in turn results in stronger customer engagement and repeat business. Furthermore, it also results in enhanced productivity and long-term loyalty.

## Impact of IR 4.0 on Hospitality Management

The 4th IR includes the integration of cyber-physical systems, IoT, big data, and AI, driving significant changes in the HM sector (Osei et al., 2020). Through IoT integration, interconnected systems allow smart devices within the hotel and restaurants to communicate in real-time enhancing HVAC, security, and guest services. Big data analytics facilitates HM stakeholders to comprehend customer insights, track operational functions, and analyze market trends, which leads to more strategic planning and precise decision making. Robust cybersecurity measures ensure enhanced security of customer data and instill trust within the evolving digitalized environment. AI and IoT technologies also support the sustainability concept that optimizes energy management, reducing environmental impact, and minimizing operational costs (Knani et al., 2022). These developments together drive the HM sector, making it more efficient, secure, and sustainable.

Increasing the customer base necessitates rigorous safeguards of client information and instilling trust among prospects, wherein the deployment of AI and IR 4.0 technologies becomes challenging (Bedi and Sharma, 2023). Integration expenses that include investment in infrastructure, software, and personnel training and development systems, also become a significant barrier. Furthermore, to make the transition smooth and worthwhile, staff must successfully handle the newest technology and make it easier for the guest to adapt. This demands an urgent need for upskilling for the workforce at each level, which will not only improve customer service but also optimize operations and facilitate data-driven decision making. With this technological innovation and advancement, the HM industry should improve its efficiency and usher in competitiveness in an increasingly digital environment.

## Case Studies on Artificial Intelligence In Hospitality Management

Here are detailed case studies of AI integration into hospitality service management in India, highlighting how different hotels and hospitality chains are leveraging AI to enhance guest experiences, streamline operations, and drive efficiency (Pillai and Sivathanu, 2020).

### *Taj Hotels: Digital Transformation and Guest Experience Enhancement*

Taj Hotels, a brand under the Indian Hotels Company Limited (IHCL), launched a digital transformation initiative to enhance guest experiences and streamline operations through the use of AI. Key applications include AI-powered chatbots that handle guest inquiries and reservations, and provide information about hotel services and local attractions, offering 24/7 support and reducing response times for greater guest convenience and satisfaction. Personalized guest services leverage AI to analyze guest data and preferences, delivering customized room settings and dining recommendations, which significantly boost guest satisfaction and loyalty. Sentiment analysis of guest reviews and feedback allows the hotel to understand guest sentiments and identify areas for improvement, facilitating proactive issue resolution and enhanced service quality. Operational efficiency is achieved through AI-driven optimization of housekeeping schedules, predictive maintenance, and effective inventory management, leading to cost reductions and timely service delivery (Sen and Kaushik, 2016). These initiatives have resulted in heightened guest satisfaction and loyalty, improved operational efficiency, cost savings, increased positive reviews, and a rise in repeat business.

### *OYO Rooms: Operational Efficiency and Dynamic Pricing*

OYO Rooms, a leading budget hotel chain, leverages AI to enhance operational efficiency and optimize pricing strategies. Through dynamic pricing, AI algorithms adjust room rates in real-time based on factors such as demand, seasonality, and competitor pricing, maximizing revenue by aligning prices with market conditions (Kumar and Singh, 2022). Additionally, AI-driven operational automation streamlines housekeeping schedules, inventory management, and maintenance tasks, reducing manual workloads and ensuring timely service delivery. These technological advancements have resulted in increased occupancy rates and revenue, improved operational efficiency and resource management, and enhanced guest satisfaction due to the prompt and efficient services provided.

### *Lemon Tree Hotels: Enhancing Guest Interactions and Operational Management*

Lemon Tree Hotels leverages AI to enhance guest interactions and improve operational management. AI-powered virtual assistants efficiently handle guest inquiries and booking modifications, and provide detailed information about hotel services, thereby enhancing guest convenience with quick and accurate responses. Additionally, sentiment analysis of guest reviews and feedback allows the hotel to understand guest sentiments and proactively address concerns, leading to improved service quality (Bedi and Sharma, 2023). These AI applications result in higher guest satisfaction scores, better-managed operations, and increased guest loyalty and positive reviews.

### *Treebo Hotels: Automation and Personalized Marketing*

Treebo Hotels are redefining hospitality with the power of AI. By utilizing AI systems for self-service check-in/check-out through kiosks or mobile apps, they're reducing waiting time and creating a smoother guest experience. This same AI personalizes marketing campaigns, sending targeted offers based on your preferences and past stays. This double-dose of AI leads to increased guest satisfaction, stronger marketing ROI, and ultimately, more repeat bookings and revenue for Treebo (Srivastava et al., 2023)

## Future Research Agendas

The integration of Artificial Intelligence (AI) in HM presents numerous research opportunities, aimed at exploring the vast potential and addressing the challenges associated with AI adoption (Gursoy and Cai, 2024). Research on AI-driven personalization should prioritize the development of advanced algorithms to enhance guest experiences by analyzing diverse data sources to predict preferences. Identifying best practices for personalized marketing, while considering the ethical use of guest data, is crucial to maintaining privacy and trust. Additionally, exploring AI's role in optimizing operational processes, such as inventory management and housekeeping, requires a cost-benefit analysis to validate financial viability and improve service quality. AI's potential in dynamic pricing and revenue management necessitates the development of models for better demand forecasting, impacting customer satisfaction and booking rates. AI-powered customer service tools like chatbots should be evaluated against human agents to ensure seamless integration and high service quality. Sentiment analysis using AI can provide real-time feedback, aiding continuous service improvement. Research on AI's contribution to sustainability should focus on optimizing energy consumption and achieving environmental standards without compromising guest comfort. Ethical considerations and data privacy are paramount, requiring measures to protect guest data and comply with regulations. Investigating AI's impact on staff roles and training will facilitate smooth AI integration, enhancing productivity. Finally, understanding consumer acceptance of AI-enabled services is vital, identifying factors influencing guest acceptance and strategies to foster it.

## Conclusion

In conclusion, the integration of Artificial Intelligence (AI) in hospitality management holds immense potential to revolutionize the industry (Buhalis and Moldavska 2022). Through AI-driven personalization, operational efficiency and automation, dynamic pricing and revenue management, customer service enhancement, sentiment analysis, and feedback management, sustainability and energy management, AI ethics and data privacy, AI integration and staff training, and consumer acceptance and behavior, hotels can enhance guest experiences, streamline operations, and drive profitability. However, future research agendas must focus on addressing challenges such as data privacy, integration costs, skill development, and ethical considerations to ensure the responsible and effective implementation of AI technologies. By exploring these research areas and advancing knowledge in AI integration, the hospitality industry can unlock new opportunities for growth and innovation, ultimately redefining the guest experience in the digital age.

## References

Bedi, K. and Sharma, N. (2023). Digital Marketing: Strategies, Trends, Implementation, and Practices. A Case of Uttarakhand Star Category Hotels. *Journal of Informatics Education and Research*, *3*(2).

Buhalis, D. and Moldavska, I. (2022). Voice assistants in hospitality: using artificial intelligence for customer service. *Journal of Hospitality and Tourism Technology*, *13*(3), 386–403.

Bulchand-Gidumal, J., William Secin, E., O'Connor, P. and Buhalis, D. (2023). Artificial intelligence's impact on hospitality and tourism marketing: exploring key themes and addressing challenges. *Current Issues in Tourism*, 1–18.

Doborjeh, Z., Hemmington, N., Doborjeh, M. and Kasabov, N. (2022). Artificial intelligence: a systematic review of methods and applications in hospitality and tourism. *International Journal of Contemporary Hospitality Management*, *34*(3), 1154–1176.

Gursoy, D. and Cai, R. (2024). Artificial intelligence: an overview of research trends and future directions. *International Journal of Contemporary Hospitality Management*. Vol. ahead-of-print No. ahead-of-print. https://doi.org/10.1108/IJCHM-03-2024-0322

Jabeen, F., Al Zaidi, S. and Al Dhaheri, M.H. (2022). Automation and artificial intelligence in hospitality and tourism. *Tourism Review*, *77*(4), 1043–1061.

Jiang, Y. and Wen, J. (2020). Effects of COVID-19 on hotel marketing and management: a perspective article. *International Journal of Contemporary Hospitality Management*, *32*(8), 2563–2573.

Knani, M., Echchakoui, S., and Ladhari, R. (2022). Artificial intelligence in tourism and hospitality: Bibliometric analysis and research agenda. *International Journal of Hospitality Management*, *107*, 103317.

Kong, H., Wang, K., Qiu, X., Cheung, C. and Bu, N. (2023). 30 years of artificial intelligence (AI) research relating to the hospitality and tourism industry. *International Journal of Contemporary Hospitality Management*, *35*(6), 2157–2177.

Kong, H., Yin, Z., Chon, K., Yuan, Y. and Yu, J. (2024). How does artificial intelligence (AI) enhance hospitality employee innovation? The roles of exploration, AI trust, and proactive personality. *Journal of Hospitality Marketing & Management*, *33*(3), 261–287.

Kumar, R. and Singh, J. (2022). OYO: Growth, Descend, Resilience, Resurgence. *Emerging Economies Cases Journal*, *4*(2), 55–71.

Law, R., Lin, K. J., Ye, H. and Fong, D.K.C. (2024). Artificial intelligence research in hospitality: a state-of-the-art review and future directions. *International Journal of Contemporary Hospitality Management*, *36*(6), 2049–2068.

Mariani, M. and Borghi, M. (2021). Customers' evaluation of mechanical artificial intelligence in hospitality services: a study using online reviews analytics. *International Journal of Contemporary Hospitality Management*, *33*(11), 3956–3976.

Mondal, S. and Samaddar, K. (2022). Responsible tourism towards sustainable development: Literature review and research agenda. *Trends in Asia Pacific Business and Management Research*, 85–122.

Mondal, S. and Samaddar, K. (2023). Reinforcing the significance of human factor in achieving quality performance in data-driven supply chain management. *The TQM Journal*, *35*(1), 183–209.

Nam, K., Dutt, C.S., Chathoth, P., Daghfous, A. and Khan, M.S. (2021). The adoption of artificial intelligence and robotics in the hotel industry: prospects and challenges. *Electronic Markets*, *31*, 553–574.

Odugbesan, J.A., Aghazadeh, S., Al Qaralleh, R.E. and Sogeke, O.S. (2023). Green talent management and employees' innovative work behavior: the roles of artificial intelligence and transformational leadership. *Journal of Knowledge Management*, *27*(3), 696–716.

Osei, B.A., Ragavan, N.A. and Mensah, H.K. (2020). Prospects of the fourth industrial revolution for the hospitality industry: a literature review. *Journal of Hospitality and Tourism Technology*, *11*(3), 479–494.

Pillai, R. and Sivathanu, B. (2020). Adoption of AI-based chatbots for hospitality and tourism. *International Journal of Contemporary Hospitality Management*, *32*(10), 3199–3226.

Samaddar, Kaushik, and Sanjana Mondal. "Reinforcing sustainable consumption practices through promoting gastronomic tourism: a cross-sectional study from India and Bangladesh." *International Journal of Tourism Cities* 10.1 (2023): 185–212.

Samaddar, K. and Mondal, S. (2024). AR and VR-based travel: A responsible practice towards sustainable tourism. *International Journal of Tourism Cities*, *10*(1), 105–128.

Sen, K. and Kaushik, T. (2016). Recent innovative measures across different functions in the Indian hospitality industry: A case study from Accor Hotels. *Worldwide Hospitality and Tourism Themes*, *8*(4), 481–489.

Srivastava, P.R., Eachempati, P., Charles, V. and Rana, N.P. (2023). A hybrid machine learning approach to hotel sales rank prediction. *Journal of the Operational Research Society*, *74*(6), 1407–1423.

Talon-Ballestero, P., Nieto-García, M. and González-Serrano, L. (2022). The wheel of dynamic pricing: Towards open pricing and one to one pricing in hotel revenue management. *International Journal of Hospitality Management*, *102*, 103184.

Yallop, A.C., Gică, O.A., Moisescu, O.I., Coroş, M.M. and Séraphin, H. (2023). The digital traveller: implications for data ethics and data governance in tourism and hospitality. *Journal of Consumer Marketing*, *40*(2), 155–170.

# 10 The Role of Artificial Intelligence (AI) in Determining the Holistic Aspect of Talent Management in the IT Industry: A Qualitative Study

Dr. Vivek Aggarwal[1*], M.V. Rama Prasad[2], Dr. Sankar Mukherjee[3], Poorvi Agrawal[4] and Md Mahabub Alam[5]

The talent acquisition landscape is undergoing a significant shift towards competency-based hiring. The purpose of this descriptive study, based on case analysis, is to explore the synergy between competency-based talent acquisition through the application of AI (Artificial Intelligence) applications, outlining how this partnership can contribute to achieving key recruitment goals and talent management elevates an organization's work environment.

This study has attempted to explore the application of AI technology in Talent management and competency development through the designing of the subjective experience of case phenomena of IBM and Google within the purposive sample of these two technological giants to ascertain the efficacy of the application of AI in solving the talent management challenges in the highly attrition oriented IT sector.

The current study inferred that AI (artificial intelligence) has a substantive impact on transformation, creating a paradigm shift in the talent acquisition process and enhancing employee competencies under the talent development mechanism. Furthermore, this heuristic study has found a positive relationship between the process of talent acquisition and post-skills and competencies development among new and existing employees under the application of AI.

## Introduction

Many researchers have rendered various meanings of the term talent from diversified angles (Ansar and Baloch 2018). The selected definition is determined by the business's strategy, the organization's structure, the environment in which

1 Professor, Galgotias University, Greater Noida, Uttar Pradesh.
2 Professor, GITAM School of Business, GITAM (Deemed to be University), Bangalore.
3 Associate Professor, M S Ramaiah Institute of Management, Bengaluru, Karnataka.
4 Research Scholar, Galgotias University, Greater Noida, Uttar Pradesh.
5 Software Architect & Engineering Manager, Draup Business Solutions Private Limited, Bengaluru, Karnataka.
Email: rmusunur@gitam.edu[2]; alapanmistu@gmail.com[3]; poorvi8266agrawal@gmail.com[4]; mahabubprof@gmail.com[5]
* Corresponding author: vivek.aggarwal@galgotiasuniversity.edu.in[1]

DOI: 10.1201/9781003559849-10

the firm competes, and other factors (CIPD, 2007). Talent is divergent by the terminology used inside the business. Piansoongnern et al., (2010) commended Morton's definition of talent as a small group of employees' knowledge, abilities, and ideologies that may generate unique value for the firm with current resources.

Talent Management is more complex than leadership development and human resource management. Organizational talent management involves more than recruitment, retention, and development, which constitute strategy, organizational culture, and change management (Milani et al., 2021). Talent Management is considered a major driver of Strategic HRM in many organizations (Sandler, 2006). A study of the Institute of Management and Administration's 2006 HR problems revealed that 75% of respondents ranked talent management as their priority. AI (Artificial intelligence) defines a wider class of technologies that allow a computer to perform various tasks requiring human acknowledgment, including adaptive decision-making (Tambe et al., 2019). The concurrence of these concerns has emerged as a key factor of performance and an analytical concern for enterprises (Hughes and Rog, 2008).

In various organizations, this often extends to the early stages of acquisition, it eventually becomes a responsibility between HR and all the recruiting managers with support from the learning organization (Greer et al., 2021). The Acquisition process is a deliberate method of illuminating, engaging, and onboarding outstanding people into the business, which has grown substantially over the past decade (Friedman et al., 2021). The strength of globalization has somewhat compelled HR professionals to reconsider their approach and change according to the changing needs and challenges (Ulrich et al., 2009), which affirm that the capabilities of all HR practitioners once needed are no longer enough in the new world of HR challenges. One way to enhance knowledge is to create models of variations of personnel functions in organizations that are placed on actions, roles, behavior, and relationships (Tyson, 1995). Since human resource (HR) plans and strategies are created over an extended period, taking into account industrial relations systems, economic conditions, anticipated societal, global, and technological changes, as well as new business operations directions, HRM is more prudent today (Compton, 2009).

Draganidis and Mentzas (2006) define a competency model as "a list of competencies made from observing satisfactory or exceptional employee performance for a specific occupation".

AI has arisen as an extreme force, penetrating many industries and transforming how people work, live, and interact. Its collision extends beyond science fiction, with real-world applications ranging from healthcare and banking to entertainment and manufacturing. The impact of AI on HR is one of the most philosophical and optimistic of these disciplines. Artificial intelligence is among the most dominant technologies that are changing the labor market (Huang and Rust, 2018).

Modern inventions such as AI, machine learning, AR/VR, and Metaverse are a few disruptive technologies that play an important role within the field of HRM, endorsing and shaping various people management functions and practices (Bersin and Chamorro-Premuzic, 2019; Malik, et al., 2023).

The application of AI extends beyond just Human Resources Management; it's also remarkable in healthcare and the energy industries (Almarashda et al., 2021). Over the last few decades, HRM has undergone a profound transformation, encompassing cross-functional and various data-driven approaches (Bresciani et al., 2021). For the first time, technology is helping to improve human intelligence, creating new challenges for HRM (Abbass, 2019). Digital recruitment, particularly through the use of artificial intelligence (AI), offers a significant advantage by increasing the number of job applications received and broadening the diversity of the applicant pool (Wilson and Daugherty, 2018).

## Literature Review

The area of talent management in the field of interest for researchers and industry practitioners has been overemphasized in the advancement of AI emergence and rolling out of its application across business domains as part of strategic talent management (Collings and Mellahi, 2009). A few consultants at McKinsey have given a new name to talent acquisition and post-nurturing as the war for talent in 1997( Axelrod et al., 2002). Talent management is the most critical function of the strategic Human Resources function, as stated in many previous research studies in HR investment and practices. Researchers used an empirical investigation in several efforts to determine the association between these variables (Gerhart, 2005). The world-famous financial consulting house Deloitte Consulting LLP has significantly studied business intelligence by connecting human capital management (Talent Management) with an organization's financial performance (Deloitte Consulting LLP, 2005).

AI is widely known for its diversity in prediction across many fields or sectors, and such potential capabilities attract attention in industries, companies, firms, or business leaders (Kiron, 2017). However, this isn't an easy path and frequently calls for advanced cognitive capabilities to grasp such a futuristic technology. The benefit of AI in recruitment flows to assess the current and past experiences from a candidate's resume and academic credentials is enormous; however, it may remain ineffective in making a good judgment or analysis based on unembodied data like their personality traits or cultural data points (Rana, 2018 ).

The significant shift in business mobility has drawn the attention of academic researchers as well as industry practitioners to investigate the challenging nature of human capital management under the lens of talent management more relevant in these times. The significant reduction of global trade barriers, driven by the processes of liberalization, privatization, and globalization, has redefined the role of human resource management, positioning it as a more strategic and integral component of organizational success (Novicevic and Harvey, 2001).

A study conducted in 2013 revealed that 54% of MSMEs (Small and Medium-sized Enterprises) have an inclusive policy for all employees under talent management mechanisms. Moreover, the research suggests that a company incorporates 29% of technical experts in talent management, whereas 10% become managerial cadets, and the rest of 7% are designated to the elite category (Festing et al., 2013).

Technical professionals drive the IT industry with a plethora of skills and competencies. There needs to be more research focused on the systematic talent management of technical professionals (Kim et al., 2014). The dual ladder system is deemed to be the most popular approach to managing technical talent (Hesketh et al., 1992). The exhilarating momentum of technologies and the changes of its dynamic character brought a new dimension to the industry 4.0 (fourth generation) revolution has created a storm in talent acquisition, talent retention, and skills and competencies development across all IT industries. This change of perspective propels the importance of more academic research in this area (Whysall et al., 2019).

This heuristic study is a subjective approach to understanding the importance of talent management in the IT sector, given ever-growing technical skills acquisition, retention, and nurturing under the holistic aspect of overall talent management as part of strategic human resource management(SHRM) in the major IT sector. Therefore, a case-based heuristic study emphasizes two major IT giants, IBM and Google, to analyze their strategic human resource practice on talent management through the application of game-changing technologies, precisely AI.

Watson Candidate Assistant (WCA), AI alerts, and AI chatter analysis are a few AI tools that transform the ambit of talent management at IBM (Guenole et al., 2018). Another renowned technology giant, Google, has integrated an AI model named Gemini (Gen AI) in the Google Workspace to streamline the talent acquisition workflows (https://workspace.google.com/solutions/ai/hr/). Many leading IT companies worldwide are paving the way for AI applications to create a robust ecosystem in their entire talent management landscape. Top global companies like Amazon, Apple, Facebook(Meta), Walmart, and Microsoft are a few leading multinational conglomerates that are institutionalizing AI implementation in their strategic HR policy(https://testlify.com/case-studies-of-successful-sourcing-programs/).

## Methodology

Heuristic study is an approach to understanding and discovering findings (Moustakas, 1990) under the aspect of phenomenological experience that elicits from human-based cognitive behavior in the field of social science and educational research. So, it is an investigation based on living experience (Sultan, 2018). Hence, the design of this study is based on two phenomenological strategic Human Resource practices executed by two world-leading IT(Information Technology) conglomerates, IBM and Google.

This study is based on secondary data obtained from various cases in IT majors throughout the world. The IBM and Google examples were chosen for a rigorous examination of the scholarly literature. This heuristic study explains the experience of researchers in examining the function of AI in comprehensive talent management (Tranfield et al., 2003). The search for cases has been restricted to those voluntarily chosen from the practices and phenomena of AI application in talent management.

The methods of cases have been selected based on a few major keywords such as “AI (Artificial Intelligence)”, “Talent Management”, Talent Acquisition”, Skills and Competencies” to understand the role and application of AI in the overall talent management exercise. The search is not confined to a stipulated period, but the two cases have been sourced on account of recent phenomena of AI application in Strategic HR practices. The quality of selected cases is based on the case rigor and its merit. Therefore, this study ensures comprehensive methods of high-quality studying and analysis of the robustness of both cases.

## Research Questions

This heuristic approach-based qualitative research posits a few questions to determine the answer. AI application in every sphere of business functions is a time-driven demand. However, it is still restricted within the policy and practical implications among large blue-chip organizations across the world. Therefore, this study has selected only one major sector of economic development in developing and developed economies, called the IT (Information and Technology) sector, as part of an illustration of how AI applications can be a potential solution provider for the most critical function of Human resource strategy as Talent Management (TM).

**Questions**

1. Can AI (Artificial Intelligence) be the panacea for solving the critical problem of Talent Management in the IT sector?
2. Is AI (Artificial Intelligence) a trustworthy integration in Talent Management across business domains across all sectors

## Research Proposition

A research proposition is a statement that defines the validity of the proposed statement to have an opportunity to be proven (Ollis, 2000). Therefore, this heuristic study has made a proposition to understand the outcome of the proposed statement through the analysis of IBM and Google Cases in the area of Talent Management under the aspect of the application of AI

**Proposition 1: There is a strong relationship between the integration of AI(Artificial Intelligence) in Strategic Human Resource Management (SHRM) with Talent Management**

## Analysis and Findings

This heuristic type of qualitative study has attempted to investigate the role and importance of holistic Talent Management (TM) in contemporary business scenarios in the Information Technology (IT) sector, particularly the large technological conglomerate companies. This study is based on phenomena-based human experience (heuristic approach), which demystifies the real-time base policy implementation in the ambit of technological disruptive innovation in exercising the strategic human resource management (SHRM) to find a panacea for the most challenging issue that has not meted out with a sustainable solution. Therefore, this study has opened multiple dimensions of technological integration with human resource function to solve the critical path of overall Talent Management in the large-scale Information Technology (IT) sector. So, this study has selected two phenomena based on disruptive innovation practices by two major IT giants in the world, IBM and Google, and their strategic human resource practice to imply the most advanced cutting-edge technology name Artificial intelligence (AI), that integrates with strategic human resource practice in talent acquisition (TA), Talent Nurturing(TN) and skills and competencies development, talent capital retention (TCR) for their employees.

The term "moonshot" of the HR era refers to IBM's TAM (Talent Acquisition and Management) business use cases with AI or Generative AI. President John F. Kennedy's 1961 seemingly impossible goal of sending a person to the moon within 10 years, when the technology for such a feat did not exist Kennedy, J.F. (2010). the Race to the Moon. AI is capable of tapping into the world of dreams.

This moonshot era of HR could do the job in many HR functions in the blink of an eye. It can act as an early guide for the future of Job description upgrades, skills demands, and employee engagement activities. IBM's business use case studies highlight how AI will help dissect the HR workflow steps and redefine the TAM landscape. Let's delve into them one by one. An AI powered insights and services at scale without ballooning headcount or cost, yet does more.

Financial allocations with AI analysis are faster and more seamless. With shifting market demand, AI applications enable HR departments to acquire and develop employee skills in lockstep. The world is moving faster every day, with vast amounts of data being added to the world. AI will be a key factor in TAM, like other fields. By making sense of the data, employees can understand complex policies way more easily than before.

Notable AI tools developed by IBM to address the above use cases include Watson Candidate Assistant (WCA), an AI candidate engagement tool that simplifies interactions for job seekers at IBM. Additionally, AI Managed Alerts tailor communication between managers and employees. The AI Chatter Analysis tool helps leaders identify issues from various sources, including social media and recommendations, to address them effectively.

Additionally, IBM created an AI-powered compensation planning assistant tool that helps line managers make better decisions by intelligently allocating the weights of various compensation factors (both crucial and non-critical). To further equalize the cost elements, the assistants are also attempting to connect IBM's internal database with data from the Bureau of Labor Statistics (BLS). Also, the tool supports manual override from the line manager against the AI recommendation to support exceptions, and AI learns from such exceptions on how the line manager's decision improves further in the future. IBM wanted to be the quality career guide in the talent space, so they built Watson Career Coach (WCC), infused with AI, to be the best career coach for an employee. WCC can help employees harness the power of AI to plan their career-like opportunities within the organization, in a different project, or create a study plan for their dream job roles. They also get personalized learning recommendations to keep themselves updated with the trends.

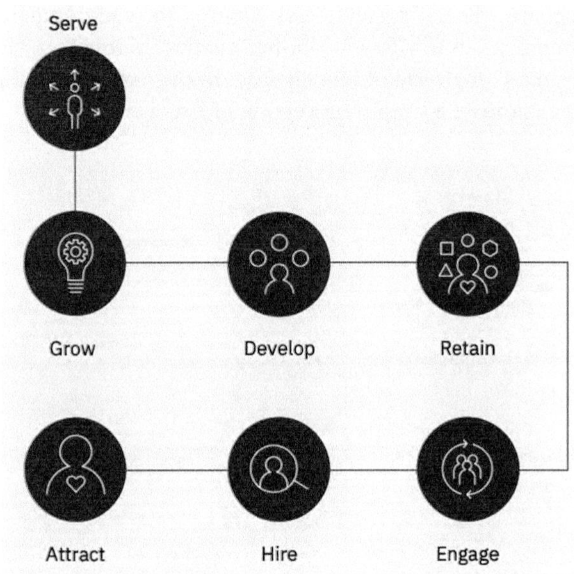


**Fig. 1** Deployment of AI in HR can occur across the entire talent lifecycle at IBM. *Source:* https://www.ibm.com/downloads/cas/A5YLEPBR

A popular Gen AI model like Google's Gemini, an AI-powered assistant, is becoming a key enabler in the Google Workspace, from drafting jobs to onboarding, speeding up hiring, and enhancing policies. Such as creating a job description is just a prompt away, an automated talent training module, and scheduling creation using AI prompts with the integration of all Google Apps at ease.

Moreover, Gemini handles everything from creating your job description for a position to posting it, including adding all the required hashtags, using an AI-powered Google workflow assistant like Google Docs. Furthermore, email outreach to candidates preparing questionnaires for an interview, creating pipelines for interview tracking, or onboarding process pipeline creation, all can be done easily with Gemini prompts with Gmail or Google Sheets.

Consider a phenomena-based case study, understanding complex policies was always been a big hurdle, Gemini just writes a simple prompt in the Google Doc policy like–"Help me with this complex and long HR policy, highlight the key contexts in bullet points, make sure to cover what's allowed and what's disallowed". A response based on the above instructions will be created, and then you can further inquire to learn more about the policy document. It is important to know that Gemini is a generative AI system; hence, even if you create a prompt or do a follow-up query prompt on the policy, but the requested information does not belong to the policy, it might give wrong information. You can avoid getting wrong information by making sure you let the AI system know with simple guided instructions, like strictly not to look outside information or make it up. Verify the response, then if required, ask Gemini to guide you further to draft an email communication to HR with further queries or doubts, or just save your understanding in a Google Doc file with ease. In the case of HR simplifying the complex, they can create a simplified version of it as well.

Findings Chart

| TECH GIANT | TOOLS | OBSERVATION |
|---|---|---|
| IBM | WCA, AI Alerts, AI Chatter Analysis | Focused on candidates interview experience and automated alerts, feedback survey and recommendation to scale up Talent Management process |
| Google | Gemini AI model integration to Google Workspace | Focused on making their existing product to be super smart and converted into AI with HR since Google Workspace products are widely used |

**Fig. 2** What the Tech Giants focused on while infusing AI with HR.
*Source:* Author's Design and Creation on the Canva App

**Challenges of AI (Artificial Intelligence) in HR (Human Resource) in Contemporary Competition of Human Resource Capital Management**
Job cut scarcity is one of the major challenges while implementing AI in HR since AI could potentially reduce or automate HR activity, resulting in lower workforce requirements or upskilling the existing employees, or restructuring changes to go through these changes, and being empathic at the same time. In a perfect world, an AI-powered platform with a human touch that works like a companion for humans will make the world a better place for tomorrow.

Privacy is a big challenge in AI implementation since personal data is shared for analysis to create a better AI system with high intelligence. However, that poses a risk of privacy concerns, and trust and should be taken seriously. A transparent AI system and robust data management with data privacy help build trust in AI. A Responsible AI (RAI) principles framework integration while building AI systems will greatly improve trust and safety.

Cybersecurity is super critical for AI. An infected AI model or AI application poses a huge risk of compromising sensitive data. Organizations and their business leaders should take extensive measures with the help of IT and SOCs (security operation centers) to make sure the AI model or AI application is secure and all safety measures are in place.

AI is prone to being biased, this can be an overwhelming problem if it is implemented without proper measures. A biased AI -powered interaction in HR (Human Resources) will hurt the sentiments of employees or candidates greatly and can damage the brand reputation on a large scale. A careful measurement of bias control mechanism along with RLHF (reinforcement learning from human feedback), i.e., a machine learning (ML) technique that uses human input to optimize AI models, helps to build a better AI model.

## Discussion

This heuristic study has a plethora of dimensions to attain a comprehensive conclusion. Regardless of the size of the organization, talent management is regarded as the central hub of the Key Responsible Areas (KRAs).. This study has unfolded the phenomenon of AI (Artificial Intelligence) application in determining the result of attaining the goal of Talent Management in the large-scale Information Technology(IT) sector and its HR (Human Resource) challenges. Moreover, this qualitative paper has shown the phenomena in reality in the area of human resource strategy to adopt the AI application in the function of Talent Management. Furthermore, this heuristic study is a testimony for other large-scale technological majors to understand and make successive decisions in accomplishing the goal of human capital management (HCM). Its sector is the most volatile industry to acquire and subsequently retain high-skilled employees. Hence, Talent Management is deemed the intuitive aspect of challenges for the HR (Human Resources) function. This study provides a silver lining for emerging IT business entities to alter their strategic human resource policy to be technology-driven talent management.

### *Limitations of the Study*

This qualitative study has its limitations. This is a heuristic investigation in a phenomenological approach to understand the complex phenomena (**Gomes 2007)** of talent management and to find the path to the solution under the application of disruptive technology. As a result, this study is constrained to the perception based on cognitive behavior (human experience). So, the application of AI in IBM and Google to solve the complex phenomena of Talent Management (TM) has its limitations because it is based on human (researchers') cognitive behavior. Moreover, only two phenomenon-based cases from two technological giants (IBM and Google) have been investigated in this study, under the heading of AI integration in Talent management. So, the applicability has its limitations because it has investigated only two tech giants (IBM and Google), not the lion's share of large-scale IT organizations.

As a result, this study has limitations as only two selective cases have been analyzed from the perspective of AI application in Talent Management.

Other research-based literature from different databases has not been considered for the study. Hence, this limitation of case-based heuristic research study is acknowledged, given the transparency of the study's score and research design (Moher et al., 2010).

## Future Research Dimension

**Artificial intelligence (AI) research in talent acquisition and management (TAM) has a lot of potential and can completely change the field.** A few major areas in the future of AI will play a pivotal role. AI-powered Application Tracking System(ATS) to track the E2E (End to End) hiring process will be interactive, with better resume relevancy creation in context with job description and more. Let's say you want to know the conversion rate of a hiring process from resume screening to interviews and interview feedback. An AI system can analyze these steps to highlight the pain points and recommend suggestions to improve the flow, thus improving the conversion rate.

An AI-powered employee benefits system can answer all the important queries for an employee 24x7 without worrying about whom to connect, when to connect, or how the HR will perceive it. Feedback sentiment analysis can enhance the understanding of a candidate's sentiment and suitability for the organization's culture. Emotional Intelligence addition in TAM will help keep the employees better engaged with clarity in the organization, and offer better decision-making possibilities to drive the success to a new high.

## Conclusion

Artificial intelligence (AI) and its applications have started to overpower contemporary business operations. The widespread application of technology with its disruptive characteristics has made a paradigm shift in traditional business operations. The policy and practice across various functions in an organization have been significantly impacted by the application of artificial intelligence (AI) throughout the entire spectrum. Under this purview of ongoing phenomena in today's business operation, this study has highlighted that the most critical aspects of strategic human resource function are Talent Acquisition (TA), Talent Retention (TR), and Talent Development under Skills and Competency enhancement. Therefore, this heuristic nature of qualitative study aims to understand the most prominent sector in the world business scenario, called the Information Technology (IT) Industry. Moreover, this business sector comprises the most skilled employees. Thus, the most important and difficult aspect of human resource management is talent management (TM). The key to overcoming these significant obstacles and examining talent management as a whole is strategy. The high rate of attrition is the most arduous problem that HR comes across in this sector. Hence, this qualitative study seeks to understand the current phenomenon-based practices of two major IT sectors (IBM and Google) in Holistic Talent Management regarding the application of Artificial Intelligence (AI). Heuristic research is the cognitive behavior developed based on human experience. Therefore, this study concludes based on the phenomena of AI application in Talent Management practice by IBM and Google that AI application is the panacea to finding an application-based solution for Talent Management in the Information Technology (IT) business landscape. Applying this AI advancement in the TAM (Talent Acquisition and Management) is crucial for all IT organizations, if not already adopted, to stay in the race for business growth under cutthroat competition. Moreover, keeping a tab on the future development of AI, be it from the big giants or new age AI companies or startups, who can further reshape the TAM workflows with disruptive innovations or develop a new terminology for talent management and acquisitions will be super critical for any organization, including IT industry in future.

## References


Abbass, H.A. (2019). Social integration of artificial intelligence: functions, automation allocation logic, and human-autonomy trust. *Cognit. Comput.* 11, 159–171. doi: 10.1007/s12559-018-9619-0

Almarashda, H.A.H.A., Baba, I. bin, Ramli, A.A., Memon, A.H. and Rahman, I.A. (2021). Human Resource Management and Technology Development in Artificial Intelligence Adoption in the UAE Energy Sector. *Journal of Applied Engineering Sciences*, 11(2).

Ansar, N. and Baloch, A. (2018). Talent and talent management: definition and issues. *IBT Journal of Business Studies (JBS)*, *1*(2).

Axelrod, R., Ford, G.R., Riolo, R.L. and Cohen, M.D. (2002). Beyond geography: Cooperation with persistent links in the absence of clustered neighborhoods. *Personality and social psychology review*, *6*(4), 341–346.

Bersin, J. and Chamorro-Premuzic, T. (2019). New ways to gauge talent and potential. *MIT Sloan management review*, *60*(2), 1.

Bresciani, S., Ciampi, F., Meli, F. and Ferraris, A. (2021). Using big data for co-innovation processes: Mapping the field of data-driven innovation, proposing theoretical developments, and providing a research agenda. *Int. J. Inf. Manage.* 60, 102347. doi: 10.1016/j.ijinfomgt.2021.102347

Chartered Institute of Personnel and Development, 2007. Talent management: Strategy, Policy, Practice. Chartered Institute of Personnel and Development, London.

Collings, D.G. and Mellahi, K. (2009). Strategic talent management: A review and research agenda. *Human resource management review*, *19*(4), 304–313.

Compton, R. (2009). Towards an Integrated Model of Strategic Human Resource Management – An Australian Case Study, Research and Practice in Human Resource Management, 17(2), pp. 81–93.

Draganidis F. and Mentzas G. (2006). Competency-Based Management: A Review of Systems and Approaches. Information Management and Computer Security, Vol. 14, No. 1, pp. 51–64.

Festing, M., Schäfer, L. and Scullion, H. (2013). Talent management in medium-sized German companies: an explorative study and agenda for future research. *Intern. J. Hum. Res. Manag.* 24, 1872–1893. doi: 10.1080/09585192.2013.777538

Friedman, G. and Greenfield, C. (2021). Integrating Culture in Successful RIA Mergers and Acquisitions. *Springer Books*.

Gerhart, B. (2005). Human resources and business performance: Findings, unanswered questions, and an alternative approach. *Management revue*, 174–185.

Gomes, W.B. (2007). Distinção entre procedimentos técnico e lógico na análise fenomenológicaRevista da Abordagem Gestáltica, 13(2), 228–240.

Greer, C.R. (2021). *Strategic human resource management*. Pearson Custom Publishing.

Guenole, N. and Feinzig, S. (2018). The business case for AI in HR. *With Insights and Tips on Getting Started. Armonk: IBM Smarter Workforce Institute, IBM Corporation.*

Hesketh, B., McLachlan, K. and Gardner, D. (1992). Work adjustment theory: An empirical test using a fuzzy rating scale. *Journal of Vocational Behavior*, *40*(3), 318–337

Hughes, J. and E. Rog, 2008. Talent management: A strategy for improving employee recruitment, retention and engagement within a hospitality organization. *International Journal of Contemporary Hospitality Management*, *20*: 743–757.

Huang, M.H. and Rust, R.T. (2018). Artificial intelligence in service. *Journal of service research*, *21*(2), 155–172.

Kim, S., Kim, D., Cho, S.W., Kim, J. and Kim, J.S. (2014). Highly efficient RNA-guided genome editing in human cells via delivery of purified Cas9 ribonucleoproteins. *Genome Research*, *24*(6), 1012–1019.

Kiron, D. (2017). What Managers Need to Know About Artificial Intelligence. MIT Sloan Management Review.

Malik, A., Budhwar, P., Mohan, H. and NR, S. (2022). Employee experience–the missing link for engaging employees: insights from an MNE's AI-based HR ecosystem. *Hum. Resour. Manage.* 62, 97–115. doi: 10.1002/hrm.22133

Milani, R., Setti, I. and Argentero, P. (2021). Learning agility and talent management: A systematic review and prospects. *Consulting Psychology Journal: Practice and Research*, *73*(4), 349.

Moher, D., Liberati, A., Tetzlaff, J., Altman, D.G., and Prisma Group. (2010). Preferred reporting items for systematic reviews and meta-analyses: the PRISMA statement. *International journal of surgery*, *8*(5), 336–341.

Moustakas, C. (1990). Heuristic research: Design, methodology, and applications. Sage Publications.

Novicevic, M.M. and Harvey, M. (2001). The changing role of the corporate HR function in global organizations of the twenty-first century. *International Journal of Human Resource Management*, *12*(8), 1251–1268.

Ollis, D. F. (1995). The research proposition. Chemical Engineering Education, *29*(4), 222–229.

Piansoongnern, O. and Anurit, P. (2010). Talent Management: Quantitative and Qualitative Studies of HR Practitioners in Thailand. *International Journal of Organizational Innovation*, *3*(1).

Rana, D. (2018). The Future of HR in the Presence of AI: A Conceptual Study. SSRN Electronic Journal. https://doi.org/10.2139/ssrn.3335670S.F. Sandler, 'Critical issues in HR drive 2006 priorities: #1 is talent management', *HR Focus*, *83*(1) (2006) 1 and 13–15.

Sandler, S.F. (2006). Critical issues in HR drive 2006 priorities: #1 is talent management. *HR Focus*, *83*(1), 13–15.

Tambe, P., Cappelli, P. and Yakubovich, V. (2019) "Artificial Intelligence in Human Resources Management: Challenges and a Path Forward." *California Management Review*, (2019). Accessed July 20, 2024. https://doi.org/10.1177/0008125619867910.

Tansley, C., 2011. What do we mean by the term "talent" talent management? Industrial Commercial Training, *43*(5): 266–274.

Tranfield, D., Denyer, D. and Smart, P. (2003). Towards a methodology for developing evidence-informed management knowledge using systematic review. *British journal of management*, *14*(3), 207–222.

Tyson, Shaun (1995). Human resource strategy: Towards a general theory of human resource management. Great Britain: Pitman Publishing.

Ulrich, D., Allen, J., Brockbank, W., Younger, J. and Nyman, M. (2009). HR Transformation: Building human resources from the outside in. New York: McGraw-Hill.

Whysall, Z., Owtram, M. and Brittain, S. (2019). The new talent management challenges of Industry 4.0. *Journal of Management Development*, *38*(2), 118–129.

Wilson, J. and Daugherty, P.R. (2018), "Collaborative intelligence: humans and AI are joining forces", *Harvard Business Review*.

# 11 | AI Transforming the Future of Human Resource Management

S. Neaba[1], Mani Deepak Choudhry[2*], Dr M Sundarrajan[3] and Dr Alka Agnihotri[4]

The rapid advancement of Artificial Intelligence (AI) is transforming various aspects of organizational functions, with Human Resource Management (HRM) being no exception. AI's potential to revolutionize HR functions has generated significant interest and concern among HR professionals, scholars, and organizations. As AI technologies evolve, they will profoundly impact how HR tasks are performed, from recruitment and talent management to employee engagement and development. AI offers numerous benefits, including enhanced efficiency and accuracy, but also raises important ethical and strategic considerations. The adoption of AI in HRM is expected to bring about significant changes in how organizations operate, making it essential to understand its implications for the future of work. Numerous studies have looked into the possible uses of AI in data analytics and hiring. This chapter provides an in-depth exploration of the impact of AI on HRM, offering insights into the transformative changes in organizations.

## Introduction to AI in Human Resource Management

Artificial intelligence is the wind of change blowing through many industries, and human resource management has not been left behind. With organizations' struggles in this digitalized world, incorporating AI into HRM practices becomes a strategic driver towards efficiency, accuracy, and strategic decision-making. This chapter thus explores how AI is reshaping traditional HRM functions into new roles, reshaping the workforce, and creating new opportunities for employees and employers (Shukla et al., 2023). From recruitment and talent management to employee engagement and performance evaluation, AI will redefine the future of HRM.

[1] Research Scholar, Department of Management Studies, National Institute of Technology, Calicut, Kerala, India.
[2] Department of Computing Technologies, School of Computing, SRM Institute of Science and Technology, Kattankulathur Campus, Chengalpattu, Tamil Nadu, India.
[3] Department of Networking and Communications, School of Computing, SRM Institute of Science and Technology, Kattankulathur Campus, Chengalpattu, Tamil Nadu, India.
[4] Associate Professor, Galgotias University, Greater Noida, Uttar Pradesh.
* Corresponding author: manideec@srmist.edu.in

DOI: 10.1201/9781003559849-11

One of the key areas through which AI will produce a more profound effect in HRM would be in recruitment. The traditional approaches toward recruitment often come with a lot of waste of time, are biased, and resource-intensive. AI-powered tools let human resource managers automate candidate screening, predict job performance, and reduce unconscious bias for efficient and fair hiring (Nishar 2022). By employing machine learning algorithms and natural language processing, AI systems can analyze vast amounts of data, identify patterns, and generate data-driven recommendations to enhance the accuracy and effectiveness of recruitment strategies.

Beyond recruitment, AI has a place even in changing talent management by offering HR professionals greater insight into employee performance, potential, and career development needs (Zhang and Chen, 2024). Such AI-driven analytics can identify high-potential employees, recommend personally relevant training programs, and predict potential attrition risks, therefore assisting organizations in taking proactive initiatives to manage their talent pipelines. This step toward data-driven talent management leads to better employee development while aligning workforce capabilities with overall business success to achieve organizational goals (Arslan et al., 2022).

Other key areas in which AI is making a big difference include employee engagement and experience. AI-driven chatbots and virtual assistants are currently being deployed to increase the effectiveness of employee communication, offer real-time support, and customize employee interactions. Tools like these can analyze employee feedback and sentiment in real-time, helping HR professionals address concerns promptly and improve overall satisfaction in the workplace. AI allows organizations to cultivate more engaged and motivated employees by providing a more personalized and responsive HR experience.

The role of AI in HRM will increase with the development of the technology further in the future, toward more intelligent and adaptive HR systems. On the other hand, some increasingly relevant and important ethical and practical considerations accompanying the integration of AI into HRM are data privacy, algorithmic bias, and upskilling HR professionals (Jarrahi et al., 2023; Kuhn et al., 2021; Votto et al., 2021; Pan and Froese, 2023; Jindal et al., 2021). The challenges addressed in the chapter are debated to discuss how organizations can manage the complexities associated with AI adoption into HRM to ensure that AI is used responsibly and effectively in shaping the future of work.

## Overview of AI and its Relevance to HRM

Artificial Intelligence has, in a very short period, become one of the leading drivers of industry transformation, not bypassing human resource management. The point lies in its ability to potentially change the traditional HR function into efficient data-driven operations that respond to the needs of employees and employers alike (Benbya et al., 2020). AI in HRM has several applications: recruitment, performance management, employee engagement, and learning and development.

For instance, AI-driven algorithms can go through hundreds of resumes to pick out the best candidates, greatly speeding up the process of hiring while making it less resource-intensive. Alternatively, AI tools could analyze behavioral patterns to predict employee turnover, thereby enabling the organization to take proactive steps toward retaining talent. It facilitates individualized employee experiences by tailoring learning and development programs to meet the needs and career aspirations of each employee, which directly enhances their satisfaction and productivity. It also gives human resource professionals insight into workforce trends and dynamics through AI-driven analytics. This is the power of AI through the processing of vast arrays of data, it is possible to find patterns and correlations that may not otherwise be apparent, most conducive to more informed decision-making as depicted in Fig. 1. In this respect, it empowers the HR Department to drive the organization more strategically toward its goals. For instance, AI optimizes workforce planning by way of predicting future staffing needs against historical data and market trends, so that an organization is well-prepared for changes in demand (Kaushal et al., 2023).

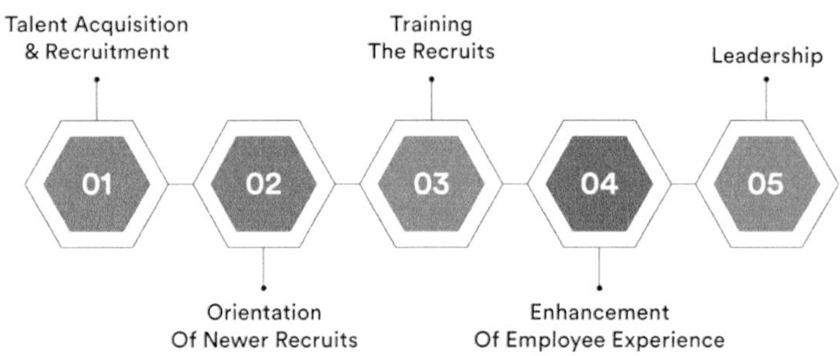


**Fig. 1** Application Specific of AI in HRM.

In Fig. 1, the entire employment lifecycle process is described, from hiring to leadership development. Each stage becomes important in building a strong, engaged, skilled workforce that can meet organizational goals.

The first step, Talent Acquisition and Recruitment, involves a search for individuals who best fit the organization in terms of skill set, culture, and values. Indeed, effective recruitment ensures candidates are sourced, interviewed, and evaluated in terms of their potential to contribute to the company's long-term vision. In the modern landscape, AI-driven tools enhance the recruitment process through automation of preliminary screening, skill gap identification, and predictive analytics to look into the suitability of the candidate for the particular role. These tools can help recruiting decisions become more inclusive and less biased while keeping the company's overall objectives in mind.

Once the correct people are recruited, the second most important phase for their induction is the **Orientation of New Recruits**. Orientation is usually done to help the employee settle into the company as smoothly as possible. It exposes them to the mission of the company, the culture, and its expectations. Many times, it's an elaborate orientation walk-through regarding their roles, responsibilities, and the structure of the teams they will be working with. A successful orientation program makes the recruits feel welcome and sets the pace for the future in the organization. AI can also contribute in this stage by providing customized onboarding journeys that will take the newbies through necessary training, resources, and role-related information. Such a personalized experience ensures that the recruits get everything they need to become productive team members.

The next process, **Training the Recruits**, plays an important role in helping employees gain the required competencies for their job roles. The training programs thus take on board everything from systems of performing the job at hand to soft skills and leadership qualities. Continuous learning is one of the ways of maintaining an agile and competent workforce, especially in those industries where technology changes day in and day out. AI-powered learning management systems further this training process by tailoring learning paths about the performance of the individual to help employees strengthen not just their weak points but also their strengths. This leads to 24×7 growing through a blend of AI and human-driven training programs to take up new challenges.

By helping employees feel engaged, valued, and inspired to contribute to the organization's success, the fourth step—improving the employee experience—is essential to keeping talent on board. The process for enhancing employee experience entails giving regular feedback, opportunities for career development, and activities aimed at ensuring their well-being. Of course, increasing the productivity and endurance of the engaged employees is a significant positive. AI-driven engagement platforms support the organization in analyzing the feedback and behaviors of employees to extract valuable insights for improvement in workplace culture. Organizations can build a supportive ecosystem that leads employees towards job satisfaction and productivity by offering them a mix of mechanisms of feedback, career progression facilities, and wellness programs.

Finally, the development of **Leadership** is the highest point of this process, which involves identifying and cultivating the organization's future leaders. As staff develop in their jobs, they must be given opportunities to develop leadership skills designed to equip them for more extensive responsibilities. Such leadership training can be in the form of mentorship, coaching, or even leading projects or teams. AI-powered enablement can make it easier to find high-potential workers possessing the skills and moral qualities needed to lead; it also makes it possible to create personalized growth plans and monitor these resources. In this way, the organization will continuously develop a pipeline of leaders competent to accept challenges and lead the company toward success in the times to come.

The above steps together thus form a comprehensive approach toward employee lifecycle management, wherein the organization recruits not only the right talent but also grows and retains talent by focusing on growth, engagement, and leadership development. AI integrated into this process enhances efficiency, personalization, and data-driven decision-making, making the workforce more adaptive and future-ready.

Moreover, AI is critical to improving diversity and inclusion in companies. Since AI tools are known to reduce human bias during recruitment and employee performance appraisal, they tend to provide a fair working environment (Chowdhury et al., 2023). For example, tools analyzing job descriptions ensure that they do not contain language that may subconsciously exclude certain groups of persons from applying. Similarly, AI can track and provide reports on diverse demographics, thus assisting organizations in monitoring their progress and areas that require improvement. In its fullness, relevance to HRM is relevant to opportunities for efficiency gains, informed decision-making, bringing more personalization, and equity in experiences among employees. As AI technologies improve, their influence on HRM will only increase, which will keep driving innovation and transformation in how organizations treat their human resources.

## Historical Background and Evolution of HR Technology

The clear backdrop to understanding the current significance of AI in HRM lies in the evolution of Human Resource technology (Chowdhury et al., 2023; Bankins 2021). Notably, HR technology has been evolving through several distinct phases, which reflect both the broader technological shifts and changing organizational needs as depicted in Fig. 2.

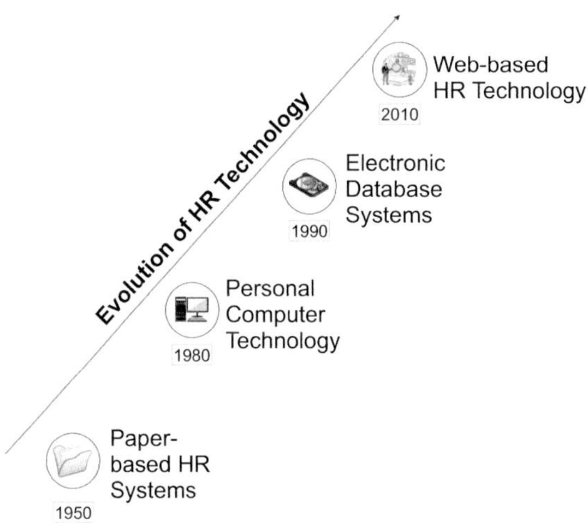


**Fig. 2** Evolution of HR Technology.

## The Pre-Digital Era: Before the 1980s

**HR management was entirely done by hand in the beginning. HR specialists used paper-based methods to handle payroll, employee records, and other administrative duties. During this time, face-to-face communication and physical documentation were heavily relied upon. HR's responsibilities were**

**mostly administrative, including hiring, maintaining compliance with labor regulations, and keeping records.**

### *The Advent of Computerization (1980s)*

It is in this environment that the function of human resource management underwent a digital revolution in the 1980s with the invention of **HR Information Systems (HRIS)**. Truly among the very first systems automating the core function of HR were payroll processing, employee record management, and benefit administration. HRIS reduced the time and effort needed to do these tasks, enabling HR departments to manage larger workforces efficiently. These systems, however, were essentially transactional, largely designed to automate administrative tasks as opposed to developing and offering meaningful insights into key strategic human resource matters.

### *Integrate and Expand (1990s)*

During the 1990s, there was a turn in HR technology from disparate, stand-alone systems to more integrated applications. **Enterprise Resource Planning (ERP)** systems emerged. These integrated the HR function with other business processes, like finance and supply chain management. This gave an organization better coordination across departments and allowed a holistic view of the operations of an organization. During this period, **Applicant Tracking Systems (ATS)** also became more prevalent, which made the recruitment process easier by automating the process of keeping tabs on candidates through the hiring pipeline. Performance management tools have evolved to help organizations evaluate and manage employee performance more systematically.

### *Cloud-based Solutions Started to Become Prominent in the 2000s*

The 2000s brought along the general adoption of cloud computing, shifting HR technology into something more available, scalable, and flexible. Cloud-based HR platforms like Workday and SuccessFactors empowered organizations to run their HR globally with real-time data access from any place in the world (Zehir et al., 2020; Yathiraju, 2022). These platforms also included deeper analytic capabilities, which provided richer insights into workforce trends for HR professionals and enabled them to make more data-driven decisions. Focus began to shift from purely transactional HR to strategic HRM, and the agenda of talent management, employee engagement, and organizational development evolved (Kambur and Yildirim, 2023).

### *The AI Revolution (the 2010s to the Present)*

The latest paradigm in the waves of evolution of HR technology is heralded by the integration of AI and machine learning. AI-driven tools are transforming every area of HRM, from recruitment and onboarding to performance management and employee engagement. AI-driven analytics provide HR professionals with new eyes into workforce dynamics, enabling them to drive more predictive and proactive management. For example, AI can predict employee turnover by looking at engagement scores, performance metrics, and even social media activity. On the recruitment side, AI tools screen resumes and conduct initial interviews, freeing up HR professionals to do work that adds value. AI also plays a very critical role in terms of employee experience. Individual employees can have personalized learning and development programs created about their needs and career aspirations, which are AI-driven. Other ways it improves employee engagement include when AI-powered chatbots provide instant answers to HR-related queries and even help in onboarding and training.

### *Future Ahead*

**As AI continues to develop, its integration into HRM will only become more profound.** Future HR technologies could use more sophisticated capabilities of AI, namely, natural language processing and deep learning, to take HR functions a step further. The AI evolution in HRM will go much more in the direction of a personalized, efficient, and data-driven way of managing human capital, thereby making HR a very strong strategic partner for achieving organizational goals. Thus, the historical evolution of HR technology mirrors a progression from manual, paper-and-pencil processes to sophisticated AI-driven solutions. In addition to increasing the effectiveness of HR operations, it has transformed HR's position inside a company from one of administrative assistance to one of a strategic partner. Probably most disruptive, AI is just the newest phase of a journey that brought new ways of organizing how organizations attract, manage, and develop their human resources.

## Aspects of AI in HRM

The face of human resource management is changing due to artificial intelligence, transferring from normal linear processes, which will improve into much more efficient and data-driven processes. In the area of recruitment and talent management, AI will shift how organizations recognize and nurture potential candidates. These organizations save time and leverage that efficiency by screening applications through AI-driven tools like resume screening algorithms, predictive analytics, and recruitment chatbots as depicted in Fig. 3. Needless to say, it accelerates the recruitment process but provides an added advantage of accuracy while fitting candidates to job roles, showing less bias, and making the workplace much more diverse.

Talent management is another critical area where AI is making its significant presence felt. The AI-driven platforms may identify and recognize current skills gaps, provide recommendations for required training, and construct individual

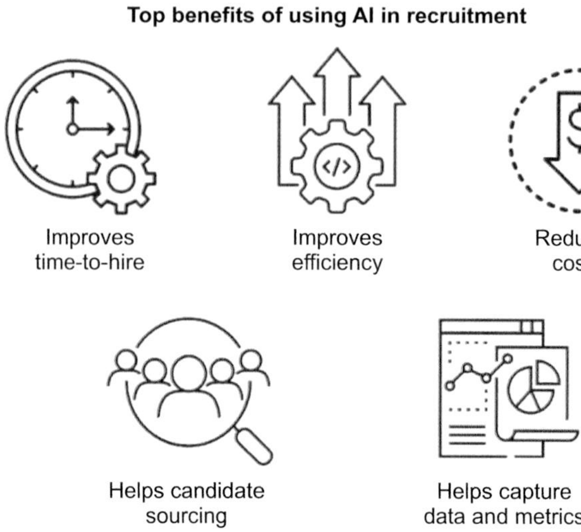


**Fig. 3** AI in Recruitment.

development plans based on big data analysis of employee performance, skills, and career advancement. In that way, staff will keep changing and growing relevant to the organization's needs (Thangaraja et al., 2024; Kadirov et al., 2024). AI can also provide insights on potential turnover risks, allowing the HR manager to take preventive steps to save the top talent and lead a more engaged and loyal workforce.

AI is also reshaping employee engagement, another key aspect of organizational success. With AI applied in sentiment analysis, pulse surveys, and real-time feedback mechanisms, it becomes easier to measure employee satisfaction and identify its problem areas (Paramita et al., 2024). AI delivers meaningful insights to the HR manager to design more personalized engagement activities that will enable relevant conversations with the workforce. What's more, AI-driven virtual assistants and platforms will facilitate such communication and collaboration that the sense of being connected and valued will remain with the employees, irrespective of location. AI is not only smoothing HR processes but is also making staff much more engaged, motivated, and productive.

## AI in Recruitment and Talent Acquisition

Artificial intelligence is entering the recruitment and talent-acquisition functions and changing how organizations identify, evaluate, and hire talent. Traditionally, hiring has been a very time-consuming and sometimes subjective process, relying heavily on manual screening and personal judgment. But now, with the advent of AI, companies can automate and make many facets of the recruitment process better, right from candidate sourcing to the final selection. AI-driven tools and platforms use advanced algorithms, machine learning, and natural language processing to go through humungous data in a quick and enviable degree of accuracy. In a sense, this will reduce bias, assist recruiters in making data-driven judgments, and improve overall productivity. Thus, AI is making the recruitment process seamless and helping organizations to get the best talent faster and more efficiently, thereby gaining a competitive edge in the market. AI's contribution to hiring and talent acquisition will not be restricted to automation; it also offers accuracy and personalization that have never been achievable.

The accuracy with which AI technologies can check candidate profiles against the job descriptions, let alone foresee future performance from past data, is unmatched. In building patterns and trends through candidate behavior and performance, the AI tools bring to the table insights that used to be the preserve of experienced HR practitioners. These insights thus improve candidate experience and quality of hire, reduce turnover rates, and ensure unbiased hiring. Other than that, AI is likely to help firms reduce unconscious bias in the recruitment process, thus creating a more diverse and inclusive workplace. With companies starting to leverage AI in their recruitment strategy, efficiency, accuracy, and success in talent acquisition are very clearly noticeable.

## AI-Driven Recruitment Tools and Platforms

AI-driven recruitment tools and platforms are increasingly changing how organizations of today identify, attract, and acquire talent. Such tools mobilize advanced algorithms and machine learning techniques toward making recruitment more efficient, objective, and scalable. They can process millions of résumés in a fraction of the time any recruiter can, whereby an analysis keyed on essential qualifications identifies matching candidates for job openings based on the understanding of the candidate's profile and the job requisites.

The first and foremost benefit that can be derived from using recruitment tools based on AI is that these help to do away with the load of biases, not only imposed by the hiring team but by the previous biased scenarios set up by the old data sets. Since such tools are based on data and objective criteria, there is a very good chance that the evaluation process doesn't show any bias towards any candidate, compared to manual evaluation. In doing so, unconscious biases, most prevalent in human decision-making, should be kept to a minimum. AI platforms learn from their environment as they go about their job and keep refining for better selection in line with evolving business goals (Agnihotri et al., 2024; Kalia and Mishra, 2023).

Other artificially intelligent-based platforms help even further in candidate engagement and experience through communication at a personal level. For instance, a chatbot could discuss with the candidate in real time, answering their questions and guiding them through the application process while updating them on their application status. This works in favor of not just the candidate but also the recruitment team, allowing them to focus more on strategic activities.

### AI Talent Pipeline Tools

Enables organizations to create a more powerful pipeline of talent. They can look through social media profiles, online portfolios, and even previous job histories to create a list of qualified applicants for any future openings. These applicants may not be actively seeking right now, but they would be a good fit. Only then does such a proactive approach toward talent acquisition open up a wider and more diverse pool of applicants?

A few of the most well-liked AI-driven recruitment tools and platforms are described below.

### HireVue

It uses video interviewing and assessment, powered by AI, to make judgments about candidates based on verbal and non-verbal cues like tone and facial expressions. It's several machine learning algorithms that analyze video responses for a score that recruiters can use to rank candidates in terms of suitability for the role. Interview scheduling can also be automated on the platform, which further reduces the need for manual coordination.

### Pymetrics

This is a neuroscience-driven artificial intelligence platform using games and AI assessments to understand the cognitive and emotional attributes of candidates. It aims for a very fair and impartial hiring decision by matching the candidate from the pool to a specific post based on his or her skills and deficiencies. The Pymetrics machine learning algorithms advance organically as more and more data is added to them, leading to better accuracy in candidate-to-job fit.

### Entelo

Entelo applies AI and predictive analytics in talent sourcing automation. This platform crawls through millions of social media profiles, resumes, and job boards to find candidate matches. It takes machine learning inputs to predict how likely a potential candidate is to change jobs. It can also prioritize passive candidates based on experience and qualifications. Entelo reduces bias by anonymizing demographic data during candidate evaluation.

### Ideal

Ideal is an AI-driven recruitment automation platform that prioritizes candidate matching, shortlisting, and resume screening. Ideal analyzes and grades applicants in real time by integrating with your internal applicant tracking system. Ideal continuously optimizes candidate ranking using historical hiring decision data, improving hire quality and cutting down on recruiting time.

### *XOR*

**To engage candidates, schedule interviews, and automate initial recruitment tasks, XOR provides AI-powered recruitment chatbots. Its chatbot communicates with the candidate through texting, calling, or chatting on Facebook Messenger or WhatsApp, allowing businesses to stay in touch around the clock. These technologies can shorten the time to hire by pre-screening candidates using questions.**

### *Hiretual*

Hiretual is an AI sourcing tool that empowers recruiters to source candidates from over 750 million profiles across various platforms. The platform leverages machine learning for parsing candidates' fits to job descriptions in skills, experience, and qualifications. It can also predict hiring trends and candidate behavior, thus providing the recruiter with valuable insight into the talent pool for informed decisions.

### *Textio*

Textio is an artificial intelligence-based job description and recruitment communication improvement platform. The site scans job postings using natural language processing and suggests improved language that is more inclusive and appeals to the largest number of candidates. This helps companies attract more diverse candidates and makes sure the language better fits their values and brand.

These tools and platforms assist businesses in improving their recruitment strategies through more accurate, speedy, and fair hiring using AI.

In a nutshell, AI-based recruitment tools and platforms can be termed a radical step in human resource management. It automates routine tasks, decision-making, and gives an organization far greater depth of insight into candidate potential by which it can make even more enlightened decisions on hiring and create hard-hitting capable teams.

## Enhancing Candidate Screening and Selection Processes

AI-driven improvements in candidate screening and selection procedures mean the use of complex algorithms and machine learning techniques to remodel and further enhance the processes by which organizations recognize, assess, and onboard employees. AI-driven tools can trawl huge amounts of data regarding candidates, including their resumes, social media profiles, and even video interviews, to appraise qualifications, skill profiles, and cultural fitting more precisely and effectively than traditional methods (Nechytailo, 2023).

AI could then enhance these processes with the help of NLP, parsing, and understanding resume content so that it would assist the system in matching candidates' profiles with job descriptions much more accurately. Alternatively, AI can be used for predictive analytics to estimate the potential success of a candidate in a given role by using data from experiences, and hence avoid mismatches and increase the effectiveness of hiring.

It can enhance fairness and objectivity in the screening that it goes through by eliminating unconscious bias. Training the machine learning model without looking into relevant experience and qualifications, rather than demographic factors affecting human judgment, can avoid such practice. AI-driven video interviewing tools will further filter candidates through a more granular scale using verbal and non-verbal analysis involving tone, facial expression, and body language, which reveal more information on communication skills and personality traits. Apart from attaining efficiency and accuracy, AI also increases the pace of recruitment and frees human resources to strategic activities such as engaging with the best talent and developing a long-term recruitment strategy. Automating some of these mundane tasks, like resume screening or the first look at candidate applications, AI frees up some very valuable time for the HR professional to make some meaningful investment in human interaction and relationship-building with the candidate pool (Sundarapandiyan Natarajan et al., 2024; Prabhakar, 2023; Rodgers et al., 2023).

On the more practical side, examples include HireVue, which uses AI to analyze video interviews, and data-driven recruitment solutions like LinkedIn's Talent Insights. These tools have been observed to significantly reduce time-to-hire and move the quality of hires forward hence, there is some tangible return in using improved AI-based screening and selection processes.

## Case Studies and Real-World Applications

Case studies in applied AI-driven recruitment and talent acquisition disrupt such processes through real-life proofs. These portray practical ways in which organizations put AI to work in driving efficiency, reducing bias, and improving candidate experiences.

a. **AI-Powered Recruitment at Unilever (Woods et al., 2020):** For the Singapore-based global consumer goods firm, Unilever, an AI-driven recruitment process helped the company efficiently sort through candidates. This aided Unilever in fast-tracking their recruitment for entry-level positions with the use of game-based assessments and AI solutions via video interviewing. Average time to hire was reduced from four months to two weeks for Unilever. AI algorithms judged candidates based on video interviews where the verbal responses, facial expressions, and body language were processed for a rounded view of a human. In this way, it created an unbiased, highly predictive forecast for future performance. It has also saved a great human workload for the recruiters in that it allows them more time for higher-level, continuous work. Therefore, with the induction of an AI-powered recruitment process, Unilever changed the way it hires people, especially for low-level positions. With the inclusion of game-based assessments and AI-powered video interviews, the company managed to shorten the usually very long recruitment cycle. Because AI can analyze and process such vast amounts of data about candidates, Unilever was able to reduce the average time it takes to hire somebody from four months to two weeks, not losing any quality in its candidates.

These game-based assessments ranged from cognitive abilities to personality traits and decision-making, in a way that was quite engaging yet informative to the company. Once these were taken, the process was further refined with AI-driven video interviews. Rather than just assessing the verbal response, the AI technology analyzed the facial expressions, body language, and even tone of voice from a candidate. This gave a holistic view of each applicant that was far beyond the scope of a traditional interview.

Artificial intelligence in Unilever's recruitment process helped ensure a much more objective process. The algorithms targeted to pick out candidates lacked unconscious bias, sometimes affecting human judgment. Judging based on pure data from video assessments and game-based exercises meant that the output of this system could predict the actual performance of a candidate more precisely.

The technology also greatly relieved the workload of recruiters. It reduced manual work, like screening and evaluating a large number of applications. It freed human recruiters to be more strategic in their talent acquisition and employee development efforts and made the whole process of recruitment more effective. Such an AI-powered platform quickened the pace, brought more equity into hiring, and freed up valuable resources to let recruiters work on higher-level tasks that require more human insight.

b. **Hilton Worldwide's chatbot for candidate engagement (Benbya et al., 2020):** Hilton Worldwide used a recruitment chatbot, more familiarly known as "Connie," in its continuum to raise candidate engagement and also to ensure that candidate applications get processed much faster. The tool makes use of NLP during interactions with the applicants by answering their questions and helping them go through the application process. This AI-driven tool was quite effective in giving effort-free service to the candidates by insourcing all the information and support on time to the candidates, thereby enhancing employer branding to an even greater extent and increasing candidate satisfaction. Further, it is critical to mention that Hilton Worldwide launched an AI-powered recruitment chatbot, "Connie." This was a bold move in the improvement of candidate experience and effective management of the recruitment process. The chatbot, with the help of NLP, would allow smooth interaction between a candidate and the company. The chatbot was allowed to let the candidates ask questions, know the availability of any position in the company, and guide them through the application process.

Not only was it faster, but with Connie on board, information was relayed to candidates in real time and a very consistent manner. The chatbot would immediately answer queries and support candidates around the clock without human recruiters having to deal with repetition. This AI-driven tool cuts delay in application processing, enabling a candidate to move through the stages faster.

Moreover, Connie made sure the responses to candidates were prompt and accurate, hence greatly improving the candidate experience. Easy access to information and support will make them feel looked after and listened to, which in turn enhances Hilton's employer branding. Candidates who had felt valued and supported throughout the process were a lot more satisfied. This better experience of candidates thus impacted their brand perception about Hilton as being tech-savvy, innovative, and employee-focused.

Connie's implementation showed just how AI can elevate the recruitment process: not by increasing the speed at which applications get handled but by building better engagement, enhancing the image of the company, and hence proving to be a far easier and more delightful experience for prospective employees.

c. **IBM Watson Recruitment (Pham and Paille, 2020):** Famed for cognitive computing, IBM's Watson uses artificial intelligence in recruitment to predict the success and fit of a candidate for the role. Later trickling down through inboxes or in social media profiles, it digs out past decisions on hiring to fish out the most fitting resumes. The support of AI helped IBM reduce unconscious bias within the hiring processes to ensure a more diverse workforce. Watson also enables the detection of patterns and trends that even a human recruiter would probably miss, hence leading to more enlightened hiring decisions. IBM Watson Recruitment leverages its advanced cognitive computing capabilities to revolutionize the hiring process, making it more efficient, unbiased, and insightful. By utilizing AI, Watson can predict a candidate's success and suitability for a role, based on an analysis of their qualifications, experience, and fit with the company culture. Watson takes into account historical data from past hiring decisions, digging into resumes, social media profiles, and other relevant data sources to identify the most promising candidates. This approach ensures that hiring managers are presented with the best possible talent without spending excessive time manually filtering applications.

One of the standout features of IBM Watson Recruitment is its ability to reduce unconscious bias in the hiring process. AI algorithms are programmed to focus solely on merit-based criteria, avoiding the influence of factors like gender, race, or background that might subconsciously affect human decision-making. By focusing purely on skills, experience, and potential fit, Watson helps foster a more diverse and inclusive workforce, a key priority for many organizations today.

In addition to minimizing bias, Watson's AI can detect patterns and trends in data that human recruiters might overlook. This includes subtle correlations between certain candidate attributes and success in a role, as well as market and industry trends that could influence hiring outcomes. These insights enable recruiters to make more informed, data-driven hiring decisions, leading to better matches between candidates and job roles.

Overall, IBM Watson's AI-driven recruitment process enhances the overall efficiency and accuracy of hiring, leading to a more diverse, skilled, and satisfied workforce. It transforms recruitment from a manual, time-consuming process into a more strategic and predictive function that benefits both the company and the candidates.

d. **How Vodafone is Leveraging AI for Volume Hiring?** Inundated by hundreds of applications for customer service positions, AI was more than a necessity for Vodafone (Ganatra and Pandya, 2023). From a numbers point of view, the introduction of a platform allowing the firm to automate quite a large portion of its initial screening made thousands of applications pour in in the quest to identify the most highly qualified contenders matched against pre-specified criteria. The system was also checking language qualification from candidates based on particular job requirements against the most wanted skills in the job specification to ensure those who don't have the required qualification in communication skills never move forward. This approach saved time and, at the same time, achieved the hiring of better-quality candidates. Vodafone faces quite a challenge handling hundreds of applications for customer service positions, and that is where AI became instrumental in streamlining its volume hiring process. The company has engaged an AI-powered recruitment platform meant to automate much of the initial candidate screening. That system enables Vodafone to process thousands of applications efficiently by sifting through those applications based on pre-set criteria that determine the most qualified candidates to advance.

   One of the key benefits of this AI-powered approach was that it allowed for the assessment of candidates' language qualifications and their communication skills-core in customer service. It compared applicants' levels of language proficiency and other job-related skills against the particular requirements listed in the job description. Anyone not meeting the minimum qualifications concerning communication or any other key skills was weeded out early in the process from moving on into the recruitment cycle.

   This AI-based screening saved Vodafone a lot of time and screened the candidates closer to the needs of the company. The automation freed the recruiters from tedious and repetitive tasks like reviewing a high volume of applicants and moved them to more strategic aspects of recruitment-thorough candidate interviews and final selection.

   With the implementation of AI in volume hiring, Vodafone saw better-quality hires faster, improving the overall efficiency and effectiveness of their recruitment process. This approach hastened the time-to-hire, with increased precision in candidate selection to ensure that only the best-fit candidates moved on to successive stages of hiring.

The case studies show how high the benefits have been from using AI in recruitment and talent acquisition. AI in recruitment could allow for speed, accuracy, diversity, and inclusion in hiring processes that drive better business results for organizations.

## AI in Talent Management and Employee Development

In business today, that is changing at a million miles per hour; talent management and employee development are the two areas that come to the fore as those on which organizations are now focusing to remain competitive. Artificial Intelligence is revolutionizing these areas by facilitating more personalized, data-driven approaches to managing and developing talent. Today, AI analyses gargantuan volumes of data through the identification of skills gaps and the ability to make predictive assertions on future talent needs while developing tailored development programs that align with organizational goals and at the same time link to the expectations expected from one's career. This is very significant for the effectiveness of talent management strategies (Foster et al., 2023), ensuring that more meaningful and engaging employee experiences can be built.

Business AI in talent management goes way beyond simple automation of talent management to a deep understanding and insight into the potential and performance of any employee. Advanced AI algorithms in this space would review an employee's process to provide real-time feedback and recommendations for developmental opportunities (Jorzik et al., 2024) as depicted in Fig. 4. Only at this depth of insight will organizations be in a position to create dynamic learning environments within which people can grow and readjust to new challenges. Furthermore, AI-driven talent management systems can spot high potential very early on and ensure the right support and resources for their growth (Kadirov et al., 2024). It can also be used to build up a culture of continuous learning and development and achieve higher satisfaction and retention within an organization.

**Fig. 4** Employee Life Cycle Process.

Figure 4 is depicted above in a detailed view:

## Attraction

The Attraction stage is quite significant as it draws potential candidates toward an organization. In this phase, the key area of concentration is showcasing those factors that make the company an attractive workplace. The organizations invest a lot in carving an employer brand that portrays their culture, values, and benefits. This is conveyed through social media, the company website, and recruitment marketing campaigns. An online presence with credible content and employee testimonials goes a long way in attracting potential candidates. In today's competitive job market, how well a company markets itself can make all the difference in attracting top talent. This involves building a positive employer brand and providing a good candidate experience to attract suitable people who share values with the organization.

## Recruitment

Recruitment is the process by which organizations locate, assess, and acquire candidates to fill job openings. This stage includes key processes such as vacancy advertising, candidate sifting, interviewing, and testing. The effective techniques of recruitment are the descriptions made in detail concerning the post that one needs to recruit, using various channels of recruitment and technology at hand, such as an applicant tracking system or AI-powered assessment tools, which make the process easier. Then the candidates have to be screened in detail to test for job requirements and cultural fit. Effective recruitment not only helps an organization find the right candidate but also aligns talent acquisition with an organization's strategic objectives and contributes to its success.

## Onboarding

Perhaps a very crucial period in effectively integrating a new hire into a job is the beginning of their journey through what is known as Onboarding. Information, training, and support are provided to a person in this stage to put them at ease in the new work environment. Successful onboarding does require structured orientation programs with new hires that introduce them to company policies, the people in the organization, and the organizational culture. It also requires role-specific training to help employees quickly ramp up in their roles. By providing a welcoming atmosphere, along with tools to help individuals understand their roles and how those roles fit into the goals of the organization, effective onboarding boosts employee satisfaction and time to productivity, as well as overall retention.

## Development

The Development stage focuses on the ongoing enhancement and growth of employees' competencies and career prospects. Apart from this, organizations invest in several development initiatives so that their workforce can keep pace with the evolution of demands that a job requires. Continuous learning opportunities through training programs, workshops, and mentorship comprise this stage. Career development plans are also designed in such a way that they help meet the career aspirations of the employees individually and merge these with the needs of the company itself for personal and professional growth. By supporting the careers of their employees and helping them to enhance their skills, companies not only contribute to the workforce with better capabilities but also boost the rate of retention along with satisfaction, developing an active and skilled team.

## Retention

Retention strategies are those concepts aimed at maintaining competent employees committed to and concerned with the organization. This stage calls for a supportive work environment that fosters job satisfaction and ensures competitive compensation and benefits. Recognition programs offering employee achievement awards, flexibilities, and career advancement opportunities are part of a successful retention strategy. Know the needs of your employees and use their input to develop a work culture that limits turnover. High retention means the continuation of institutional knowledge and reduces some of the hiring and training costs associated with new employees. All of these factors play to the organization's advantage in the success of its long-term operations.

## Separation

Separation is when an employee leaves the organization, which may be voluntary or otherwise. This stage addresses the separation process in a professional manner that commands respect. The separations may be classified under two categories: voluntary and non-voluntary, where non-voluntary includes layoffs or terminations, while voluntary includes resignations and retirements. While the former cases should also be treated with care, they require different approaches. An exit interview serves as a tool for soliciting any feedback about an employee's experience, along with areas of improvement. In other words, with a formal offboarding process, one can be sure that all the administrative tasks, not to mention time-consuming ones such as company property returns and knowledge transfers, are all done efficiently. It is effective separation management that keeps good relations with former employees, while offering valuable information for future retention efforts and organizational improvements.

AI-based performance management systems leverage complex algorithms to facilitate the continuous feedback, which is data-driven, about their performances to employees. Traditional methods normally rely on annual reviews and sometimes even subjective evaluations. AI systems, in real-time, scan through a wide range of performance metrics (Asfahani, 2024). Such systems can recognize patterns and anticipate problems, making relevant suggestions that would provide managers with the ability to be proactive in performance concerns, allowing individualization of development plans. The approach seeks to ensure that feedback obtained is timely and relevant to both the employee's and the organization's goals.

Another major milestone in this respect is AI-enabled personalized learning and development programs. The AI-driven platforms can estimate any employee's skills, learning style, and career aspirations before imparting relevant training. Such platforms use data on individual performance and learning style preferences to provide the necessary resources and training that maximize efficiency in learning and employment engagement (Nosratabadi et al., 2022). This approach acquires skills relevant to achieving their career aspirations; therefore, it yields job satisfaction and retention.

One of the most important components in modern talent management, especially in talent retention and succession planning, is predictive analytics. AI algorithms break down years of historical data to point out trends related to employee turnover, performance, and career progression (Madhumita et al., 2024). Organizations can foresee any problems that may arise with employee retention by using such an analysis and taking proper action. Predictive analytics in succession planning secondly identifies high-potential employees and prepares them for future leadership, hence assurance of smooth transition and continuity for key positions within an organization.

## Ethical and Strategic Considerations of AI in HRM

In the fast-changing HRM environment, AI has become a robust force that brings substantial change into various dimensions of HR practices. Regrettably, along with this spreading notion of integrating AI technologies within HRM comes a new raft of ethical and strategic concerns that organizations have to overcome in the interests of securing its responsible and effective implementation (Somasundaram et al., 2020). Essentially, ethical considerations include all matters that pertain to bias, issues of objectivity, fairness, privacy of data, and dehumanization in decisions. To give an illustration, AI algorithms for recruitment and talent management could inadvertently perpetuate existing biases if not monitored and adjusted, which will be unfair to some of the candidates or employees. Another concern about handling personal and sensitive data within AI systems is related to the question of privacy and security of a person's information. This has been creating strategic needs within the organizations in terms of balancing efficiency gains from AI with a human touch in HR processes. AI could improve the ability of HR professionals while evaluating candidates and assessing the performance of employees; however, HR would have to ensure that the purpose and the use of technologies were aimed at complementing human judgment and interaction, not replacing them. Strategic use would thus align these technologies with organizational goals and corresponding values, making AI-driven decisions transparent and implementing regular re-examinations with changes in contentions about the impact of AI on employee experience, organizational culture, and so forth. These ethical and strategic considerations may contribute to organizations using AI in HRM to ensure energy balance in every respect while at the same time promoting a positive organizational culture.

Deep ethical implications and challenges for many organizations accompany the introduction of Artificial Intelligence (AI) in many sectors. These implications mostly concern the issues of bias, privacy, accountability, and the general social impact of the technologies.

### *Bias and Fairness*

The most critical ethical challenge revolving around AI pertains to the phenomenon of preserving or augmenting existing biases. AI systems learn from historical data, and if that data has historical prejudices or inequalities, then it's likely that the AI will reproduce those biases in its results. For example, biased data sources trained algorithms used for recruitment services that subsequently cause discriminatory practices, entailing granting undeserving preference to some candidates while denying others based on their demographic background or other factors. This presents questions of fairness and equality, as the automated decision-making process may end up being systematically prejudicial to particular groups of people. If an organization is to ensure fairness in an AI-based output, then they have to make a conscious effort toward the identification, minimization, and monitoring of bias in the AI model.

Bias and fairness in AI are critical ethical challenges that have huge implications for how those systems impact decision-making across a wide array of domains. At the root of this issue is the nature of the bias itself. Essentially, AI systems-throughout with machine learning-learn patterns from historical data. If that data contains existing social biases and inequities, then the AI will most likely mirror these biases in predictions and recommendations. For instance, if an AI system is fed historical recruitment data biased toward selecting individuals from one demographic background over another, the resultant AI system could turn around and manifest this same bias, which can be unequal concerning hiring outcomes.

Bias in AI emanates from several sources. Historical data is often a source of systemic biases. When an AI model is trained on such data, that may be further strengthened. Bias may be introduced in a system when data collection or preparation is going on. Poor methods of data collection or poor representation of classes may result in biased performance in AI models. For example, a face recognition system trained mostly on lighter-skinned people is very likely to fail when used on people with darker skin tones. Such cases show that there might be something wrong with the data collection practices the outcomes are biased. Besides biased data, algorithmic design can introduce bias into a system. If an algorithm is not well designed to handle class imbalances, it may result in worse performance for underrepresented classes, possibly perpetuating existing disparities.

Biased AI has the potential to make very deep impacts. Such AI systems can, for instance, favor certain groups of candidates in recruitment and discriminate against others, therefore continuing inequalities and making organizations less diverse. Bias may also pertain to issues of access to and the quality of services. For example, AI applied in health could be less precise for a given demographic group, leading to disparities in health outcomes. Furthermore, if the AI systems are unfair, then trust in technology and institutions making use of these systems will be compromised, perhaps provoking resistance to adopting AI and confidence in its decisions.

Eliminating bias and ensuring fairness in AI systems is best approached from multiple angles. Organizations should regularly subject AI models to checks for bias, using statistical and empirical methods to review model outputs for inequities across multiple dimensions of demographics. Additionally, the training data in AI should be ensured to be diverse and representative of all relevant demographic groups. In practice, this means collecting diverse data, correcting imbalanced data sets, and not feeding available biased data into systems because this would only perpetuate the already existing bias. This can be further prevented through the infusion of transparency into the development of algorithms and decision-making processes. Allowing insight into how algorithms work- and, therefore, their inner workings to be understandable is a sure way to advance transparency.

Incorporating human judgment into the process of AI decision-making will also be an important feature. While AI gives valuable insight, human oversight ensures that such decisions are made in line with ethical standards and principles of fairness. Second, this would involve continuous monitoring and feedback to adapt to newer data and societal changes that might impact fairness in AI over time. Finally, having ethical guidelines and a framework for AI development and deployment will help organizations navigate ways to ensure fairness, accountability, and transparency are promoted in their systems. With this in place, an organization will work toward the goal of minimizing biases in AI and assuring equity in outcomes.

### *Privacy and Data Security*

AI research and development heavily rely on large datasets, most of which are often personal information. This has given the heightened privacy of individuals whose private information has since been collected, processed, and analyzed by AI. The information on the subject should be protected from misuse and unauthorized access. More important, though, are questions of transparency in how the data is used and informed consent. Every organization should have strong data protection measures, enforce privacy policies in the workplace, and be open with people regarding their data, including privacy protection practices of data collection and usage.

AI research and development fall in the high domain of scrutiny as far as guarantees of privacy and data security are concerned, particularly because large datasets containing personal information have been used in most cases. Such a dataset naturally involves sensitive data about individuals, which is accumulated, processed, and analyzed; the discretion of information maintenance has become a huge question. Safeguarding that kind of data against misuse and unauthorized access is not only a technical demand but one of the basic ethical imperatives as well. These can only be adequately addressed through the application of effective measures for data protection by the organization. This includes the development and enforcement of a comprehensive privacy policy that regulates the collection, storage, and use of personal information. First, such a policy must comply not only with all applicable legal and regulatory frameworks but also with best practice in respect of data security. Technical measures to prevent data breaches or unauthorized disclosures include encryption, access controls, and audits.

Equally fundamental is the aspect of transparency in the use of personal data. The organizations should clearly state their data practices to these individuals to ensure that data collection, processing, and analysis are done with full knowledge and consent of the people affected. These individuals need to know the type of data that was collected, for what purpose, and for how long the data shall be kept. Transmittal of informed consent is also essential in transparency, allowing people to be responsible for personal decisions concerning their data, by opting out or not. Beyond that, transparency has to do with processes and practices regarding the handling of data in organizations. It means details about the measures taken to protect data privacy, mechanisms for addressing any breach of data, and steps to comply with regulations on privacy. By this openness and accountability, organizations cultivate trust in people, showing how much respect they have for standards that ensure full privacy and security of data. In other words, it follows that the interaction between AI research and data privacy needs to be strongly focused on technical and ethical issues. Rigorous protection of data and transparency in data practices are needed in order not to violate personal information and to respect private life in an information society.

### *Accountability and Transparency*

AI systems make decisions black-boxed to a understanding that is difficult to glean. Thus, responsibility becomes a painful activity in the understanding of decision making from such AI systems, especially in a situation where the decisions taken have consequential effects in areas like criminal justice, health care, among others. In other words, accountability is synonymous with understanding and being in a position to explain decisions that are based on AI technology. This, therefore, means that organizations have to develop auditing mechanisms, provide clear documentation on how the decisions were arrived at, and prepare to explain or justify such outcomes to stakeholders.

### *Employment and Economic Impact of AI*

Adoption of AI has significant economic and employment impacts. While it increases efficiency and the possible creation of new opportunities, AI is bound to lead to more displacement of jobs, which are routine and repetitive practices. This raises an ethical problem concerning the sharing out of benefits accruing from AI and the approaches that organizations take in the face of likely job loss. It is, therefore, crucial that organizations focus more on attempts at re-skilling and up-skilling strategies for employees who might be affected by AI-led changes and initiatives in support of workforce transition and development.

### *Social and Moral Implications*

AI adoption may affect wider social and moral dynamics. For example, artificial intelligence in surveillance and law enforcement has aired views for concerns over privacy and civil liberties. AI technology can significantly track and manipulate a population, denying them human rights in the end. Furthermore, the AI deployment on the decision-making roles traditionally conducted by humans, like judiciaries and medicine, raises appropriateness concerns about machine-driven decisions and moral normative concerns over the dispossession of human judgment in these processes.

Such ethical implications can be tackled only through a multifaceted approach to developing ethical guidelines, regulatory frameworks, and an ongoing dialogue between technologists, policy thinkers, and the public. Meeting them head-on will put organizations in a better place to ensure that their AI systems are developed and deployed in an ethical and socially responsible way.

## Conclusion

Fast-paced development of artificial intelligence is becoming a reshaping force in human resource management, with some potential for changing organizational functions. That said, emerging technologies of AI are bound to make an impact on human resource practices in areas like recruitment, talent acquisition, employee retention, and development. With the potential to fast and correctly process and analyze vast amounts of data, AI will bring along better decision-making and individual employees' development plans. For example, AI-driven recruitment tools enable easier ways of hiring by automating resume screening and initial interviews. Predictive analytics enables better talent acquisition through forecasts of hiring needs and skill gaps. AI also engages employees much better by using real-time sentiment analysis. It gives personalized learning opportunities through tailored training recommendations. At the same time, significant ethical and strategic concerns within the integration of AI into HRM have emerged, such as privacy issues and biased algorithms. In these regards, organizations are called upon to ensure high standards of data privacy and provide strict oversight to prevent bias. On another level, HR professionals will have to fit new roles of AI-driven insight, requiring continuous learning and cultural adaptation to technological change. Effective change management is called for in the integration of AI tools into existing HR processes. This chapter has identified that AI is ushering in a new era of HRM, with attributes linked to data-driven decision-making and strategic human capital management. Its influence on the future of work is due to be enhanced.

## References

Agnihotri, A., Pavitra, K.H., Balusamy, B., Maurya, A. and Bibhakar, P. (2024). Artificial Intelligence Shaping Talent Intelligence and Talent Acquisition for Smart Employee Management. EAI Endorsed Transactions on Internet of Things, 10.

Arslan, A., Cooper, C., Khan, Z., Golgeci, I. and Ali, I. (2022). Artificial intelligence and human workers interaction at team level: a conceptual assessment of the challenges and potential HRM strategies. *International Journal of Manpower*, *43*(1), 75–88.

Asfahani, A.M. (2024). Fusing talent horizons: the transformative role of data integration in modern talent management. *Discover Sustainability*, *5*(1), 25.

Bankins, S. (2021). The ethical use of artificial intelligence in human resource management: a decision-making framework. *Ethics and Information Technology*, *23*(4), 841–854.

Benbya, H., Davenport, T.H. and Pachidi, S. (2020). Artificial intelligence in organizations: Current state and future opportunities. *MIS Quarterly Executive*, *19*(4).

Chowdhury, S., Dey, P., Joel-Edgar, S., Bhattacharya, S., Rodriguez-Espindola, O., Abadie, A. and Truong, L. (2023). Unlocking the value of artificial intelligence in human resource management through AI capability framework. *Human resource management review*, *33*(1), 100899.

Foster, N., Wood, F.M., Fear, M., Pavlos, N., Raby, E. and Edgar, D.W. (2023). IBM Watson AI-enhanced search tool identifies novel candidate genes and provides insight into potential pathomechanisms of traumatic heterotopic ossification. *Burns Open*, *7*(4), 126–138.

Ganatra, N.J. and Pandya, J.D. (2023). The transformative impact of artificial intelligence on hr practices and employee experience: A review. *Journal of Management Research and Analysis*, *10*(2), 106–111.

Jarrahi, M.H., Askay, D., Eshraghi, A. and Smith, P. (2023). Artificial intelligence and knowledge management: A partnership between human and AI. *Business Horizons*, *66*(1), 87–99.

Jindal, P. and Shaikh, M. (2021). Talent Retention: A Mediator of the Relationship Between Talent Management Strategies and Succession Planning. *Asian Academy of Management Journal*, *26*(2).

Jorzik, P., Klein, S.P., Kanbach, D.K. and Kraus, S. (2024). AI-driven business model innovation: A systematic review and research agenda. *Journal of Business Research*, *182*, 114764.

Kadirov, A., Shakirova, Y., Ismoilova, G. and Makhmudova, N. (2024, April). AI in Human Resource Management: Reimagining Talent Acquisition, Development, and Retention. In *2024 International Conference on Knowledge Engineering and Communication Systems (ICKECS)* (Vol. 1, pp. 1–8). IEEE.

Kalia, P. and Mishra, G. (2023). Role of artificial intelligence in Re-inventing human resource management. In *The Adoption and Effect of Artificial Intelligence on Human Resources Management, Part B* (pp. 221–234). Emerald Publishing Limited.

Kambur, E. and Yildirim, T. (2023). From traditional to smart human resources management. *International Journal of Manpower*, *44*(3), 422–452.

Kaushal, N., Kaurav, R.P.S., Sivathanu, B. and Kaushik, N. (2023). Artificial intelligence and HRM: identifying future research Agenda using systematic literature review and bibliometric analysis. *Management Review Quarterly*, *73*(2), 455–493.

Kuhn, K.M., Meijerink, J. and Keegan, A. (2021). Human resource management and the gig economy: Challenges and opportunities at the intersection between organizational HR decision-makers and digital labor platforms. *Research in personnel and human resources management*, 39, 1–46.

Madhumita, G., Diana, P.D., Neena, P.C., Kiran, P.N., Aggarwal, S. and Nargunde, A.S. (2024, April). AI-powered Performance Management: Driving Employee Success and Organizational Growth.

In *2024 5th International Conference on Recent Trends in Computer Science and Technology* (ICRTCST) (pp. 204–209). IEEE.

Nechytailo, A. (2023). Using AI-powered tools for Improving Talent Acquisition Processes.

Nishar, S. (2022). The Role of Artificial Intelligence in Transforming Human Resource Management: A Literature Review. *Journal of Artificial Intelligence & Cloud Computing*. SRC/JAICC-167. DOI: doi. org/10.47363/JAICC/2022 (1), 155, 2–4.

Nosratabadi, S., Zahed, R.K., Ponkratov, V.V. and Kostyrin, E.V. (2022). Artificial Intelligence models and employee lifecycle management: A systematic literature review. *Organizacija*, *55*(3), 181–198.

Pan, Y. and Froese, F.J. (2023). An interdisciplinary review of AI and HRM: Challenges and future directions. *Human resource management review*, *33*(1), 100924.

Paramita, D., Okwir, S. and Nuur, C. (2024). Artificial intelligence in talent acquisition: exploring organisational and operational dimensions. *International Journal of Organizational Analysis*, 32(11), 108–131.

Pham, D.D.T. and Paille, P. (2020). Green recruitment and selection: an insight into green patterns. *International journal of manpower*, *41*(3), 258–272.

Prabhakar, N.J. (2023). Role of new emerging technologies in recruitment and selection process. *The Online Journal of Distance Education and e-Learning*, *11*(1).

Rodgers, W., Murray, J.M., Stefanidis, A., Degbey, W.Y. and Tarba, S.Y. (2023). An artificial intelligence algorithmic approach to ethical decision-making in human resource management processes. *Human resource management review*, *33*(1), 100925.

Shukla, A., Mishra, L. and Agnihotri, A. (2023). A Comprehensive Review of the Effects of Digital Technology on Human Resource Management. *Technology, Management and Business*, 31, 7–19.

Somasundaram, M.J.K.M.S., Junaid, K.M. and Mangadu, S. (2020). Artificial intelligence (AI) enabled intelligent quality management system (IQMS) for personalized learning path. *Procedia Computer Science*, *172*, 438–442.

Sundarapandiyan Natarajan, D.K.S., Subbaiah, B., Dhinakaran, D.P., Kumar, J.R. and Rajalakshmi, M. (2024). AI-Powered Strategies for Talent Management Optimization. *Journal of Informatics Education and Research*, *4*(2).

Thangaraja, T., Maharudrappa, M., Bakkiyaraj, M., Johari, L. and Muthuvel, S. (2024). AI-Powered HR Technology Implementation for Business Growth in Industrial 5.0. In *Multidisciplinary Applications of Extended Reality for Human Experience* (pp. 171–200). IGI Global.

Votto, A.M., Valecha, R., Najafirad, P. and Rao, H.R. (2021). Artificial intelligence in tactical human resource management: A systematic literature review. *International Journal of Information Management Data Insights*, *1*(2), 100047.

Woods, S.A., Ahmed, S., Nikolaou, I., Costa, A.C. and Anderson, N.R. (2020). Personnel selection in the digital age: A review of validity and applicant reactions, and future research challenges. *European Journal of work and organizational psychology*, *29*(1), 64–77.

Yathiraju, N. (2022). Investigating the use of an artificial intelligence model in an ERP cloud-based system. *International Journal of Electrical, Electronics and Computers*, *7*(2), 1–26.

Zehir, C., Karaboga, T. and Basar, D. (2020). The transformation of human resource management and its impact on overall business performance: big data analytics and AI technologies in strategic HRM. *Digital Business Strategies in Blockchain Ecosystems: Transformational Design and Future of Global Business*, 265–279.

Zhang, J. and Chen, Z. (2024). Exploring human resource management digital transformation in the digital age. *Journal of the Knowledge Economy*, *15*(1), 1482–1498.

# 12 Sustainable Delivery Planning and Delivery Management with AI for Society 5.0

M Sundarrajan[1], Mani Deepak Choudhry[2*], Akshya Jothi[3], Preethi S[4] and Krishna Kumar[5]

As e-commerce grows, the logistics sector's contribution to reducing its environmental impact must be balanced against increasing demand. Traditional methods of planning and managing deliveries often result in inefficient routes, wasted resources, and excess emissions. These Intelligent Transport Systems provide a lifeline proposition toward enhancing the growing flow of vehicles and developing the workings of traffic in cities, thus decreasing the accident rate. Massive data are released from different digital devices connected to the transportation network to form big datasets for further analysis and help with deep learning techniques. These methods can help to predict traffic performance, automate the control of traffic lights, detect lanes, and detect objects around vehicles to drive ITS safety and efficiency forward. This paper discusses some of the outstanding challenges and things marked priority in ensuring that ITS and deep learning approaches mix seamlessly to fix things like the improvement of traffic flow and transportation logistics while predicting optimal goods transportation routes.

## Introduction

Industry 4.0 is the convergence of technologies and new trends oriented towards disrupting hitherto existing processes with the hitherto unexplored power of digitalization. Industry 5.0, on the other hand, is a new way humans and machines are collaborating to work in tandem for increased production efficiency, more

1 Department of Networking and Communications, School of Computing, SRM Institute of Science and Technology, Kattankulathur Campus, Chengalpattu, Tamil Nadu, India.
2 Department of Computing Technologies, School of Computing, SRM Institute of Science and Technology, Kattankulathur Campus, Chengalpattu, Tamil Nadu, India.
3 Department of Computational Intelligence, School of Computing, SRM Institute of Science and Technology, Kattankulathur Campus, Chengalpattu, Tamil Nadu, India.
4 Department of Electronics and Communication Engineering, Dr. N.G.P. Institute of Technology, Coimbatore, Tamil Nadu, India.
5 Department of Computer Science and Engineering, Sasi Institute of Technology and Engineering, Tadepalligudem, Andhra Pradesh, India.
* Corresponding author: manideec@srmist.edu.in

DOI: 10.1201/9781003559849-12

incisively. Evidence of Industry 4.0 in the manufacturing sector has been well-documented from the Industrial Revolution and the years of digital transformation to the present. Figure 1 presents a very detailed diagram of the progress starting from the 1970s up until this century, where each phase was indicative of critical changes in the manufacturing process and how they had affected the way industries functioned.

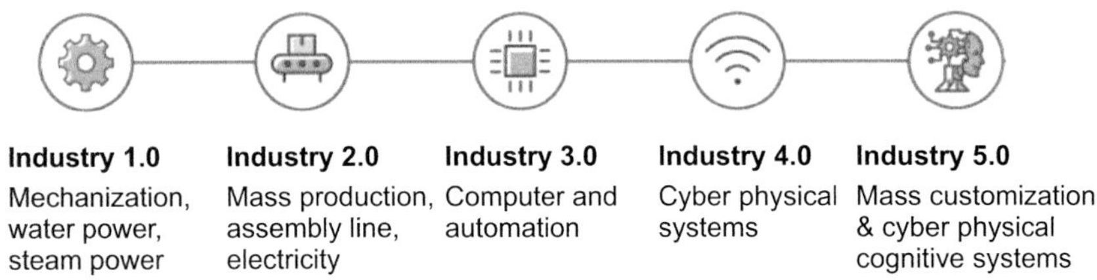


**Fig. 1** Evolution of the Industrial Revolution.

Industry 5.0 has been focusing on the symbiotic relationship between man and robot. Even as automation and state-of-the-art manufacturing take center stage, the role of the human factor is seen to be just as important (Choudhry et al., 2024a, Choudhry et al., 2024b). Industry 5.0 can be described as the run of the system through automated and highly effective methodologies; however, at the same time, it incorporates personalized and human-centered approaches. This new era of industrial revolution combines automation processes in such a way that it opens the door for new revolutions in manufacturing, especially in the medical Hub. In this process, the Internet of Things (IoT) and Internet of Services (IoS) open new ways for development. High-tech innovations, such as new manufacturing technologies, software, robotics, and sensors, guarantee strong data interchange and connectivity.

Industry 5.0 deals with the complex interactions between humans and machines, based on the synergy already existing in the environments of smart manufacturing, where humans and devices collaborate. The new stage aims at an evolution of these interactions, particularly because of the enhancement of human-machine interfaces. What Industry 5.0 is supposed to be driven by is the force of automation, Big Data, new technological policies, responsible science practice, and 3D symmetry in the design of innovation ecosystems, with safety procedures at the very front.

Integration in this era will be smoother, faster, and closely paired with human ability. Cogent computing will work in tandem with human intelligence to provide high-quality value-added products and goods. Technology will not replace human roles; instead, it enhances them in the manufacturing process of Industry 5.0. This will make humans do other important tasks instead of spending time on repetitive tasks like drilling or data entry. System supervision, real-time decision-making, and critical thinking are some of the tasks that will elevate the quality and efficiency of production processes (Kasinathan et al., 2022; Sidek et al., 2021; Vivek et al., 2024; Hariprasath et al., 2024; Sundarrajan et al., 2023).

Mechanical output converging with cognitive reasoning is not a concept too far away. Well, in Industry 5.0, data collection gets automated. This simply means more accurate inputs are possible for robotic systems or connected devices. This period is characterized by the availability of real-time data, perfect system connectivity, and interaction. For instance, a tool machine fitted with sensors can monitor its wear and tear in real time and communicate it to tool inventories to order a replacement cutting tool just in time to minimize downtime and increase productivity.

Society 5.0 is a human-centered strategy, balancing economic growth with social responsibility (Society, 5.0 2018; Foresti et al., 2020; Fukuda, 2020). Society 5.0 was originally proposed in the Fifth Science and Technology Basic Plan of Japan, defining the future society that Japan wants to realize. It reflects the new and innovative way of trade practice and accepts digital transformation in society. The central notion is concern for technological developments, which are causing changes in society. Priority is given to the common welfare of the citizens and the development of a highly intelligent society. According to (Salimova et al., 2019), it works on a wide range of spectrum concerning implications.

Human activity in work is changing and expanding dramatically with the rising power of Digitization and AI. Such a huge number of traditional jobs are bound to vanish, and an emerging need for retraining and upskilling needs to be urgently addressed. In the education sector, there will be a pressing need for evolution to cater to the emerging, innovative Society 5.0. It will further enhance not only teaching but also research in light of Society 5.0 requirements. Some critics of Society 5.0 raised their concerns over the huge amounts of personal data that would be collected and shared among different systems. In this regard, stringent security measures are most necessary. This also provides enormous potential for creating innovative solutions and services that can boost networked systems and the application areas associated with them. A human-centered society would ensure that economic growth aligns with the alleviation of social ills by achieving the integration of physical space and cyberspace seamlessly. Society 5.0 actualizes a deep convergence of the physical or real world with cyberspace or virtual space. Artificial intelligence analyzes the vast amounts of data in cyberspace, and the gained insights are applied in many forms to make human lives better in the physical world. Society 5.0 is a new approach to the integration of the two spaces in a way that will enable AI-driven big data and robots to perform changes and tasks, or assist in them, which humans used to manage. The creation relieves human beings from tiring routine tasks in which a person may not be that effective. Society 5.0 creates new value by ensuring the delivery of important products and services to people in society who need them, thus optimizing the whole social and organizational system.

Society 5.0 is the social creation paving the way toward envisioning life that will further merge the physical world and the digital into one. In Society 5.0, individuals live in cyber communities, able to leverage the power of the Internet, big data, and artificial intelligence, yet living in the real world among others. This

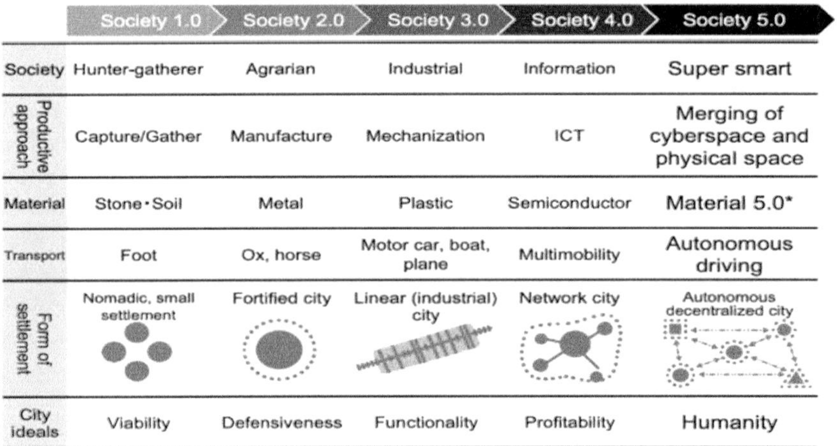


**Fig. 2** Society 1.0 to Society 5.0.

is the fifth concept in human society after the hunter-gatherer, the agricultural, the industrial, and the information societies, as illustrated in Fig. 2. Improvements in societal advancement with innovations have resulted in increased labor productivity, improved average life expectancy, and increased societal wealth. For example, wearable devices and digital tools are provided to employees in smart industries to make the operations smoother. Physically strenuous tasks that involve heavy lifting are performed by robots under the guidance of humans. The more integrated these technologies are, the better the workforce efficiency, safety, and productivity. Policymakers can incentivize organizations to offer supplementary training for future manufacturing technicians to facilitate this kind of technical change for a just transition from one technology to another.

Green logistics means strategies and practices that reduce the environmental impact of the activities involved in this industry (Kasinathan et al., 2022). Optimization of the supply chain process to minimize carbon emissions, energy use, and generation of waste is one of the aspects involved. It also comprises a vast area: transport, warehousing, packaging, and reverse logistics. A key issue for green logistics is the construction of a sustainable logistics system that would meet not only the business world's economic needs but also, at the same time, be helpful to the environment by conserving it. This will enable companies to reduce their carbon footprint over time through the introduction of green technologies and practices. The other key area of green logistics could be transportation network optimization through better fleet management with energy-efficient vehicles, route optimization, and consolidation of shipments to reduce the number of trips and fuel consumption. Besides, companies are also using increasing amounts of alternative fuels such as electricity and biofuels to power their fleets. Powered by advanced technologies like IoT and AI in logistics, many activities allow real-time tracking and data analysis to plan routes efficiently and optimize loads. These measures help companies not only in reducing the amount of greenhouse gas emissions but also result in cost savings for the business.

Sustainable methods of packaging and waste management are also insisted upon by green logistics. Companies are encouraged to use recyclable and biodegradable materials for packaging to reduce the generation of waste. Besides, reverse logistics, which means the return and recycling of products, assumes a place of importance in the green logistics framework. The process is of great importance in landfill waste reduction and in recovering valuable materials; therefore, this step provides a pathway toward a circular economy. Embracing green logistics practices allows businesses not only to showcase their care for the environment but, most importantly, to enhance brand image and customer loyalty by ensuring consumers are aware of the need for sustainability in the supply chain.

### *Background*

Logistics 4.0, in that respect, is the change in the sector, just like Industry 4.0, where technological digitalization is incorporated into every aspect of logistics (Winkelhaus, 2020). The change has primarily been epitomized by the use of the Internet of Things, smart and flexible processes, cyber-physical systems, and big data analytics. The nature of all these elements combined gives way to driverless transport systems, smart containers, intelligent warehousing, and smart shelves. These technologies raise the efficiency, effectiveness, and interconnectivity of logistics operations with other parts of the value chain. In this respect, Logistics 4.0 offers concepts that allow companies the agility and flexibility needed to react more precisely to the changed requirements of dynamic markets.

The concept of Logistics 4.0 has been widely recognized within the circle of industrial engineering and is one of the most important fields of theoretical research and practical realization. A literature review has been conducted, based on the most relevant scientific studies, to analyze core elements defining Logistics 4.0 and to estimate the readiness and maturity of various models for logistics operations transformation. During the search in databases such as Web of Science by using keywords like ‘Logistics 4.0’, ‘Smart Logistics’, ‘readiness’, and ‘maturity’, researchers were able to identify more frequently discussed elements that define the current smart logistics landscape.

The progress of the field is heading more and more toward Logistics 5.0, which has a focus on human-centered logistics. Logistics 5.0 is based on the technological foundations laid by Logistics 4.0, adding a layer of human-centric intelligence and autonomy to the mix. It refers to the development of logistics systems striving for efficiency and connectivity in a changing market environment while keeping humans and their well-being at the top of the priorities list. This shift is characterized by the holistic view of logistics, including the role of technology and people as core in the pursuit of the development of sustainable and resilient logistics solutions.

## Logistics 5.0 from Logistics 4.0

A few of the key features that define the integration into Industry 4.0 of Logistics 4.0 in the evolving landscape include: altogether personalization of service, being able to mass custom logistic solutions according to the needs of its individual customers. The frame works with an ultimate goal to increase the quality of service, which improves errors within complex environments; it will ultimately optimize overall efficiency. General customer service is the priority for the mass personalized services that the operations focus on (Winkelhaus, 2020).

Extensive literature reviews reveal the concept of Industry 5.0, especially in the context of the supply chain. It enhances the technology framework developed by Industry 4.0 through the incorporation of aspects, such as mass personalization, revolutionary technologies, and the development of a super-smart and sustainable society (Frederico, 2021). This advanced framework pinpoints a gap in the existing literature about Logistics 5.0, and it suggests a much more sophisticated approach to managing logistics processes.

This has also brought a revolution in logistics development, with the emergence of smart Internet of Things systems targeted at supporting logistics processes. Of course, technology is a critical tool towards the realization of Industry 5.0, as this will streamline logistic time and costs, whereas increasing the level of customer satisfaction and company profit (Bhargava et al., 2022). This case study examines the demand for logistics solutions that come with speed and effective means.

More recently, the interaction of digital twin and big data technologies in the Logistics 4.0 domain has been discussed. Thereby, digital twins are one of the key elements for the planning and optimization of logistic processes aimed toward risk and loss reduction (Figueiras et al., 2021). The research points out the significant role of digital twins in improving efficient and effective logistics operations.

More innovations in managing warehousing systems can be seen in the concept of a digital warehouse, intralogistics 4.0. In this regard, scientific studies in the said area have shown serious success in introducing complicated technologies in warehouse systems, thus improving the efficiency of operation of these systems (Domansk, 2019).

One of the biggest aspects that Logistics 5.0 is reliant on is environmental awareness. Studies on green intermodal freight transportation note the necessity of adopting green logistics principles and multi-objective planning of freight transportation. This kind of approach, which has been identified lately, is that it does not just deal with carbon emissions reduction but emphasizes the benefits of adopting sustainable logistics practices (Demir, 2019).

The evolving needs of flexibility and mass customization in logistics penetrate deeply from an operational to a managerial level. This paper starts addressing these needs using the paradigm referred to as Logistics Operator 4.0 by exploring the frontiers of human-computer and human-machine interaction interfaces towards control of fully automated systems and laying the foundation for the development of ergonomic standards and hybrid human-machine decision-making processes (Cimini et al., 2020).

Third, human factors are considered while digital logistics systems are being developed. Ignoring these factors can result in operator fatigue, discomfort, and even injury, which affects the performance of the operator and consequently the efficiency of the logistics system. It may be suggested that further development in such an area holds potential for better performance, quality, and well-being of the employed operators (Vijayakumar et al., 2022).

## ***Deep Learning and UAV-Based Logistics***

### *Preliminaries Deep Neural Networks*

The deep neural network will consist of multiple layers of nodes, which are all connected. Input in this case will be processed to have a result in the output layer, such as prediction or classification. The term "deep" refers to the presence of multiple layers that allow the network to learn increasingly complex features from the input. Today, DNNs are of paramount importance and applicability because they can learn and automatically extract relevant features from the data without the help of domain experts. They have been applied in a variety of fields for hundreds of tasks and purposes, such as security and industrial component recognition, all the way to their integral design for the optimum performance of the whole system. Training DNN involves the tuning of weights connecting nodes to minimize prediction errors using optimization techniques. Other variants of the DNN family of algorithms include Convolutional Neural Networks, including computer vision, Graph Neural Networks for graph-structured data, Recurrent Neural Networks for sequential data problems, and Natural Language Processing for analyzing text data, to mention a few.

- **CNN** – They are powerful because they learn the spatial hierarchy of features from the input data, which forms an image and is an important factor in understanding the visual context. They contain Convolution, Pooling, and Fully connected layers. The convolution layer is used to apply filters that identify the features, such as edges or corners, and the Pooling layer is used to reduce the dimensionality for efficient computation. These features are then converted into probabilities of each class by the fully connected layer. Applications of CNNs include, though are by no means limited to, object detection, facial identification, and image classification. What's more, they have been applied to other data types, like speech, text, and video, hence making them very versatile tools in machine learning.

  Once mainly used for simple data processing, CNNs have become integral to the modern UAV, especially because of the algorithm's robust capability in processing and analyzing visual data. In general, the basic applications of CNNs on UAVs revolve around detecting and recognizing objects. The ability to observe objects within the view of its camera, recognize, and classify them is a vital function of the CNN in carrying out tasks that range from surveillance to autonomous navigation and even search and rescue missions.

Architectures such as YOLO and SSD realize some of the best results in real-time object detection due to their efficiency and precision.

Besides object detection, CNNs also find application in image segmentation, which is the process of partitioning an image into distinct segments based on attributes. This ability is crucial in applications like land cover classification in agriculture, identification of terrain types, and detailed mapping for autonomous navigation. Thus, the well-known architecture U-Net is employed in these scenarios to return real, actionable information from visual data.

Feature extraction with the help of Convolutional Neural Networks is playing a very vital role in navigation, hence enabling UAVs to understand environmental features. Obstacle detection, route planning, and safe navigation through an environment with constraints can further realize applications of CNNs for which relevant features extracted from images are essentially required. This feature extraction is often integrated into the broader navigation system that pools visual data with information from other sensors, further enhancing overall navigational capability. This is depicted in Fig. 3.

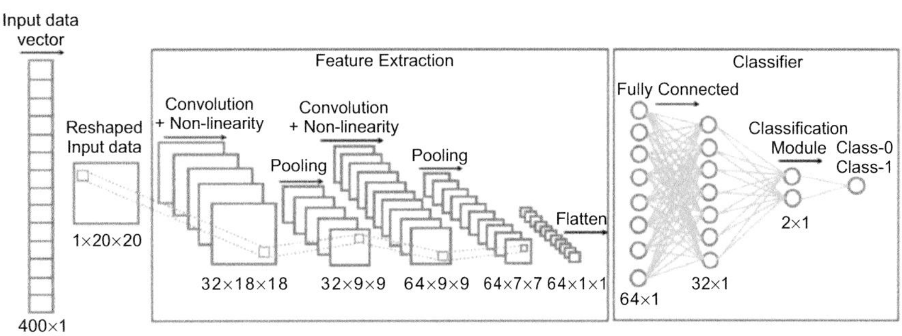


**Fig. 3** Basic UAV data-based feature extraction CNN Model.

Another major application of CNNs in UAVs involves anomaly detection. In infrastructure inspection tasks, for instance, CNNs can identify any irregularities or defects that may be present within images; for example, the cracking or corrosion of buildings and bridges. It provides important indication about the need for maintenance and/or safety assessments, to which immediate interventions or prevention may be undertaken.

CNNs further contribute to scene understanding through complex visual information analysis and interpretation, including object identification and their relationships within the scene. This enhanced understanding has great value for higher-order applications that include autonomous urban navigation or environmental monitoring, where awareness of context is critical. Another strong point of CNNs is real-time processing, which is integral to all UAV applications involving real-time decision-making. Using hardware accelerators such as GPUs and TPUs can give a large boost in CNN inference speed. High-resolution images and video streams will, therefore, be analyzed in real time, making sure UAVs accomplish tasks efficiently and promptly respond to dynamic conditions.

Finally, UAV technologies like GPS and IMU sensors can also be integrated with CNNs. These integrated technologies enhance the performance of the navigation system further by fusing spatial and motion information with visual information. For instance, CNNs will improve the performance of visual odometry, a technique that estimates motion based on visual inputs, since better features should lead to higher accuracy of navigation and control. However, some challenges also exist in deploying CNNs on UAVs, which include computation power consumption. There should be a good balance between the model complexity and the processing power for real-time performance. Other constraints include that large and diverse training datasets are needed by CNNs, ensuring the models well represent the operational environment of the UAV. It should guarantee robustness against changes in lighting conditions, weather, and other environmental factors to maintain accuracy and ensure model reliability.

- **RNN** – Recurrent Neural Networks consider not only the current input but also the previous inputs (or states of the network) when making an output at any given time step. In other words, it is composed of interacting recurrent cells that process the input and update the internal state of the network with each time step. Each network takes the previous state as well as the current turn's input and produces output accordingly, and forwards a new state to the next network in the series. One trains an RNN through a process called backpropagation through time, a modified version of the default backpropagation algorithm. This process ensures one can update the network weights based on the error at each point in time. RNNs perform well in applications where it is core to understand the temporal dependencies of the sequential data, such as language modeling and speech recognition. Nevertheless, training RNNs is very hard, mainly due to issues such as vanishing and exploding gradients. Later techniques like gradient clipping and regularization approaches, such as dropout, were developed to make training easier.

  RNNs have become of great importance to UAVs, especially in the execution of tasks that require analysis and prediction of a temporal sequence. Unlike CNNs, which work well in the processing of spatial data, RNNs are suited for sequential data and hence can be helpful with functionalities that require an understanding of time-dependent patterns for which prediction is required. In this regard, RNN applications are critical in enhancing the functionalities of UAVs in such areas as navigation and environmental monitoring. Figure 4. depicts a basic model of RNN involved with UAV.

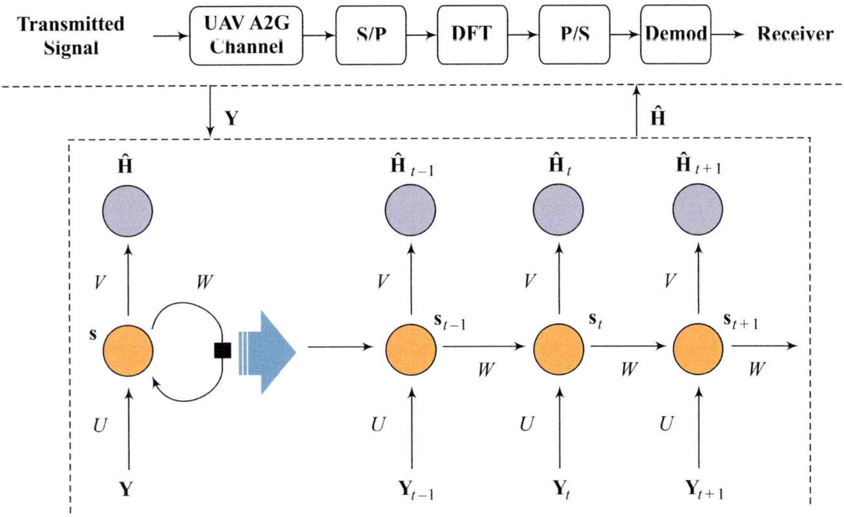


**Fig. 4** RNN for UAV.

Another critical application of RNNs in UAVs is trajectory prediction and path planning. Types of RNNs, especially those with LSTM units, are efficient in learning and predicting sequential patterns from motion data. RNN could forecast the future trajectories from the historical flight path analysis to real-time sensor data input. The UAV will decide on optimal routes and calculate evasion plans dynamically. The capability for autonomous navigation in an agent is important because the planning of safe and efficient operations requires precise and adaptive path planning.

The other beneficial area of RNNs is in analyzing and forecasting environmental conditions. Most UAV missions operate in complex and dynamic environments, and the application of RNN could be of significance in the simulation and forecasting of these changes. For example, an RNN that has been trained on weather data or even time-series input about atmospheric conditions can forecast short-term changes that may have an impact on the performance of a UAV during a flight. Subsequently, the UAV would adapt to new situations foreseen by predictive models, hence ultimately enhancing the dependability and capacity to operate UAVs.

Besides trajectory and environment predictions, the RNN will also be able to enhance mission planning and execution analysis of temporal sequences of mission data. Learning from past missions, RNNs identify patterns in them and optimize mission strategies. This could involve task scheduling, operational parameter adaptation, or resource management based on performance history data, and, therefore, these mission strategies become more productive and successful.

Another very promising application of RNNs in UAVs is in autonomous decision-making. RNNs can process sequences of sensory inputs and make real-time decisions based on learned patterns and predictions. In this context, during a search and rescue mission, an RNN could analyze a sequence of images and sensor data to identify areas of interest toward which the UAV would guide actions. This is the capability to make informed decisions in real time, which is critical for missions requiring maximum agility and maximum responsiveness.

Such things also bring challenges of their own while implementing RNNs on UAVs. Training RNNs with long sequences borders on large training data and severe computational demands, both resource burdens normally found in UAV applications. Though the RNNs can model sequential data properly, they may find challenges with exceedingly long sequences due to issues such as vanishing and exploding gradients. Advanced RNN architectures, such as LSTMs and Gated Recurrent Units, go a long way in mitigating such issues but still require careful tuning and optimization.

In short, RNNs have given significant benefits to all such UAV applications concerned with sequential data analysis and the innate prediction capability they possess. It is such capabilities for handling temporal dependencies that make them a tool of high value in such tasks as trajectory prediction, forecasting of the environment, mission planning, and autonomous decision-making. Though the training and implementation are tedious processes concerning RNNs, owing to their potential to enhance the capabilities of UAVs, they are indispensable in furthering the autonomous aerial systems.

- **GNN** – GNNs are deep neural network architectures specialized for graph-structured data, as in the case of traffic networks, social networks, or molecular structures. These networks integrate the structure of the graph and its node relationships directly into the computations. GNNs represent nodes of a graph as vectors or tensors and use message passing between nodes to update these representations with regard to a graph's structure. More formally, during each iteration of such a message-passing process, nodes aggregate information from their neighbors and update their representations using some learned update function. There have been several forms for GNNs to focus on individual problems. Some GNNs are based on graph convolutional layers to capture node features locally; others use the attention mechanism to learn global relationships between nodes. There are GNNs designed to tackle dynamic graphs changing across time and others optimized for heterogeneous graphs with different types of nodes and edges. GNNs have been applied to a wide variety of problems at hand, such as traffic prediction, social network analysis, recommendation systems, and drug discovery.

## Unmanned Aerial Vehicles (UAV)

A drone is an aircraft that does not have a human pilot flying it from inside the craft. Instead, it may be controlled remotely through radio signals or autonomously by onboard computers. Given their flexibility and cost-effectiveness, such vehicles are greatly valued, apart from not causing any environmental pollution. Thus, their usage is becoming increasingly prevalent in logistics. That will greatly reduce urban traffic congestion, noise pollution, and harmful emissions in urban centers, substituting traditional delivery vehicles such as vans and lorries; therefore, it contributes toward energy conservation and environmental protection. UAVs have been used in regional transportation, express delivery, emergency logistics, and storage management. Regional UAV transportation will provide links between central hubs and peripheral areas that are remote or otherwise inaccessible, guaranteeing effective delivery where traditional means falter. UAV express delivery, otherwise known as terminal distribution, is a process whereby drones are used to directly deliver packages to the doorstep of customers to speed up delivery time and not rely on ground transportation in urban environments. In these respects, UAVs also have a very important place in emergency logistics by delivering important supplies in crises and storehouse management by automating jobs like inventory control and inspections. These UAV distribution systems mainly fall under branch line transportation, connecting major distribution centers, and terminal distribution, such as the last mile of delivery to the final user. Not only do UAVs increase operational efficiency in integrating into logistic operations, but they are a step toward sustainable development goals by reducing the ecological impact that traditional ways of conducting logistics have.

## Integration of DL and UAVs for Sustainable Delivery Management

### *DL Integration*

The challenges before the modern transportation system are severe growth in population and the consequential increase in the number of vehicles on the road. The challenges, therefore, have to be met, and it is mandatory, for more advanced and cost-effective solutions to arrive at these burning issues: traffic congestion, pollution, traffic accidents, and managing efficient flow. To address these issues, several advanced technologies like smart cards, GPS, sensors, video detectors, and social media have been developed under Intelligent Transportation Systems. All these technologies jointly make transportation networks highly efficient and safe.

ITS has categorized objectives to enhance road safety and increase transport efficiency, or minimize pollution from the environment. With the multimodal information sources, the ITS systems can analyze better with intelligent techniques and advanced algorithms; they filter the relevant information and process it for decision-making that is timely and accurate, proactively. This approach can manage traffic flow more effectively, avoiding accidents and transit operations. With the changing scenario, procedures change for the integration of intelligent methods to improve the performance of traffic management to promote safer driving.

All these brought to light many new complexities associated with the modern transportation systems. Machine learning techniques have begun to emerge as a force in many domains. It is especially possible to deal with large and complex data sets, mostly deep learning, through the analysis of data with dynamics for the discovery of patterns and underlying structures that can not be directly inferred in the beginning. Such exploration of patterns allows deep learning models to make accurate predictions and decisions for systems to scale up and adapt to diverse quality-of-service requirements. Extract meaning from vast volumes of data to help develop better systems in transportation management.

This merging of machine learning, deep learning, and ITS is a phenomenal development in transportation. Such technologies reflect data-driven, sophisticated approaches to managing traffic, optimizing routes, and predicting demand. With the growth in the volume of data produced from the transportation system, the place of machine learning within ITS for improved efficiency and effectiveness becomes more pronounced. It can be adapted to every new advanced technology to provide new concepts of services, address the challenges of the modern transport system, and create much better mobility solutions that are both sustainable and efficient.

Transport operators need to find a way of obtaining both reliable and low-cost predictions about the arrival times of different transport modes. The correctness of the arrival time forecasting is of significant importance to the administrators and operators for several reasons. First, it helps in resource implementation and management, including human resources, equipment, and spatial resources. Knowing the time of vehicle or shipment arrival helps an operator to be well prepared and to allocate resources effectively to bring idle time down and avoid congestion within operational areas.

Furthermore, with arrival time prediction, costs are reduced and operations become more efficient. Administrators, if they can predict actual arrival time, will be able to schedule in such a way that waiting time for the vehicles is minimized, thus reducing operational costs related to time and resource wastage. Proper allocation of resources will also improve service levels and hence customer satisfaction, since arrivals and departures on time play a big role in the smooth flow of operations in a warehouse, terminal, or port.

Not only are there operation-related benefits, but dependable predictions support strategic decisions in a meaningful way. With an extremely clear understanding of the arrival patterns and their time frames, we can expect the transportation operators to work out effective handling of inventory management as well as to plan for the right workforce and equipment utilization. This gives strategic long-term planning insight within the vision and lessens the risks in not having unexpected delays or not having enough resources.

Several data mining techniques were applied to measure the possibility of making an arrival time prediction, even though the correlation between the independent variables and the dependent variable, tardiness or the difference between planned and actual arrival times, was close to nil (Spoel et al., 2017). Five techniques of data mining in use are Decision Trees, K Nearest Neighbors (Breiman, 2017) , Support Vector Machines (Mining, 2006) , and their corresponding ensemble classifiers: Ad-aBoost.M1 (Cortes and Vapnik, 1995, Freund and Schapire 1996) and Random Forest (Breiman, 2001).

UAVs, integrated with the other machines, can have extensive capabilities in manufacturing processes, unit delivery, supervision, or can even be used to manage and optimize other connected machines, as shown in Fig. 5. The supervising UAV will be operated from the control point. The operator will collect information from the sensors and connected machines about the status of current and future tasks, analyzing factory efficiency and possible problems. If the operator of the factory receives data about defective or inefficient machine operation, the supervising UAV can be sent in place to provide visual data and direct connection between the malfunctioning robot and the operator. This application requires a stable wireless connection to the UAV, and the chance that the link is blocked by machines or disturbed by poor propagation conditions must be minimized.

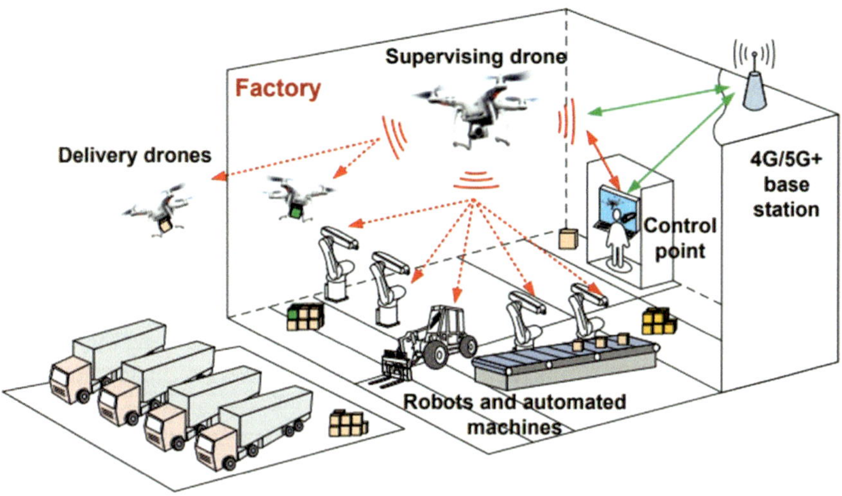


**Fig. 5** Integration of UAVs into factories

In a nutshell, having accurate predictive arrival times is an integral part of the effective management of transportation. These, therefore, enable optimal allocation of resources, operational efficiency, and strategic planning to end up with more manageable operations and increased performance within transportation and logistics networks.

## UAV Integration

Integrating unmanned aerial vehicles into logistics delivery management is the new frontier in ferrying goods. The process starts with an initial placement of orders and pre-flight planning for the UAV. The system, upon order, would estimate the best route depending on the conditions and specifications of the package at that time. Equipped with high-tech navigation systems, UAVs could fly autonomously or even semi-autonomously to provide accurate and timely delivery, hence reducing dependence on traditional delivery systems and increasing efficiency and time factors (Macrina et al., 2020; Boysen et al., 2021).

In this regard, UAVs dynamically adjust their flight paths at the commencement of every delivery using real-time data. Equipped with advanced sensors and GPS technology, a UAV can continuously monitor weather conditions, air traffic, and probable obstacles. This will enable the UAV to adapt to varying conditions and avoid hazards, thereby ensuring a safe and reliable delivery (Chung et al., 2020). Real-time adjustments help in keeping the delivery schedules intact in bad weather or under any other disruption.

The other big factor when it comes to UAV logistics management is traffic optimization. In respect to this, UAV systems can deduce and avoid congested areas by analyzing real-time traffic data in respect to historical delivery patterns. This is attained through algorithms that integrate traffic flow data with route planning. Airlift UAVs can, in this way, navigate around high-traffic areas and congested urban regions to result not only in better delivery time frames but also reduced fuel consumption and carbon emissions related to ground transport.

Other than that, UAVs ensure efficient last-mile delivery. This has something to do with the fact that UAVs have a disproportionate impact on the last-mile delivery segment of any logistics chain, usually the most complex and expensive part. The feature of reaching far-off places or areas inaccessible by other means gives the edge to the UAVs in making the delivery more efficiently and reliably than conventional ways (Moshref-Javadi and Winkenbach 2021; Li et al., 2021). Therefore, it enhances customer satisfaction by allowing them to get the ordered products on time, even in areas that conventional delivery vehicles find very difficult to reach.

Furthermore, the use of UAVs in logistics sets a foundation for future route optimization and demand prediction. Having captured and analyzed huge amounts of data, the UAV systems can iteratively improve their algorithms for route planning and traffic management. Improvements in the future concerning AI and machine learning will further promote such capabilities, ensuring more efficiencies and cost savings in logistics delivery management. While technology continues to change, UAVs have a very large potential for disruption in logistics.

Although deep learning-based object detection methods for UAV remote sensing images are mainly borrowed from traditional digital images in the computer vision community, the limitation of small UAV platforms and imaging acquisition conditions inevitably causes problems of particularity perspective, complex background, scale and direction diversity, and issues related to small sizes. UAV remote sensing images can be acquired at different altitudes, and ground objects can be any size, even for intraclass. Therefore, solutions to scale diversity are cross-referenced in this review. There are two main approaches to solving this problem through deep learning, as illustrated in Fig. 6. The most commonly used is the multi-scale feature map, which is the output of multiple filters on multiple feature maps (MFM) or multiple filters on a single feature map (SFM). The other is a dilated/deformable convolution kernel. It points out that systematic expansion supports the exponential expansion of the receptive field without loss of resolution or coverage.

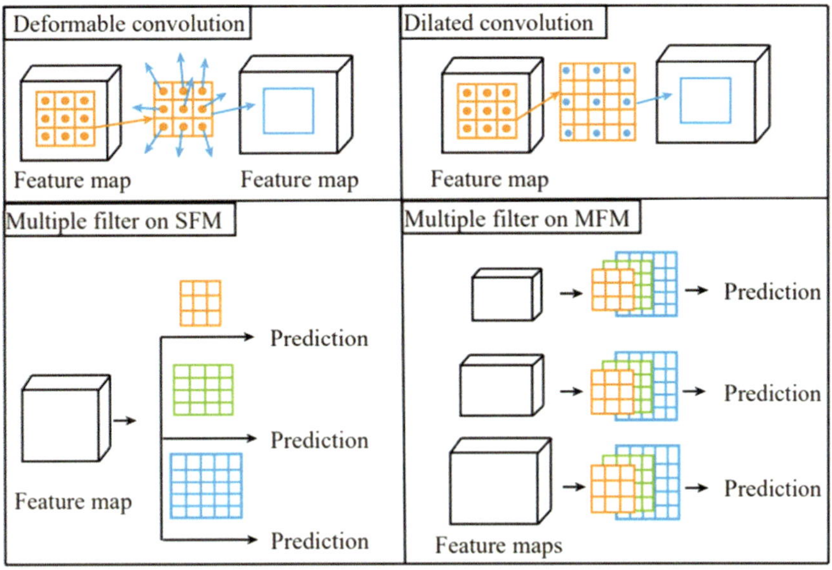


**Fig. 6** Scale Diversity Strategies.

The UAV flying altitude inevitably causes most objects to be shown in scale diversity, small object size, and dense arrangement, resulting in less feature information that can be extracted. Many works deal with the small object detection problem through the same network design for scale diversity, including RRNet, HRDNet, Cascade network, UAV-YOLO, MPFPN, depthwise-separable attention-guided network (DAGN), GANet, and FSSSD, ResNeXt-d. In these methods, accurate feature information learned from small objects is highly important. In addition, some new networks are based on YOLOv4 or Efficientdet-D7 networks, e.g., DNOD, which are developed to improve the detection speed.

Objection direction from an optical remote sensing image is related to its actual parking location. The classic CNNs, which benefit from using a rectangular convolution kernel, are sensitive to object direction. Figure 7 shows four commonly used solutions based on deep learning.

## Discussion

Despite the significant advances in deep learning within Intelligent Transportation Systems (ITS), several challenges persist. One major issue is ensuring the security of deep learning networks, which must learn from and generalize across varied datasets. Even minor variations in input data can lead to substantial discrepancies in the network's output, potentially causing instability and vulnerabilities. To

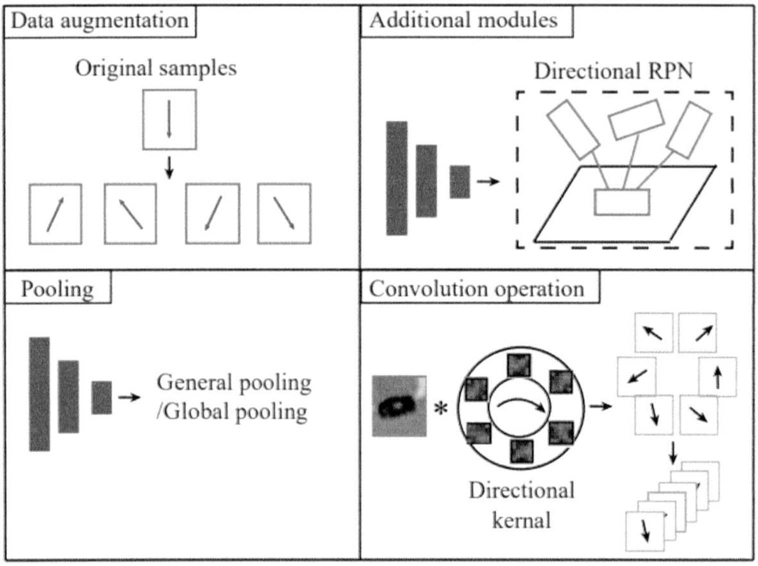


**Fig. 7** Direction Diversity Methods.

mitigate this, it is crucial to establish robust defensive mechanisms to safeguard the network's integrity from malicious attacks, such as data injection by hackers, which could compromise the system's functionality and reliability.

Another challenge is the scarcity of comprehensive and validated datasets in the ITS domain. While extensive datasets are available for other areas like image recognition and health, the ITS field lacks sufficient data resources. Existing datasets, such as those from Data.gov and the University of Sydney's Intelligent Vehicles and Safety Systems, are limited. This data shortage hampers the ability to train deep learning models effectively, especially given the dynamic and unpredictable nature of traffic patterns. The variability in traffic flow during different times of the day poses difficulties for developing models that can adapt to these changes, requiring sophisticated approaches like multi-layered models and deep reinforcement learning to address these issues.

Unmanned Aerial Vehicles (UAVs) face significant challenges in path planning, particularly in urban environments. The low-altitude operations required for industrial applications introduce complexities that necessitate advanced path planning algorithms. Factors such as altitude, wind speed, temperature, and humidity must be considered to make informed decisions for specific flight scenarios. Future research should focus on improving the comprehensiveness of environmental construction, enhancing path planning efficiency, and optimizing the cooperative operation of UAVs with distribution vehicles. Combining various algorithms may enhance real-time decision-making and adaptability in complex urban settings.

Furthermore, the evolution of UAV technology towards clustering and intelligent systems highlights the need for more sophisticated path planning methods. Current algorithms typically address single UAV operations, but future developments should explore methods for managing UAV clusters. Integrating UAV path planning with last-mile delivery logistics could significantly reduce distribution costs, which currently account for over 30% of logistics expenses. By focusing on efficient route optimization and operational coordination, UAVs can address key challenges in last-mile distribution and enhance overall logistical efficiency.

Limited by flight stability and the load capacity of a micro-mini-UAV, the altitude of an airborne remote sensing sensor needs to be adjusted quickly and accurately in real-time so that ground objects are always in the monitoring field of vision. Meanwhile, rapid processing and analysis of high-quality remote sensing images obtained by a UAV system in real-time is the key to miniature UAV remote sensing. When considering all the deep learning methods, the most direct way is to choose the right platform, including an ARM, mobile, and embedded platform, or to trim up the classic network architecture to minimize unnecessary channels in the convolutional layer. Multiple object tracking (MOT) for UAV video has attracted increasing research interest in recent years due to the flexibility of the camera in the drone platform. The popular DL-based MOT methods are not usually optimal for drone video data, due to new challenges, e.g., large viewpoint change and scales in drone platforms. Figyre 8 shows the development of typical methods for MOT.

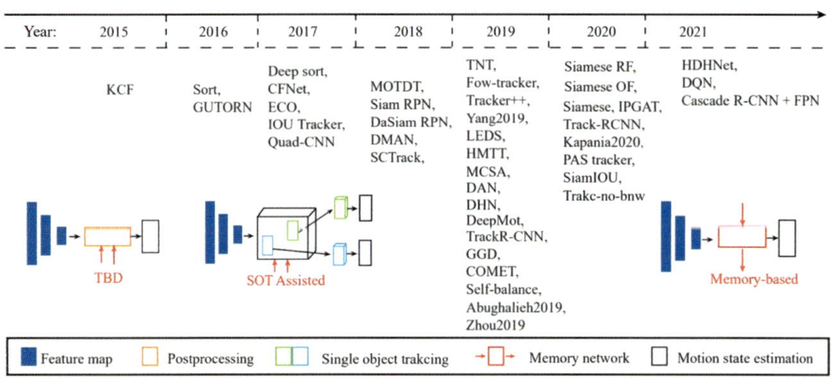


**Fig. 8** Development of methods for UAV object tracking.

## Conclusion

Deep learning methods are transforming transportation services, such as logistics and automated driving environments, by utilizing extensive data from digital devices connected within vehicular networks and publicly available datasets. This chapter explores how integrating deep learning with Intelligent Transportation

Systems (ITS) can address various challenges and unlock substantial benefits, including the enhancement of autonomous vehicle networks and the provision of personalized services based on detailed behavioral and contextual information. This integration aims to improve the overall experience and services provided by ITS. Moreover, the chapter highlights the evolving role of Unmanned Aerial Vehicles (UAVs) in logistics, showcasing their distinct advantages in terms of cost-efficiency, environmental protection, and energy savings. UAVs offer a reduction in carbon emissions and lower energy consumption compared to traditional delivery vehicles, contributing to sustainability. Effective path planning for UAVs is essential for optimizing routes, speeding up distribution, reducing costs, and increasing efficiency. Given the increasing concerns about air pollution and traffic congestion, this chapter argues that the application of UAVs in logistics represents a promising, environmentally friendly alternative to conventional ground-based delivery methods.

## References

Bhargava, A., Bhargava, D., Kumar, P.N., Sajja, G.S. and Ray, S. (2022). Industrial IoT and AI implementation in vehicular logistics and supply chain management for vehicle mediated transportation systems. *International Journal of System Assurance Engineering and Management*, 13(Suppl 1), 673–680.

Boysen, N., Fedtke, S. and Schwerdfeger, S. (2021). Last-mile delivery concepts: a survey from an operational research perspective. Or *Spectrum*, *43*(1), 1–58.

Breiman, L. (2001). Random forests. *Machine learning*, 45, 5–32.

Breiman, L. (2017). Classification and regression trees. *Routledge*.

Choudhry, M.D., Sivaraj, J., Munusamy, S., Muthusamy, P.D. and Saravanan, V. (2024a). Industry 4.0 in Manufacturing, Communication, Transportation, and Health Care. *Topics in Artificial Intelligence Applied to Industry* 4.0, 149–165.

Choudhry, M.D., Jeevanandham, S., Sundarrajan, M., Jothi, A., Prashanthini, K., and Saravanan, V. (2024b). Future Technologies for Industry 5.0 and Society 5.0. *Automated Secure Computing for Next-Generation Systems*, 403–414.

Chung, S.H., Sah, B. and Lee, J. (2020). Optimization for drone and drone-truck combined operations: A review of the state of the art and future directions. *Computers & Operations Research*, 123, 105004.

Cimini, C., Lagorio, A., Romero, D., Cavalieri, S. and Stahre, J. (2020). Smart logistics and the logistics operator 4.0. IFAC-PapersOnLine, *53*(2), 10615–10620.

Cortes, C. and Vapnik, V. (1995). Support-vector networks. *Machine learning*, *20*, 273–297.

Demir, E., Hrušovský, M., Jammernegg, W. and Van Woensel, T. (2019). Green intermodal freight transportation: bi-objective modelling and analysis. *International Journal of Production Research*, *57*(19), 6162–6180.

Domansk, R. 2019. Logistics 4.0. In Warehousing—Current State and Trends: Business Logistics in Modern Management, Proceedings of the 2019 19th International Scientific Conference Business Logistics in Modern Management, Osijek, Croatia, 10–11 October 2019; EFOS: Osijek, Croatia, 2019

Figueiras, P., Lourenço, L., Costa, R., Graça, D., Garcia, G. and Jardim-Gonçalves, R. (2021, June). Big data provision for digital twins in industry 4.0 logistics processes. In *2021 IEEE International Workshop on Metrology for Industry* 4.0 & IoT (MetroInd4. 0&IoT) (pp. 516–521). IEEE.

Foresti, R., Rossi, S., Magnani, M., Bianco, C.G.L. and Delmonte, N. (2020). Smart society and artificial intelligence: big data scheduling and the global standard method applied to smart maintenance. *Engineering*, *6*(7), 835–846.

Frederico, G.F. (2021). From supply chain 4.0 to supply chain 5.0: Findings from a systematic literature review and research directions. *Logistics*, *5*(3), 49.

Freund, Y. and Schapire, R.E. (1996, July). Experiments with a new boosting algorithm. *In icml* (Vol. 96, pp. 148–156).

Fukuda, K. (2020). Science, technology and innovation ecosystem transformation toward society 5.0. *International journal of production economics*, 220, 107460.

Hariprasath, V.Y., Mukesh, S., Aruna, T.N., Gayana, R., Akshya, J., Choudhry, M.D. and Sundarrajan, M. (2024, April). Path Planning Solution for Intelligent Robots Using Ex* RRT Algorithm in Disaster Relief. In *2024 5th International Conference on Recent Trends in Computer Science and Technology (ICRTCST)* (pp. 413–418). IEEE.

Kasinathan, P., Pugazhendhi, R., Elavarasan, R.M., Ramachandaramurthy, V.K., Ramanathan, V., Subramanian, S., Kumar, S., Nandhagopal, K., Raghavan, R.R.V., Rangasamy, S. and Devendiran, R. (2022). Realization of sustainable development goals with disruptive technologies by integrating industry 5.0, society 5.0, smart cities and villages. *Sustainability*, *14*(22), 15258.

Li, H., Chen, J., Wang, F. and Bai, M. (2021). Ground-vehicle and unmanned-aerial-vehicle routing problems from two-echelon scheme perspective: A review. *European Journal of Operational Research*, *294*(3), 1078–1095.

Macrina, G., Pugliese, L.D.P., Guerriero, F. and Laporte, G. (2020). Drone-aided routing: A literature review. *Transportation Research Part C: Emerging Technologies*, 120, 102762.

Mining, W.I.D. (2006). *Introduction to data mining* (pp. 2–12). New Jersey: Pearson Education, Inc.

Moshref-Javadi, M. and Winkenbach, M. (2021). Applications and Research avenues for drone-based models in logistics: A classification and review. *Expert Systems with Applications*, 177, 114854.

Salimova, T., Guskova, N., Krakovskaya, I. and Sirota, E. (2019, April). From industry 4.0 to Society 5.0: Challenges for sustainable competitiveness of Russian industry. In *IOP conference series: materials science and engineering* (Vol. 497, p. 012090). IOP Publishing.

Sidek, S., Khadri, N.A.M., Hasbolah, H., Yaziz, M.F.A., Rosli, M.M., and Husain, N.M. (2021, August). Society 5.0: green logistics consciousness in enlightening environmental and social sustainability. *In IOP Conference Series: Earth and Environmental Science* (Vol. 842, No. 1, p. 012053). IOP Publishing.

Society 5.0 (2018-11-13). Available online: https://www.keidanren.or.jp/en/policy/2018/095.html (accessed on 10 August 2024).

Spoel, V.D., Chintan, A. and Hillegersberg, V. (2017). Predictive analytics for truck arrival time estimation: A field study at a European Distribution Center. *International Journal of Production Research*, *55*(17), 5062–5078.

Sundarrajan, M., Jothi, A., Choudhry, M.D., Rose, B., Jayapratha, T. and Nithya, V. (2023). Effective Path Planning of Cyber-Physical Systems for Precision Agriculture. In *Contemporary Developments in Agricultural Cyber-Physical Systems* (pp. 223–239). IGI Global.

Vijayakumar, V., Sgarbossa, F., Neumann, W.P. and Sobhani, A. (2022). Framework for incorporating human factors into production and logistics systems. *International Journal of Production Research*, *60*(2), 402–419.

Vivek, N., Suriya, A., Kamala, V., Chinnasamy, N.V., Akshya, J., Sundarrajan, M. and Choudhry, M.D. (2024, April). Integrating Deep Q-Networks and YOLO with Autonomous Robots for Efficient Warehouse Management. *In 2024 5th International Conference on Recent Trends in Computer Science and Technology (ICRTCST)* (pp. 419–424). IEEE.

Winkelhaus, S. 4.0: *A systematic review towards a new logistics system.* 2020, 58. DOI: https://doi.org/10.1080/00207543.2019, 1612964, 18–43.

# Index

# About the Editors

**Dr Alka Agnihotri** is currently working as Professor of Human Resources & Organization Behavior in the School of Business, Galgotia's University, Greater Noida, India. She has two decades of professional experience. She obtained a Doctor of Philosophy in management from Amity University, Noida, India. She has a double postgraduate and double NET qualification (MBA & MPA). She has published several research papers in Scopus indexed journals (with best paper awards) and conferences. Alka has 18 years of experience in consultancy, research, training, corporate life and academics. Her technical skills include SAP-ERP in HR Module, SPSS, AMOS, NVivo, SLR, Bibliometric Analysis using R, etc. She is a corporate trainer and has conducted workshops on leadership, stress management, time management, business communication & leadership, etc. She has got patents published and has also written a book on HRM, AI in management, Leadership etc topics with couple of books indexed in Scopus. She is also working as reviewer and editor for many international journals including Scopus indexed journals. She has won awards in research including the InSc Young Researcher Award 2021 awarded by Institute of Scholars and Galgotias University.

**Dr Anuja Pandey** is a distinguished academician and thought leader in marketing and management education, with over 25 years of experience in teaching, research, and institutional leadership. As Professor of Marketing and Head of the India Case Research Centre at AIMA, she has been instrumental in advancing India-centric case research and promoting the use of analytics in management pedagogy. Her academic contributions are deeply rooted in marketing analytics, digital transformation, and AI-readiness frameworks, with a strong emphasis on applied research and public policy consulting. She has led several high-impact research projects funded by government ministries, including studies on AI implementation, emerging technology adoption, and advertising ethics. Dr. Pandey has mentored over 150 India-centric teaching cases, published 23 refereed journal papers, and 12 case studies in marketing analytics published by Wiley. Her editorial leadership at the AIMA-Journal for Management & Research and the launch of Casepedia have significantly enriched the Indian case research ecosystem. She has supervised multiple PhD scholars, presented at international conferences, and collaborated with global institutions like Harvard Business School, The Case Centre (UK), and EFMD. Her work bridges academia and industry, with a focus on data-driven decision-making, AI integration in governance, and capacity-building in analytics education

**Dr Balamurugan Balusamy** is currently working as an Associate Dean Academics in Shiv Nadar Institution of Eminence, Delhi-NCR. Prior to this assignment he was Professor, School of Computing Sciences & Engineering and Director International Relations at Galgotias University, Greater Noida, India. His contributions focused on Engineering Education, Block chain and Data Sciences. His Academic degrees and twelve years of experience working as a faculty in a global University like VIT University, Vellore has made him more receptive and prominent in his domain. He does have 200 plus high impact factor papers in Springer, Elsevier and IEEE. He has done more than 200 Edited and authored books and collaborated with eminent professors across the world from top QS ranked university. Prof. Balamurugan Balusamy has served up to the position of Associate Professor in his stint of 12 years of experience with VIT University, Vellore. He had completed his Bachelors, Masters and PhD Degrees from Top premier institutions from India. His passion is teaching and adapts different design thinking principles while delivering his lectures. He has visited 15 plus countries for his technical course. He serves in the advisory committee for several startups and forums and does consultancy work for industry on Industrial IOT. He has given over 195 talks in various events and symposium. He has spearheaded and conducted more than 10 IEEE and ACM International conferences up to date.

For Product Safety Concerns and Information please contact our
EU representative GPSR@taylorandfrancis.com Taylor & Francis
Verlag GmbH, Kaufingerstraße 24, 80331 München, Germany